Library Wars

4

Love & War

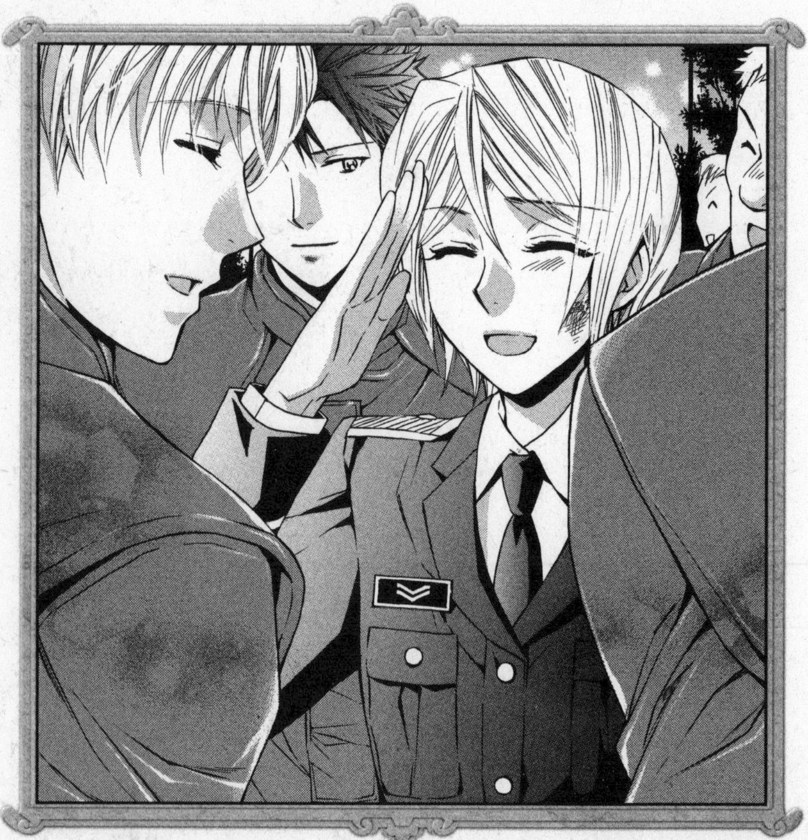

STORY & ART BY Kiiro Yumi ORIGINAL CONCEPT BY Hiro Arikawa

Library Wars
Love & War

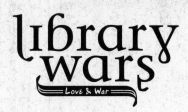

Contents

The Library Freedom Act

Libraries have the freedom to acquire their collections.

Libraries have the freedom to circulate
materials in their collections.

Libraries guarantee the privacy of their patrons.

Libraries oppose any type of censorship.

When libraries are imperiled,
librarians will join together
to secure their freedom.

library wars

Love & War

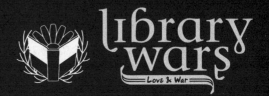

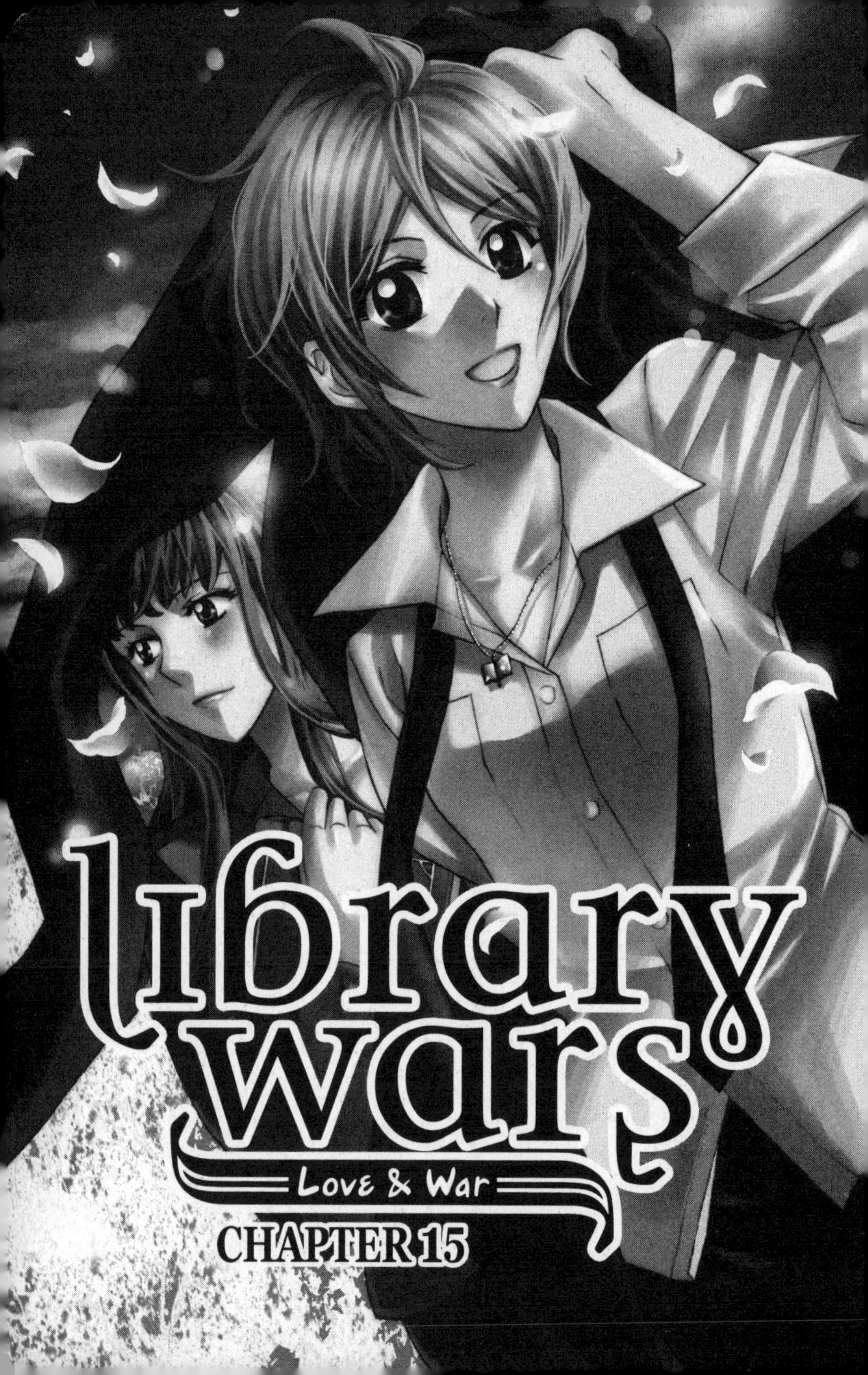
library wars
Love & War
CHAPTER 15

Library Wars LOVE&WAR Volume 4

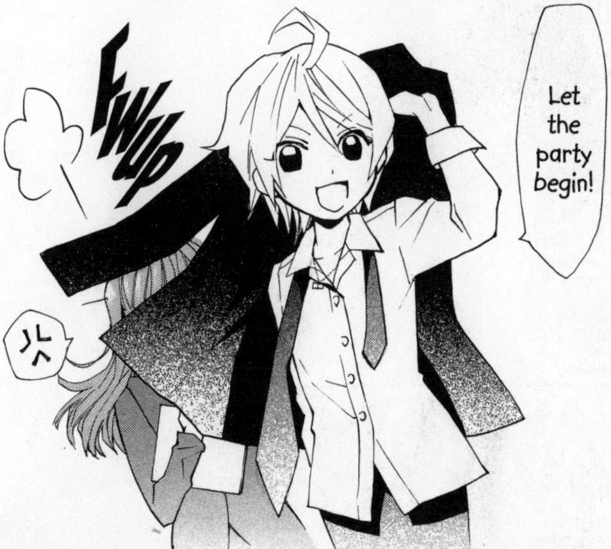
Let the party begin!
FWUP

Hope you enjoy the story!

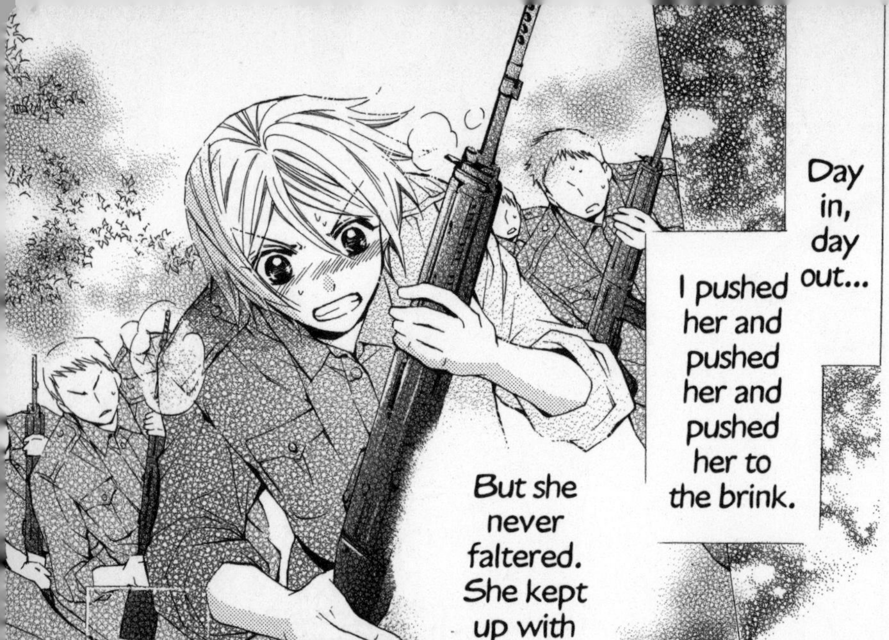
Day in, day out...
I pushed her and pushed her and pushed her to the brink.
But she never faltered. She kept up with me.
But then...

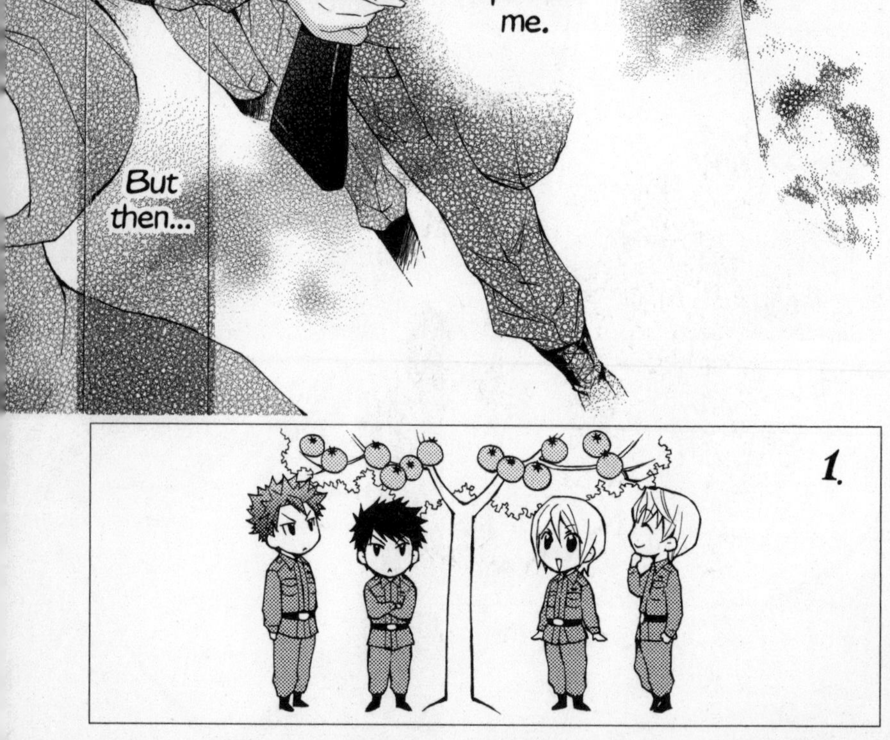
1.

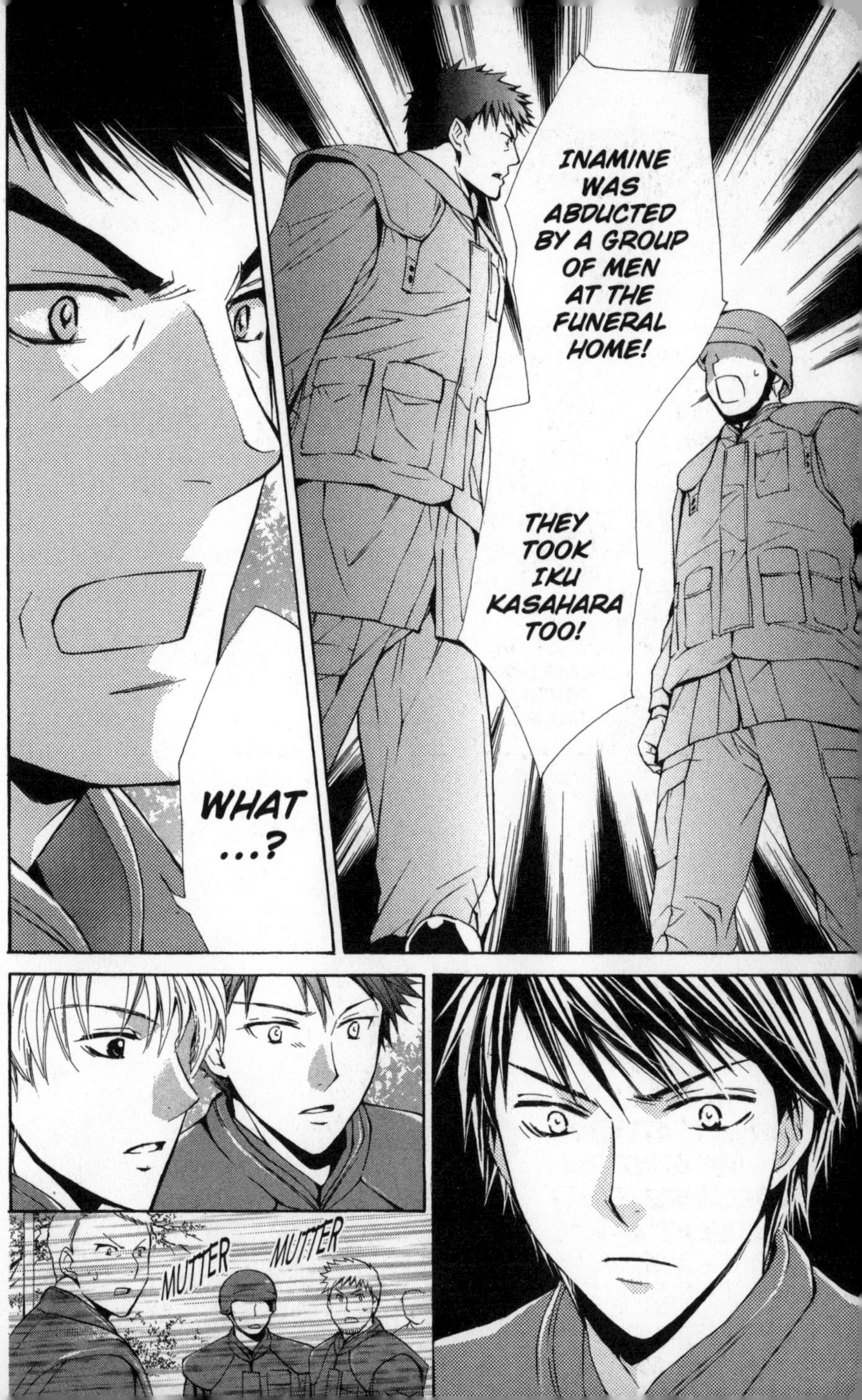
INAMINE WAS ABDUCTED BY A GROUP OF MEN AT THE FUNERAL HOME!
THEY TOOK IKU KASAHARA TOO!
WHAT ...?
MUTTER
MUTTER

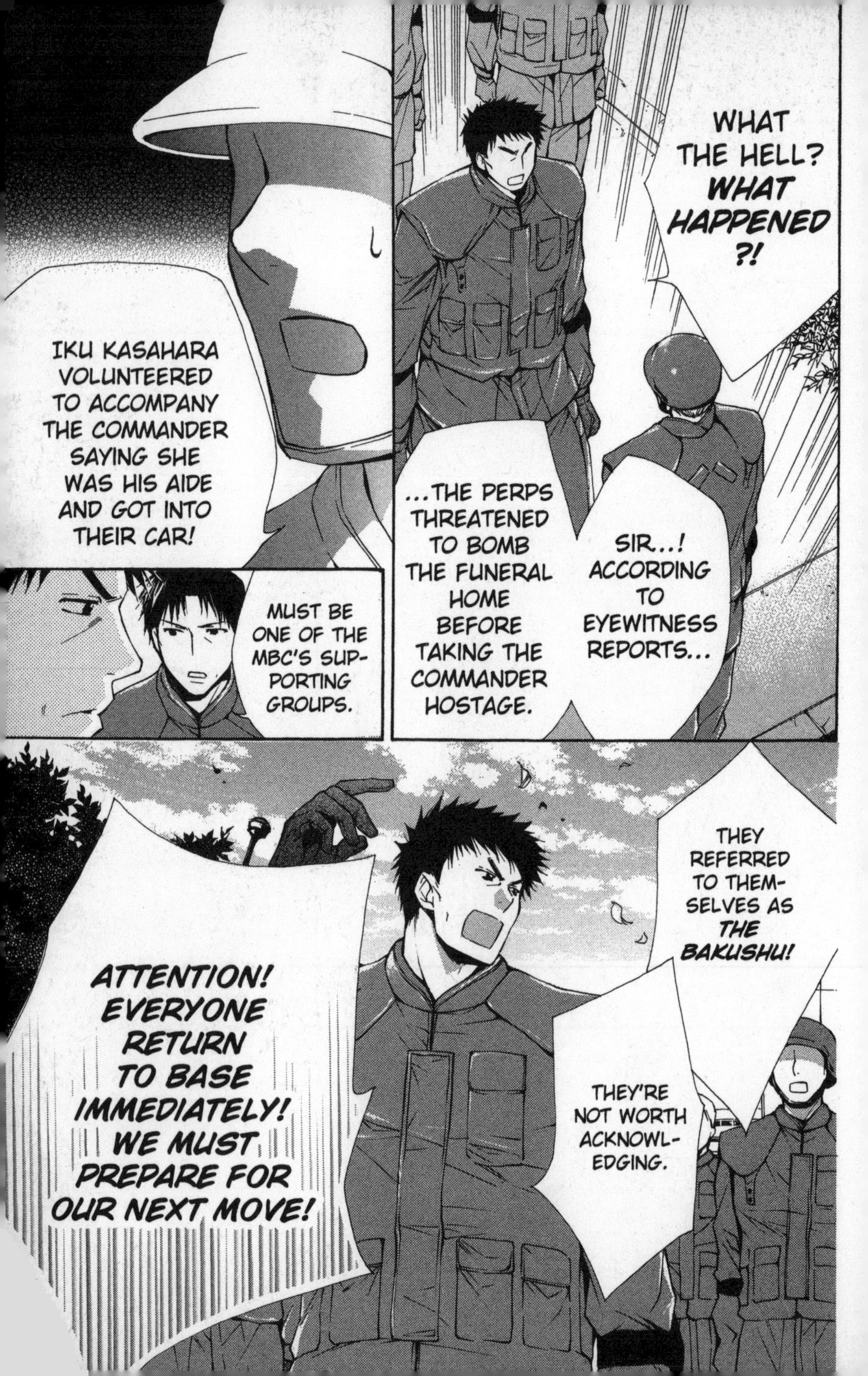
WHAT THE HELL? *WHAT HAPPENED?!*
SIR...! ACCORDING TO EYEWITNESS REPORTS...
...THE PERPS THREATENED TO BOMB THE FUNERAL HOME BEFORE TAKING THE COMMANDER HOSTAGE.
IKU KASAHARA VOLUNTEERED TO ACCOMPANY THE COMMANDER SAYING SHE WAS HIS AIDE AND GOT INTO THEIR CAR!
MUST BE ONE OF THE MBC'S SUP-PORTING GROUPS.
THEY REFERRED TO THEM-SELVES AS *THE BAKUSHU!*
THEY'RE NOT WORTH ACKNOWL-EDGING.
ATTENTION! EVERYONE RETURN TO BASE IMMEDIATELY! WE MUST PREPARE FOR OUR NEXT MOVE!

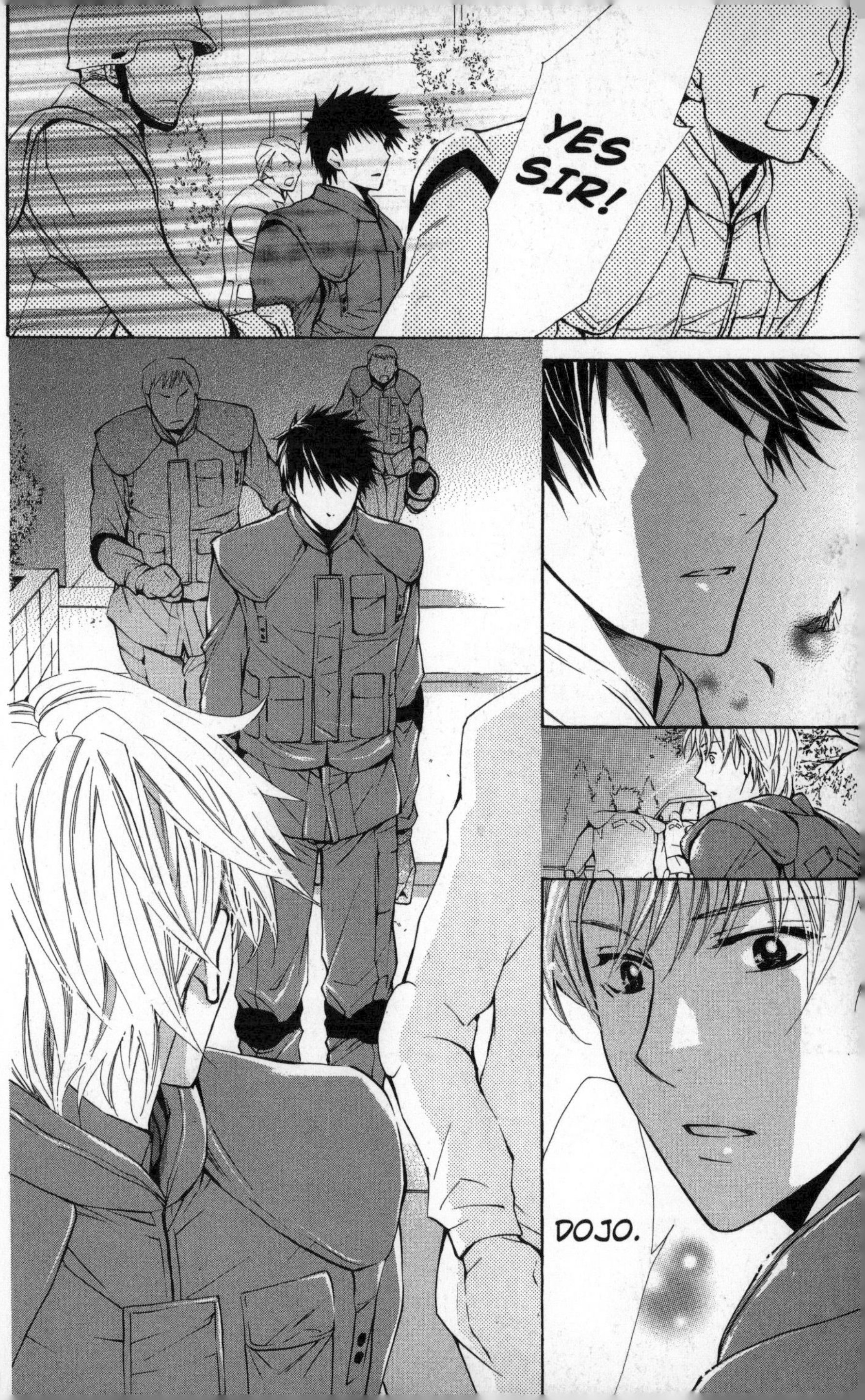
YES SIR!
DOJO.

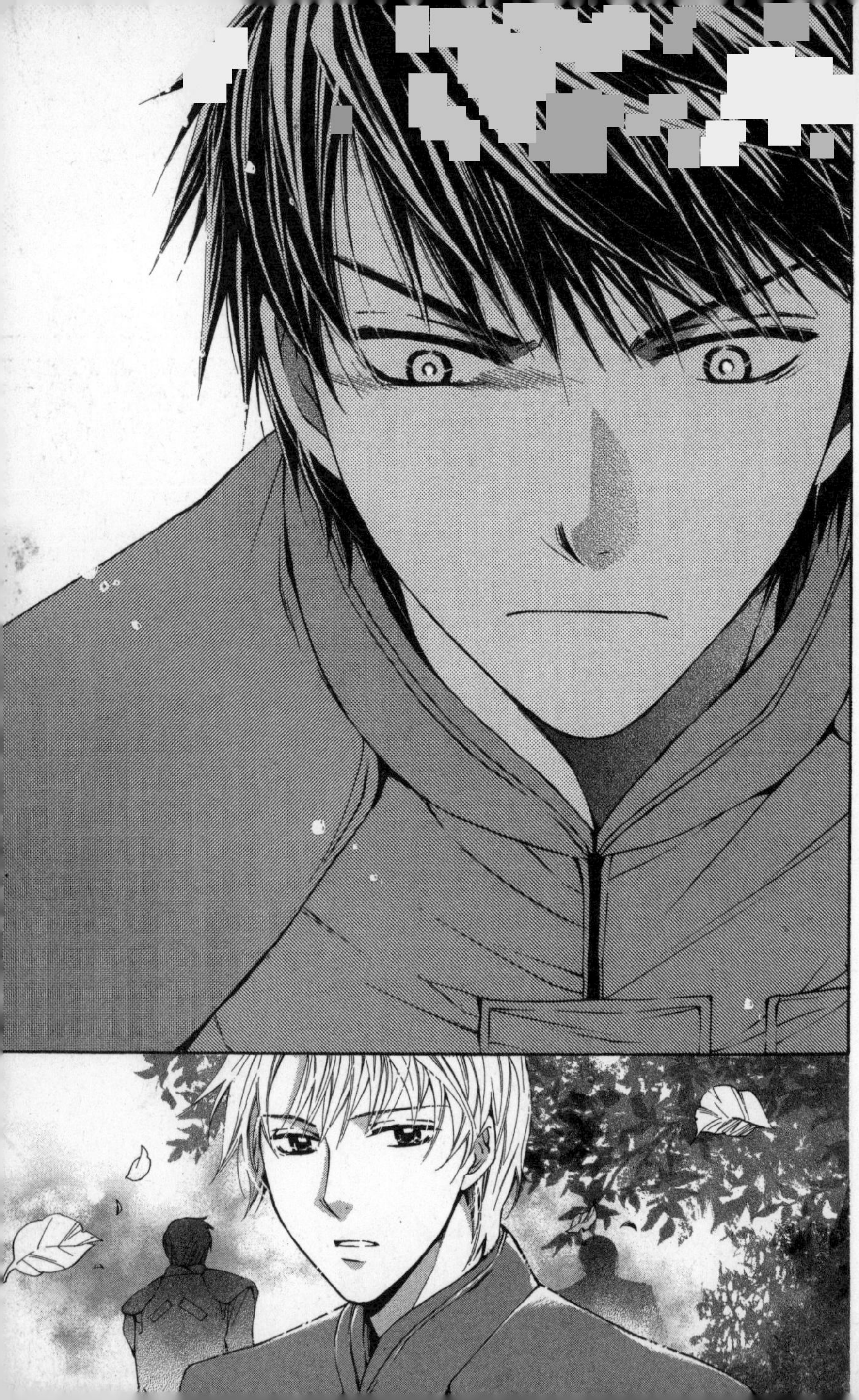

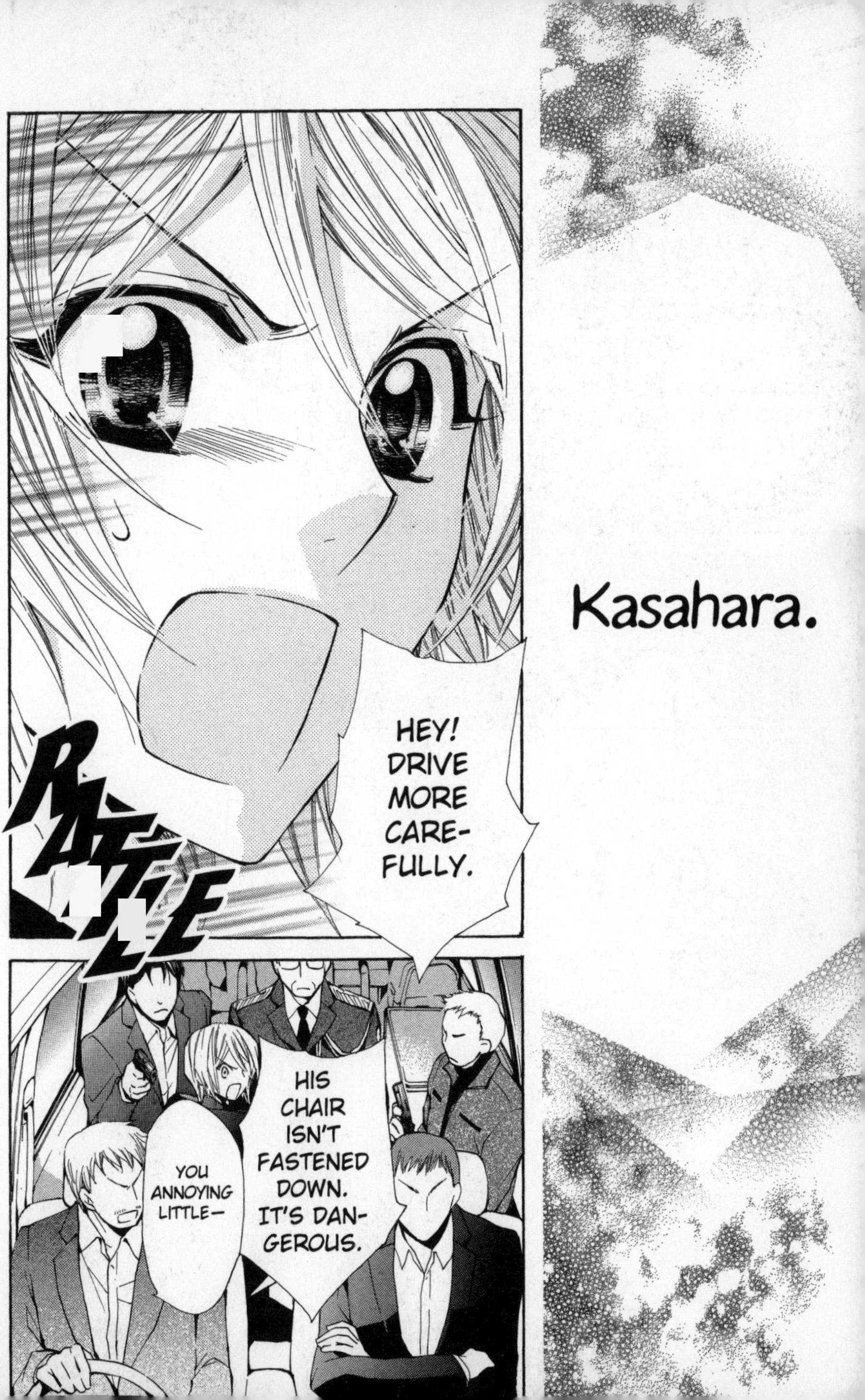
Kasahara.
HEY! DRIVE MORE CAREFULLY.
RATTLE
HIS CHAIR ISN'T FASTENED DOWN. IT'S DANGEROUS.
YOU ANNOYING LITTLE—

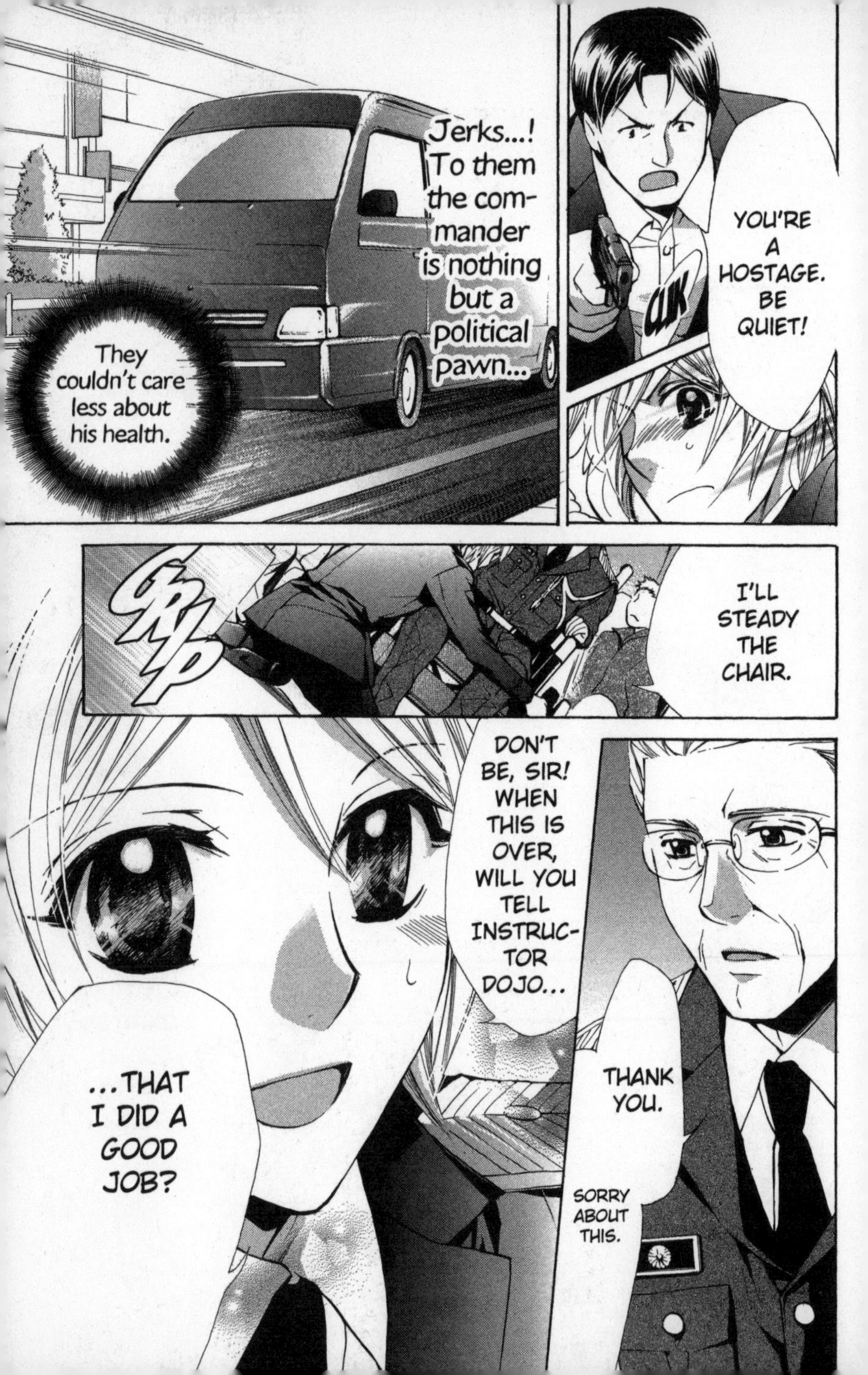
YOU'RE A HOSTAGE. BE QUIET!
CLIK
Jerks...! To them the commander is nothing but a political pawn...
They couldn't care less about his health.
I'LL STEADY THE CHAIR.
GRIP
THANK YOU.
SORRY ABOUT THIS.
DON'T BE, SIR! WHEN THIS IS OVER, WILL YOU TELL INSTRUCTOR DOJO...
...THAT I DID A GOOD JOB?

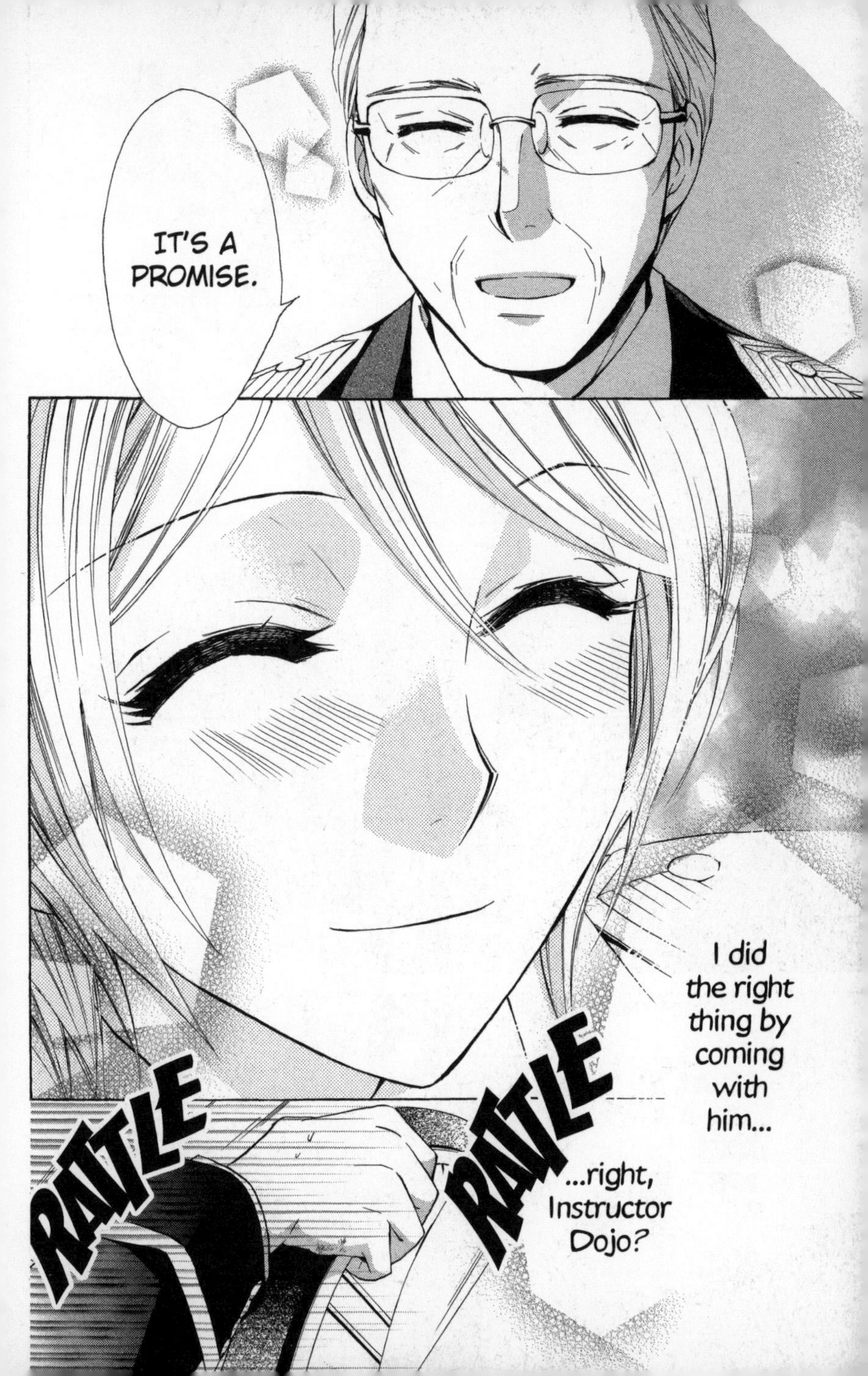
IT'S A PROMISE.
I did the right thing by coming with him...
RATTLE RATTLE
...right, Instructor Dojo?

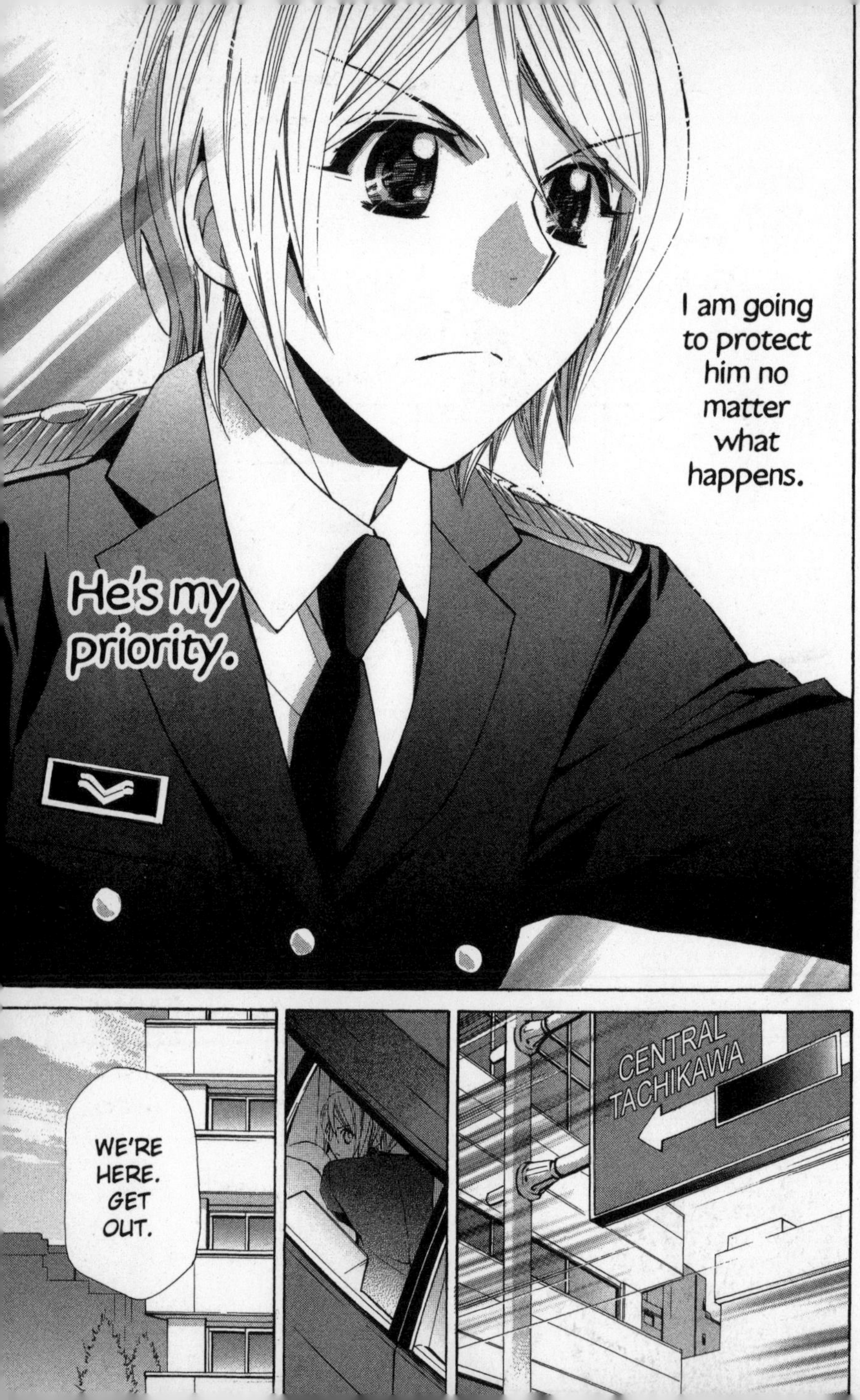
I am going to protect him no matter what happens.
He's my priority.
CENTRAL TACHIKAWA
WE'RE HERE. GET OUT.

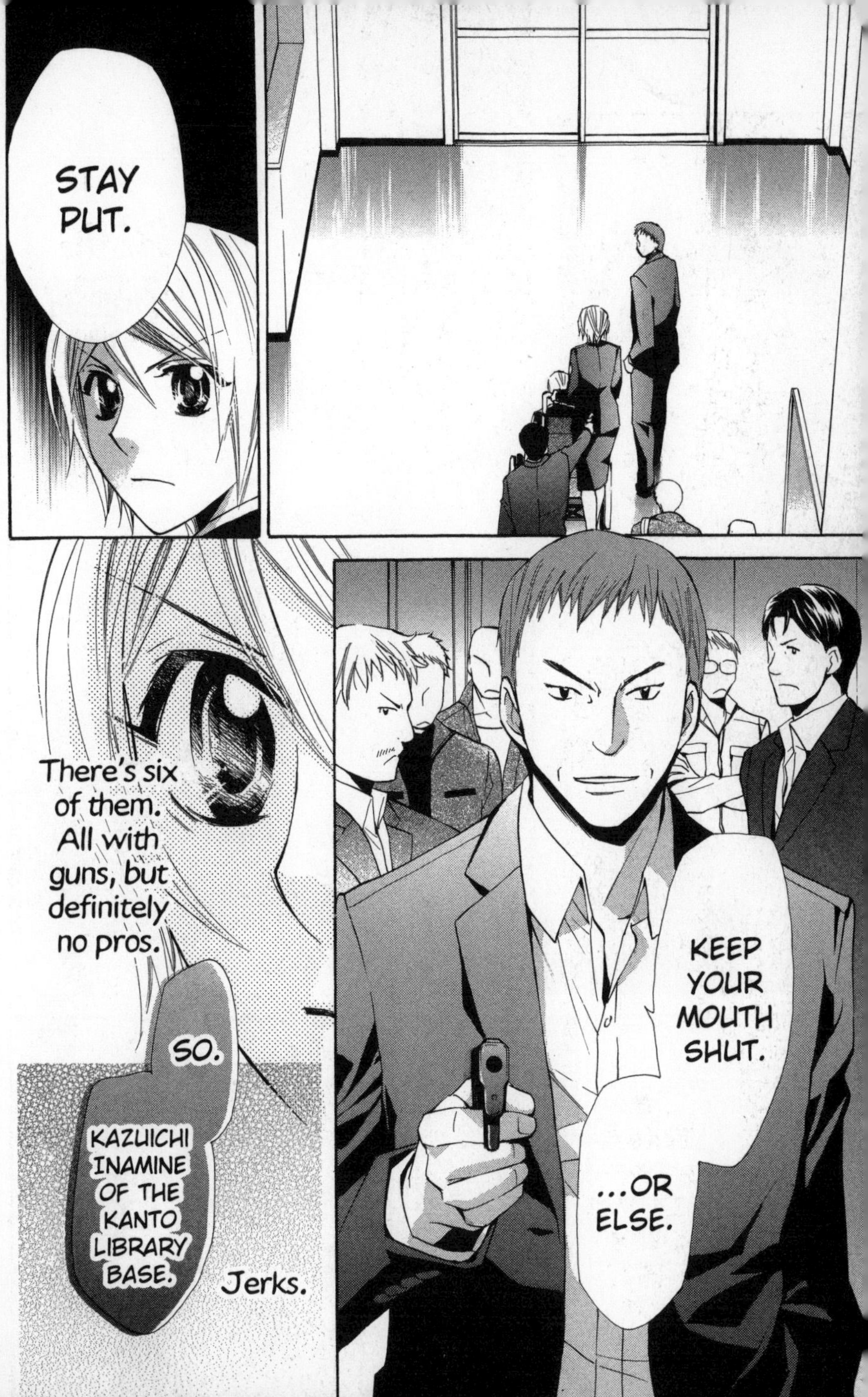
STAY PUT.
KEEP YOUR MOUTH SHUT.
...OR ELSE.
There's six of them. All with guns, but definitely no pros.
SO.
KAZUICHI INAMINE OF THE KANTO LIBRARY BASE.
Jerks.

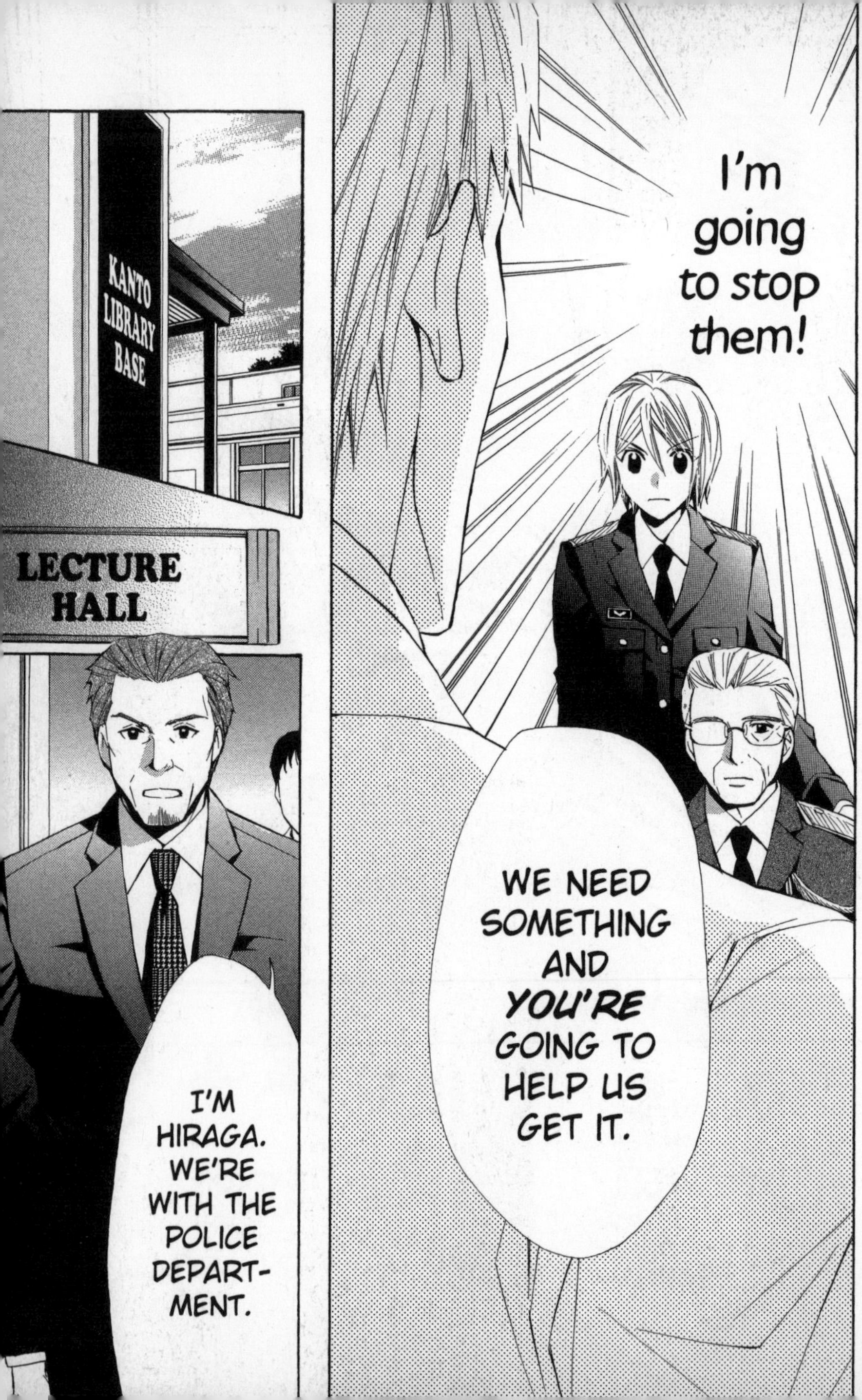
I'm going to stop them!
WE NEED SOMETHING AND *YOU'RE* GOING TO HELP US GET IT.
KANTO LIBRARY BASE
LECTURE HALL
I'M HIRAGA. WE'RE WITH THE POLICE DEPART-MENT.

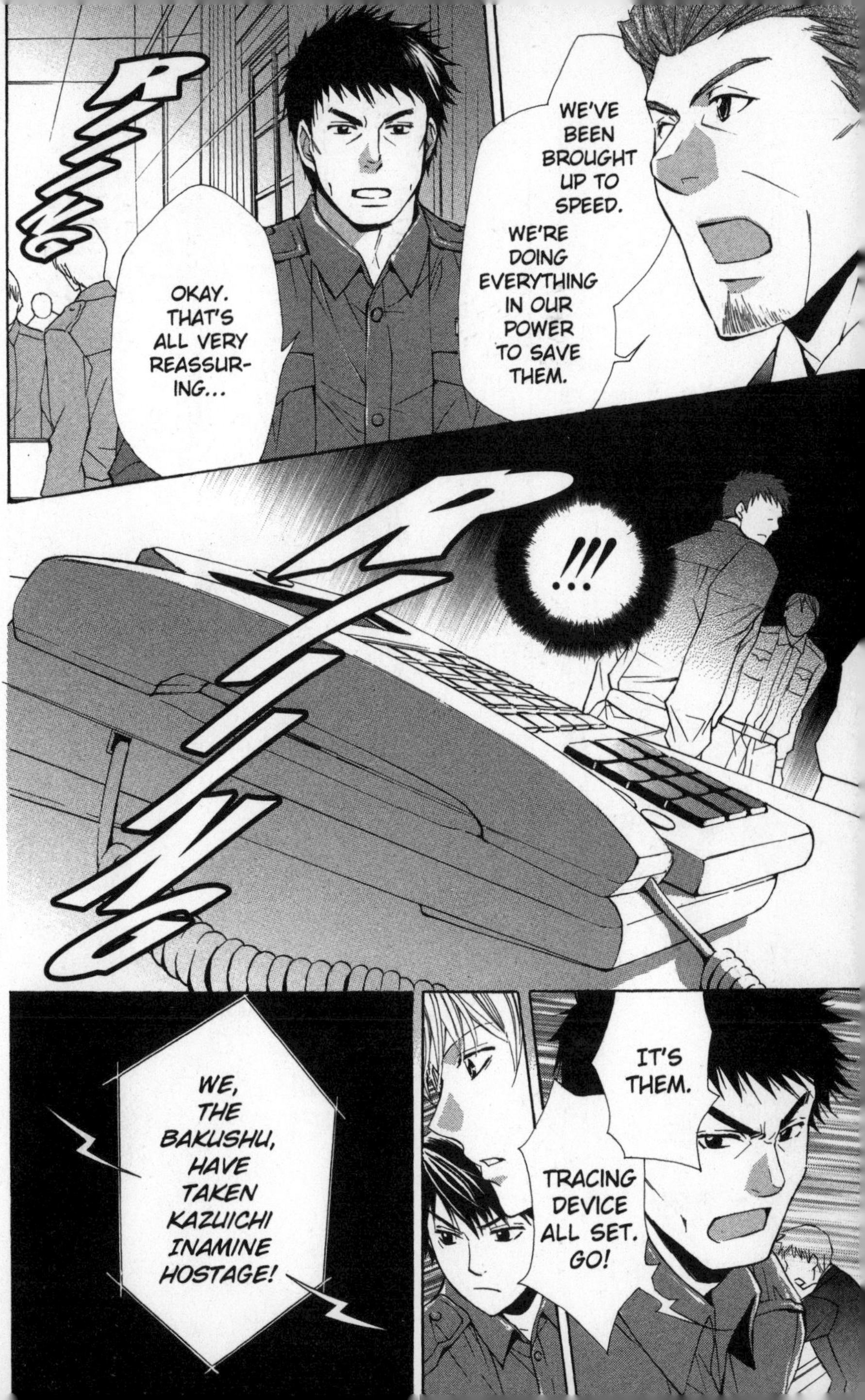
WE'VE BEEN BROUGHT UP TO SPEED.
WE'RE DOING EVERYTHING IN OUR POWER TO SAVE THEM.
RIIING
OKAY. THAT'S ALL VERY REASSURING...
!!!
RIIING
IT'S THEM.
TRACING DEVICE ALL SET. GO!
WE, THE BAKUSHU, HAVE TAKEN KAZUICHI INAMINE HOSTAGE!

1

*

Hello,
I'm Kiiro Yumi.

Welcome to *Library Wars* volume 4.

Volume 4! Yes! I know this is cliché, but it's like a dream come true.

I couldn't have come this far without everyone who makes the *LaLa* version of *Library Wars* possible.

Thank you very, very much.

I hope you enjoy this to the last page.

*

*

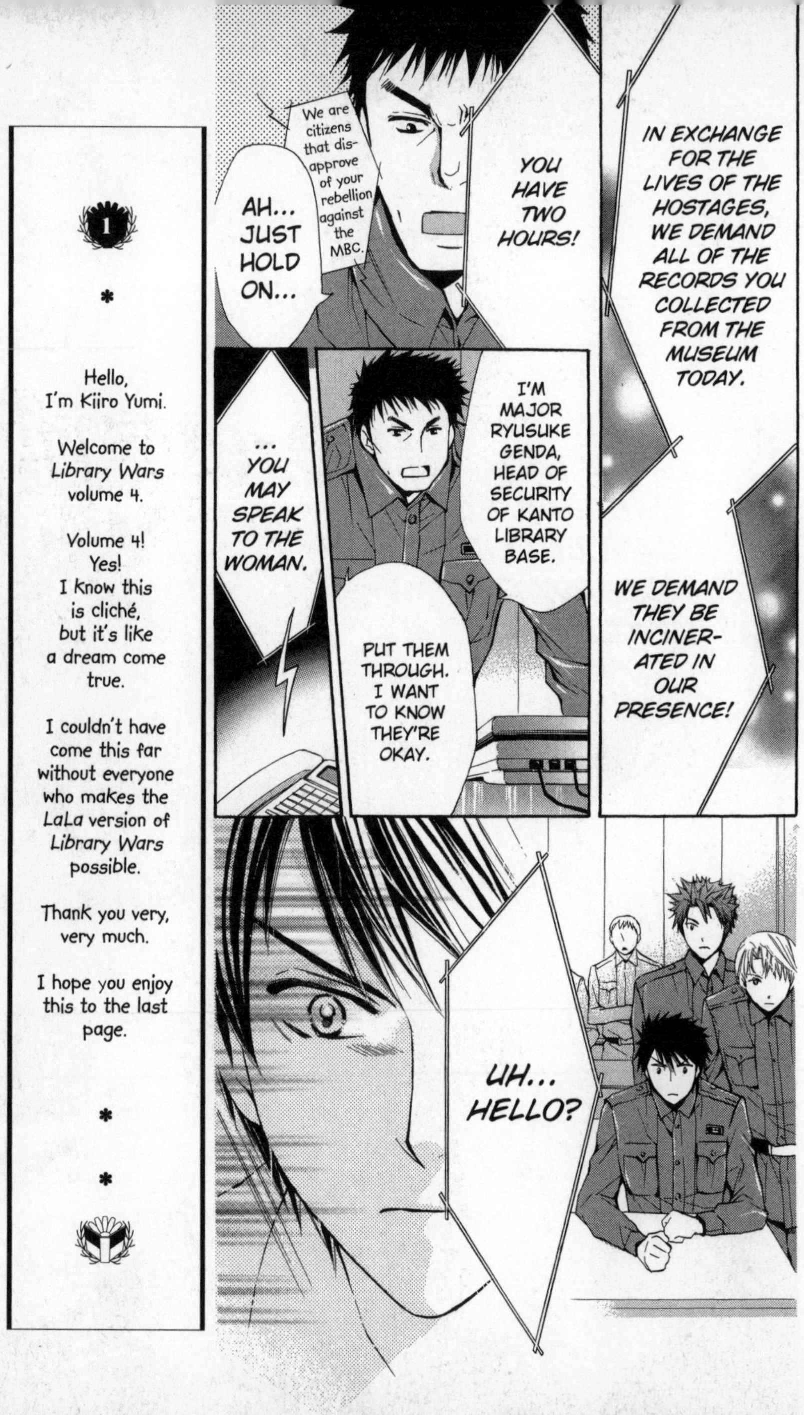
IN EXCHANGE FOR THE LIVES OF THE HOSTAGES, WE DEMAND ALL OF THE RECORDS YOU COLLECTED FROM THE MUSEUM TODAY.
WE DEMAND THEY BE INCINER-ATED IN OUR PRESENCE!
YOU HAVE TWO HOURS!
We are citizens that dis-approve of your rebellion against the MBC.
AH... JUST HOLD ON...
I'M MAJOR RYUSUKE GENDA, HEAD OF SECURITY OF KANTO LIBRARY BASE.
PUT THEM THROUGH. I WANT TO KNOW THEY'RE OKAY.
... YOU MAY SPEAK TO THE WOMAN.
UH... HELLO?

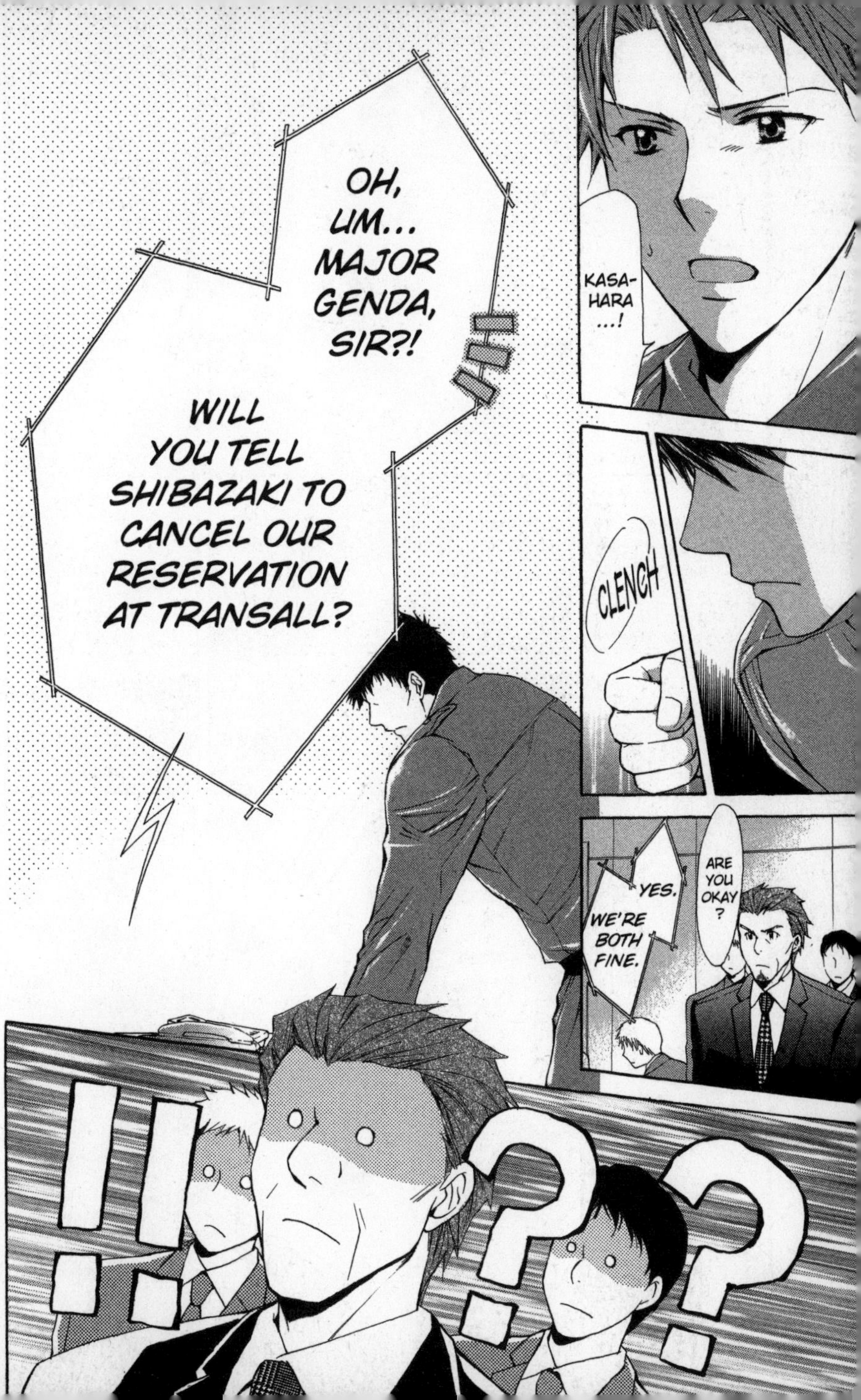
KASA-HARA...!
CLENCH
ARE YOU OKAY?
YES. WE'RE BOTH FINE.
OH, UM... MAJOR GENDA, SIR?!
WILL YOU TELL SHIBAZAKI TO CANCEL OUR RESERVATION AT TRANSALL?
!!
??

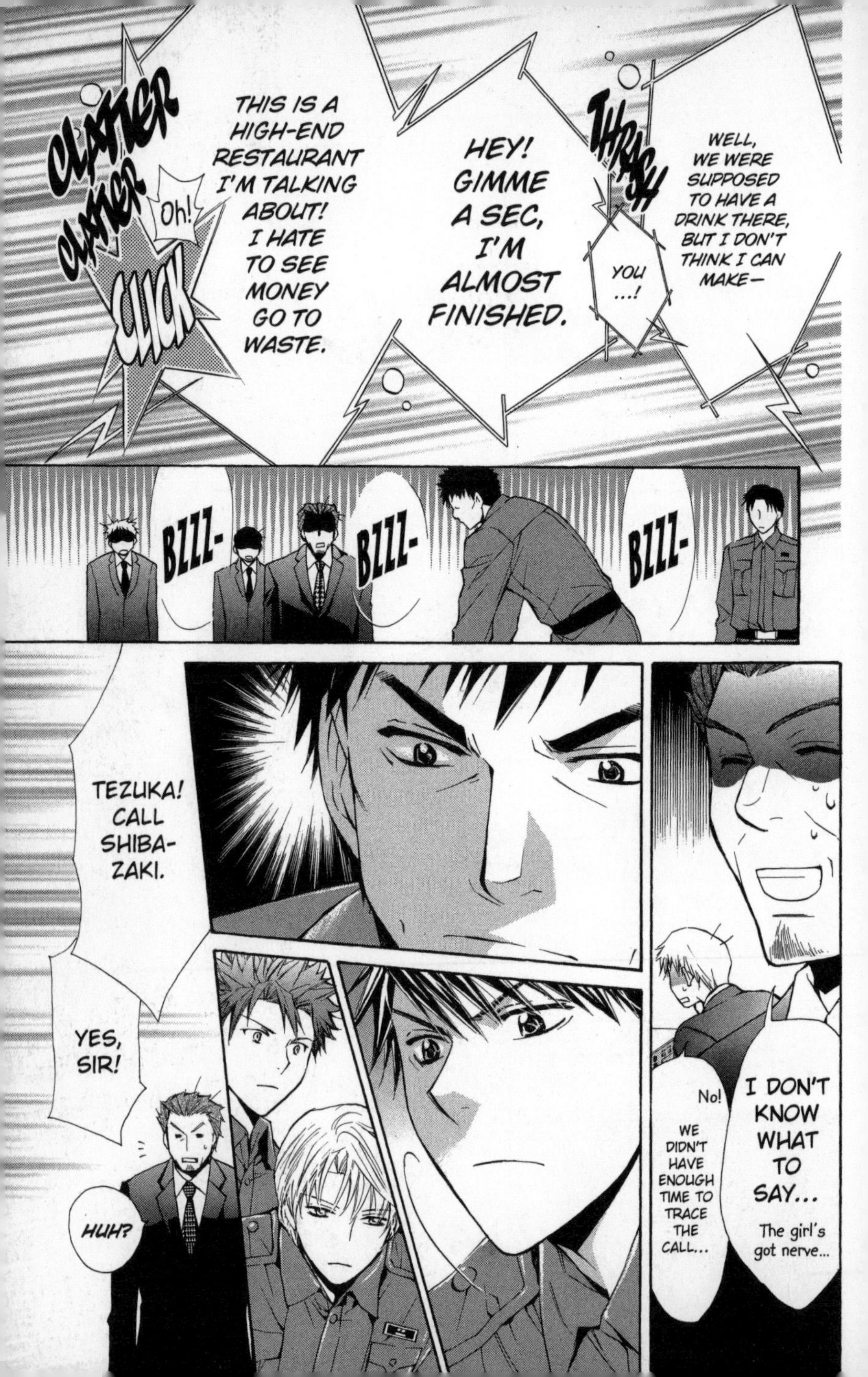
WELL, WE WERE SUPPOSED TO HAVE A DRINK THERE, BUT I DON'T THINK I CAN MAKE—
THRASH
YOU ...!
HEY! GIMME A SEC, I'M ALMOST FINISHED.
THIS IS A HIGH-END RESTAURANT I'M TALKING ABOUT! I HATE TO SEE MONEY GO TO WASTE.
Oh!
CLATTER CLATTER
CLICK
BZZZ-
BZZZ-
BZZZ-
I DON'T KNOW WHAT TO SAY...
The girl's got nerve...
No!
WE DIDN'T HAVE ENOUGH TIME TO TRACE THE CALL...
TEZUKA! CALL SHIBA-ZAKI.
YES, SIR!
HUH?

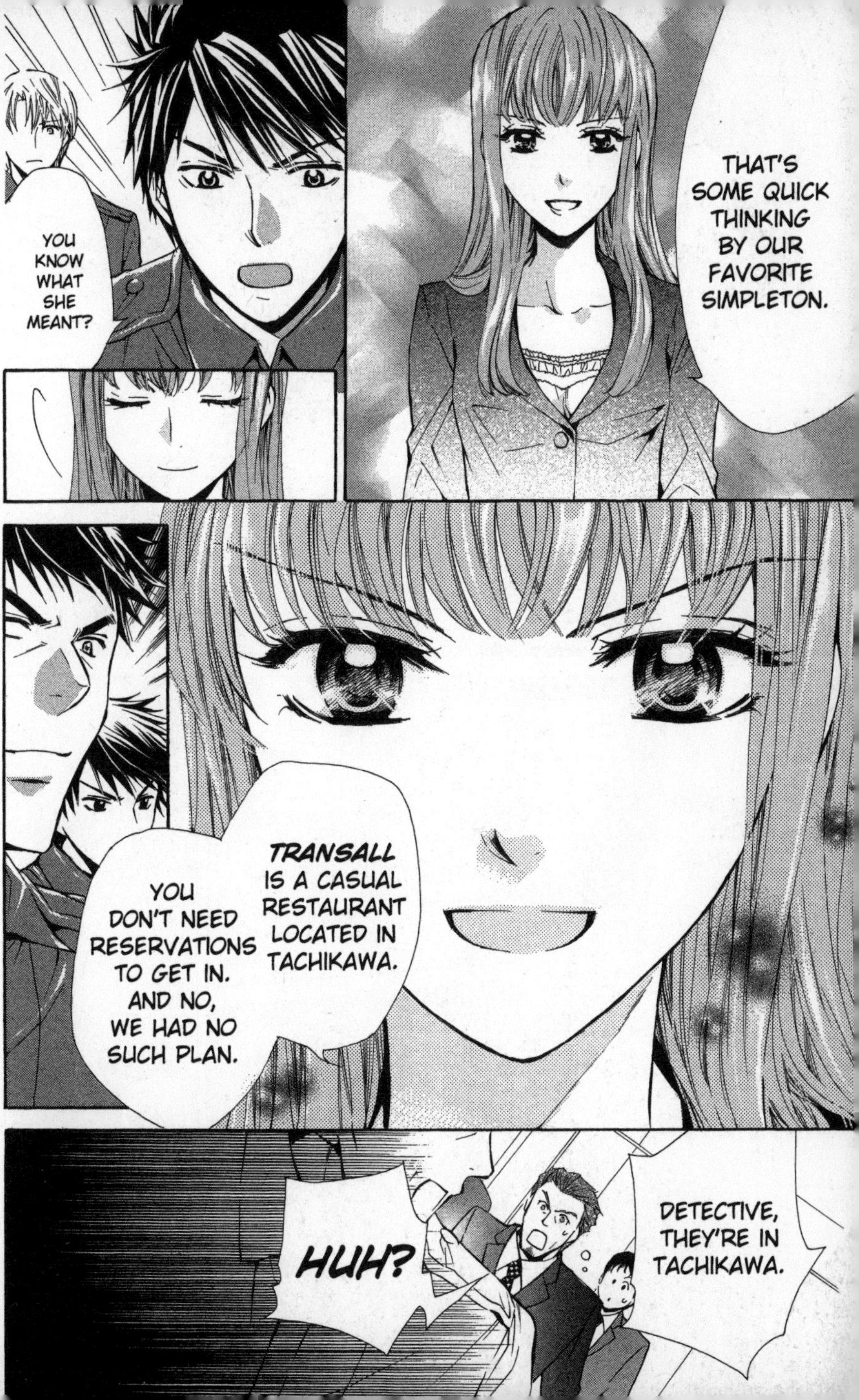
THAT'S SOME QUICK THINKING BY OUR FAVORITE SIMPLETON.
YOU KNOW WHAT SHE MEANT?
TRANSALL IS A CASUAL RESTAURANT LOCATED IN TACHIKAWA.
YOU DON'T NEED RESERVATIONS TO GET IN. AND NO, WE HAD NO SUCH PLAN.
DETECTIVE, THEY'RE IN TACHIKAWA.
HUH?

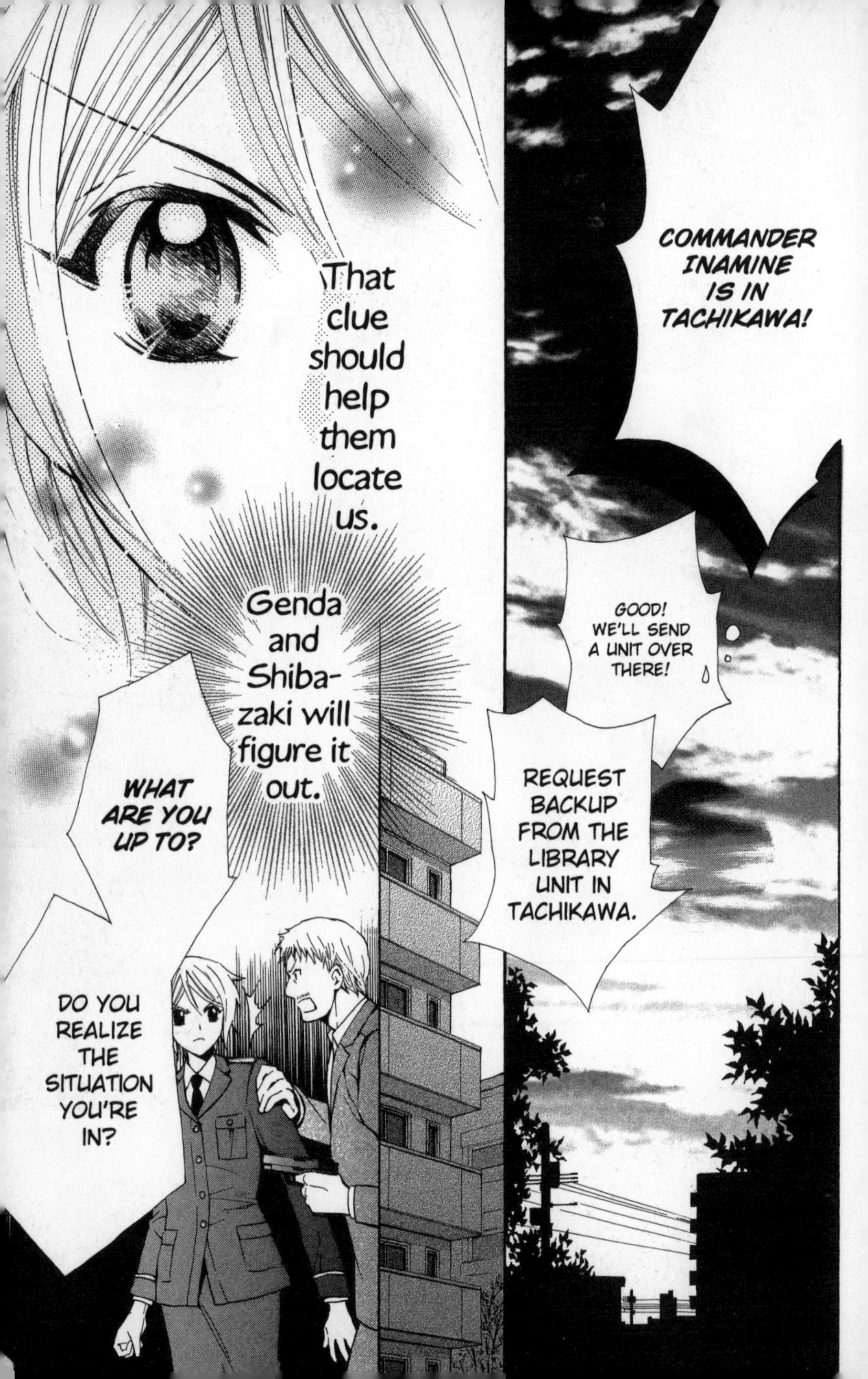
COMMANDER INAMINE IS IN TACHIKAWA!
GOOD! WE'LL SEND A UNIT OVER THERE!
REQUEST BACKUP FROM THE LIBRARY UNIT IN TACHIKAWA.
That clue should help them locate us.
Genda and Shiba-zaki will figure it out.
WHAT ARE YOU UP TO?
DO YOU REALIZE THE SITUATION YOU'RE IN?

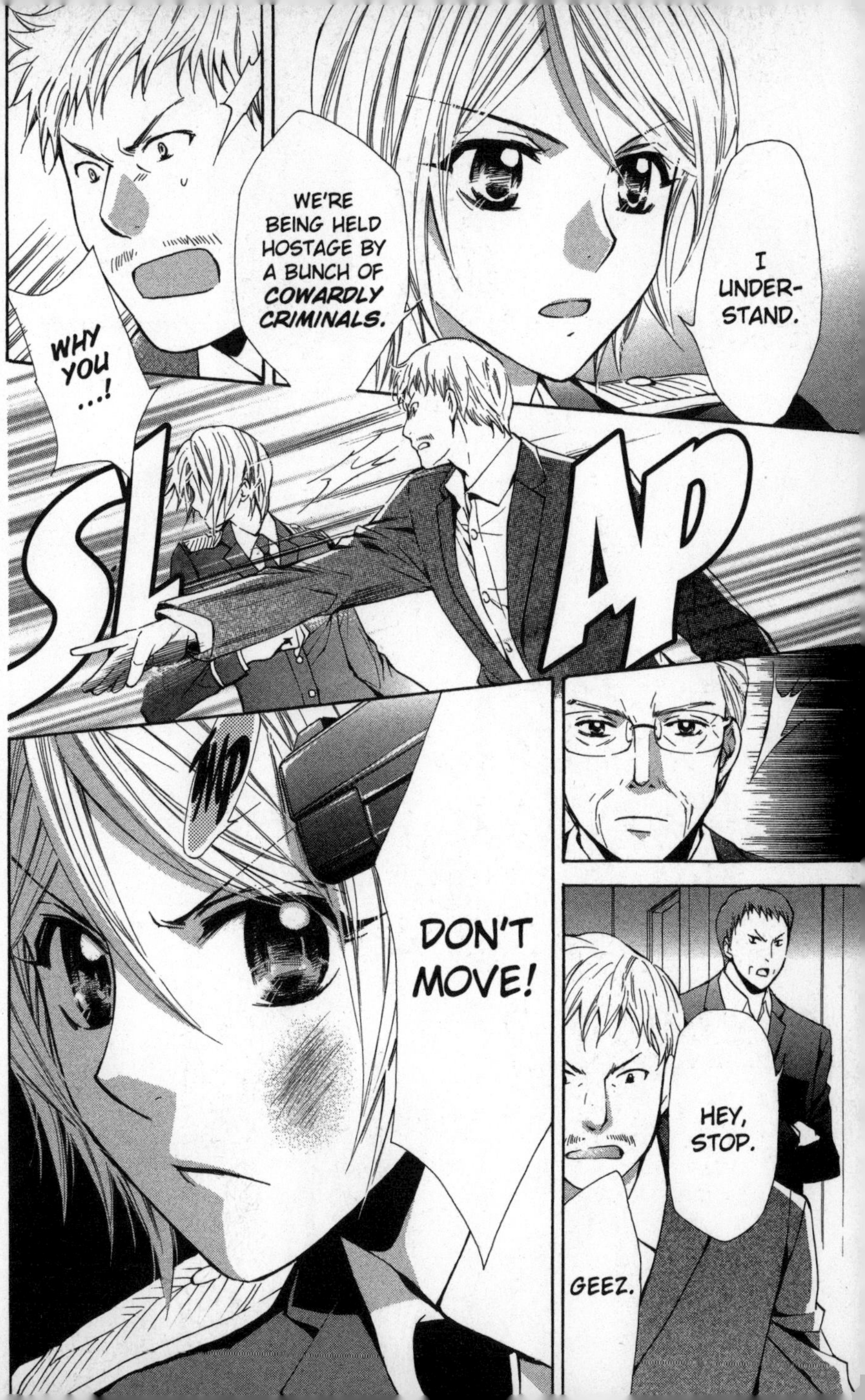
I UNDERSTAND.
WE'RE BEING HELD HOSTAGE BY A BUNCH OF COWARDLY CRIMINALS.
WHY YOU ...!
SLAP
HEY, STOP.
GEEZ.
DON'T MOVE!

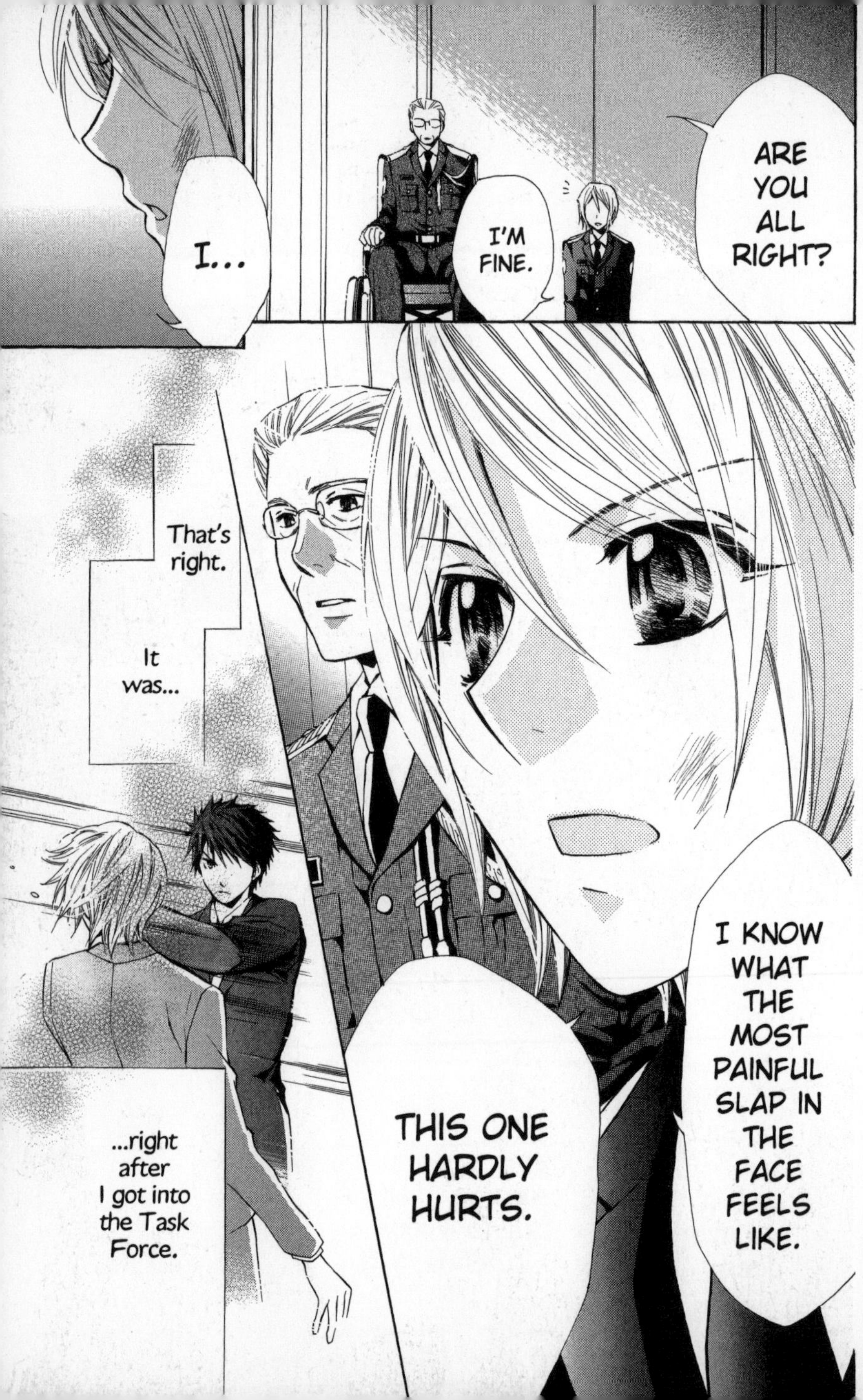
ARE YOU ALL RIGHT?
I'M FINE.
I...
I KNOW WHAT THE MOST PAINFUL SLAP IN THE FACE FEELS LIKE.
THIS ONE HARDLY HURTS.
That's right.
It was...
...right after I got into the Task Force.

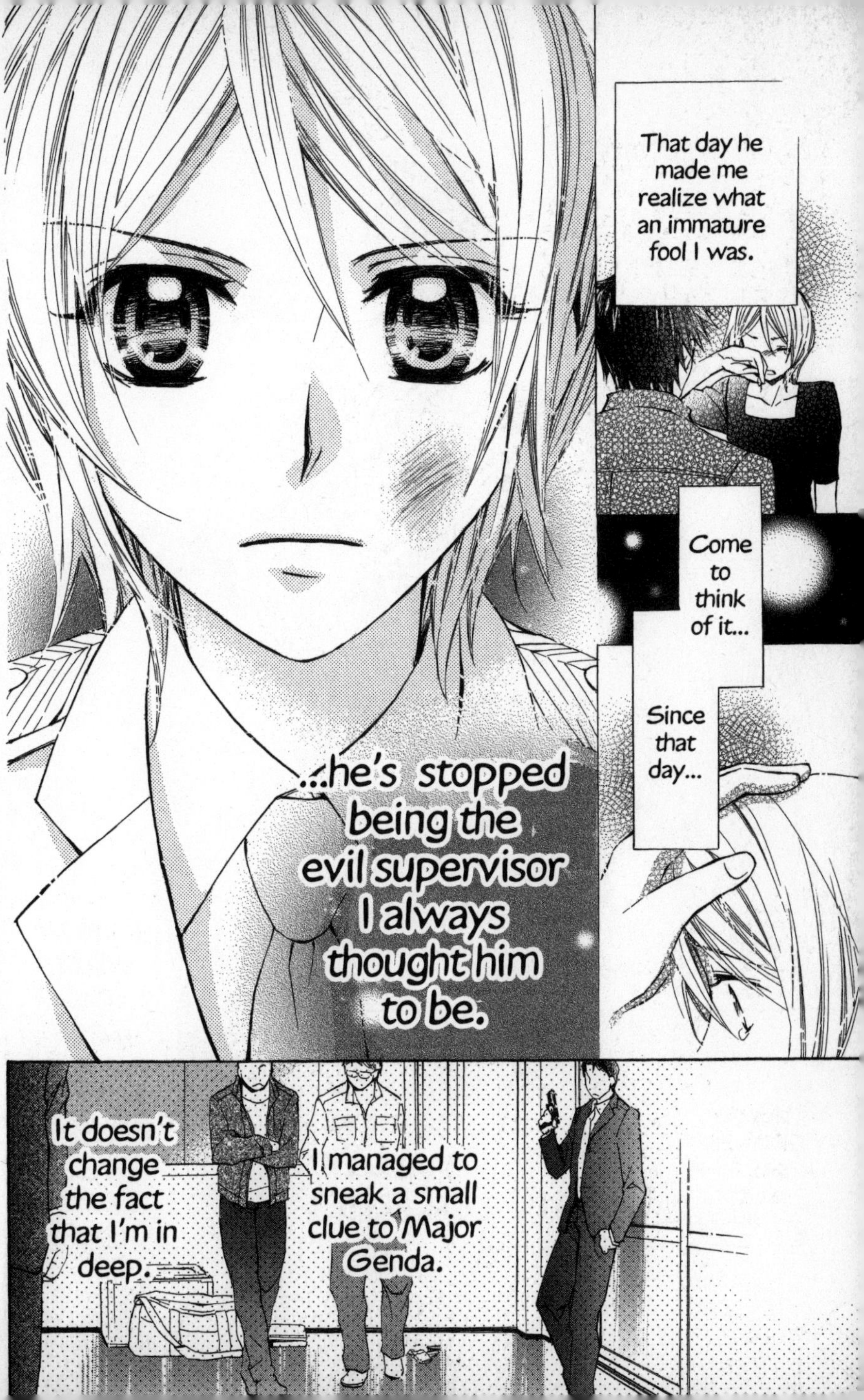
That day he made me realize what an immature fool I was.
Come to think of it...
Since that day...
...he's stopped being the evil supervisor I always thought him to be.
I managed to sneak a small clue to Major Genda.
It doesn't change the fact that I'm in deep.

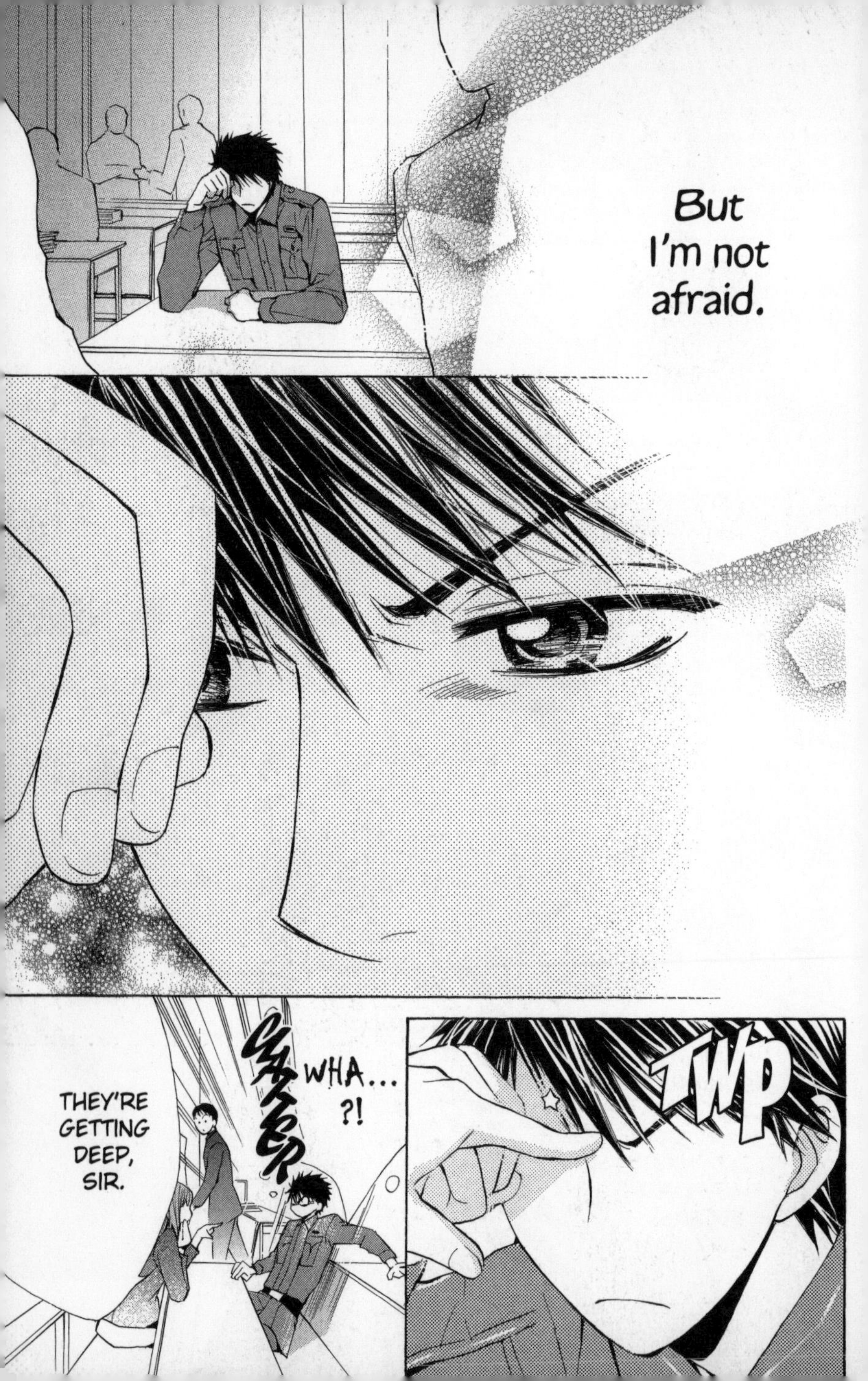
But I'm not afraid.
TWP
WHA... ?!
CLATTER
THEY'RE GETTING DEEP, SIR.

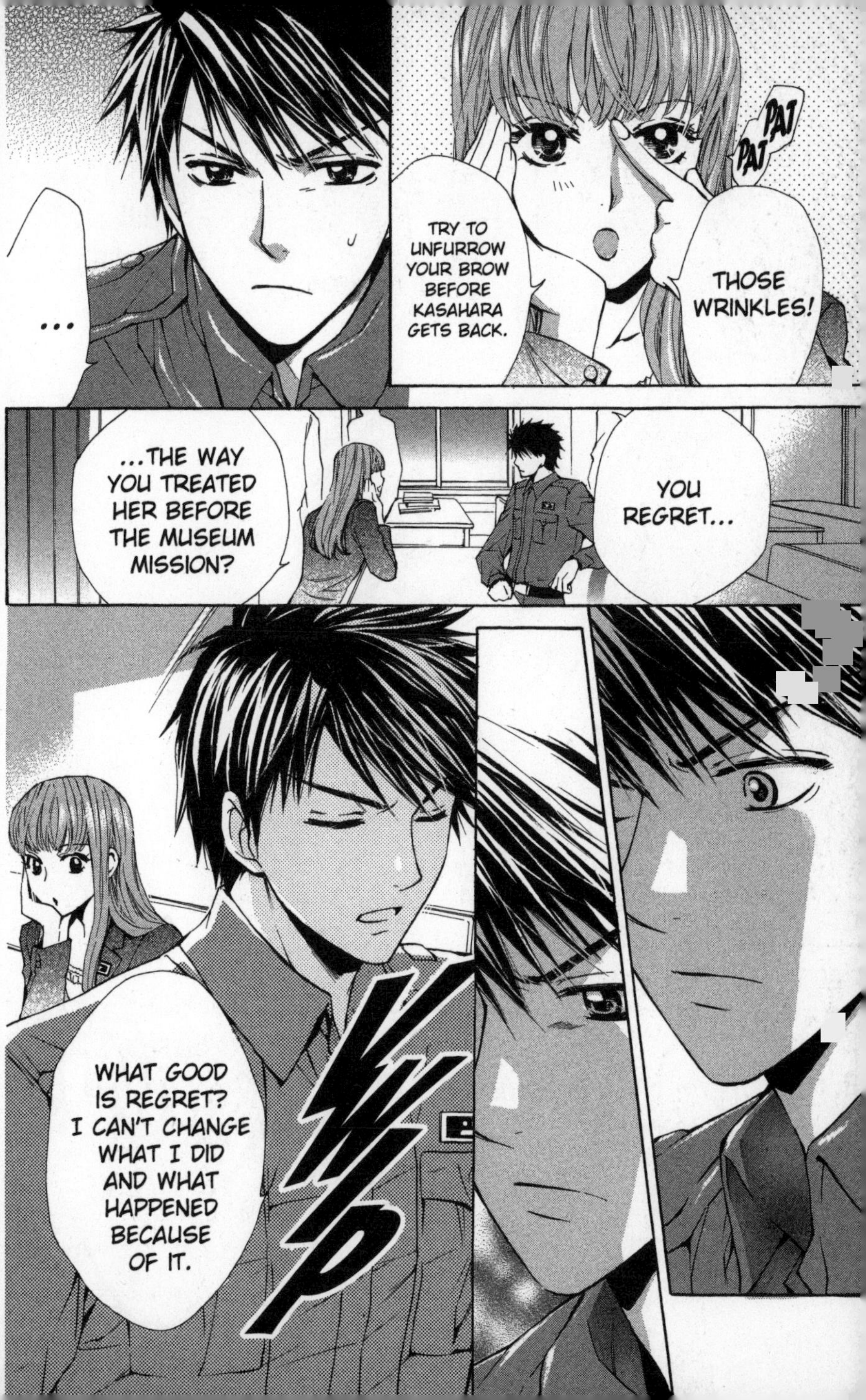
PAJ PAJ
THOSE WRINKLES!
TRY TO UNFURROW YOUR BROW BEFORE KASAHARA GETS BACK.
...
YOU REGRET...
...THE WAY YOU TREATED HER BEFORE THE MUSEUM MISSION?
WHIP
WHAT GOOD IS REGRET? I CAN'T CHANGE WHAT I DID AND WHAT HAPPENED BECAUSE OF IT.

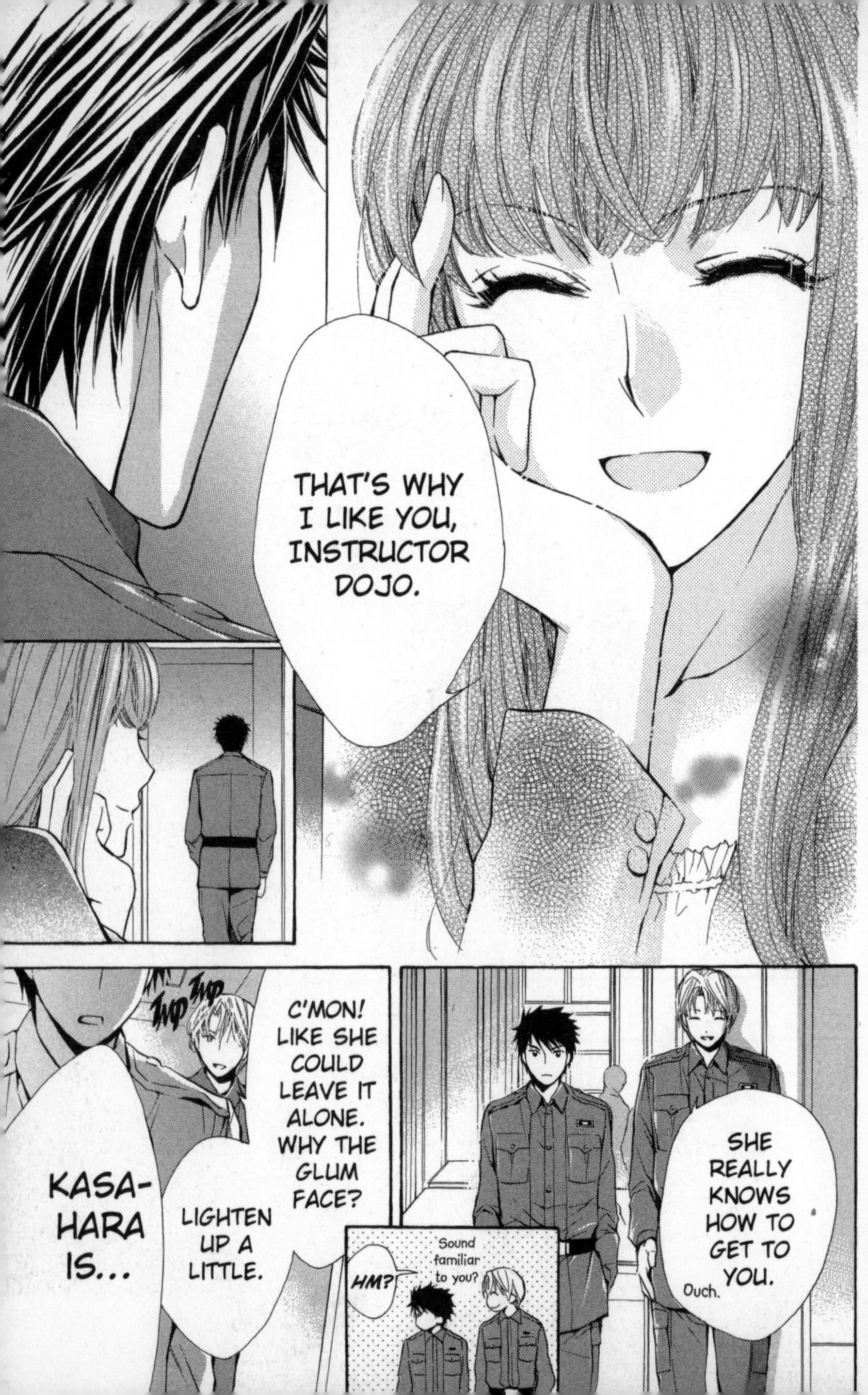
THAT'S WHY I LIKE YOU, INSTRUCTOR DOJO.
SHE REALLY KNOWS HOW TO GET TO YOU.
Ouch.
Sound familiar to you?
HM?
C'MON! LIKE SHE COULD LEAVE IT ALONE. WHY THE GLUM FACE?
LIGHTEN UP A LITTLE.
KASA-HARA IS...

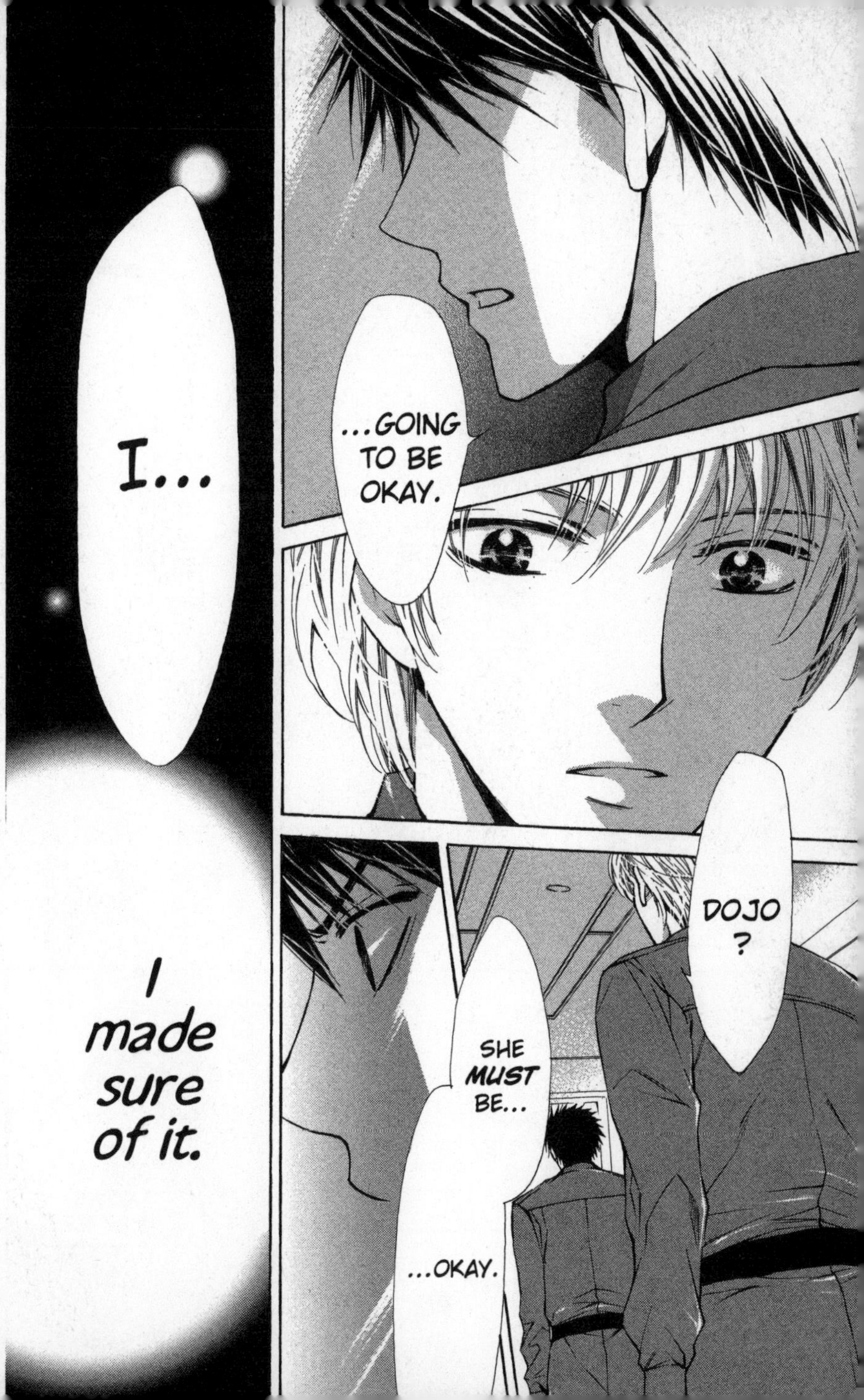
...GOING TO BE OKAY.
DOJO?
SHE *MUST* BE...
...OKAY.
I...
I made sure of it.

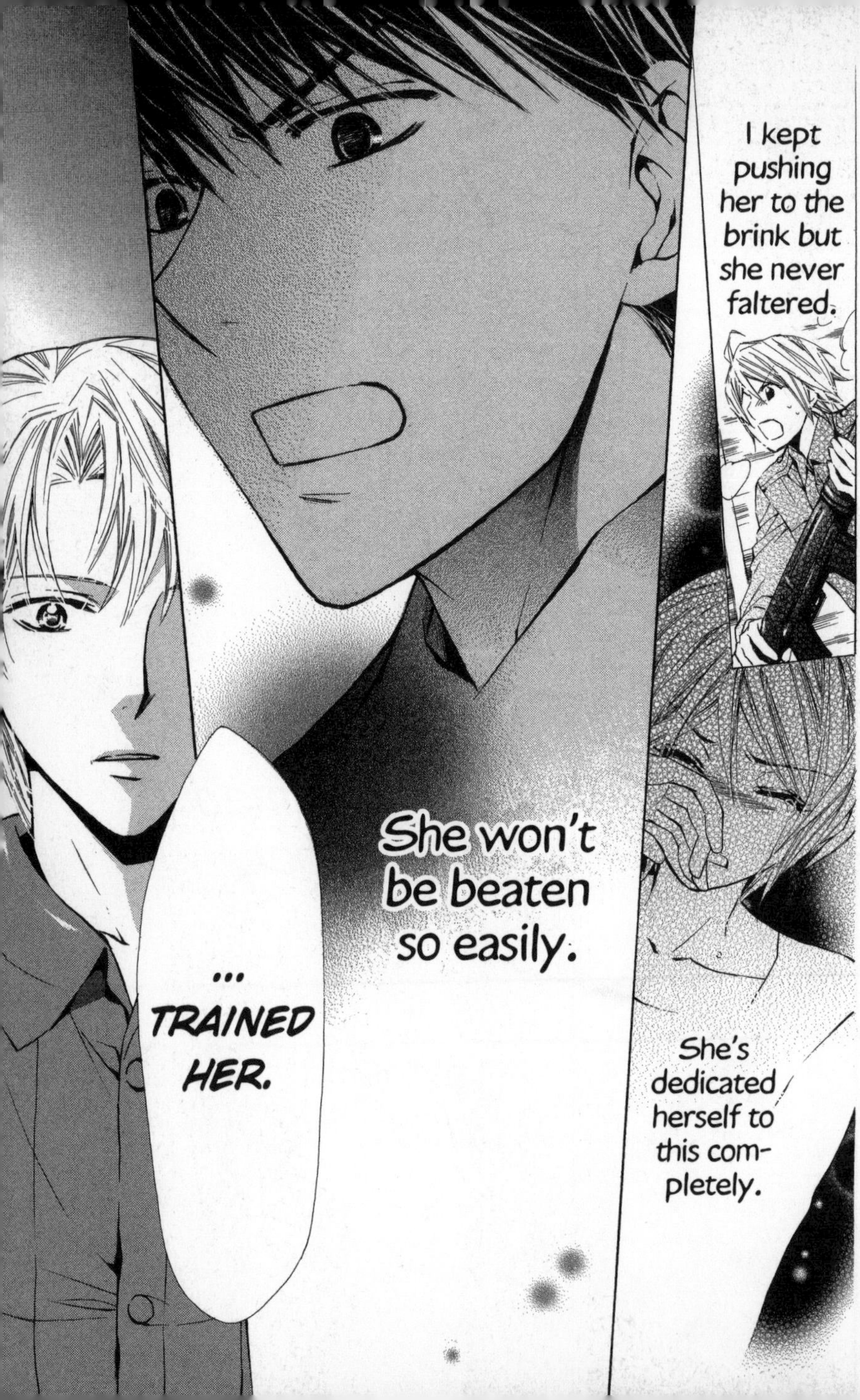
I kept pushing her to the brink but she never faltered.
She's dedicated herself to this com-pletely.
She won't be beaten so easily.
... TRAINED HER.

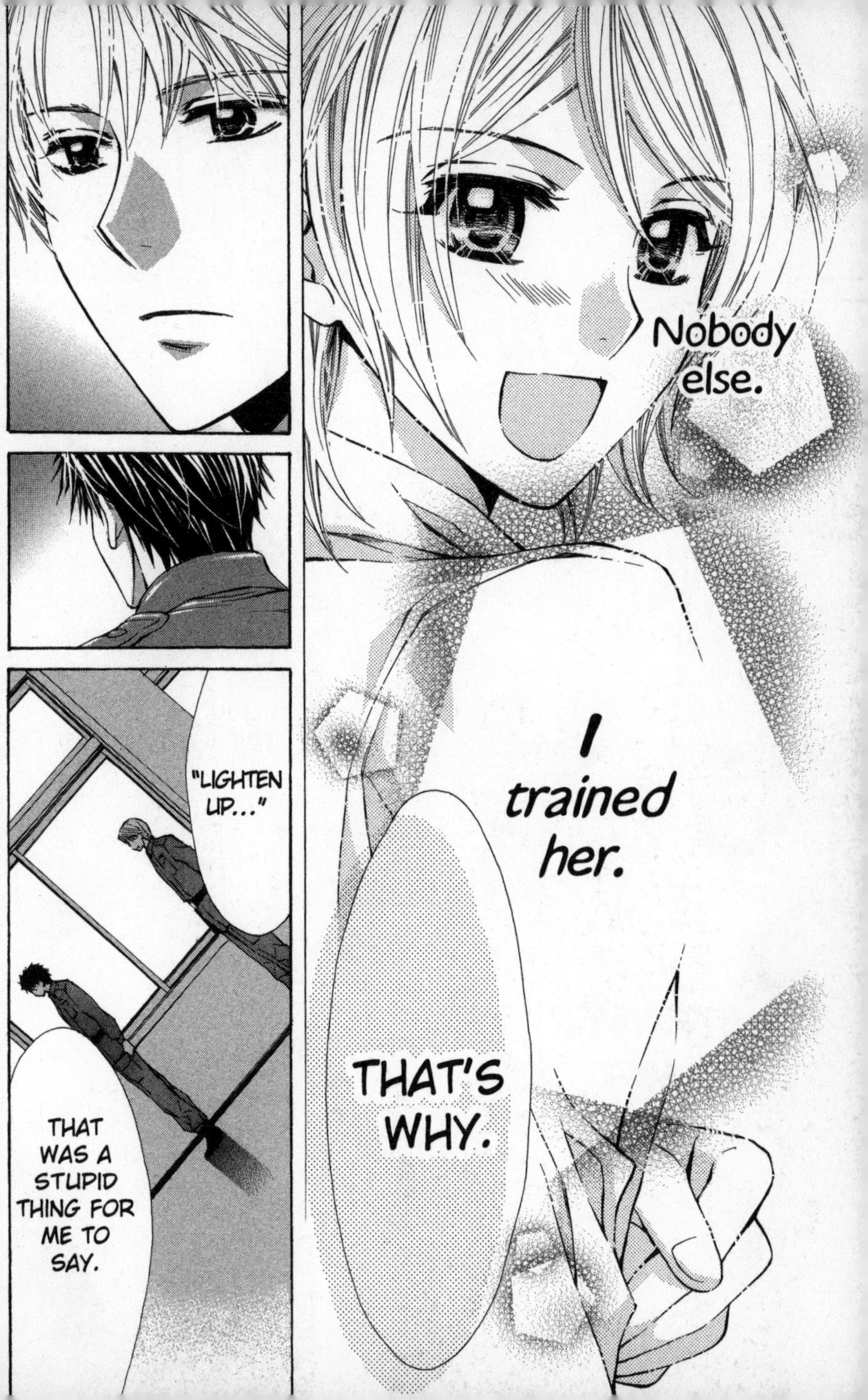
Nobody else.
I trained her.
THAT'S WHY.
"LIGHTEN UP..."
THAT WAS A STUPID THING FOR ME TO SAY.

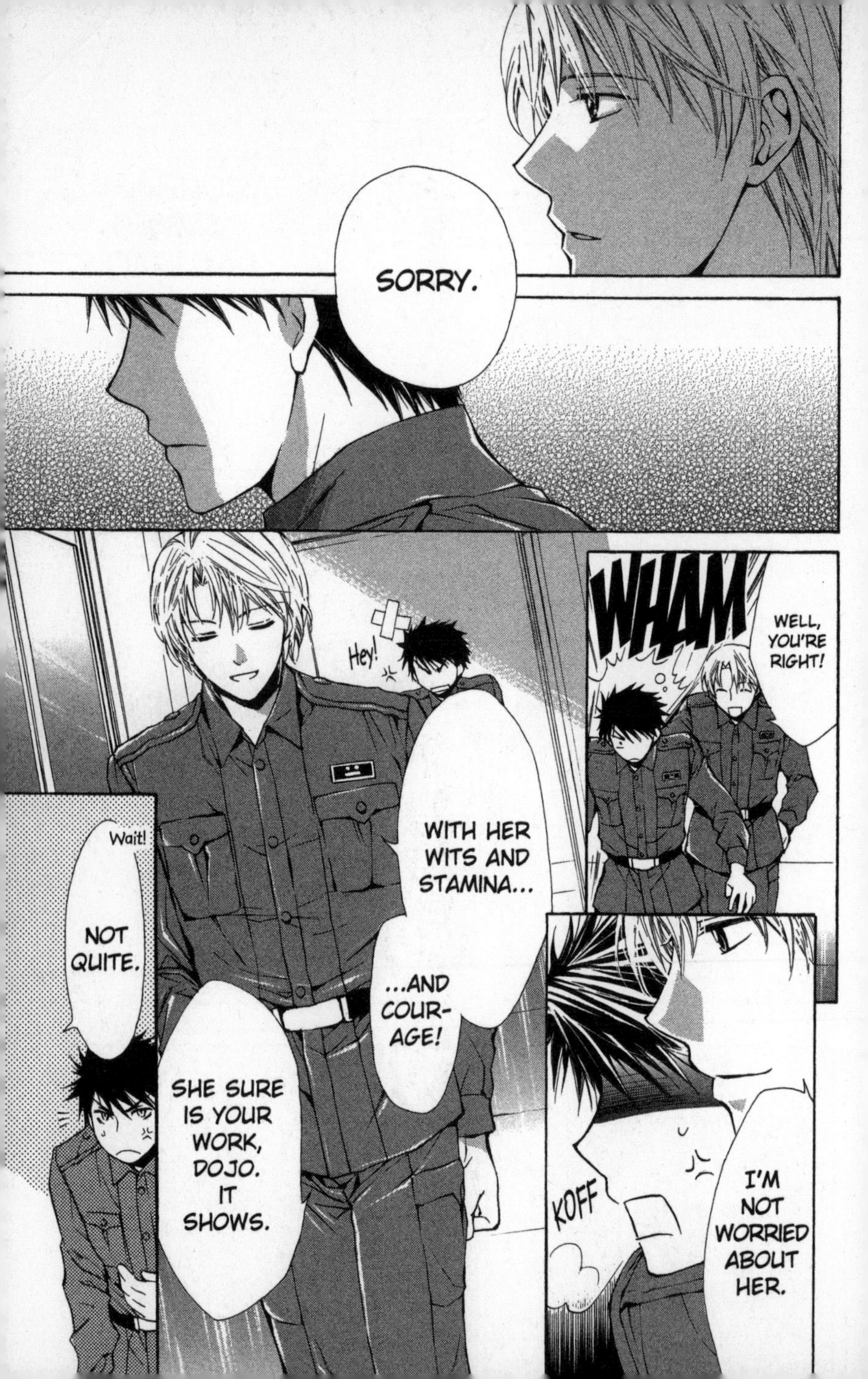
SORRY.
WHAM
WELL, YOU'RE RIGHT!
KOFF
I'M NOT WORRIED ABOUT HER.
Hey!
WITH HER WITS AND STAMINA...
...AND COURAGE!
SHE SURE IS YOUR WORK, DOJO. IT SHOWS.
Wait!
NOT QUITE.

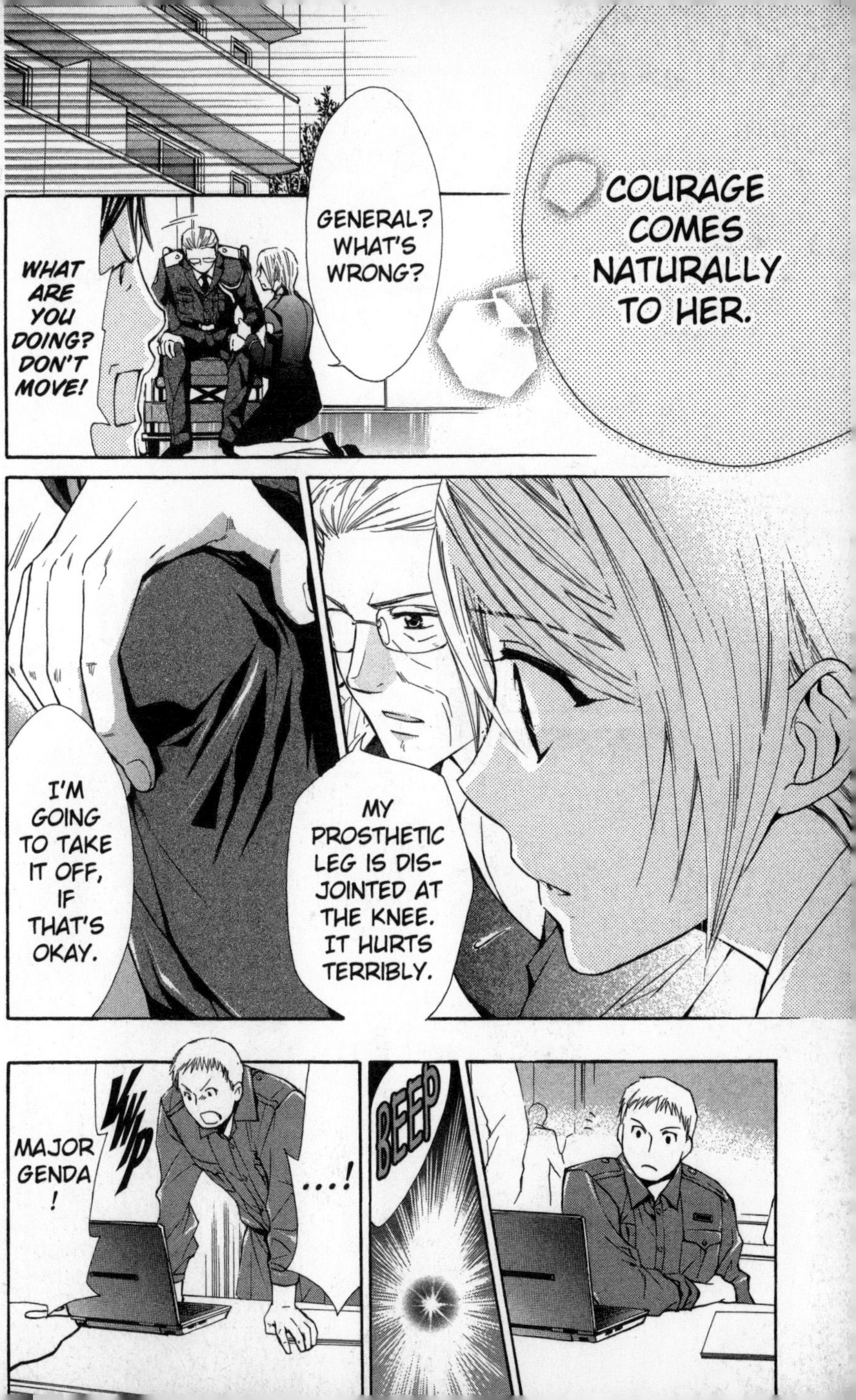
COURAGE COMES NATURALLY TO HER.
GENERAL? WHAT'S WRONG?
WHAT ARE YOU DOING? DON'T MOVE!
MY PROSTHETIC LEG IS DIS-JOINTED AT THE KNEE. IT HURTS TERRIBLY.
I'M GOING TO TAKE IT OFF, IF THAT'S OKAY.
BEEP
...!
WHIP
MAJOR GENDA!

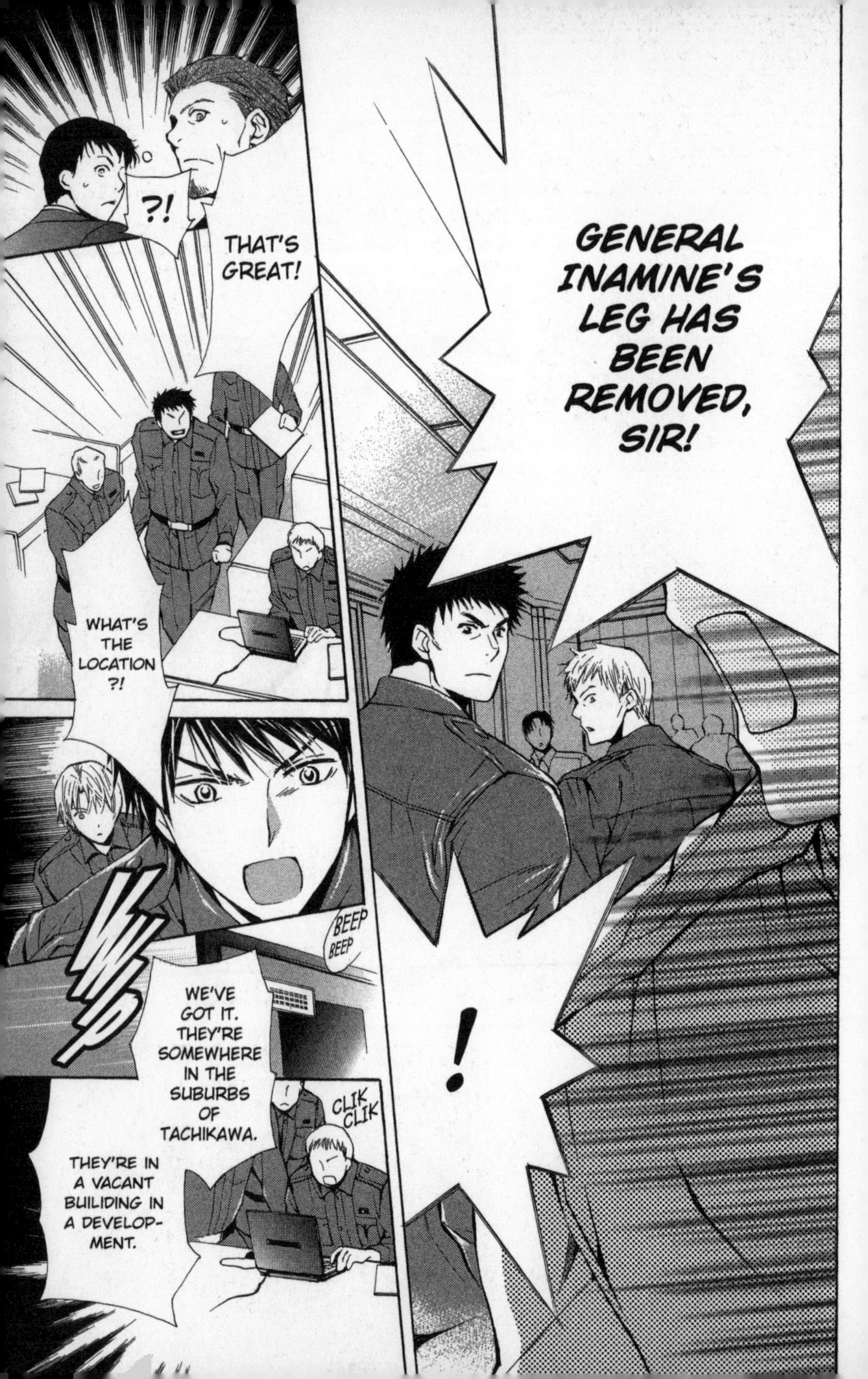
GENERAL INAMINE'S LEG HAS BEEN REMOVED, SIR!
!
?!
THAT'S GREAT!
WHAT'S THE LOCATION ?!
WHIP
BEEP BEEP
WE'VE GOT IT. THEY'RE SOMEWHERE IN THE SUBURBS OF TACHIKAWA.
CLIK CLIK
THEY'RE IN A VACANT BUILIDING IN A DEVELOP-MENT.

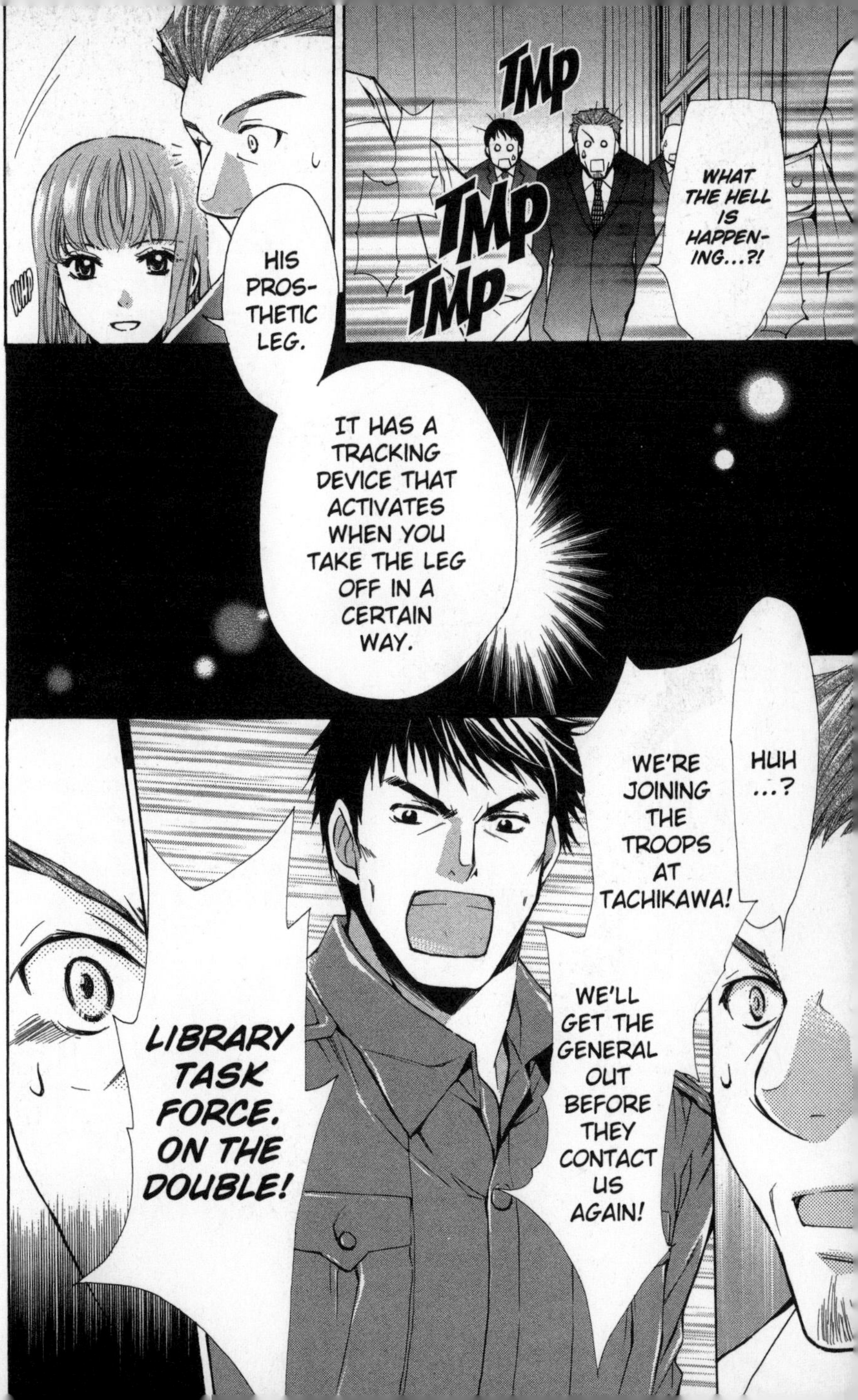
TMP
WHAT THE HELL IS HAPPEN-ING...?!
TMP TMP
HIS PROS-THETIC LEG.
WHP
IT HAS A TRACKING DEVICE THAT ACTIVATES WHEN YOU TAKE THE LEG OFF IN A CERTAIN WAY.
HUH ...?
WE'RE JOINING THE TROOPS AT TACHIKAWA!
WE'LL GET THE GENERAL OUT BEFORE THEY CONTACT US AGAIN!
LIBRARY TASK FORCE. ON THE DOUBLE!

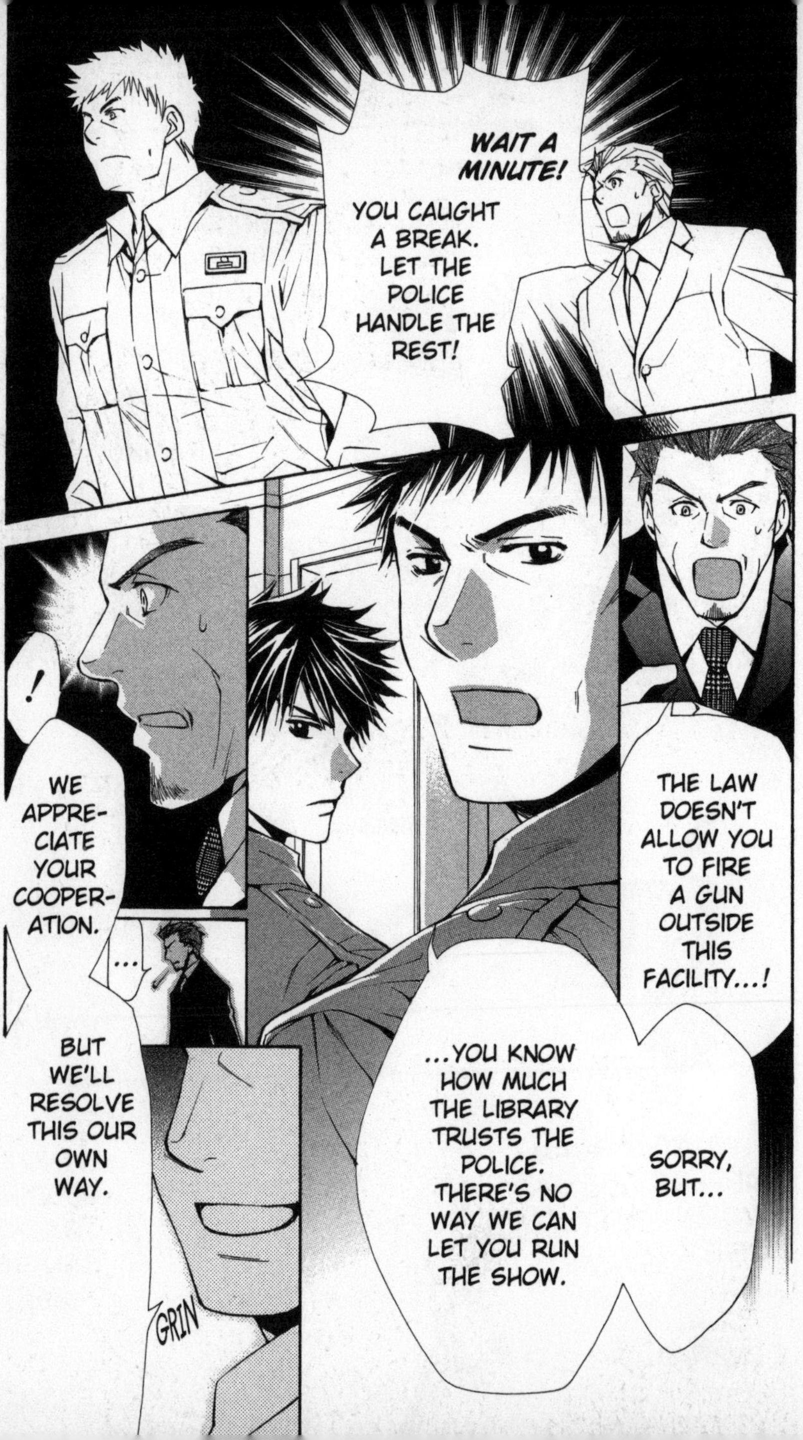
WAIT A MINUTE!
YOU CAUGHT A BREAK. LET THE POLICE HANDLE THE REST!
THE LAW DOESN'T ALLOW YOU TO FIRE A GUN OUTSIDE THIS FACILITY...!
SORRY, BUT...
...YOU KNOW HOW MUCH THE LIBRARY TRUSTS THE POLICE. THERE'S NO WAY WE CAN LET YOU RUN THE SHOW.
!
WE APPRECIATE YOUR COOPERATION.
...
BUT WE'LL RESOLVE THIS OUR OWN WAY.
GRIN

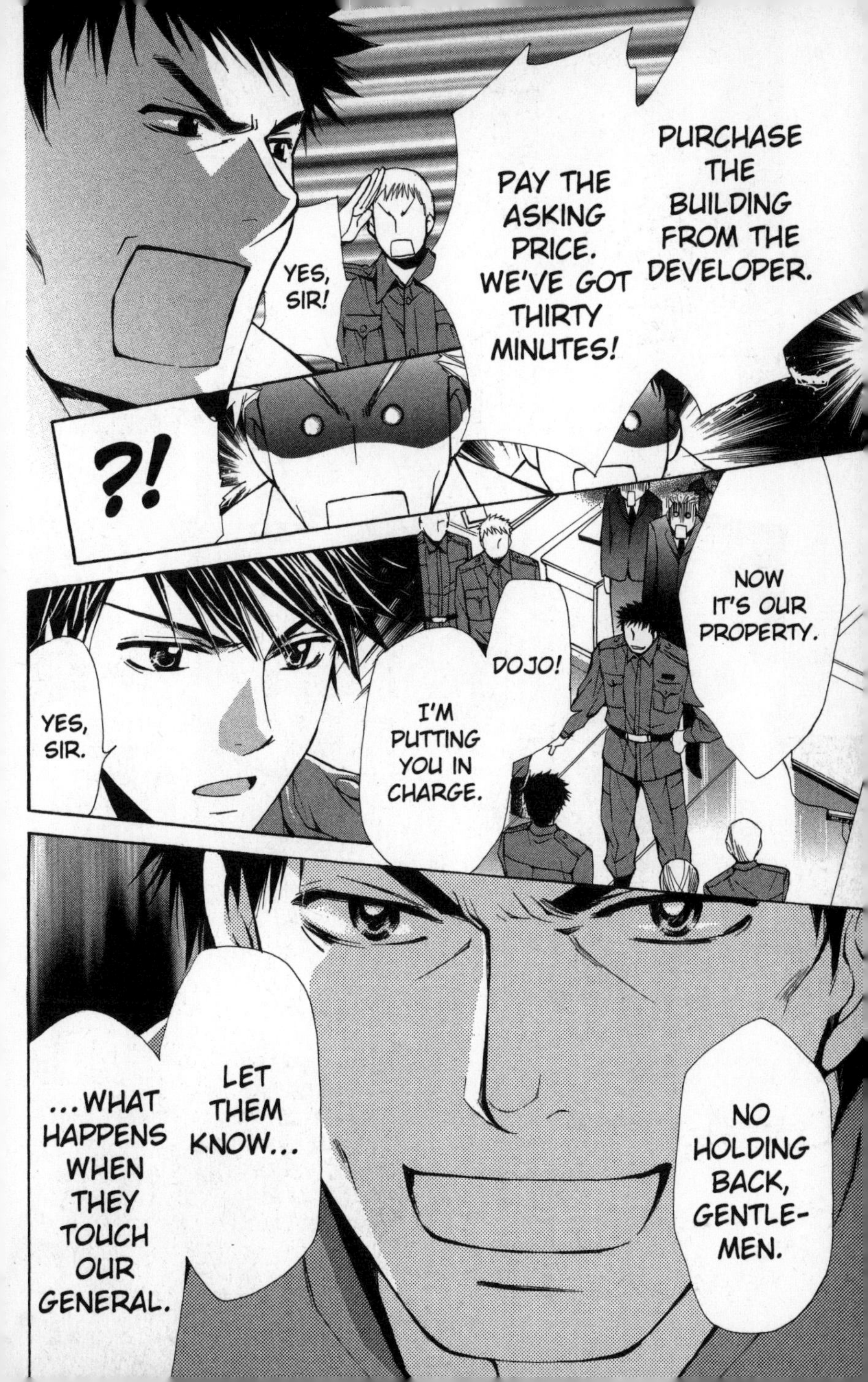
PURCHASE THE BUILDING FROM THE DEVELOPER.
PAY THE ASKING PRICE. WE'VE GOT THIRTY MINUTES!
YES, SIR!
?!
NOW IT'S OUR PROPERTY.
DOJO!
I'M PUTTING YOU IN CHARGE.
YES, SIR.
NO HOLDING BACK, GENTLEMEN.
LET THEM KNOW...
...WHAT HAPPENS WHEN THEY TOUCH OUR GENERAL.

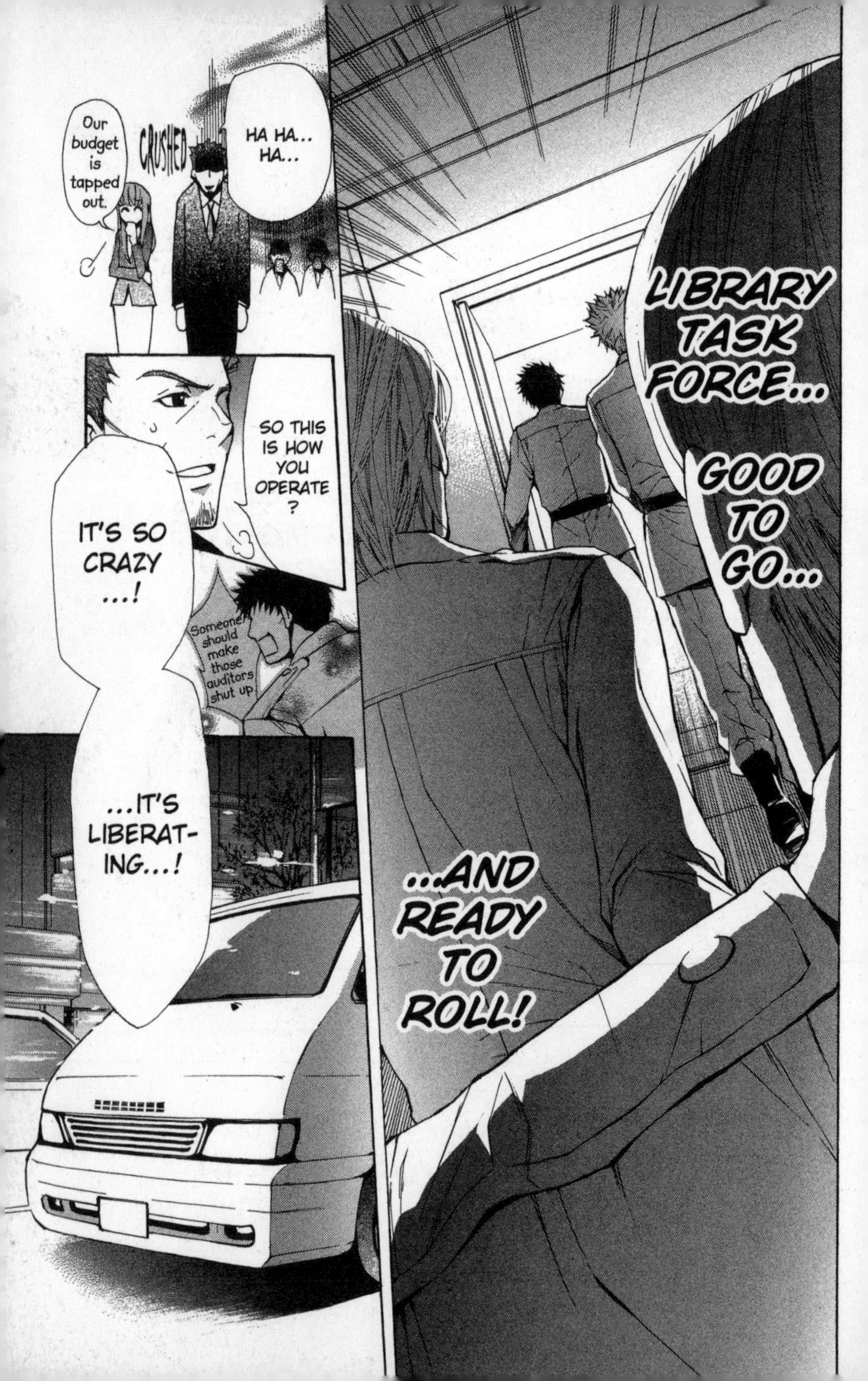
LIBRARY TASK FORCE...
GOOD TO GO...
...AND READY TO ROLL!
HA HA... HA...
CRUSHED
Our budget is tapped out.
SO THIS IS HOW YOU OPERATE?
IT'S SO CRAZY...!
Someone should make those auditors shut up
...IT'S LIBERATING...!

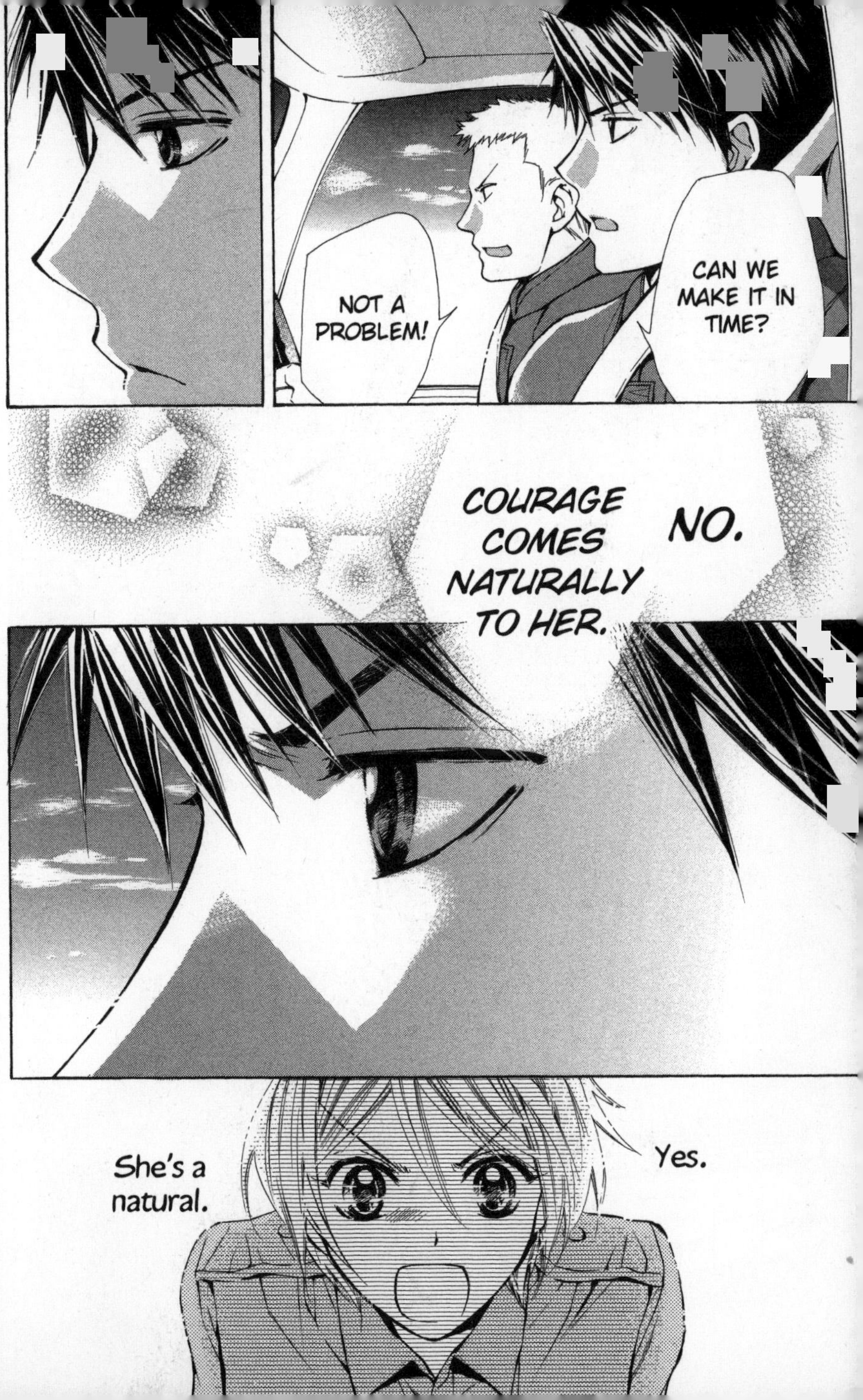
CAN WE MAKE IT IN TIME?
NOT A PROBLEM!
NO.
COURAGE COMES NATURALLY TO HER.
Yes.
She's a natural.

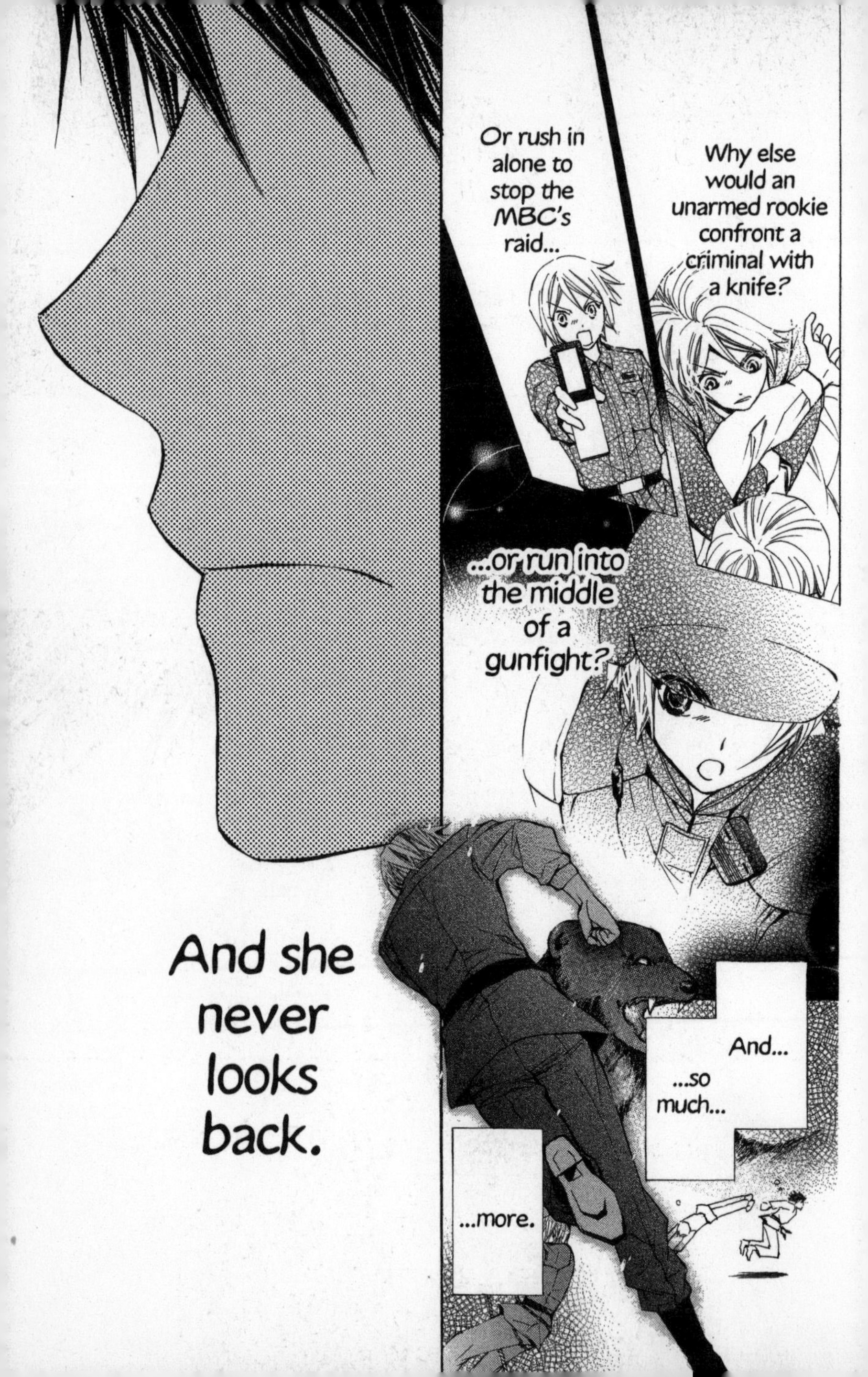
Why else would an unarmed rookie confront a criminal with a knife?
Or rush in alone to stop the MBC's raid...
...or run into the middle of a gunfight?
And...
...so much...
...more.
And she never looks back.

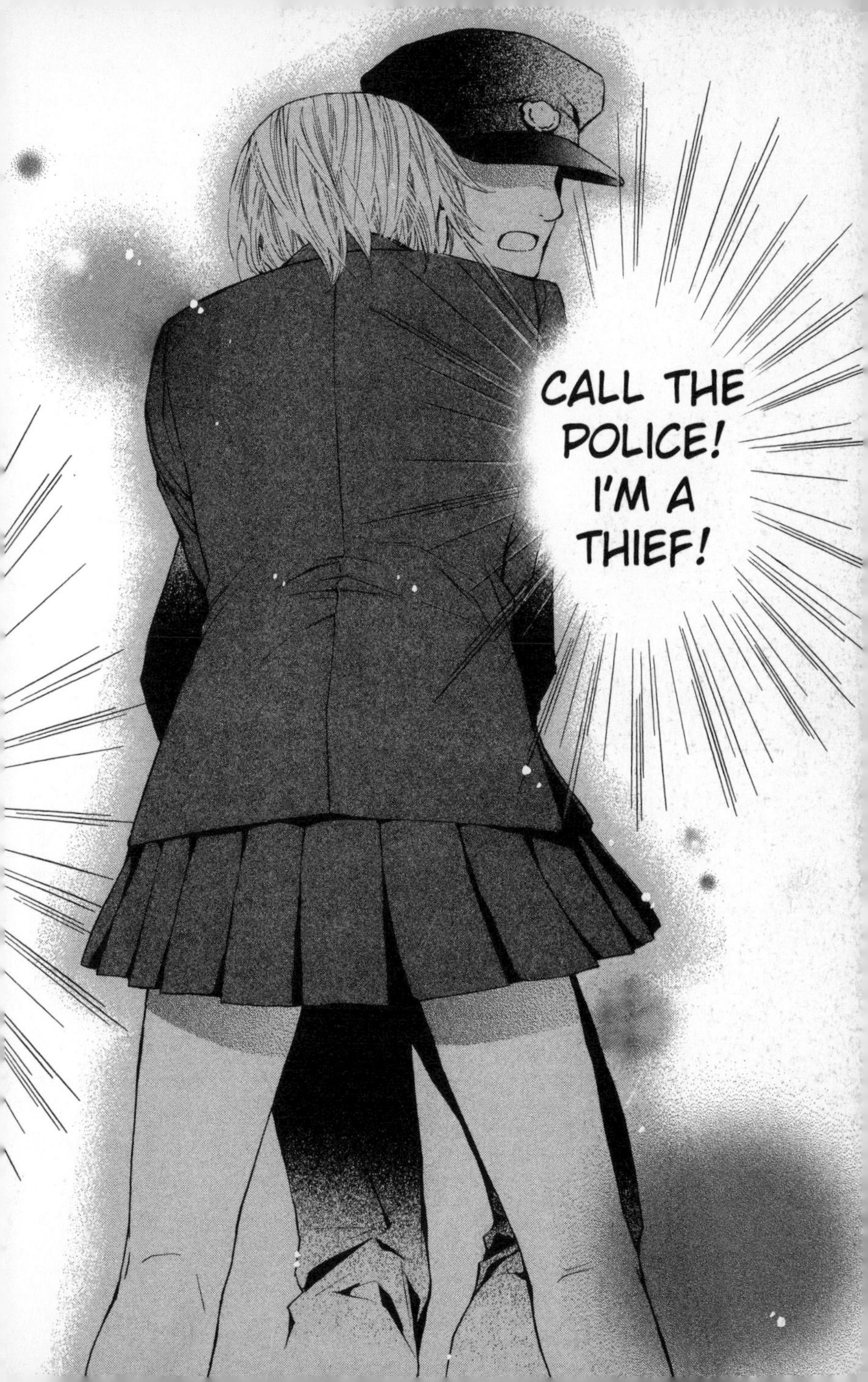
CALL THE POLICE! I'M A THIEF!

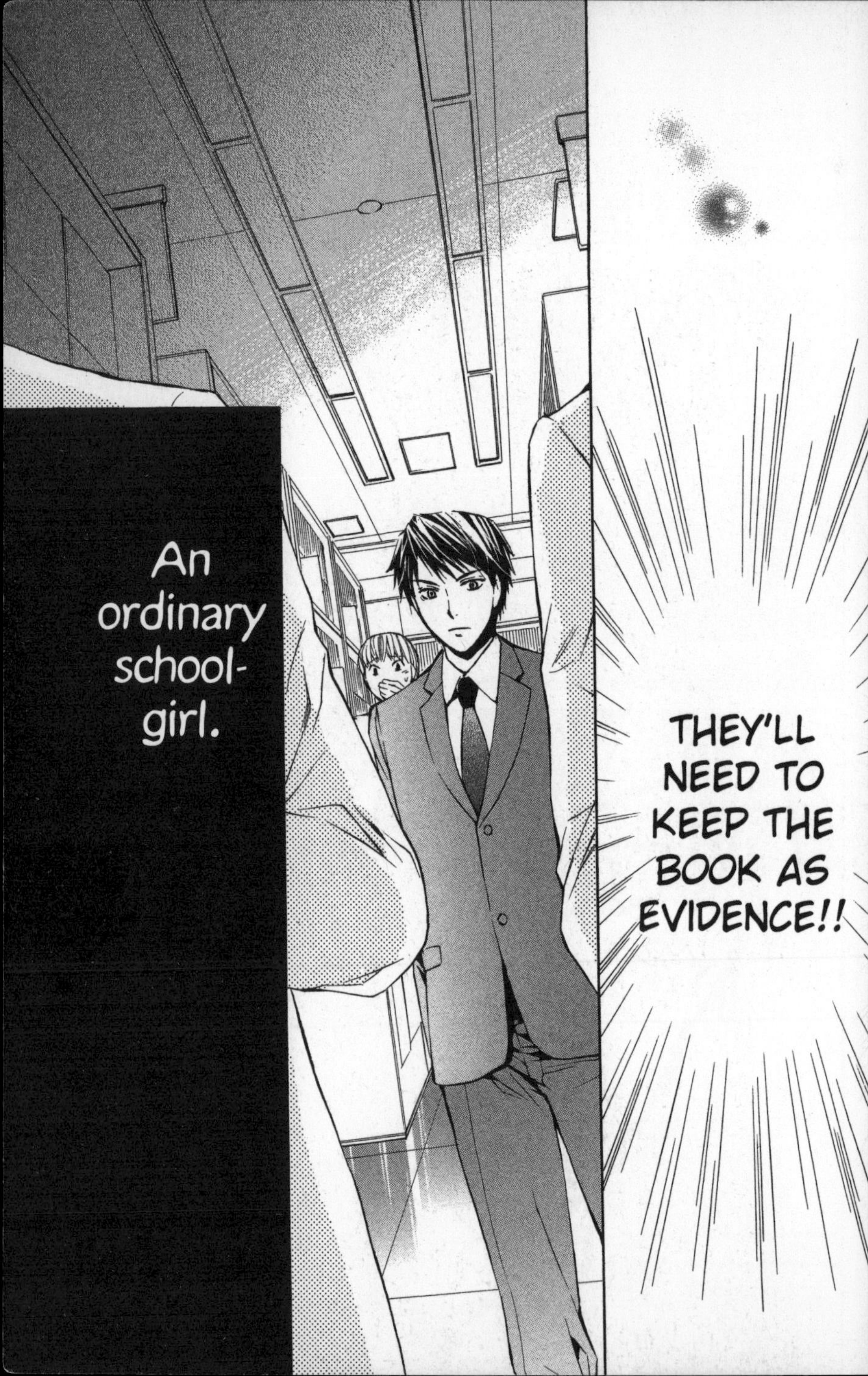
THEY'LL NEED TO KEEP THE BOOK AS EVIDENCE!!
An ordinary school-girl.

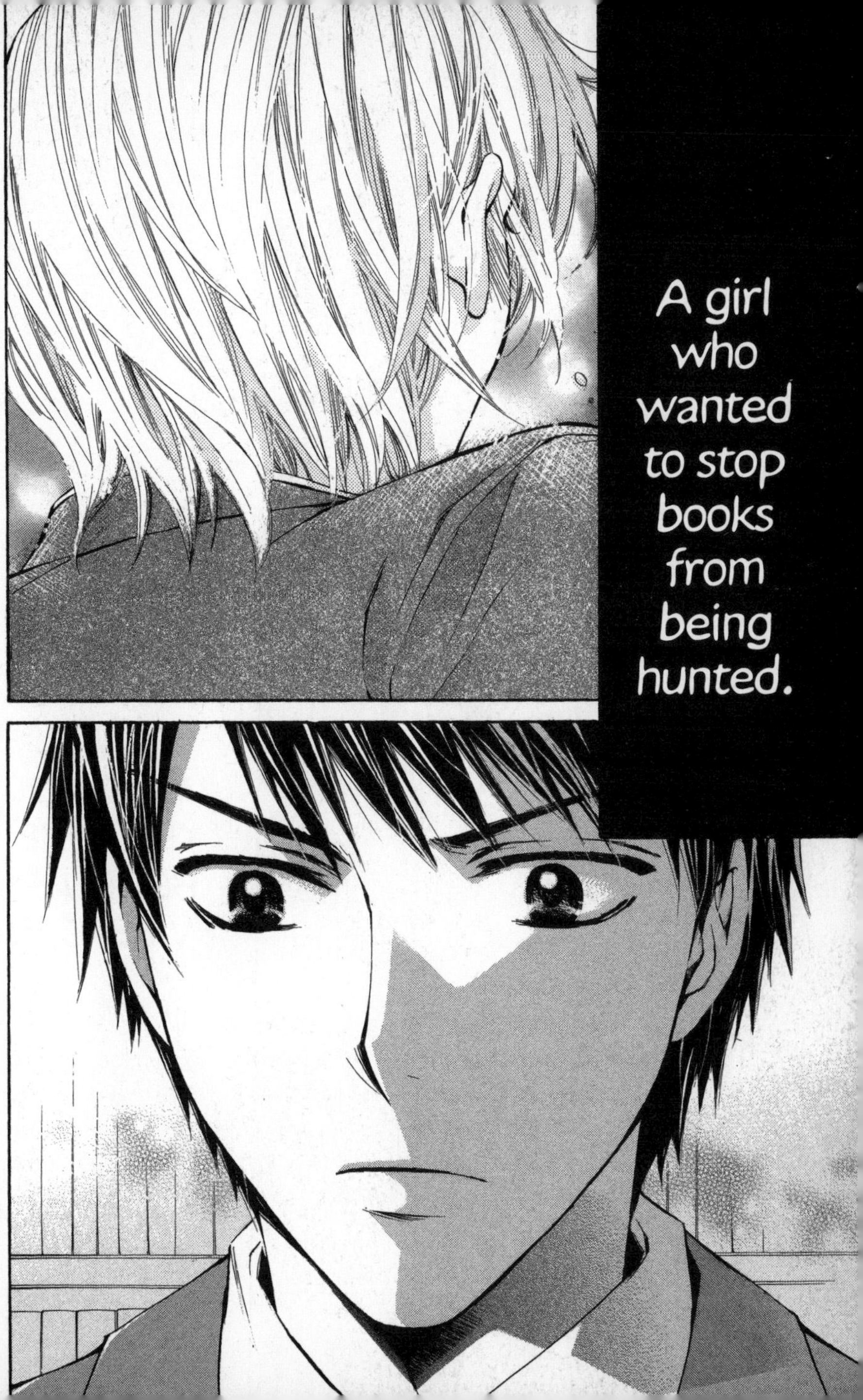
A girl who wanted to stop books from being hunted.

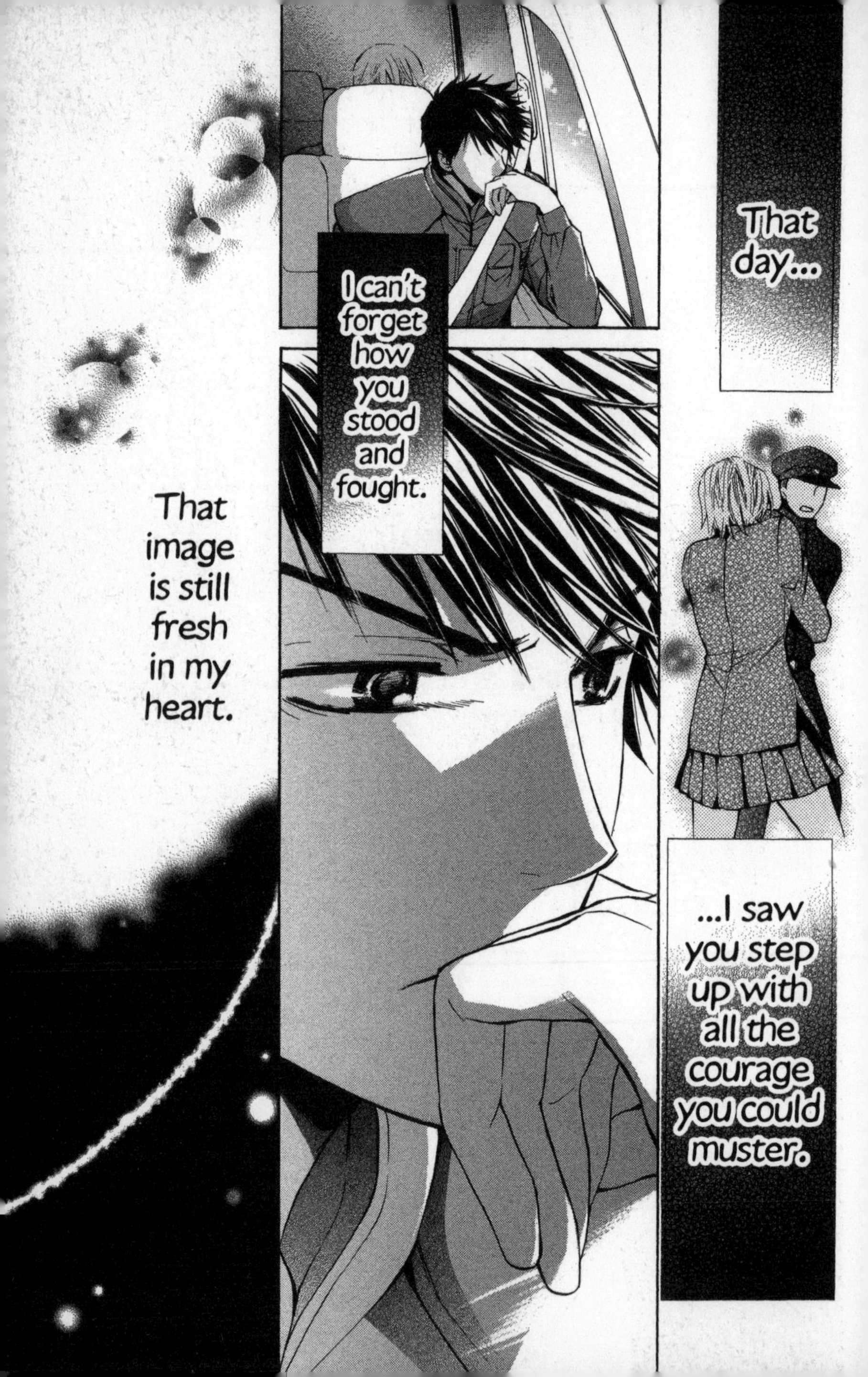
That day...
...I saw you step up with all the courage you could muster.
I can't forget how you stood and fought.
That image is still fresh in my heart.

The Worst Pain

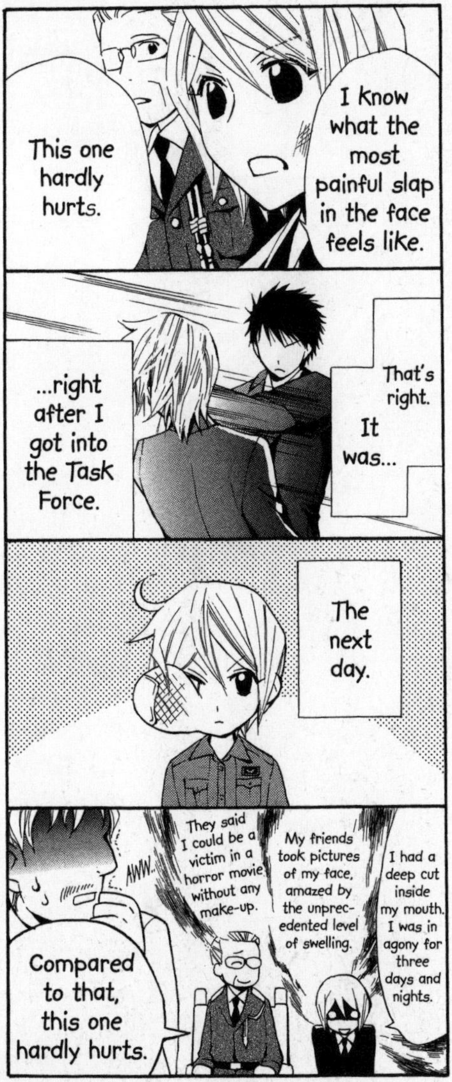
I know what the most painful slap in the face feels like.
This one hardly hurts.
That's right.
It was...
...right after I got into the Task Force.
The next day.
I had a deep cut inside my mouth. I was in agony for three days and nights.
My friends took pictures of my face, amazed by the unprecedented level of swelling.
They said I could be a victim in a horror movie without any make-up.
AWW..
Compared to that, this one hardly hurts.

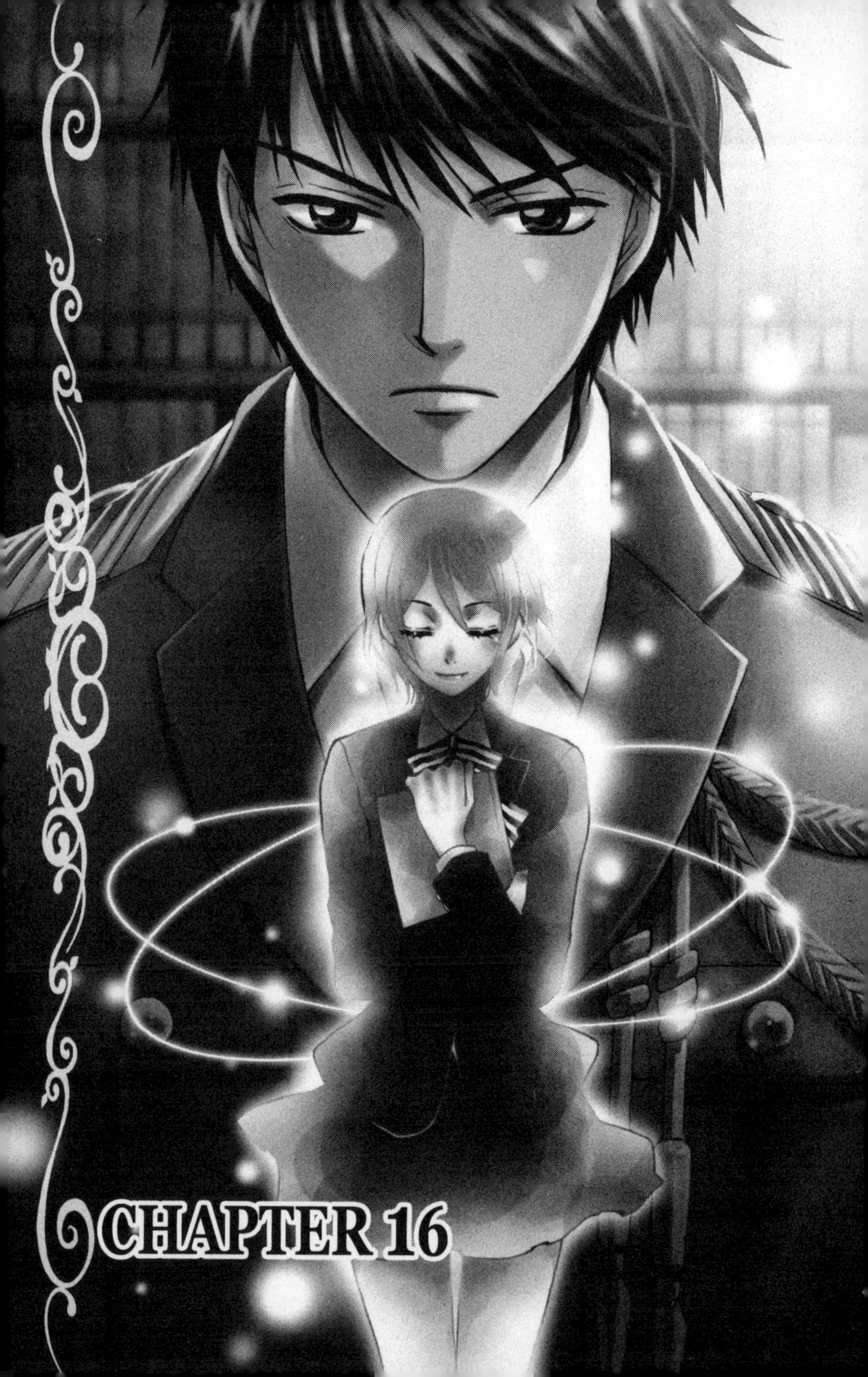
CHAPTER 16

Daydreamer: She's a Natural

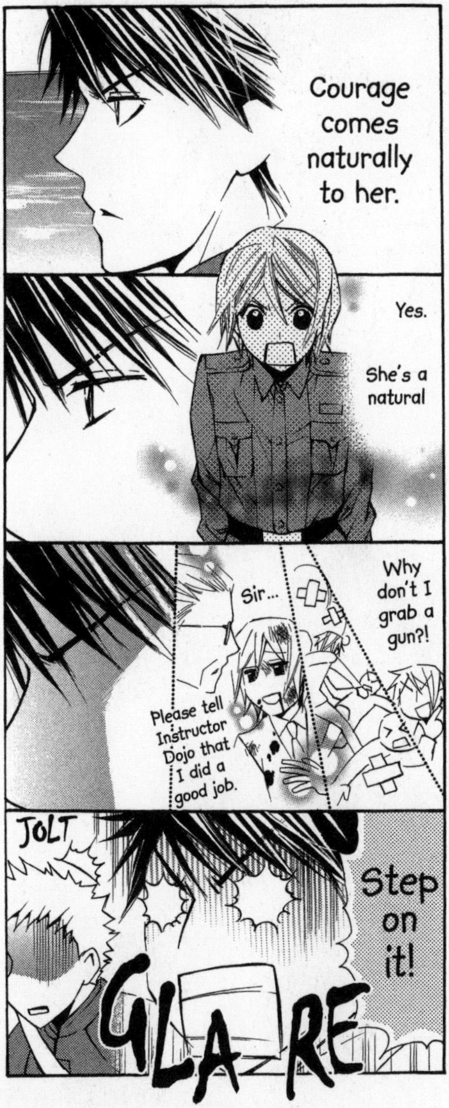
Courage comes naturally to her.
Yes.
She's a natural
Why don't I grab a gun?!
Sir...
Please tell Instructor Dojo that I did a good job.
Step on it!
JOLT
GLARE

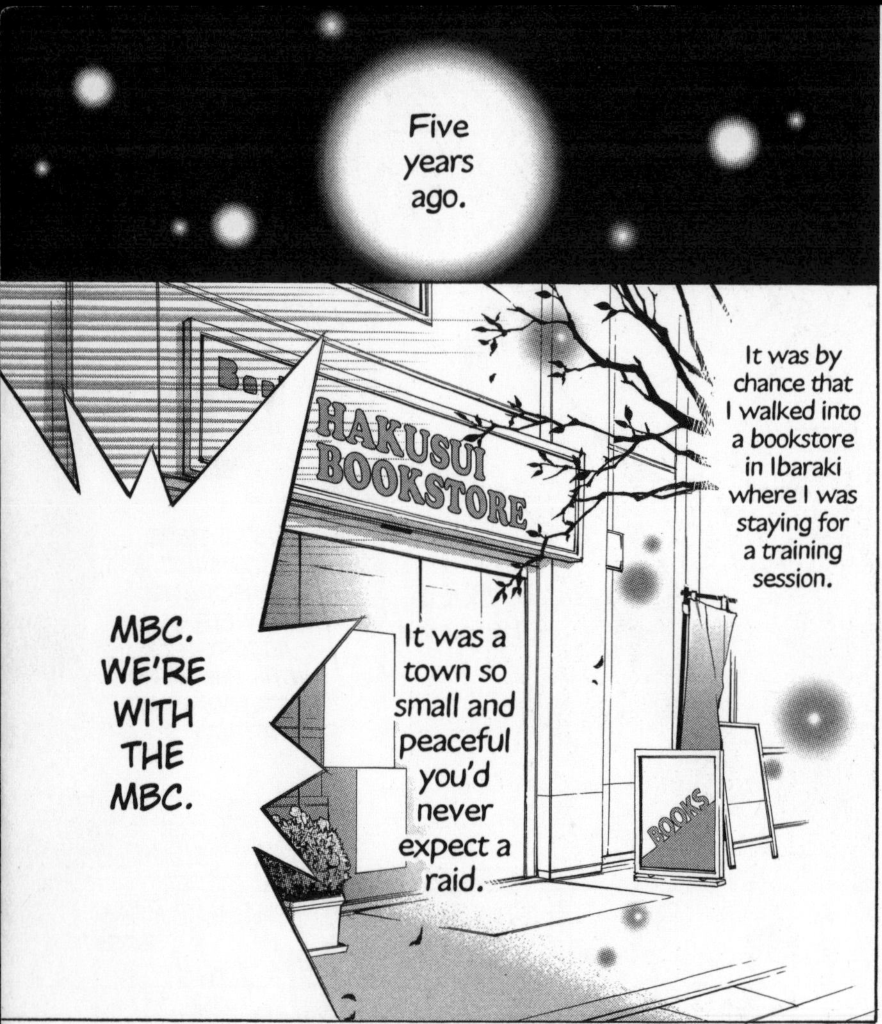
Five years ago.
HAKUSUI BOOKSTORE
It was by chance that I walked into a bookstore in Ibaraki where I was staying for a training session.
It was a town so small and peaceful you'd never expect a raid.
BOOKS
MBC. WE'RE WITH THE MBC.
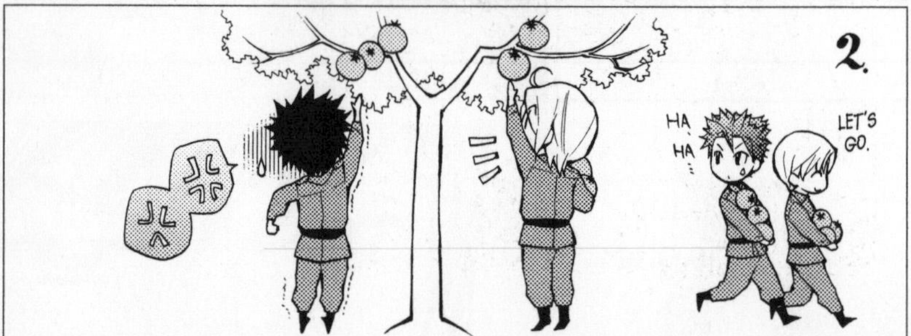
2.
LET'S GO.
HA HA

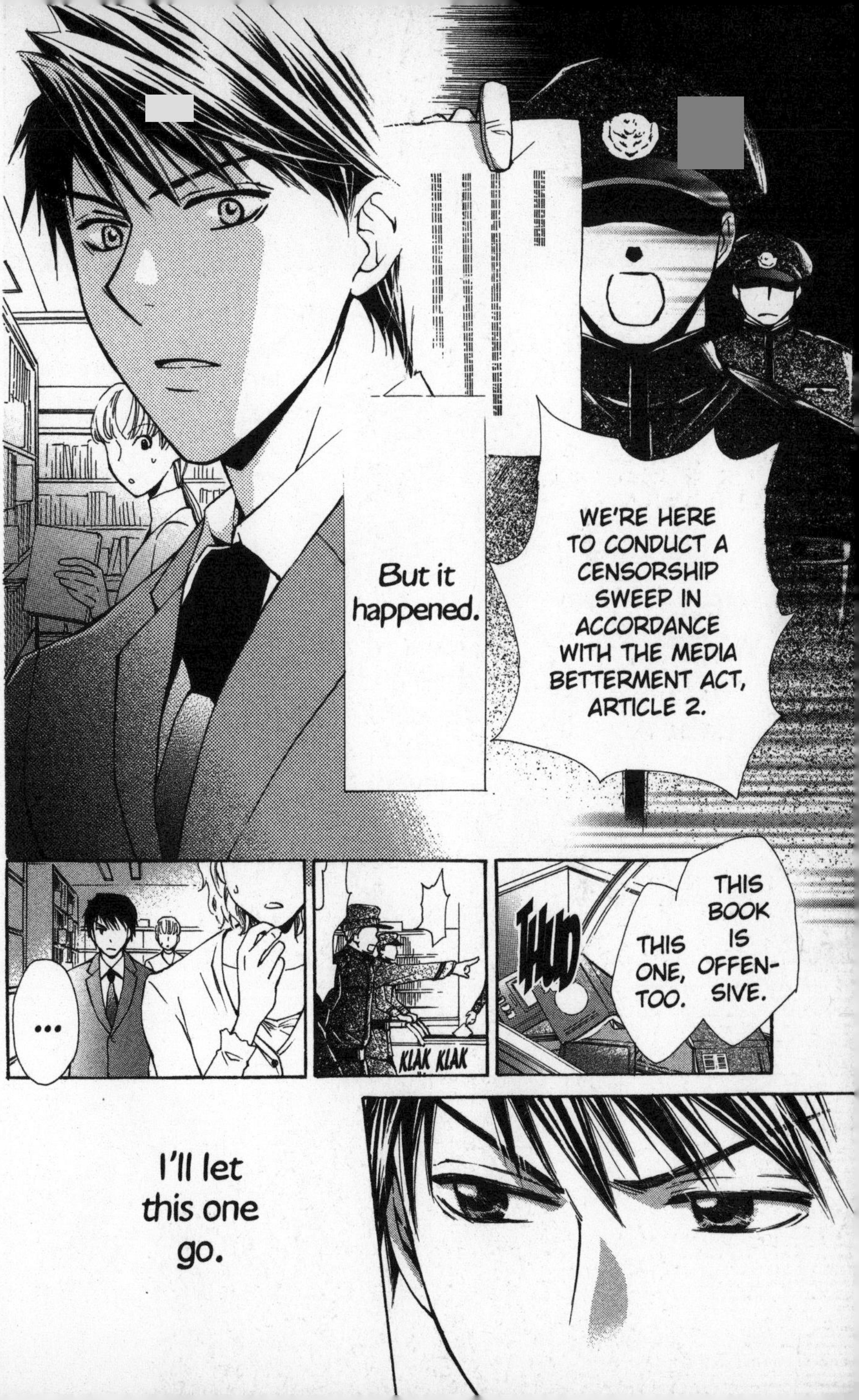
WE'RE HERE TO CONDUCT A CENSORSHIP SWEEP IN ACCORDANCE WITH THE MEDIA BETTERMENT ACT, ARTICLE 2.
But it happened.
THIS BOOK IS OFFEN-SIVE.
THIS ONE, TOO.
THUD
KLAK KLAK
...
I'll let this one go.

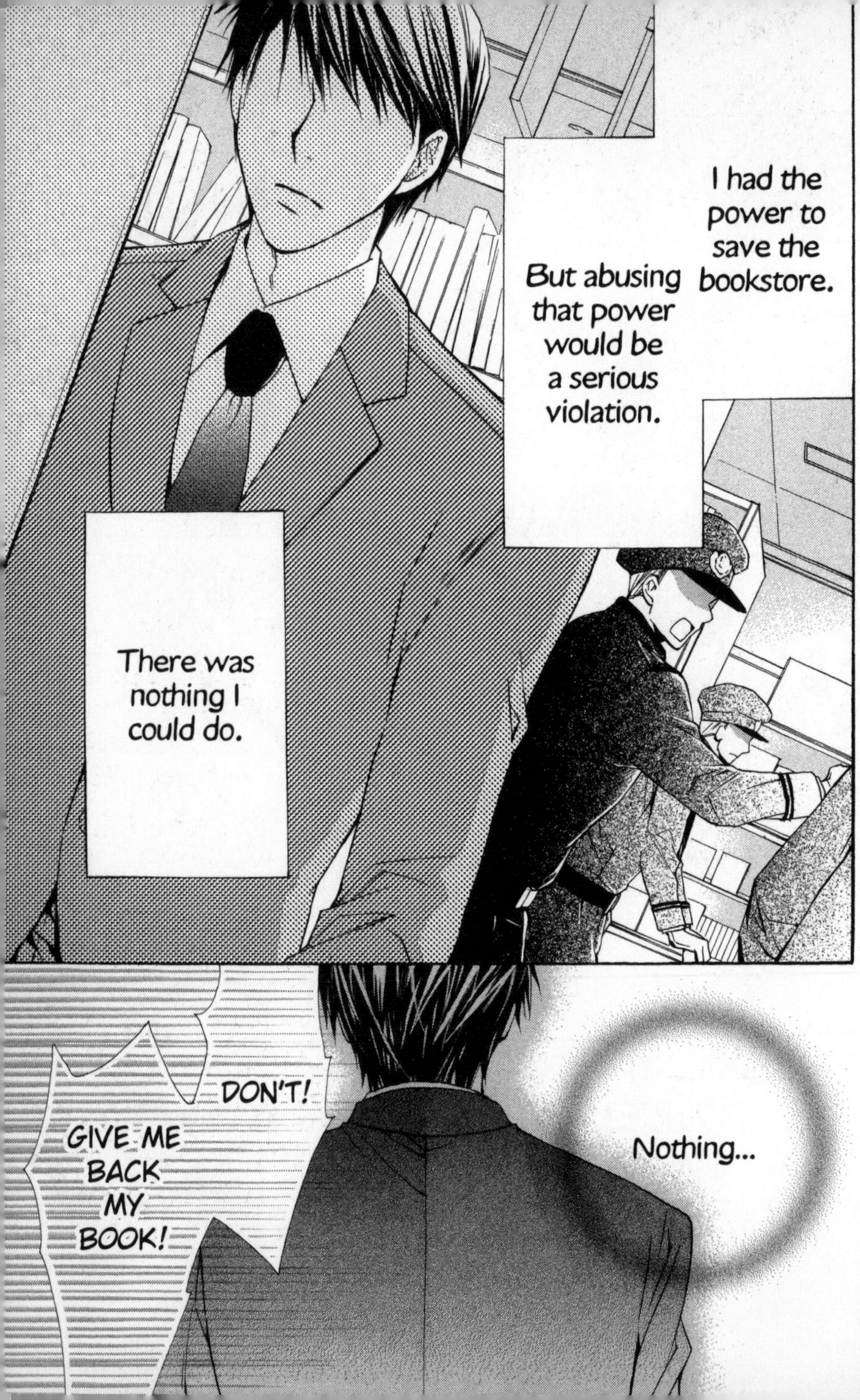
I had the power to save the bookstore.
But abusing that power would be a serious violation.
There was nothing I could do.
Nothing...
DON'T!
GIVE ME BACK MY BOOK!

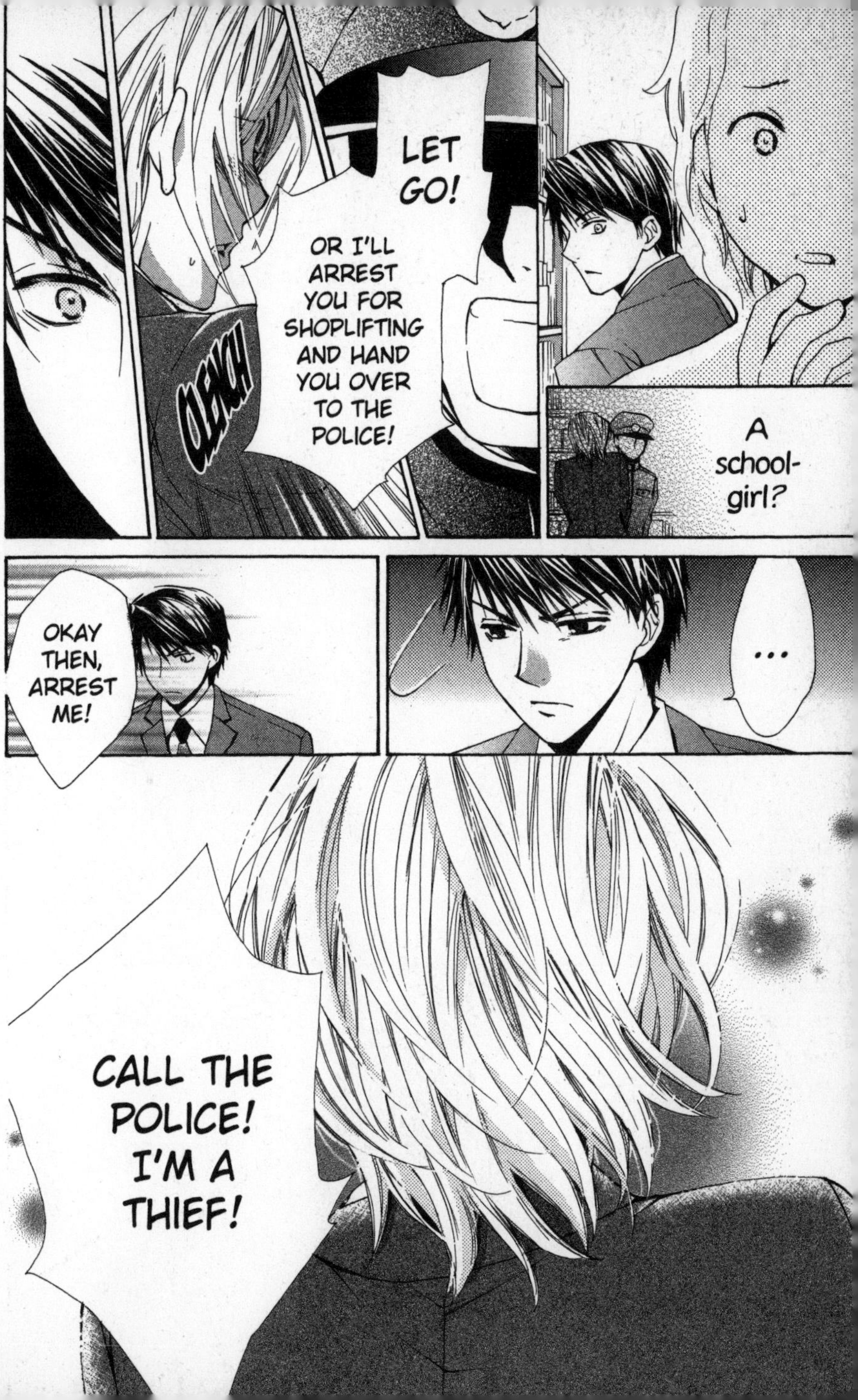

A school-girl?
LET GO!
OR I'LL ARREST YOU FOR SHOPLIFTING AND HAND YOU OVER TO THE POLICE!
CLENCH
...
OKAY THEN, ARREST ME!
CALL THE POLICE! I'M A THIEF!

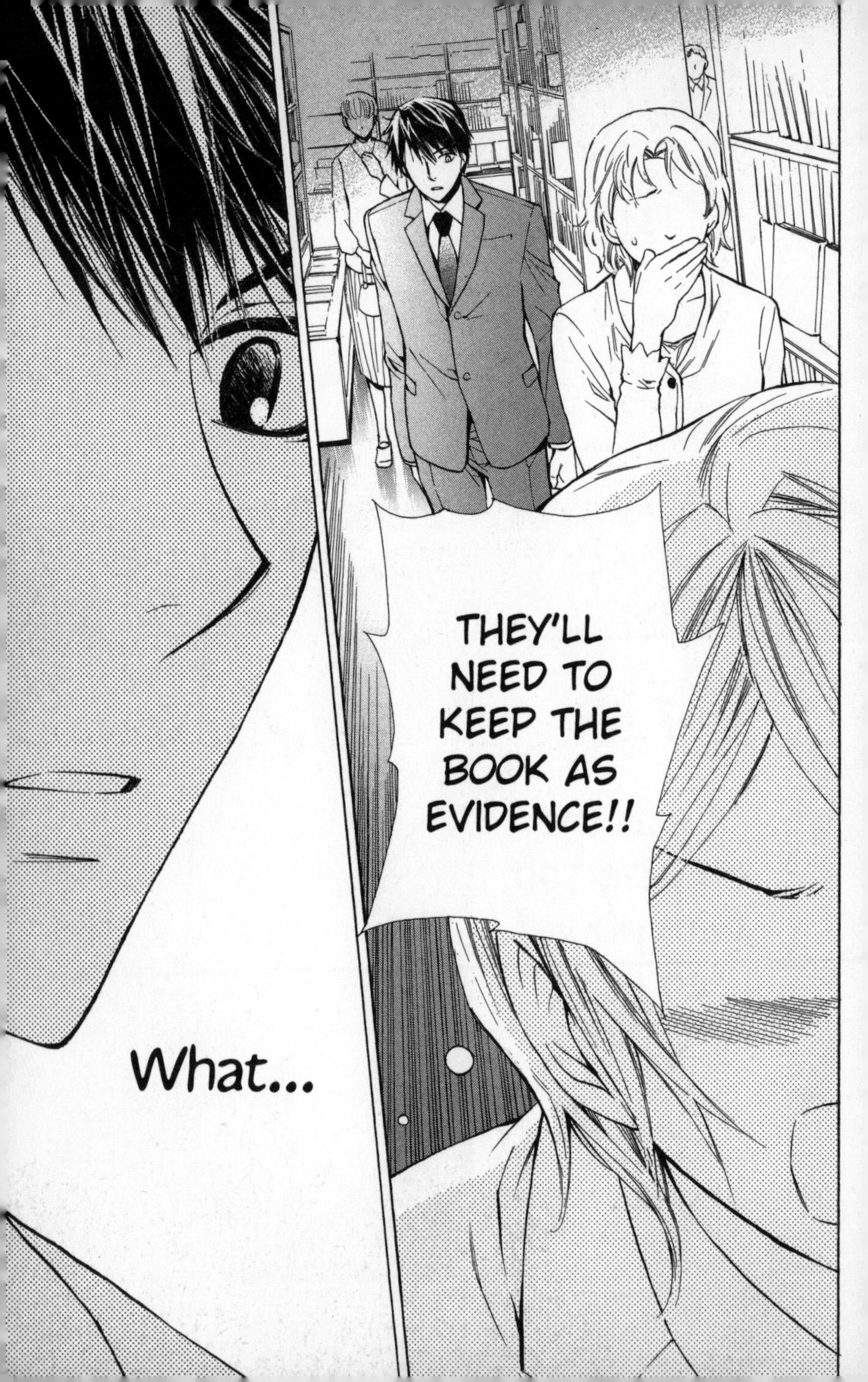
THEY'LL NEED TO KEEP THE BOOK AS EVIDENCE!!
What...

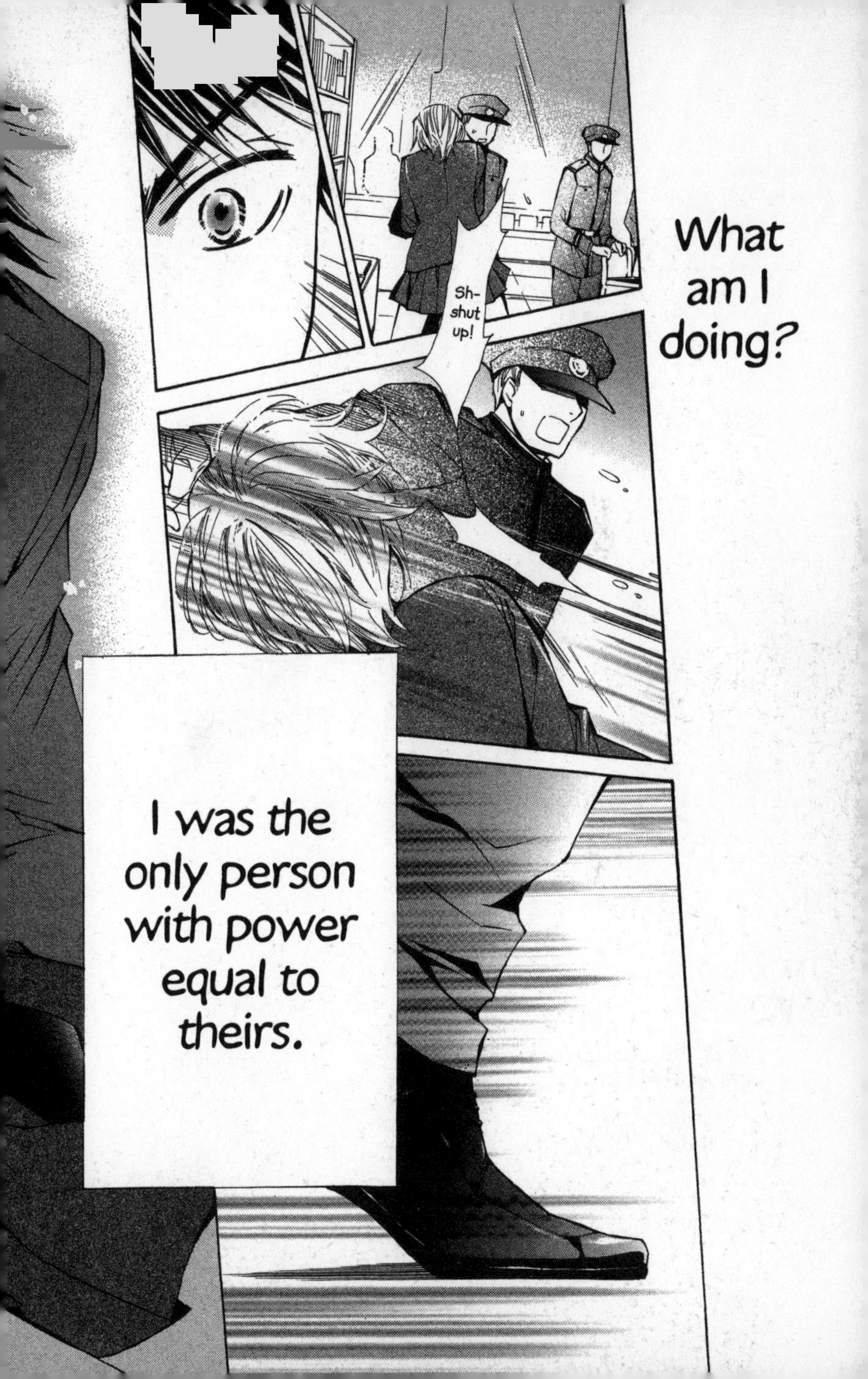
What am I doing?
Sh- shut up!
I was the only person with power equal to theirs.

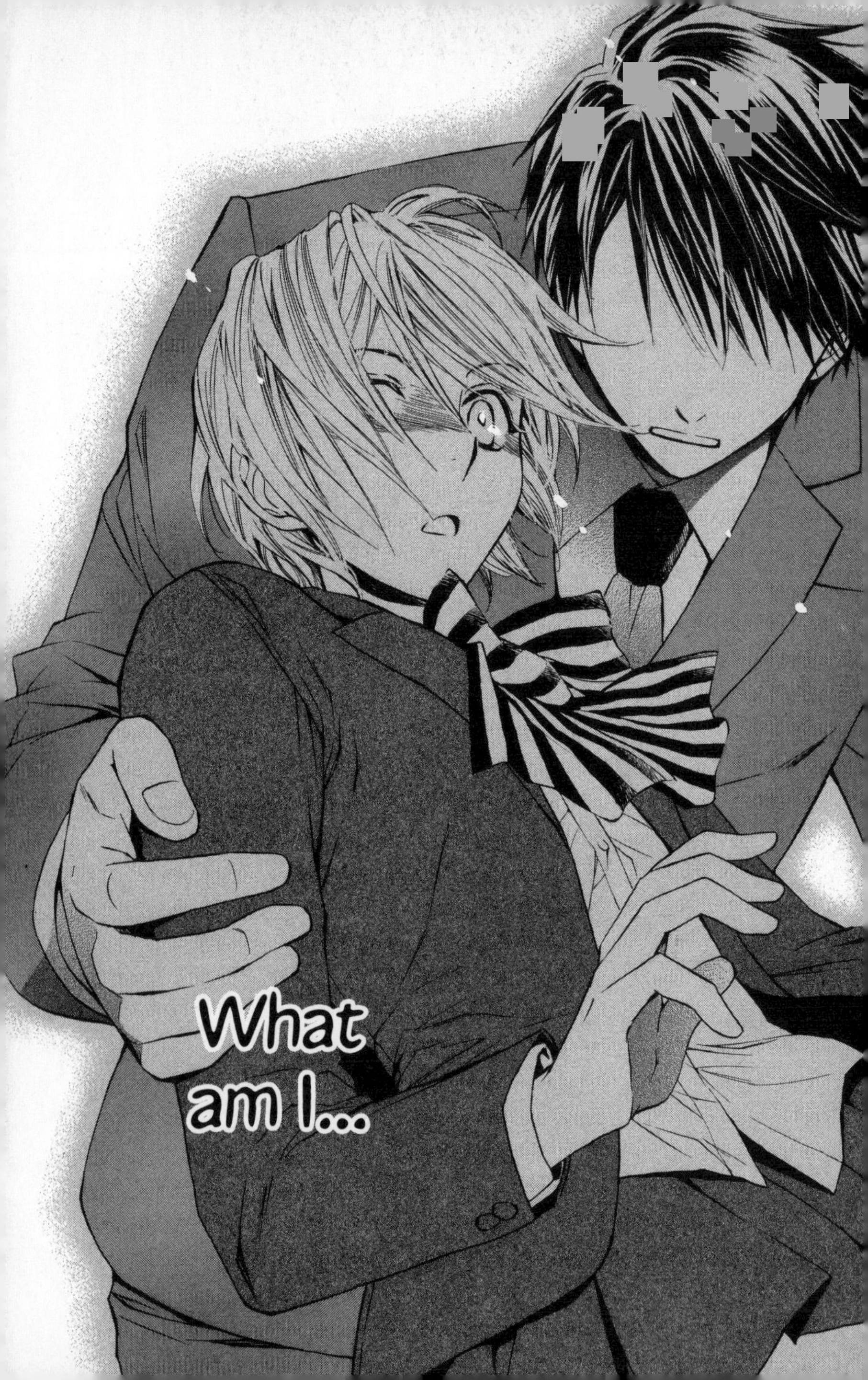
What am I...

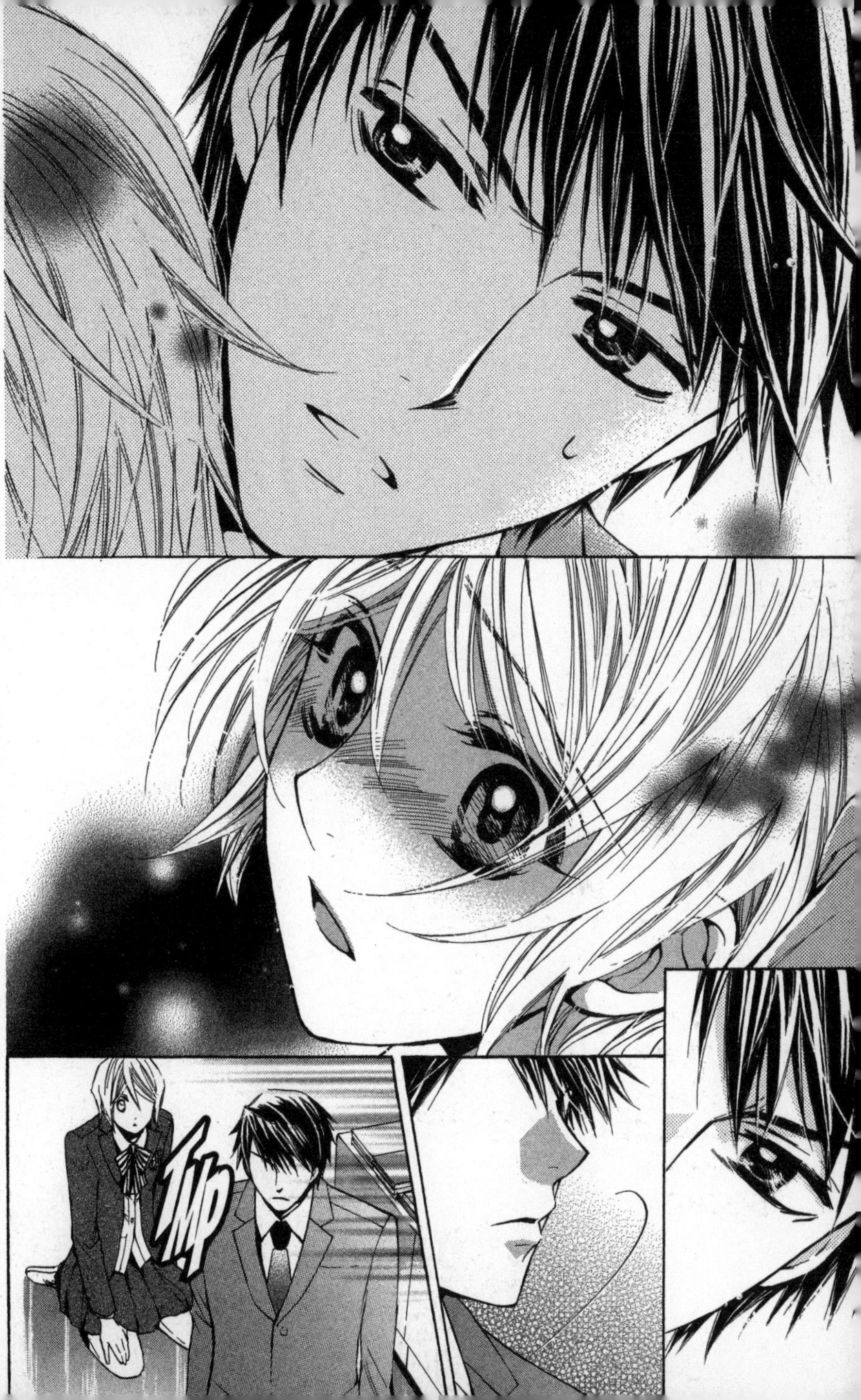
TMP

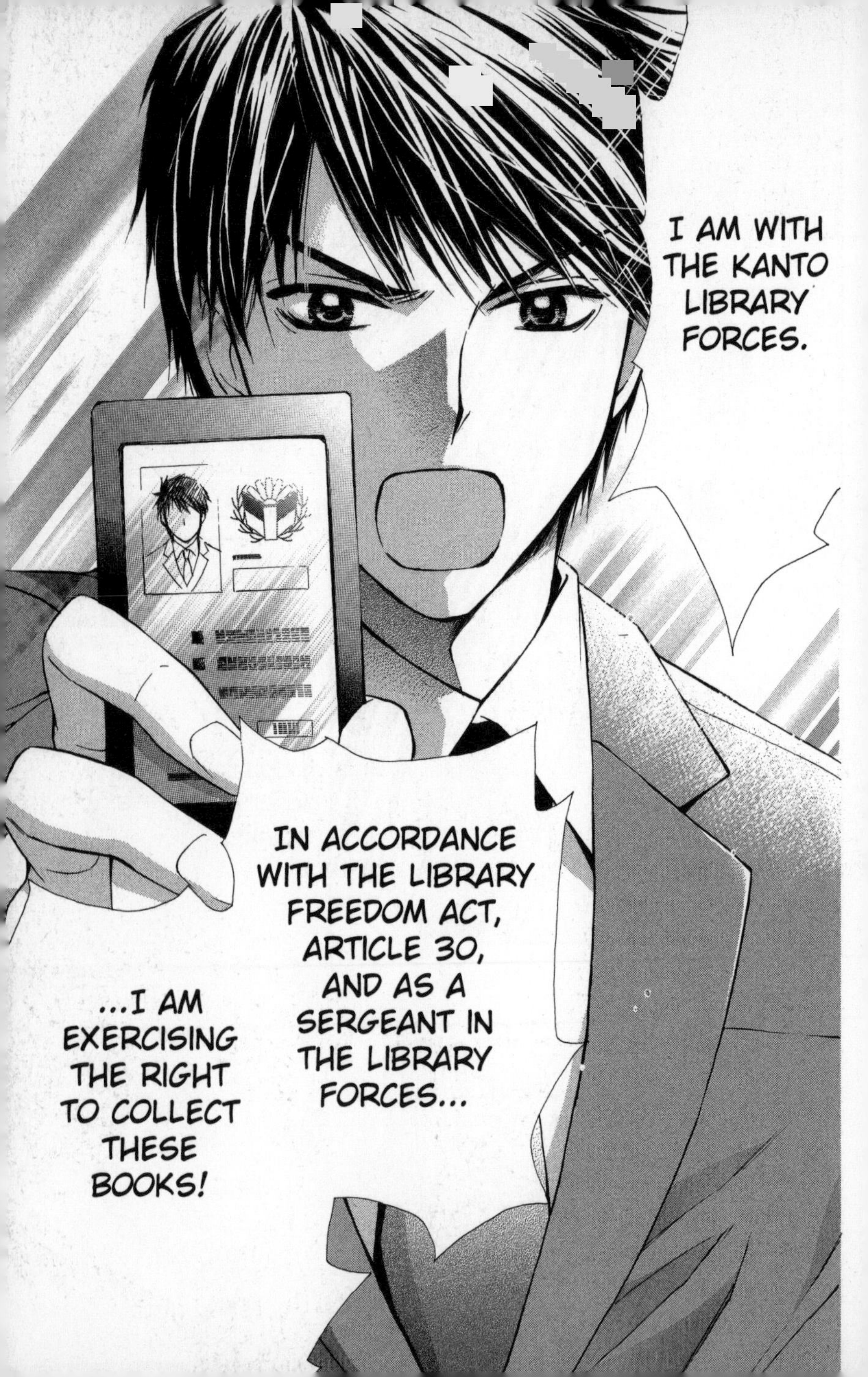
I AM WITH THE KANTO LIBRARY FORCES.
IN ACCORDANCE WITH THE LIBRARY FREEDOM ACT, ARTICLE 30, AND AS A SERGEANT IN THE LIBRARY FORCES...
...I AM EXERCISING THE RIGHT TO COLLECT THESE BOOKS!

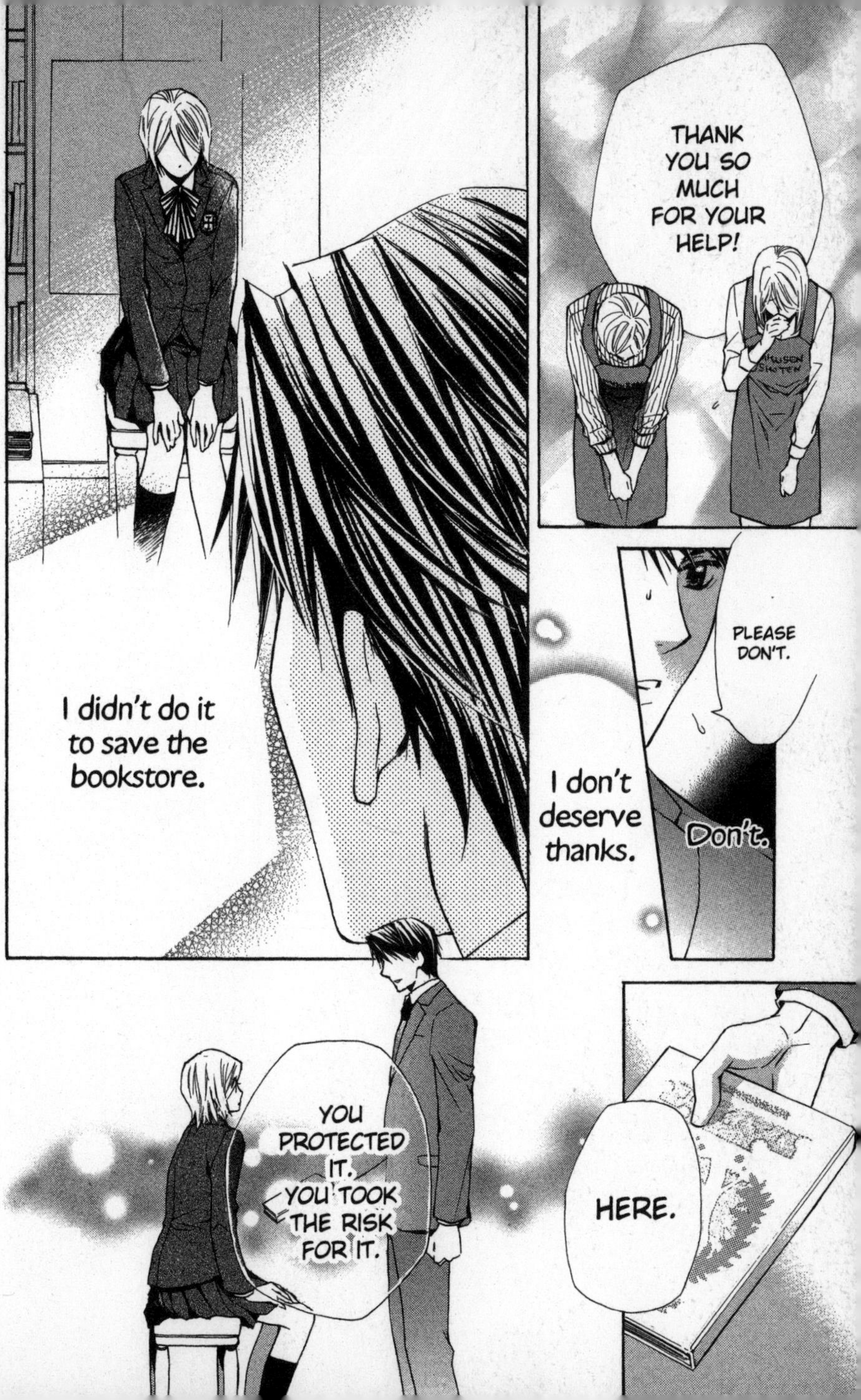
THANK YOU SO MUCH FOR YOUR HELP!
PLEASE DON'T.
Don't.
I don't deserve thanks.
I didn't do it to save the bookstore.
HERE.
YOU PROTECTED IT. YOU TOOK THE RISK FOR IT.

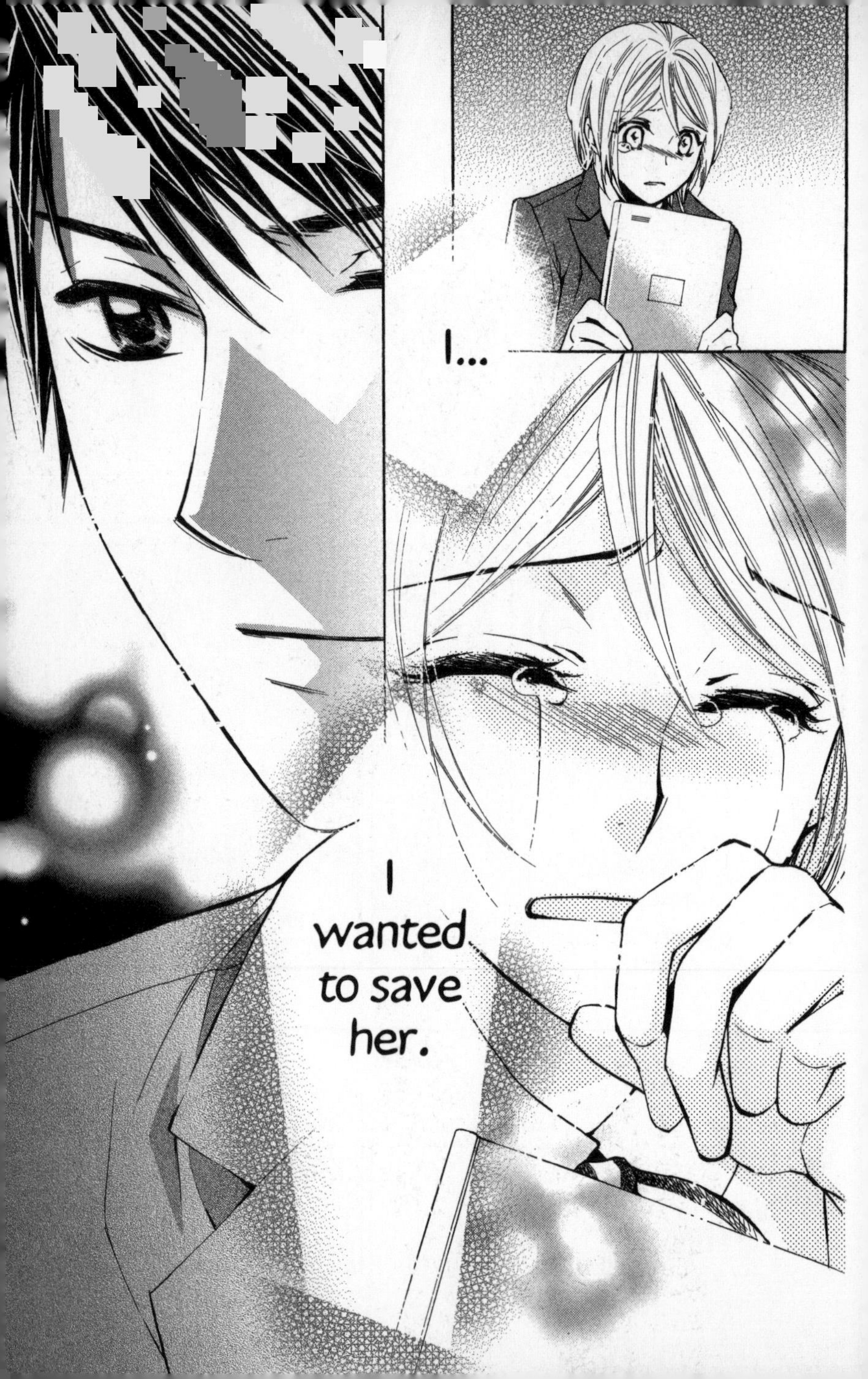
I...
I wanted to save her.

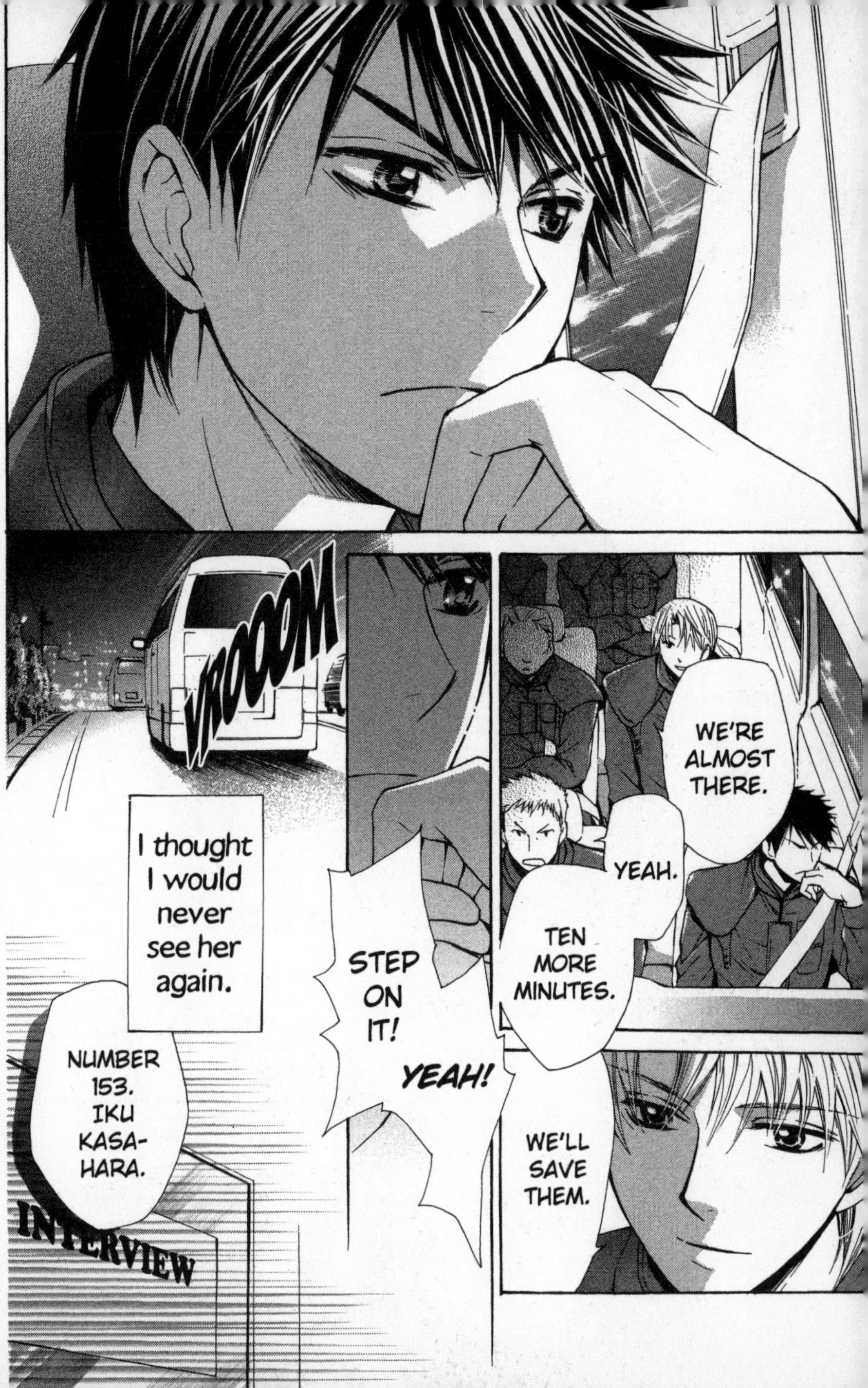
WE'RE ALMOST THERE.
YEAH.
TEN MORE MINUTES.
WE'LL SAVE THEM.
STEP ON IT!
YEAH!
VROOOM
I thought I would never see her again.
NUMBER 153. IKU KASA-HARA.
INTERVIEW

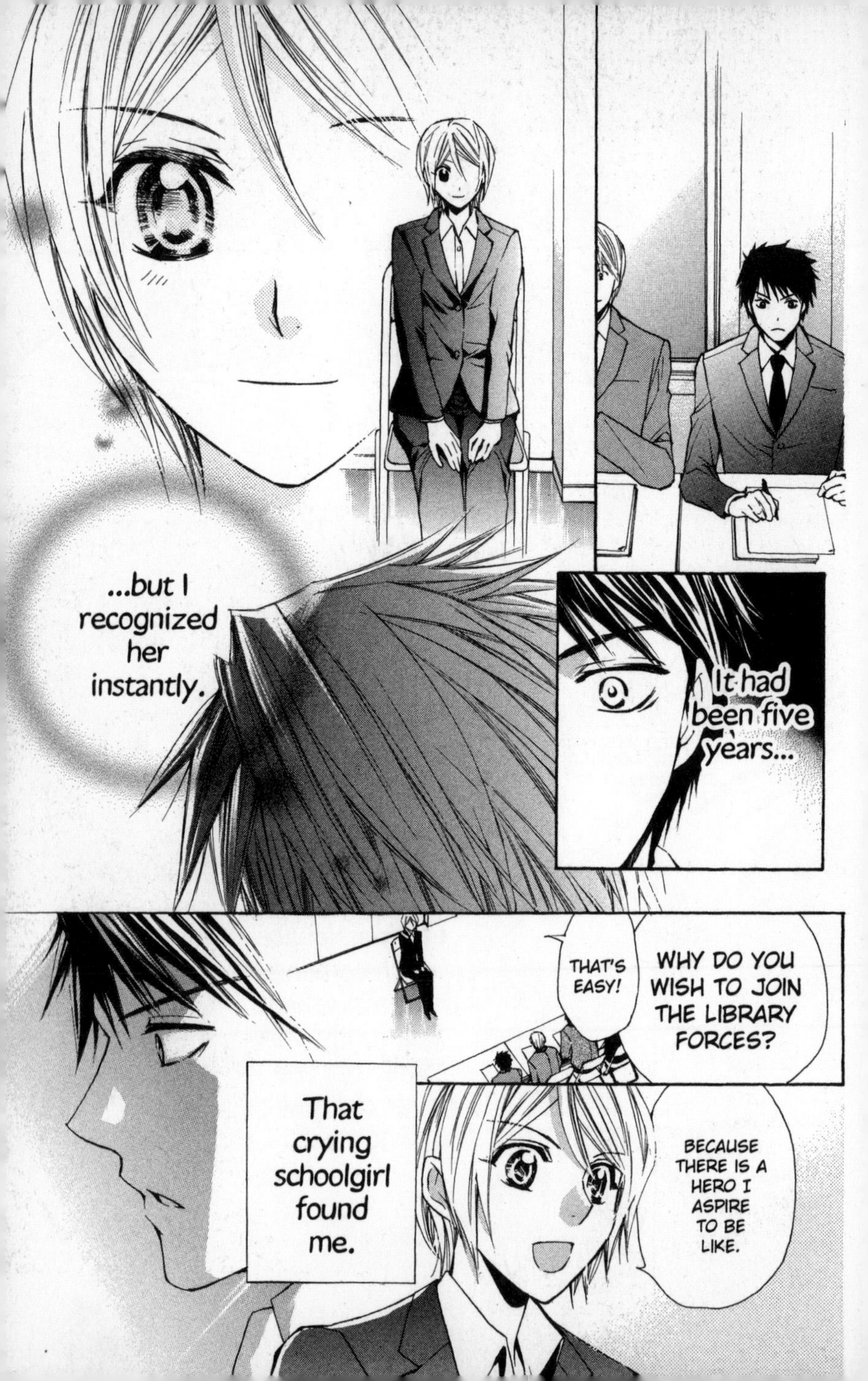
It had been five years...
...but I recognized her instantly.
WHY DO YOU WISH TO JOIN THE LIBRARY FORCES?
THAT'S EASY!
BECAUSE THERE IS A HERO I ASPIRE TO BE LIKE.
That crying schoolgirl found me.

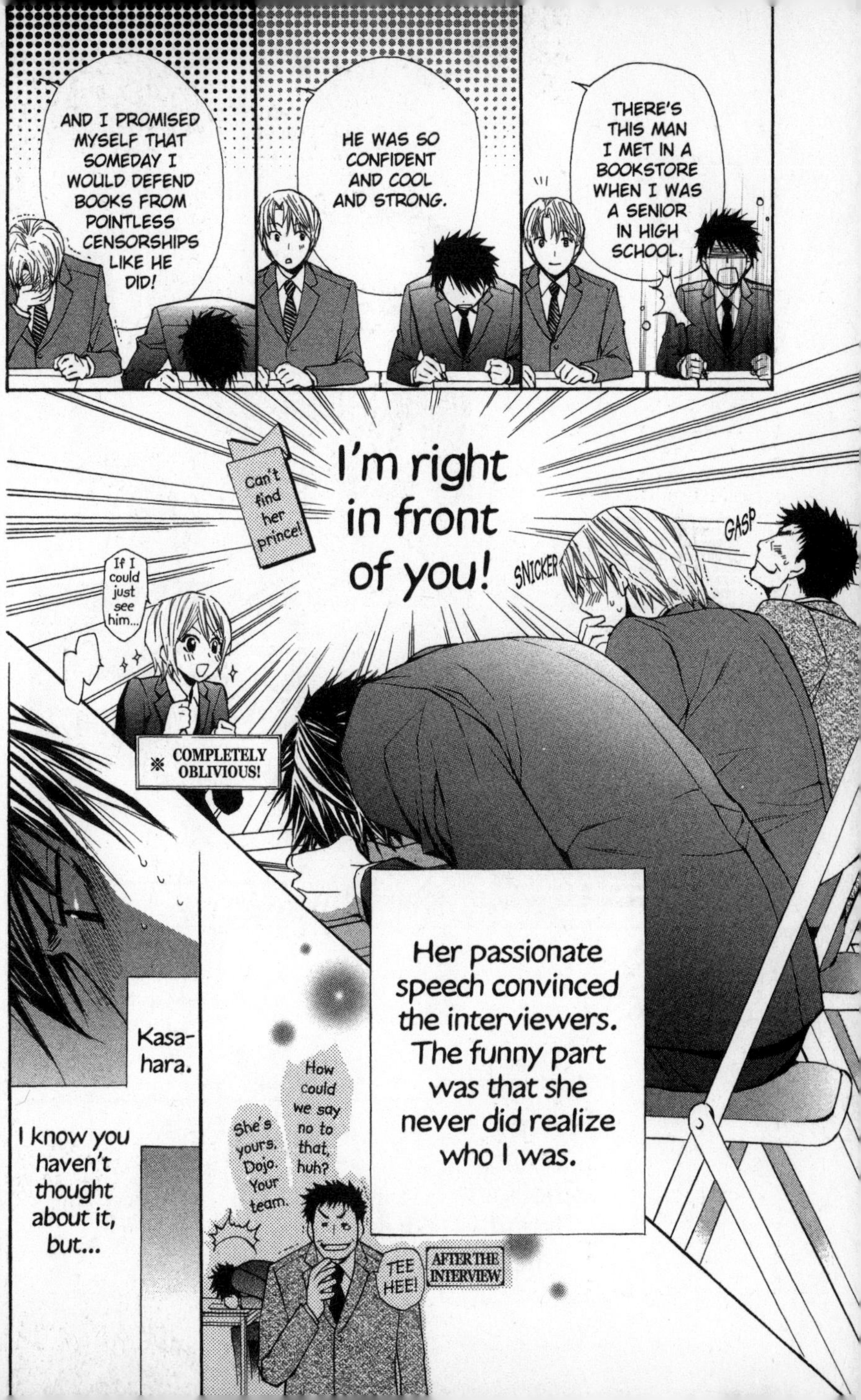
THERE'S THIS MAN I MET IN A BOOKSTORE WHEN I WAS A SENIOR IN HIGH SCHOOL.
HE WAS SO CONFIDENT AND COOL AND STRONG.
AND I PROMISED MYSELF THAT SOMEDAY I WOULD DEFEND BOOKS FROM POINTLESS CENSORSHIPS LIKE HE DID!
GASP
SNICKER
I'm right in front of you!
Can't find her prince!
If I could just see him...
※ COMPLETELY OBLIVIOUS!
Her passionate speech convinced the interviewers. The funny part was that she never did realize who I was.
Kasa-hara.
I know you haven't thought about it, but...
How could we say no to that, huh?
She's yours, Dojo. Your team.
TEE HEE!
AFTER THE INTERVIEW

2

*

There is a comic strip after each chapter.
I enjoy doing these four-panel comic strips and other bonus strips with petite characters, though sometimes I have a tough time coming up with a story!

The bonus chapters at the end of the tankoban are a lot easier to create.

I really admire professional comic strip artists.
They have to come up with two strips for each page...!

And they're so zany....!

I wish I had it in me to make those creative strips.

*

*

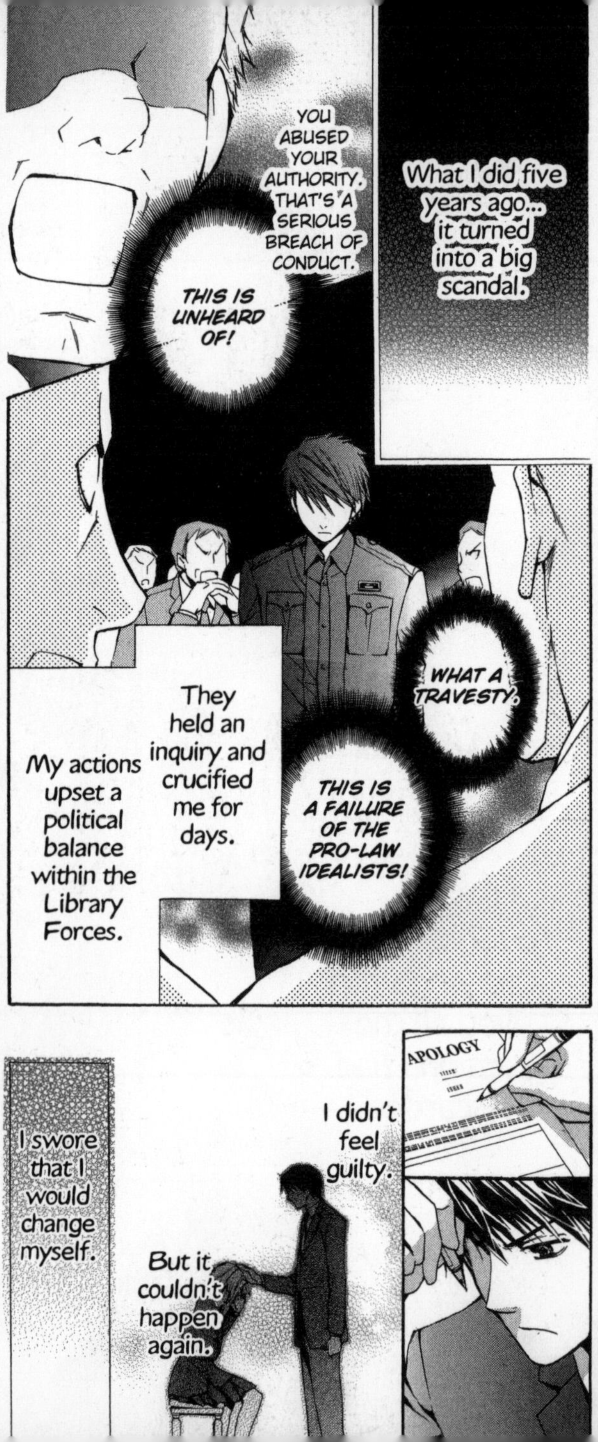
What I did five years ago... it turned into a big scandal.
YOU ABUSED YOUR AUTHORITY. THAT'S A SERIOUS BREACH OF CONDUCT.
THIS IS UNHEARD OF!
WHAT A TRAVESTY.
THIS IS A FAILURE OF THE PRO-LAW IDEALISTS!
They held an inquiry and crucified me for days.
My actions upset a political balance within the Library Forces.
APOLOGY
I didn't feel guilty.
But it couldn't happen again.
I swore that I would change myself.

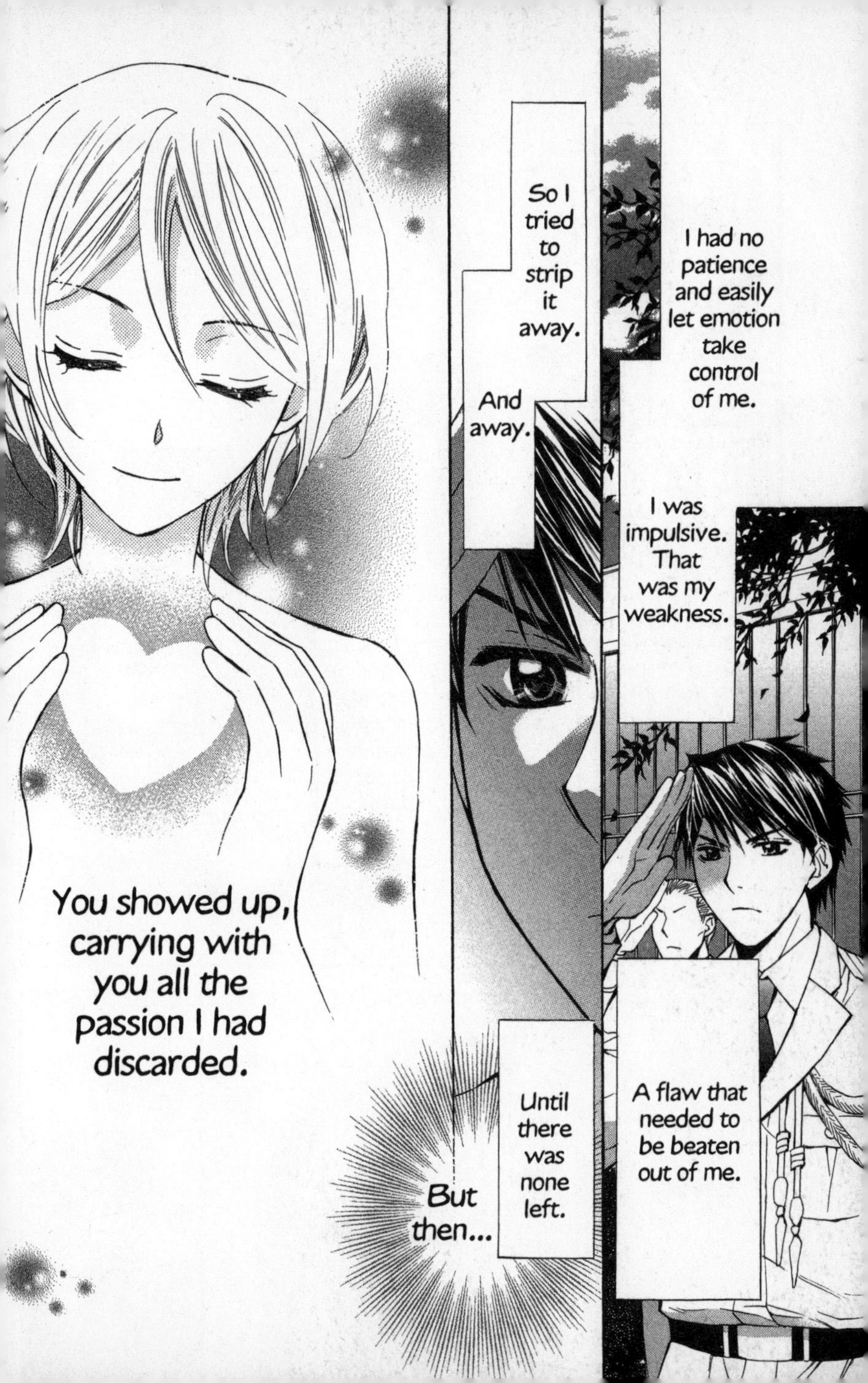
I had no patience and easily let emotion take control of me.
I was impulsive. That was my weakness.
A flaw that needed to be beaten out of me.
So I tried to strip it away.
And away.
Until there was none left.
But then...
You showed up, carrying with you all the passion I had discarded.

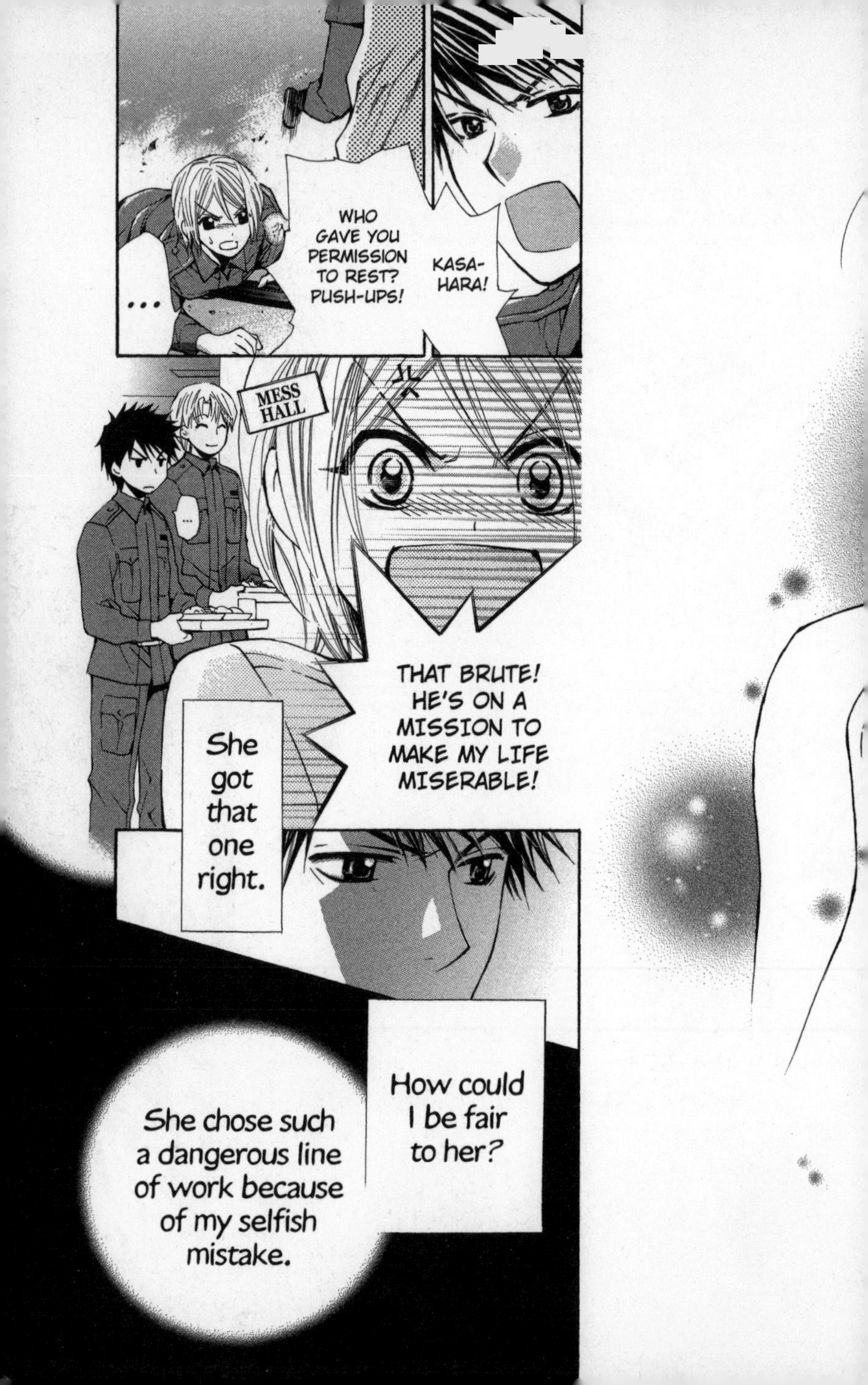
KASA-HARA!
WHO GAVE YOU PERMISSION TO REST? PUSH-UPS!
...
MESS HALL
THAT BRUTE! HE'S ON A MISSION TO MAKE MY LIFE MISERABLE!
...
She got that one right.
How could I be fair to her?
She chose such a dangerous line of work because of my selfish mistake.

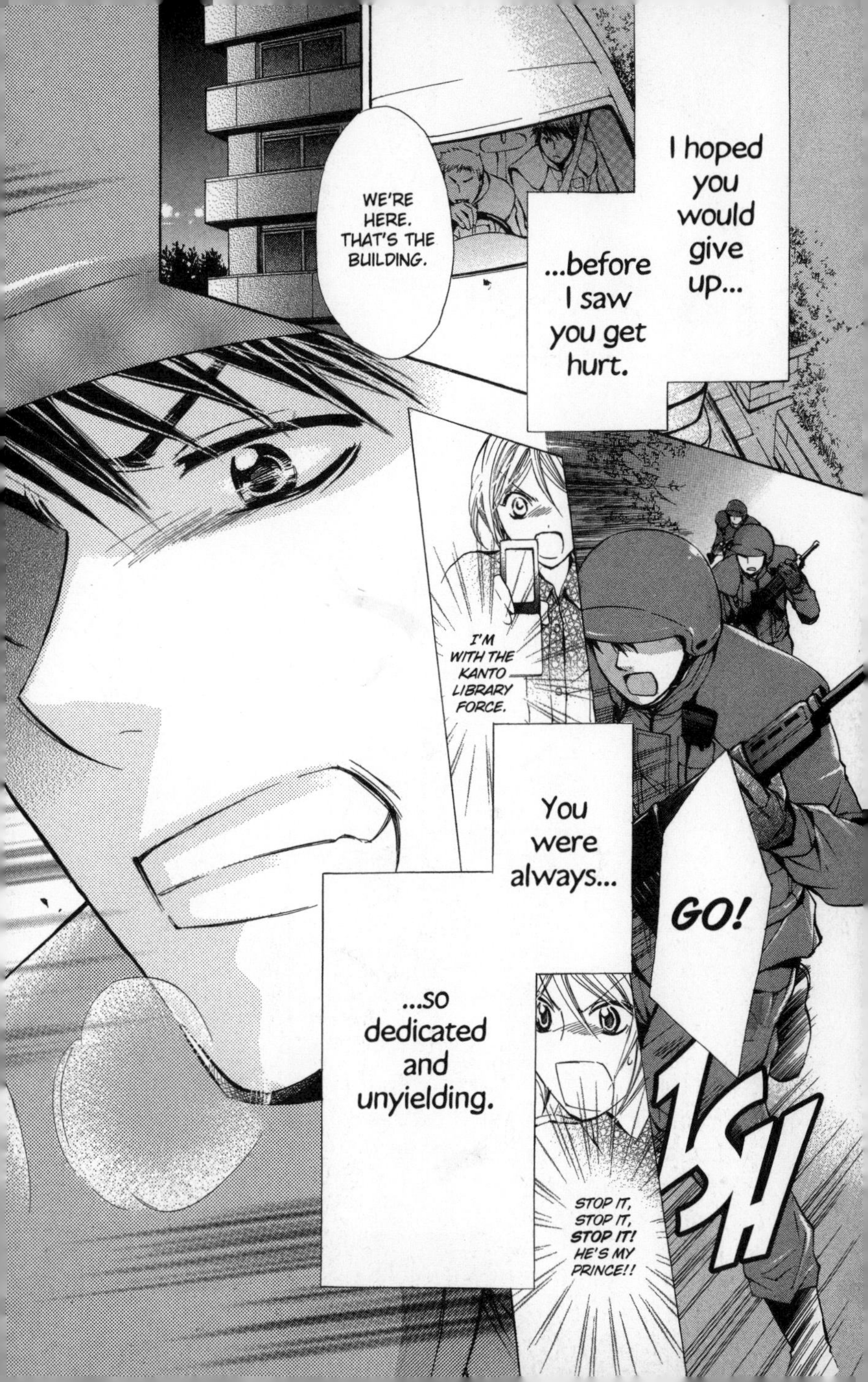
I hoped you would give up...
...before I saw you get hurt.
WE'RE HERE. THAT'S THE BUILDING.
GO!
You were always...
I'M WITH THE KANTO LIBRARY FORCE.
...so dedicated and unyielding.
STOP IT, STOP IT, STOP IT! HE'S MY PRINCE!!

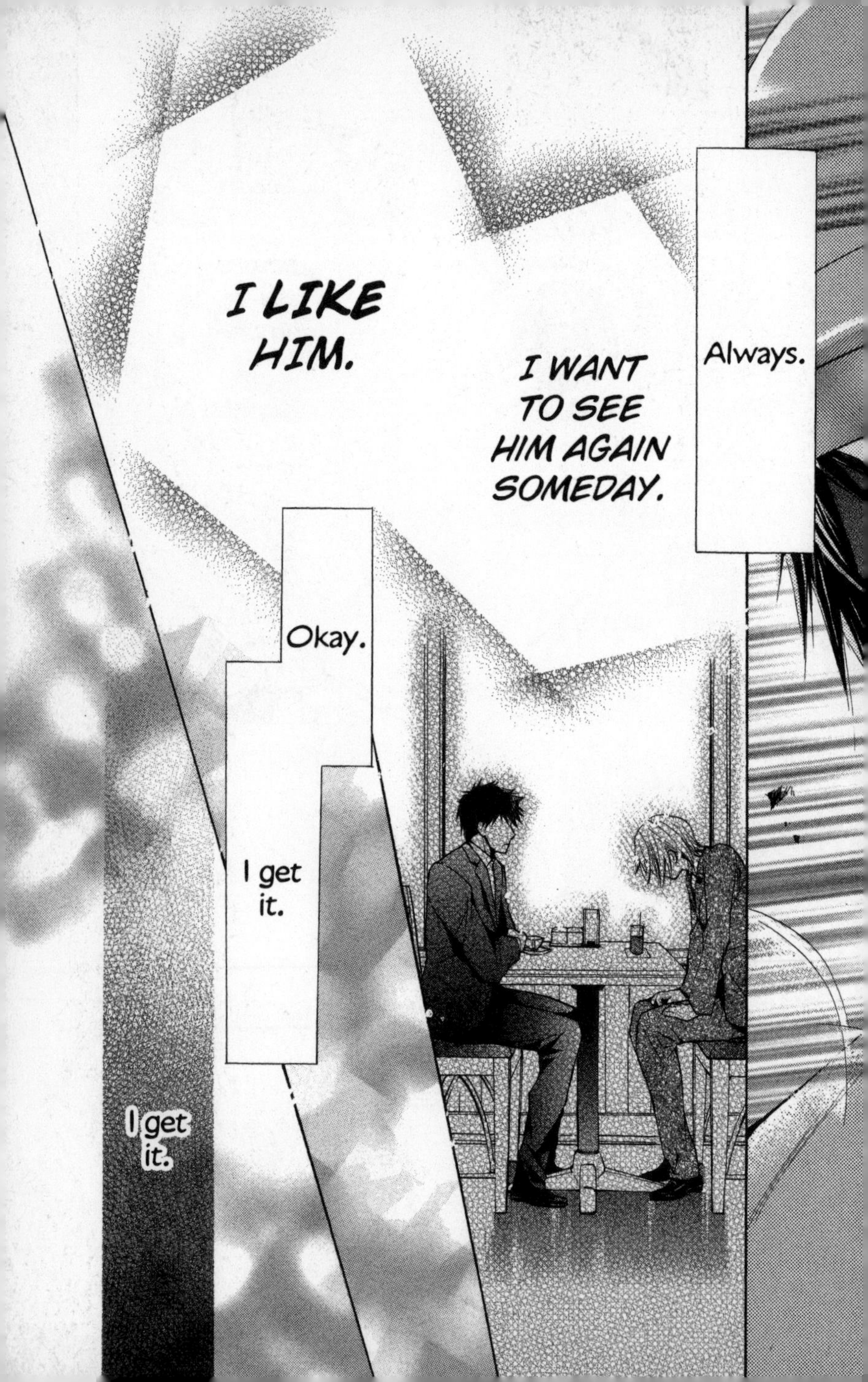
Always.
I WANT TO SEE HIM AGAIN SOMEDAY.
I LIKE HIM.
Okay.
I get it.
I get it.

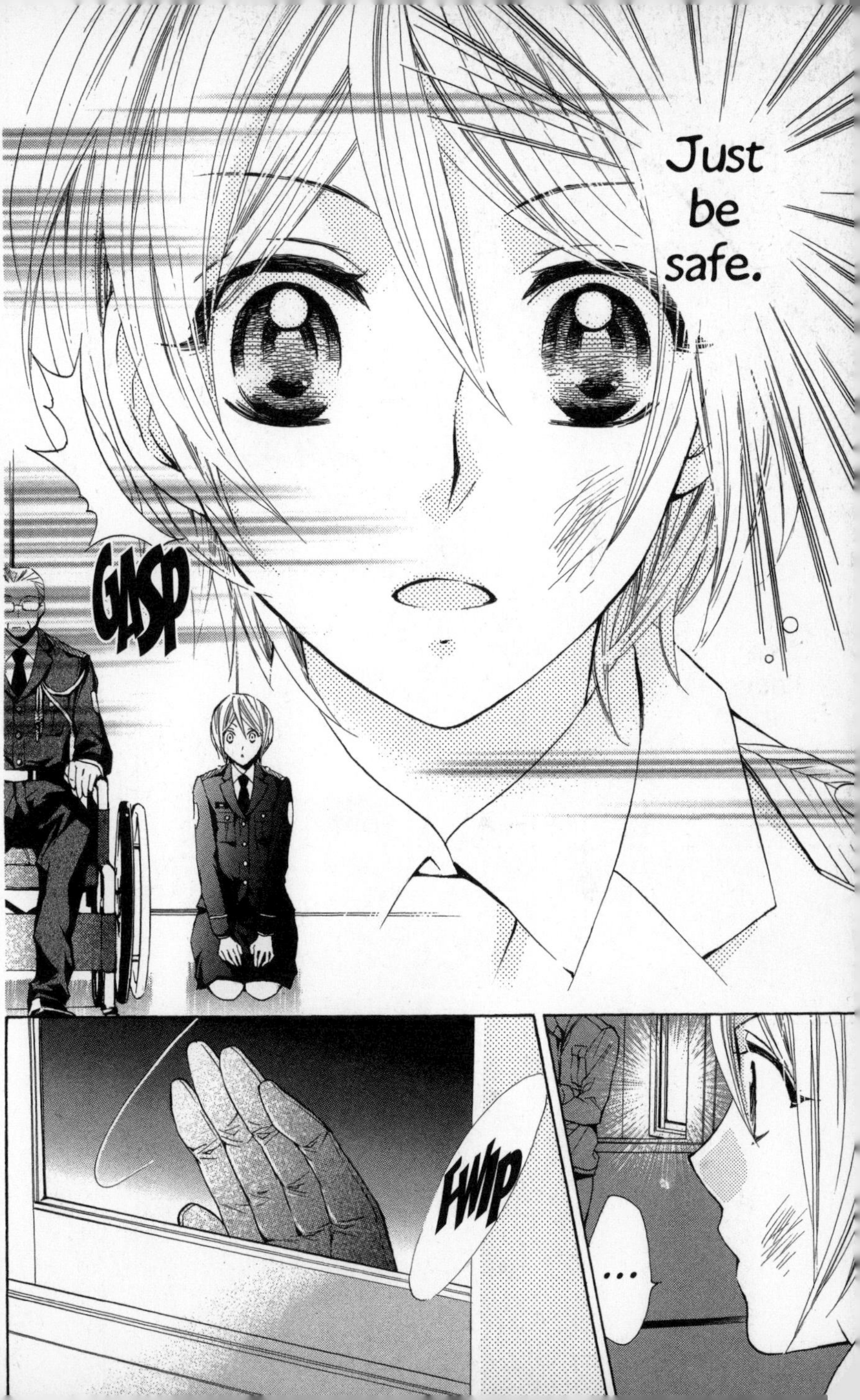
Just be safe.
GASP
...
FWIP

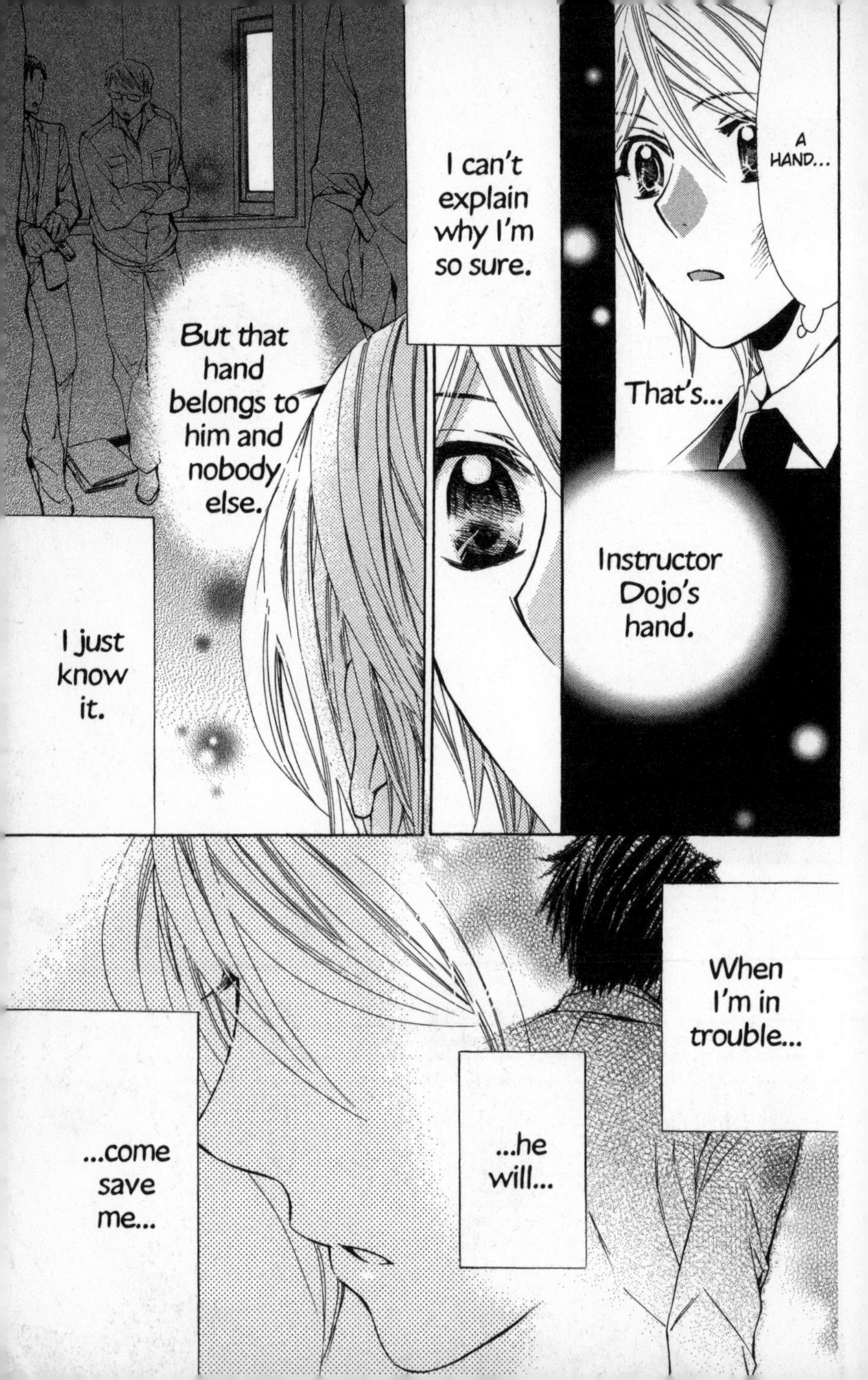
A HAND...
That's...
Instructor Dojo's hand.
I can't explain why I'm so sure.
But that hand belongs to him and nobody else.
I just know it.
When I'm in trouble...
...he will...
...come save me...

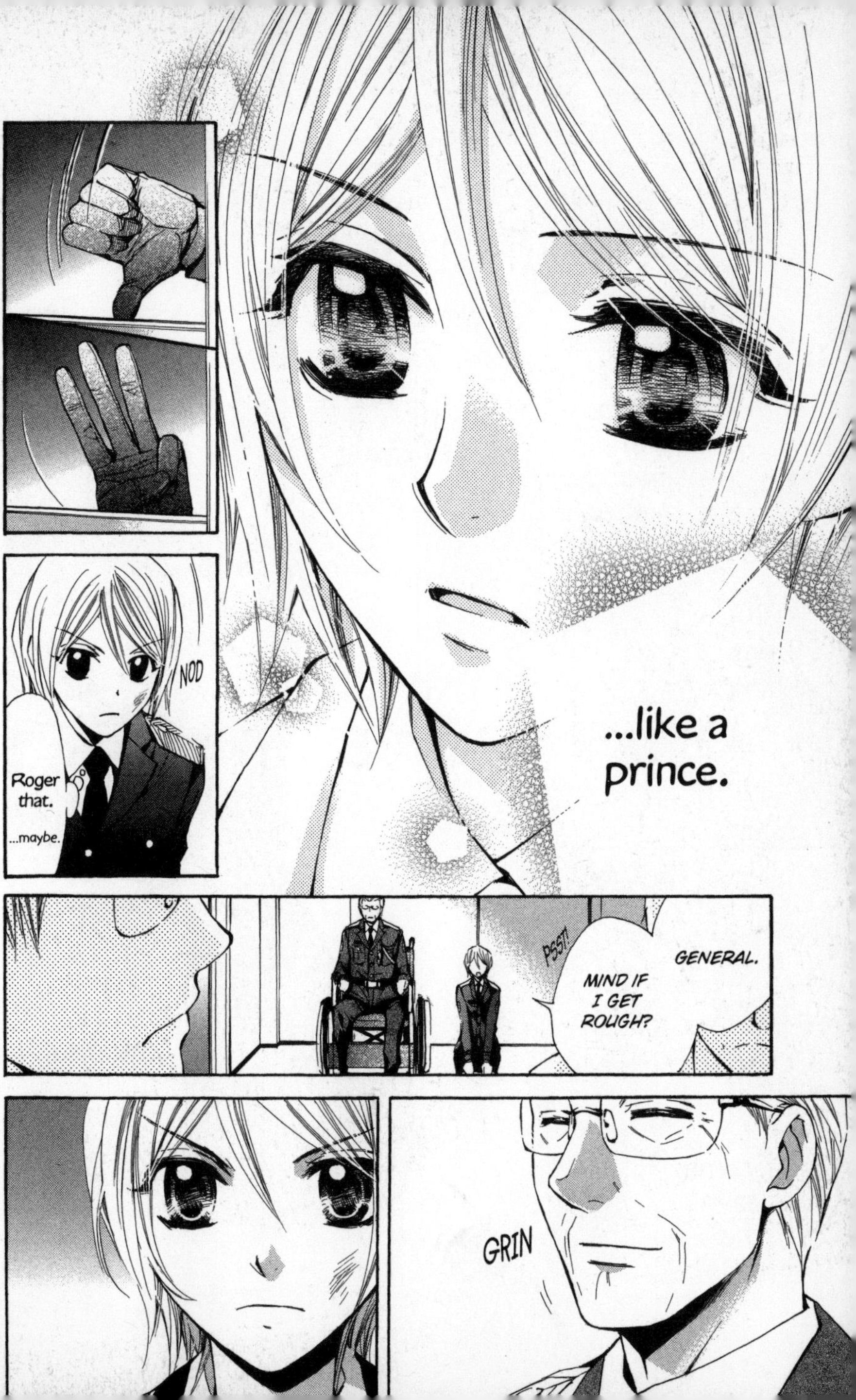
...like a prince.
NOD
Roger that.
...maybe.
GENERAL.
PSST!
MIND IF I GET ROUGH?
GRIN

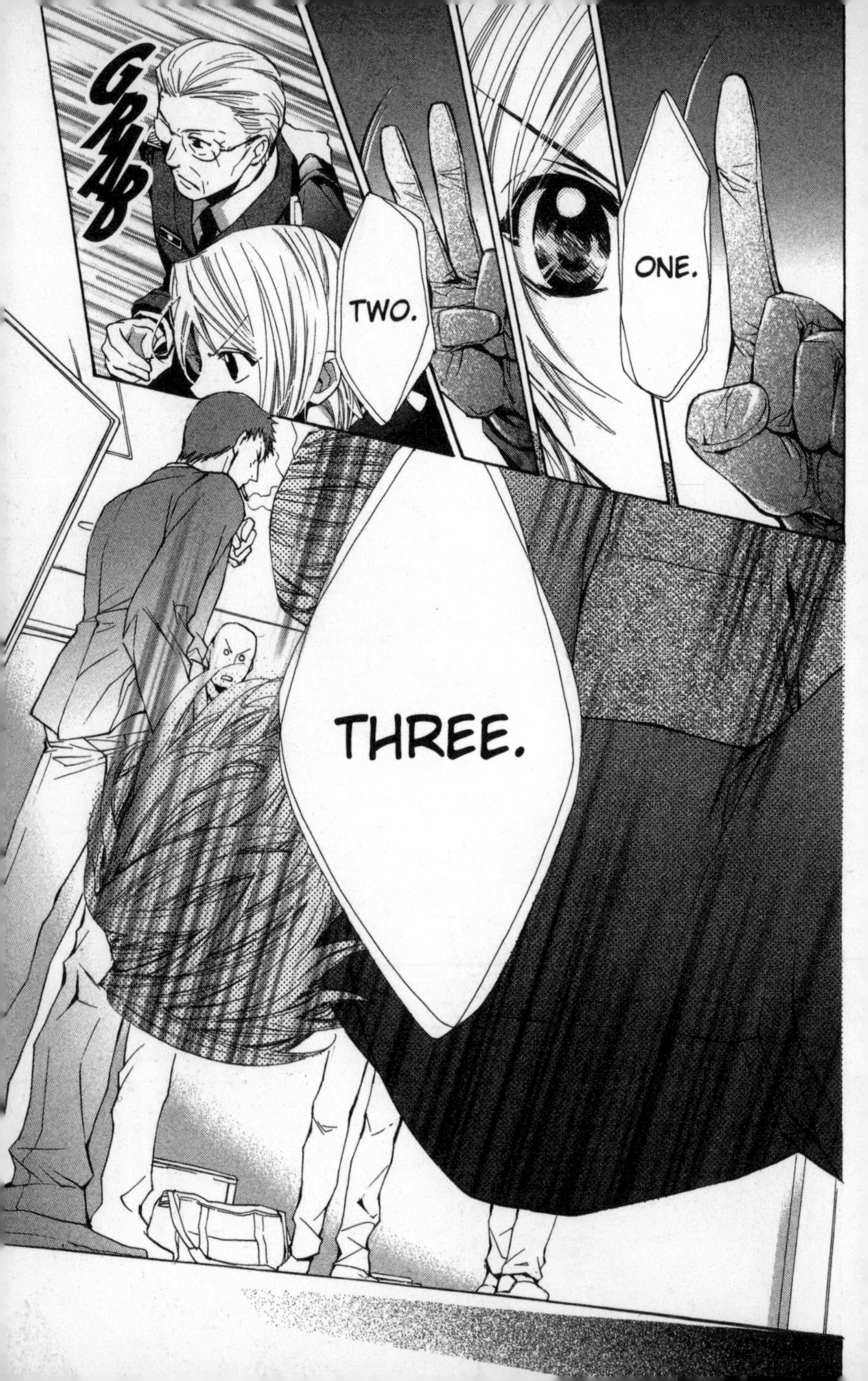
ONE.
TWO.
GRAB
THREE.

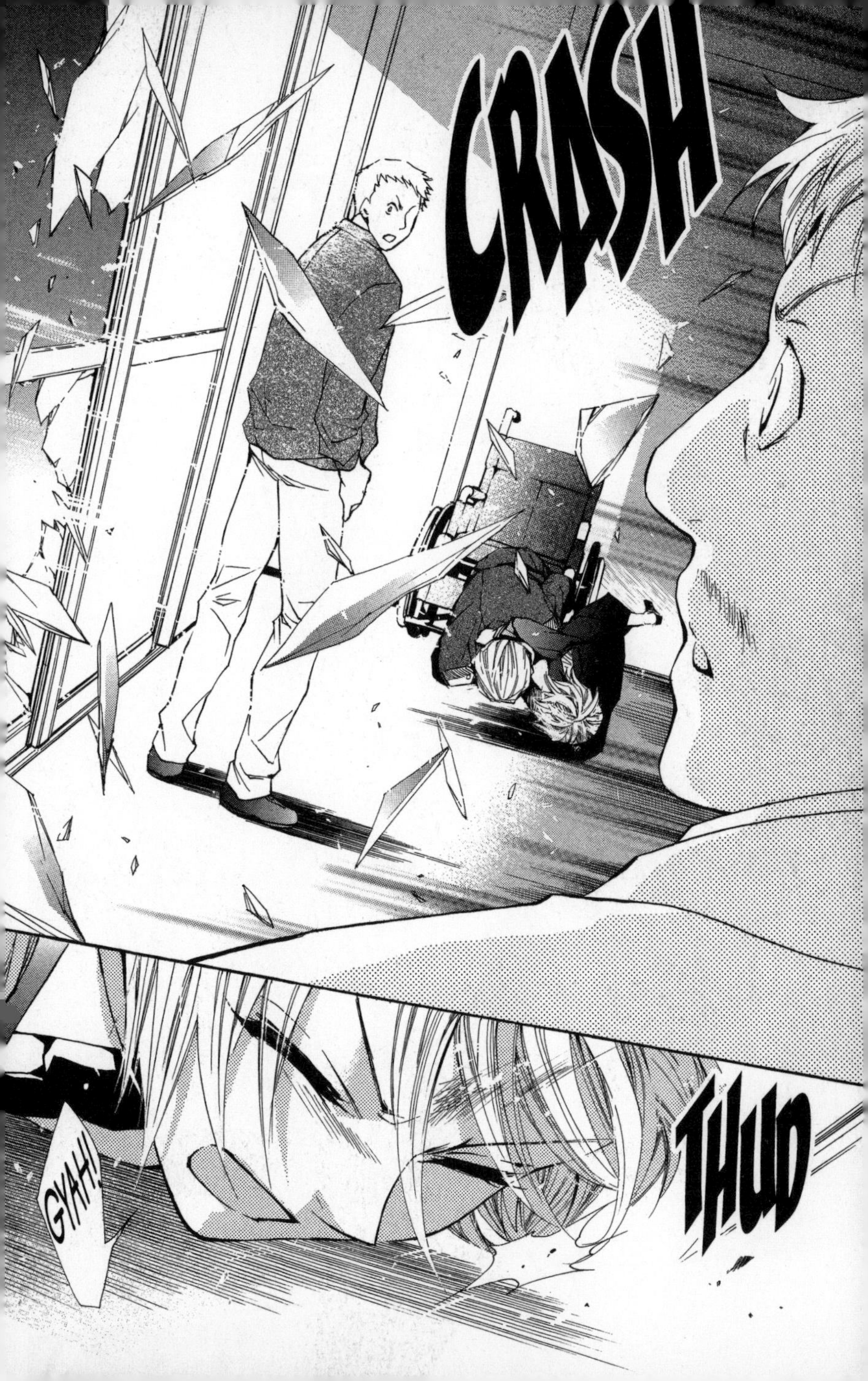
CRASH
THUD
GYAH!

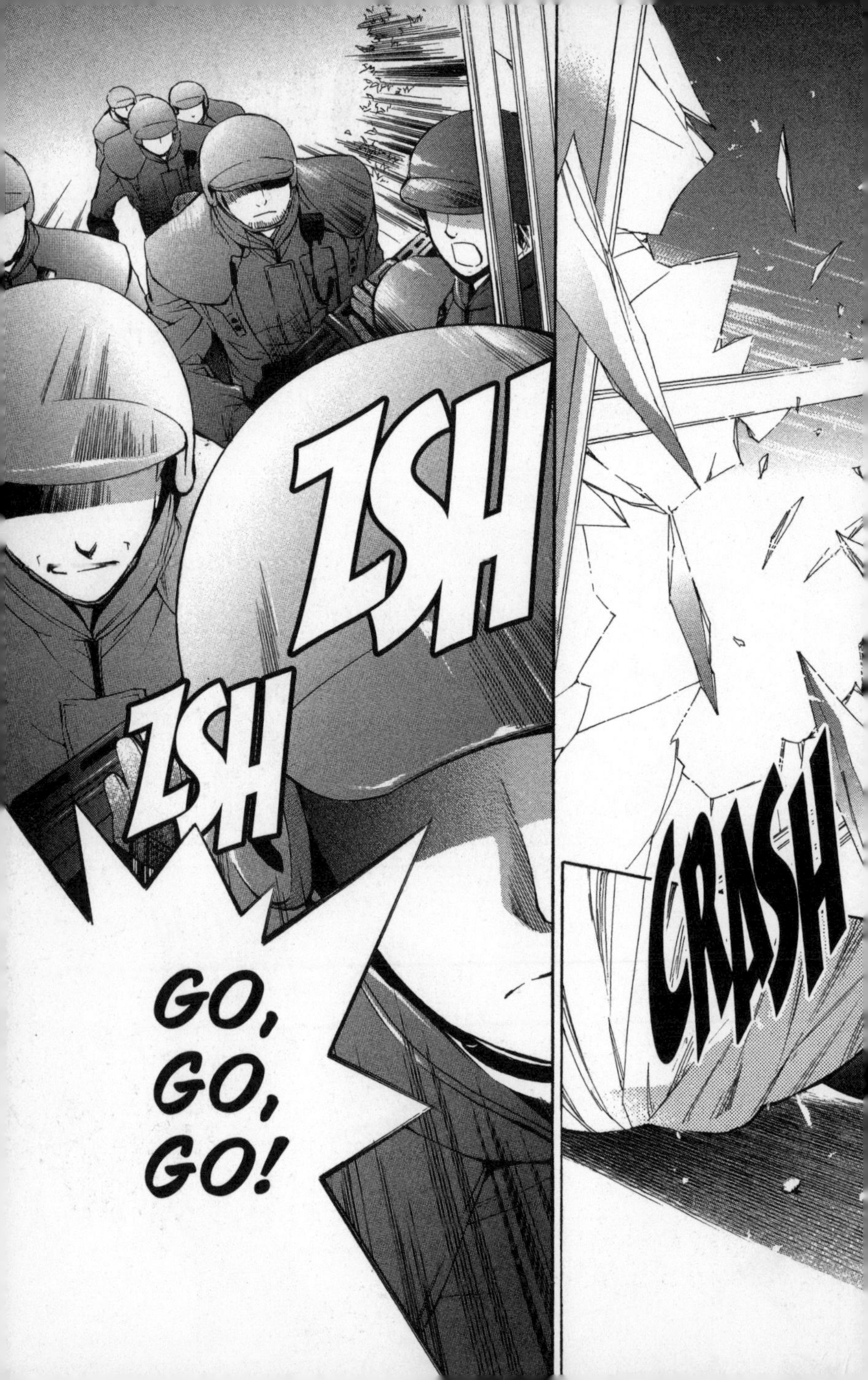
CRASH
ZSH
ZSH
GO, GO, GO!

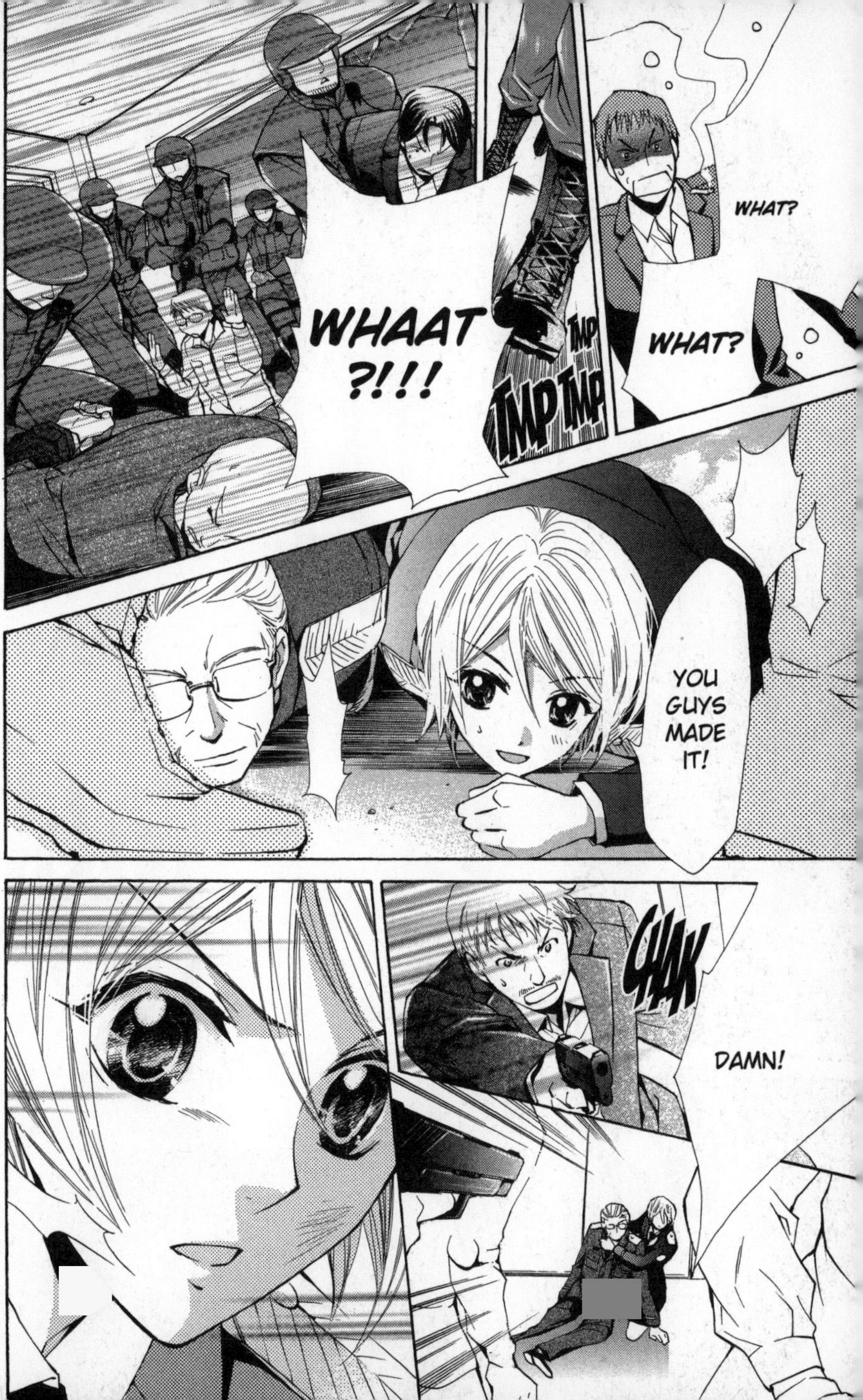
WHAT?
WHAT?
TMP TMP TMP
WHAAT ?!!!
YOU GUYS MADE IT!
CHAK
DAMN!

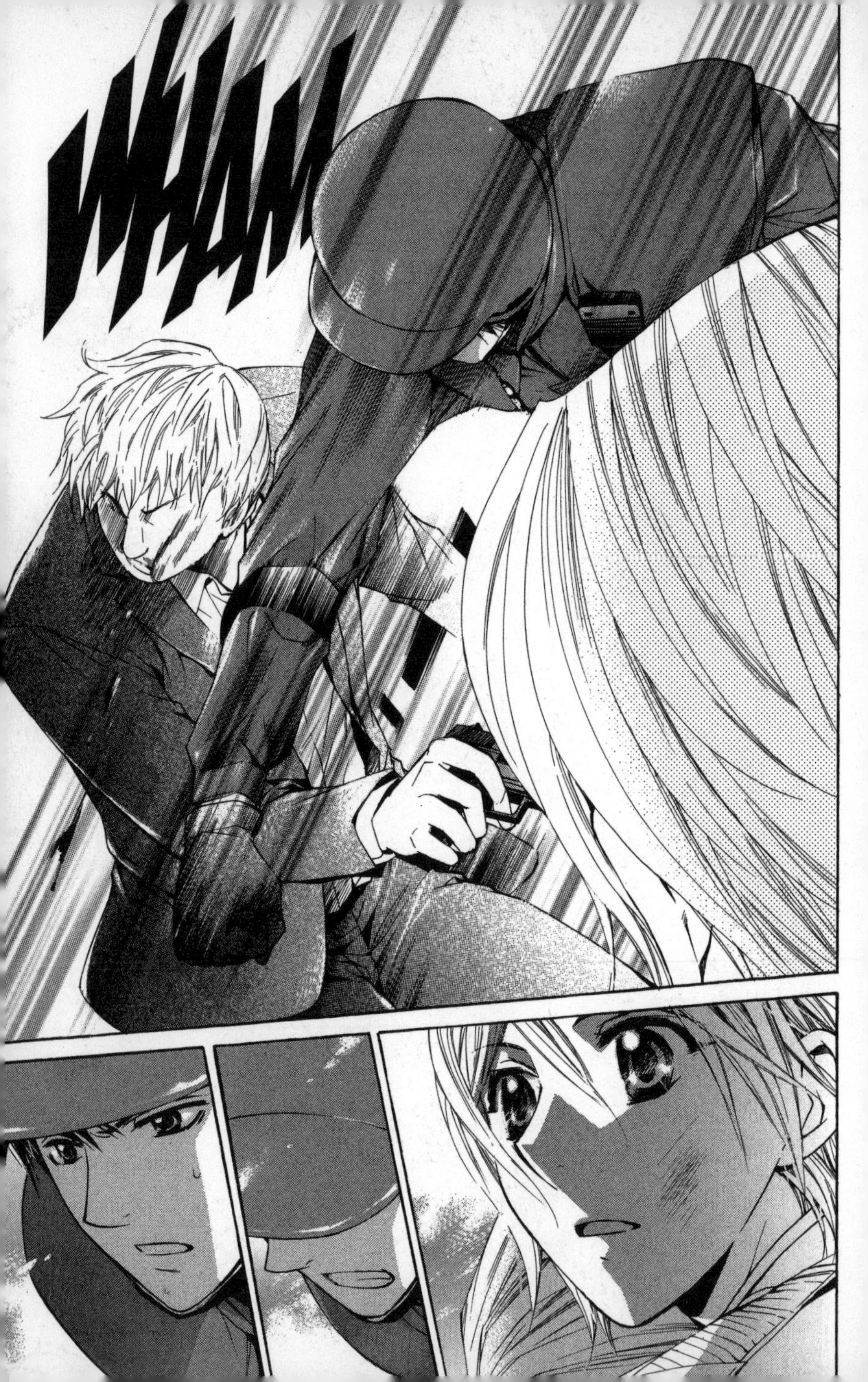
WHAM

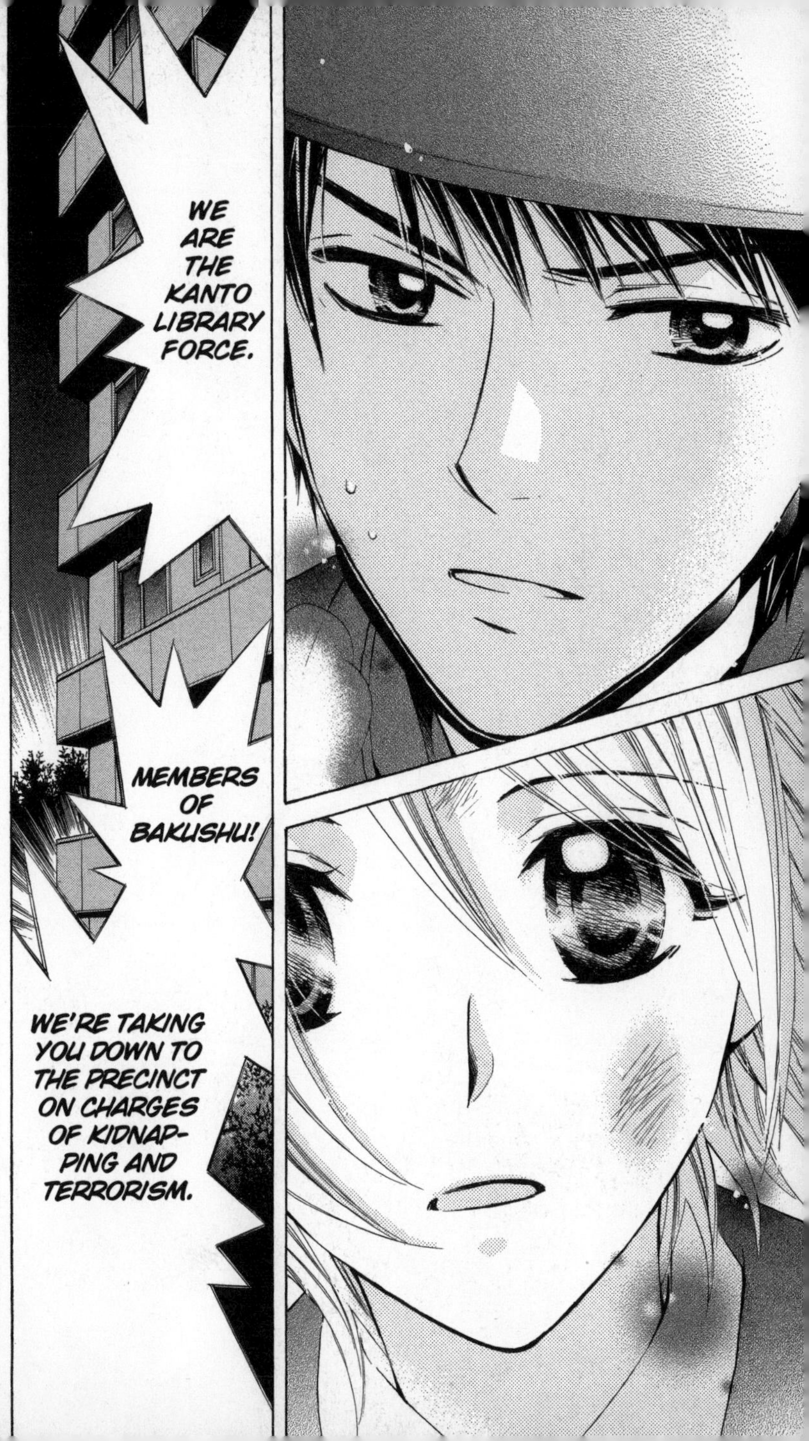
WE ARE THE KANTO LIBRARY FORCE.
MEMBERS OF BAKUSHU!
WE'RE TAKING YOU DOWN TO THE PRECINCT ON CHARGES OF KIDNAP-PING AND TERRORISM.

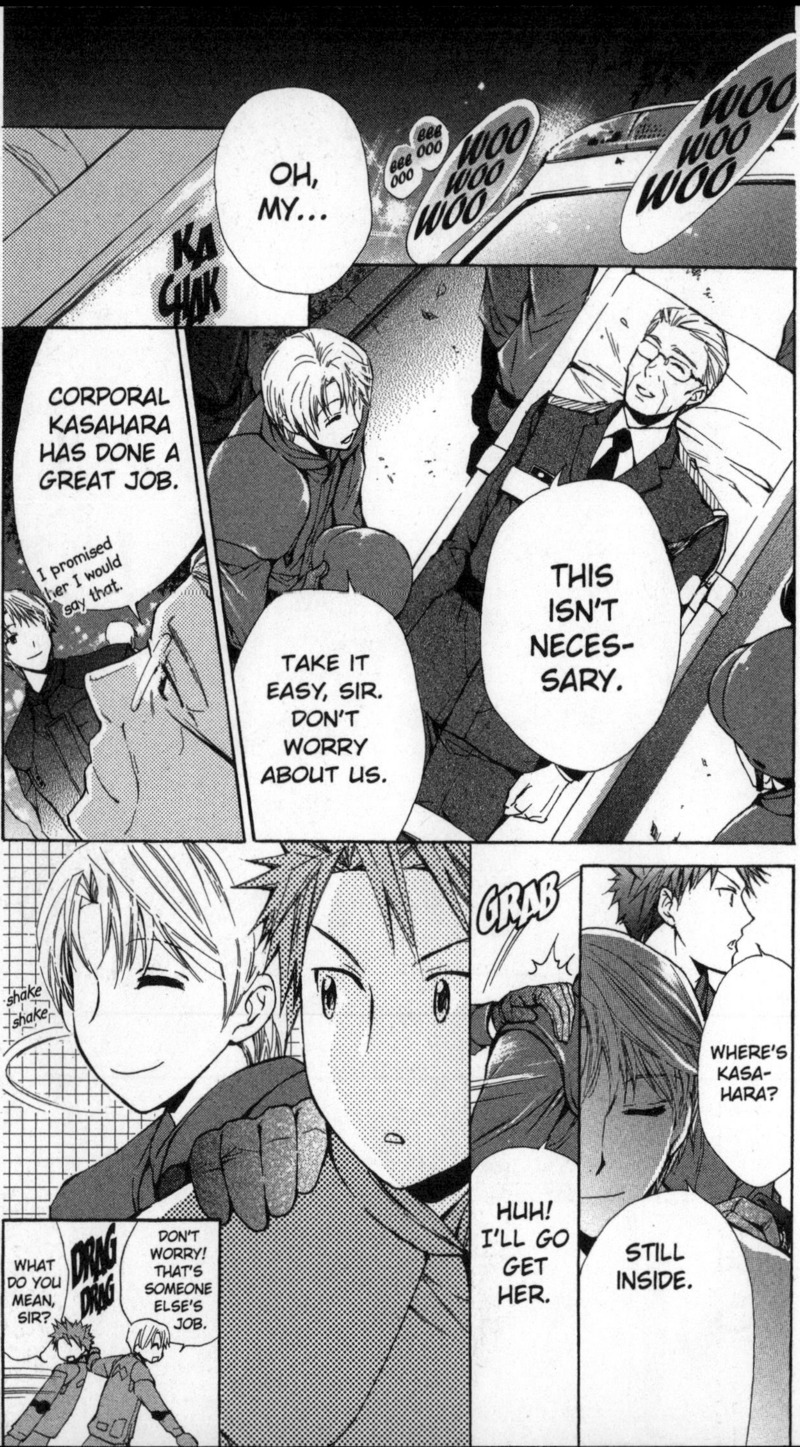
WOO WOO WOO
WOO WOO WOO
eee ooo eee ooo
OH, MY...
KA CHAK
THIS ISN'T NECES-SARY.
TAKE IT EASY, SIR. DON'T WORRY ABOUT US.
CORPORAL KASAHARA HAS DONE A GREAT JOB.
I promised her I would say that.
GRAB
WHERE'S KASA-HARA?
STILL INSIDE.
HUH! I'LL GO GET HER.
shake shake
DON'T WORRY! THAT'S SOMEONE ELSE'S JOB.
DRAG DRAG
WHAT DO YOU MEAN, SIR?

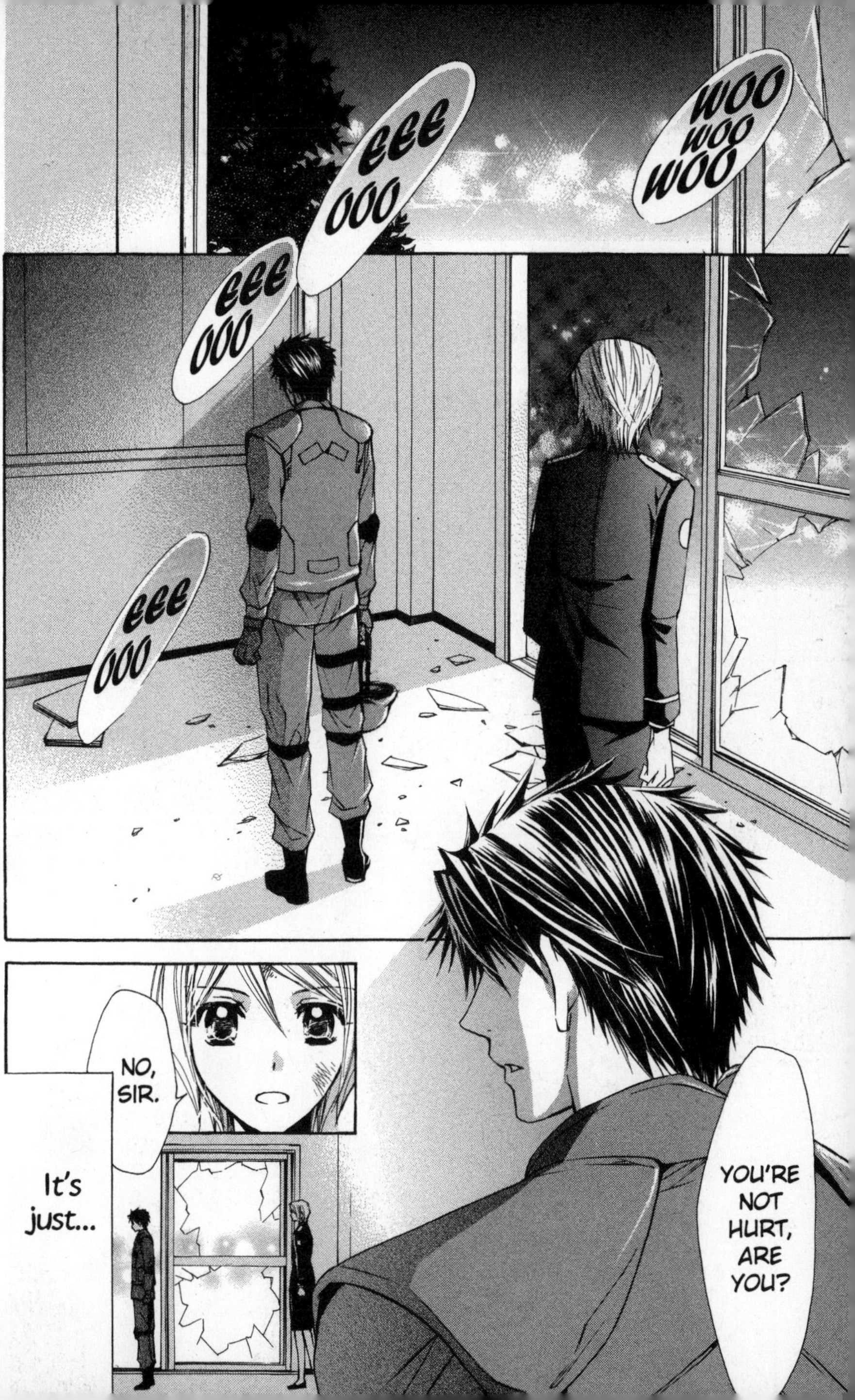
WOO WOO WOO
EEE OOO
EEE OOO
EEE OOO
YOU'RE NOT HURT, ARE YOU?
NO, SIR.
It's just...

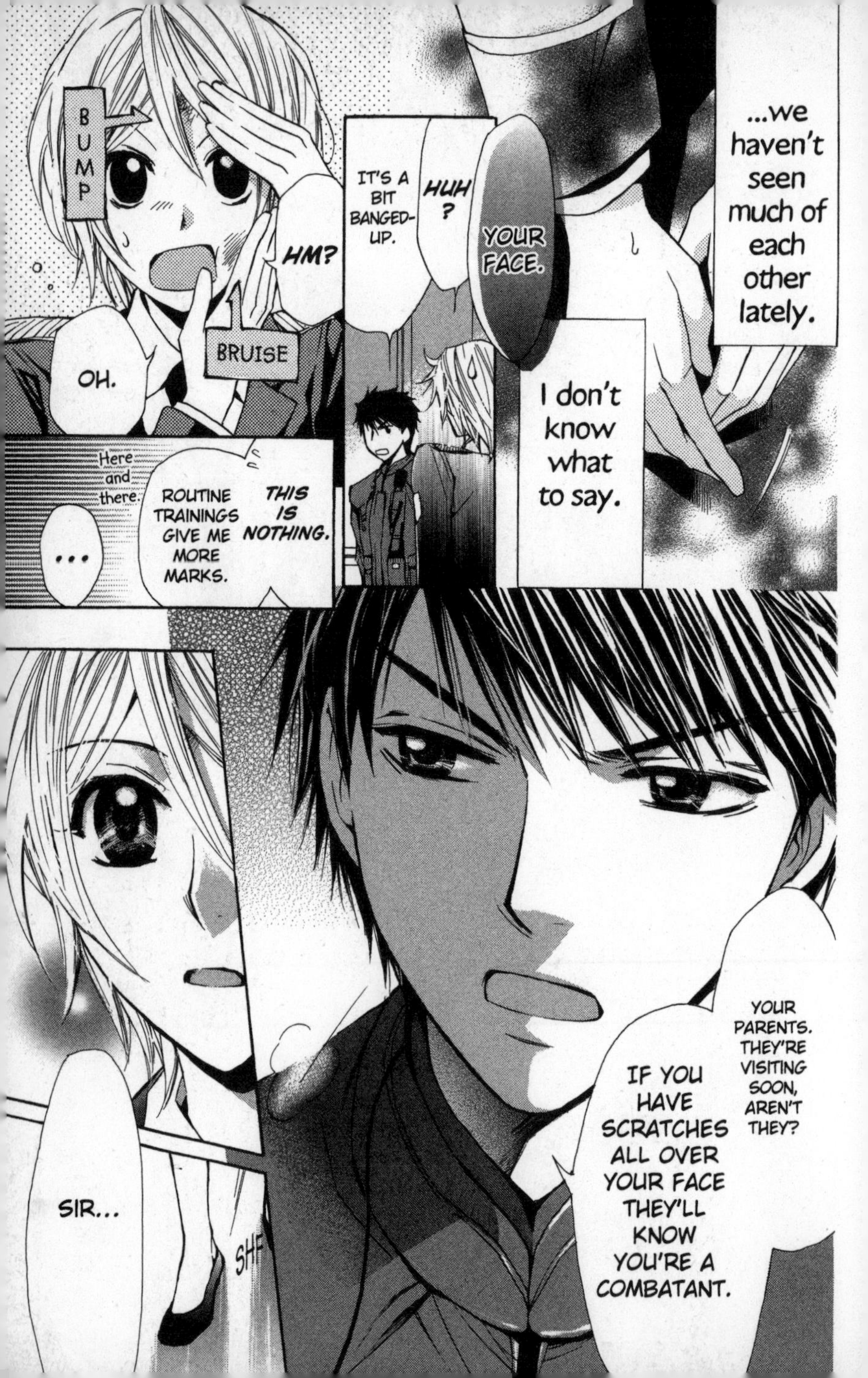
...we haven't seen much of each other lately.
I don't know what to say.
YOUR FACE.
HUH?
IT'S A BIT BANGED-UP.
HM?
BUMP
BRUISE
OH.
THIS IS NOTHING.
ROUTINE TRAININGS GIVE ME MORE MARKS.
Here and there.
...
YOUR PARENTS. THEY'RE VISITING SOON, AREN'T THEY?
IF YOU HAVE SCRATCHES ALL OVER YOUR FACE THEY'LL KNOW YOU'RE A COMBATANT.
SHF
SIR...

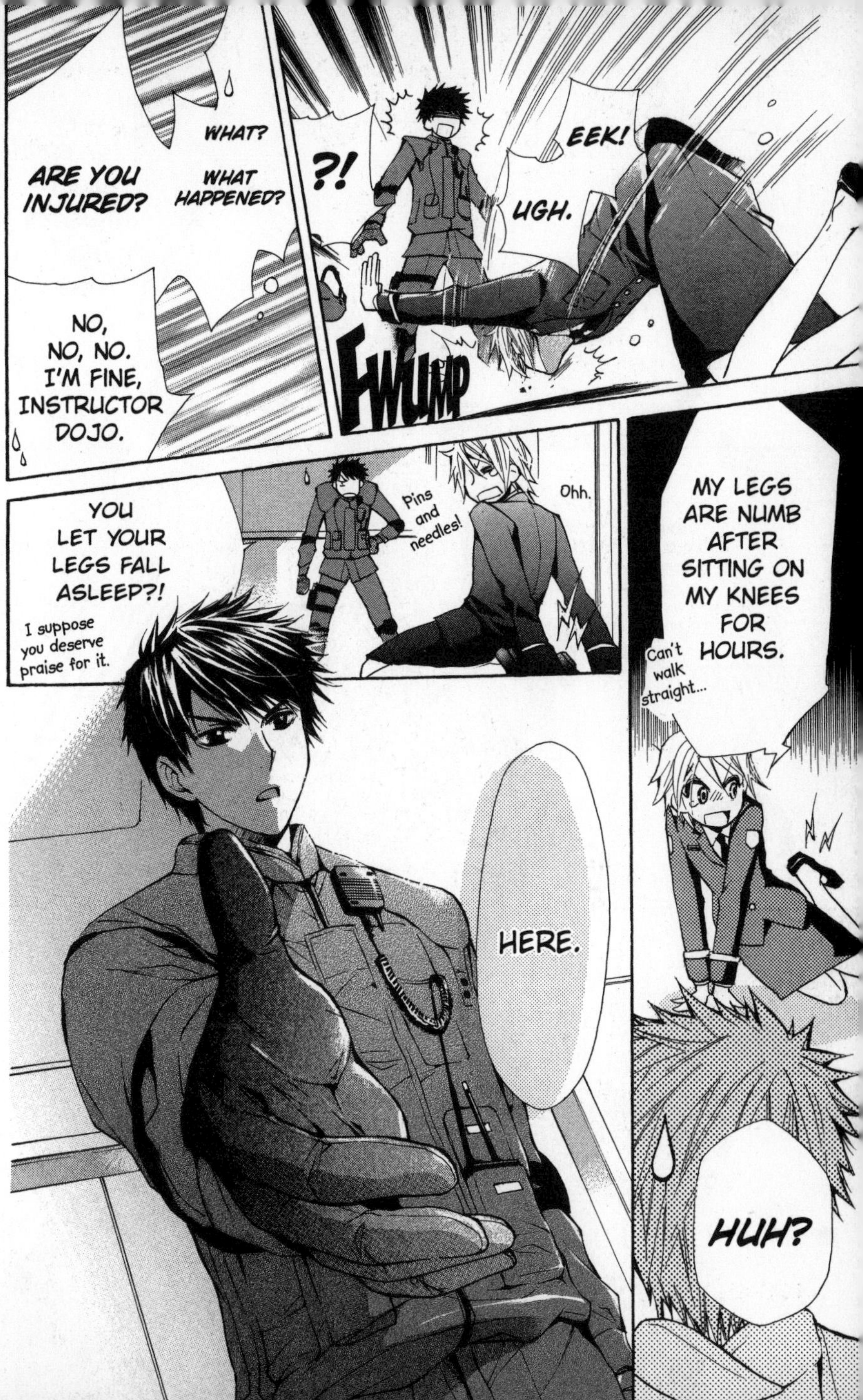
EEK!
UGH.
?!
FWUMP
WHAT?
WHAT HAPPENED?
ARE YOU INJURED?
NO, NO, NO. I'M FINE, INSTRUCTOR DOJO.
MY LEGS ARE NUMB AFTER SITTING ON MY KNEES FOR HOURS.
Can't walk straight...
Ohh.
Pins and needles!
YOU LET YOUR LEGS FALL ASLEEP?!
I suppose you deserve praise for it.
HERE.
HUH?

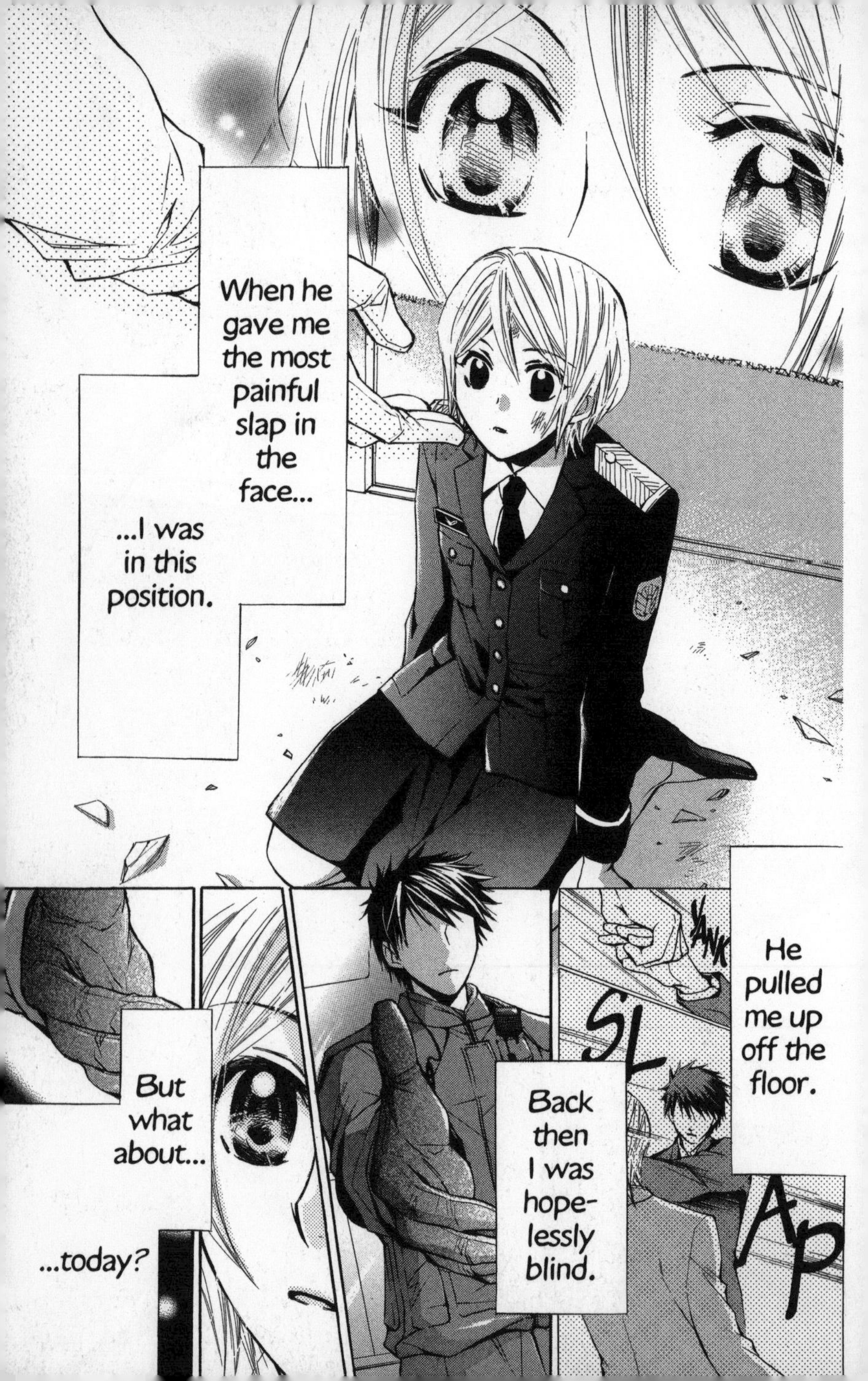
When he gave me the most painful slap in the face...
...I was in this position.
YANK
He pulled me up off the floor.
SL
AP
Back then I was hopelessly blind.
But what about...
...today?

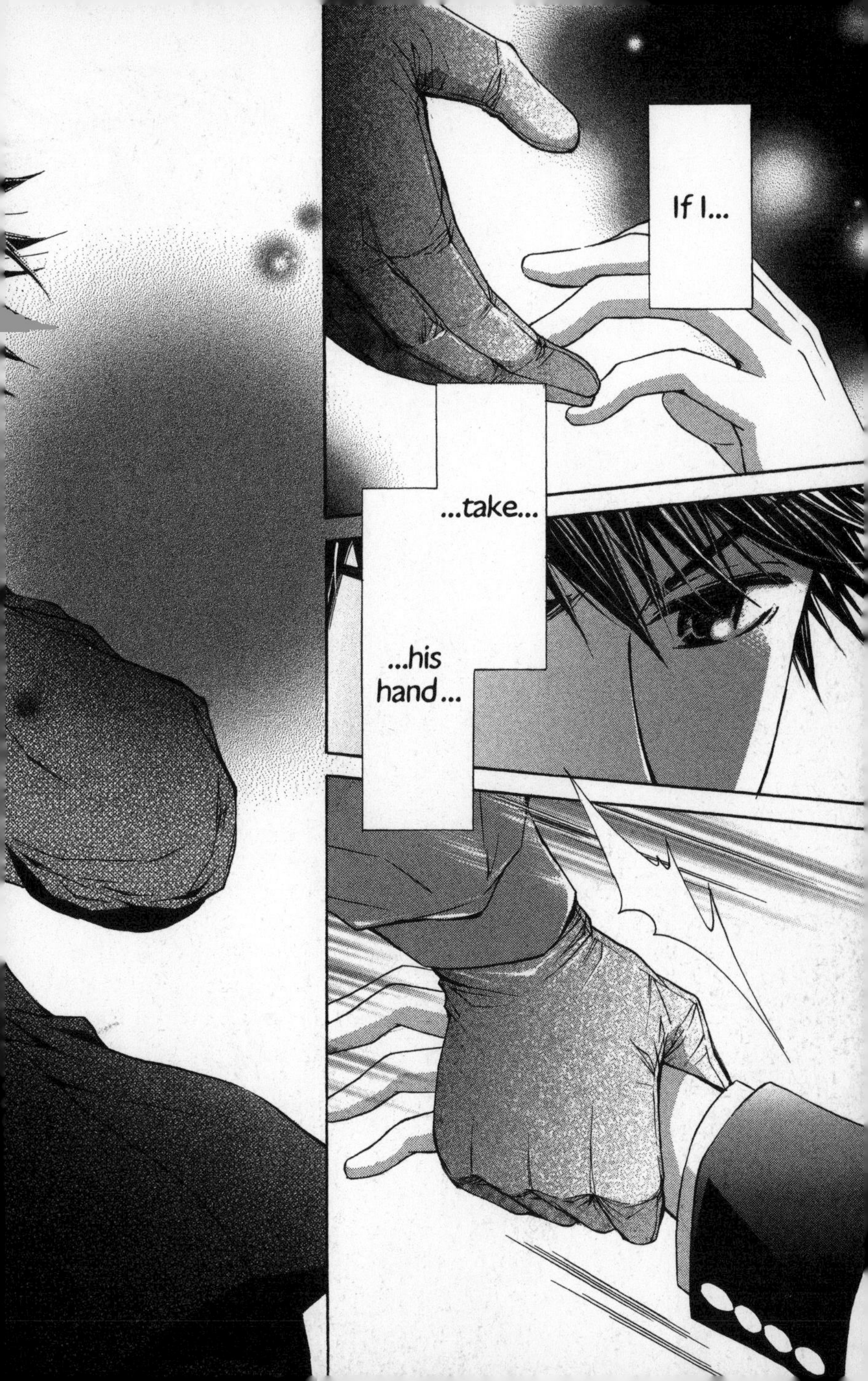
If I...
...take...
...his hand...

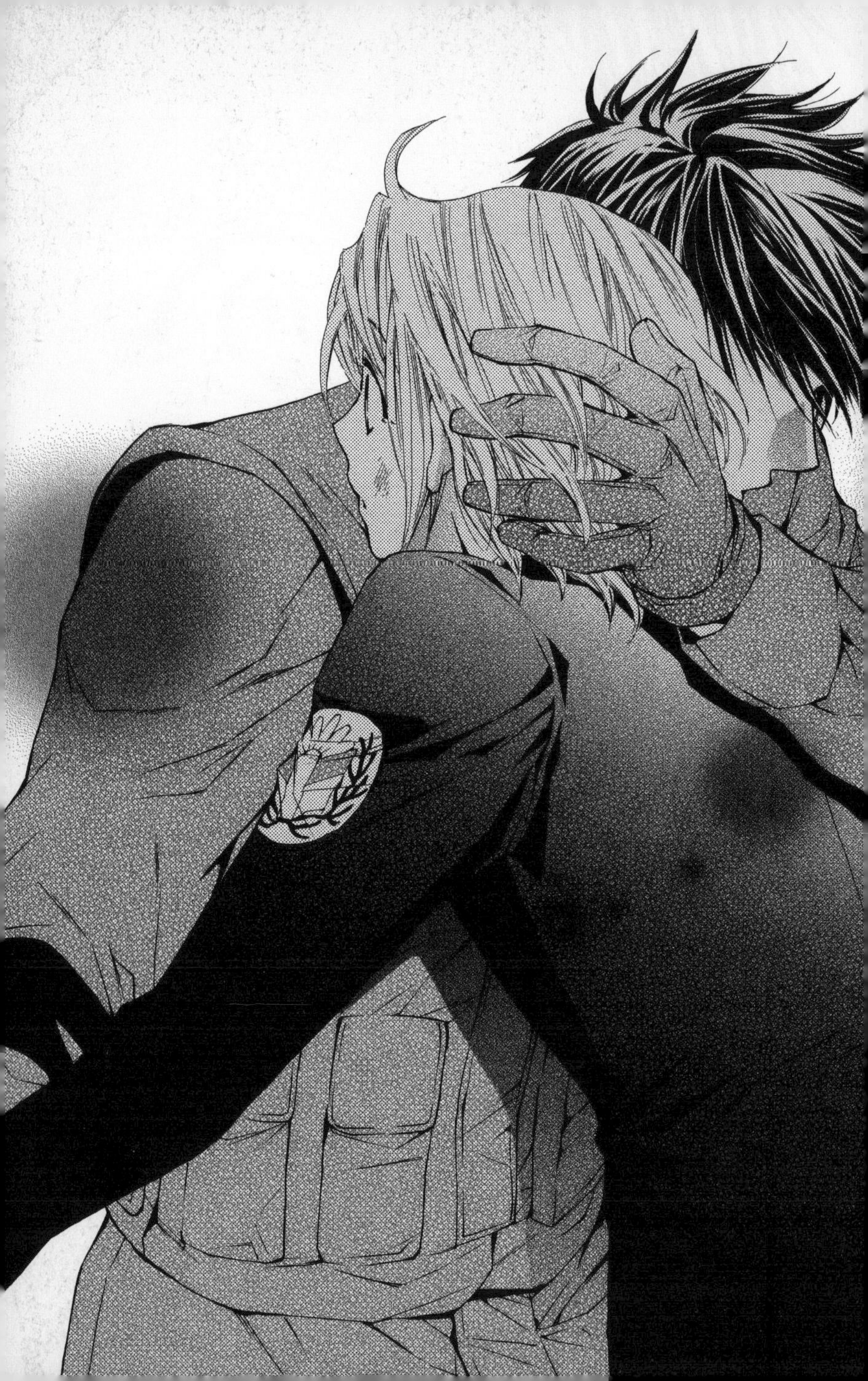

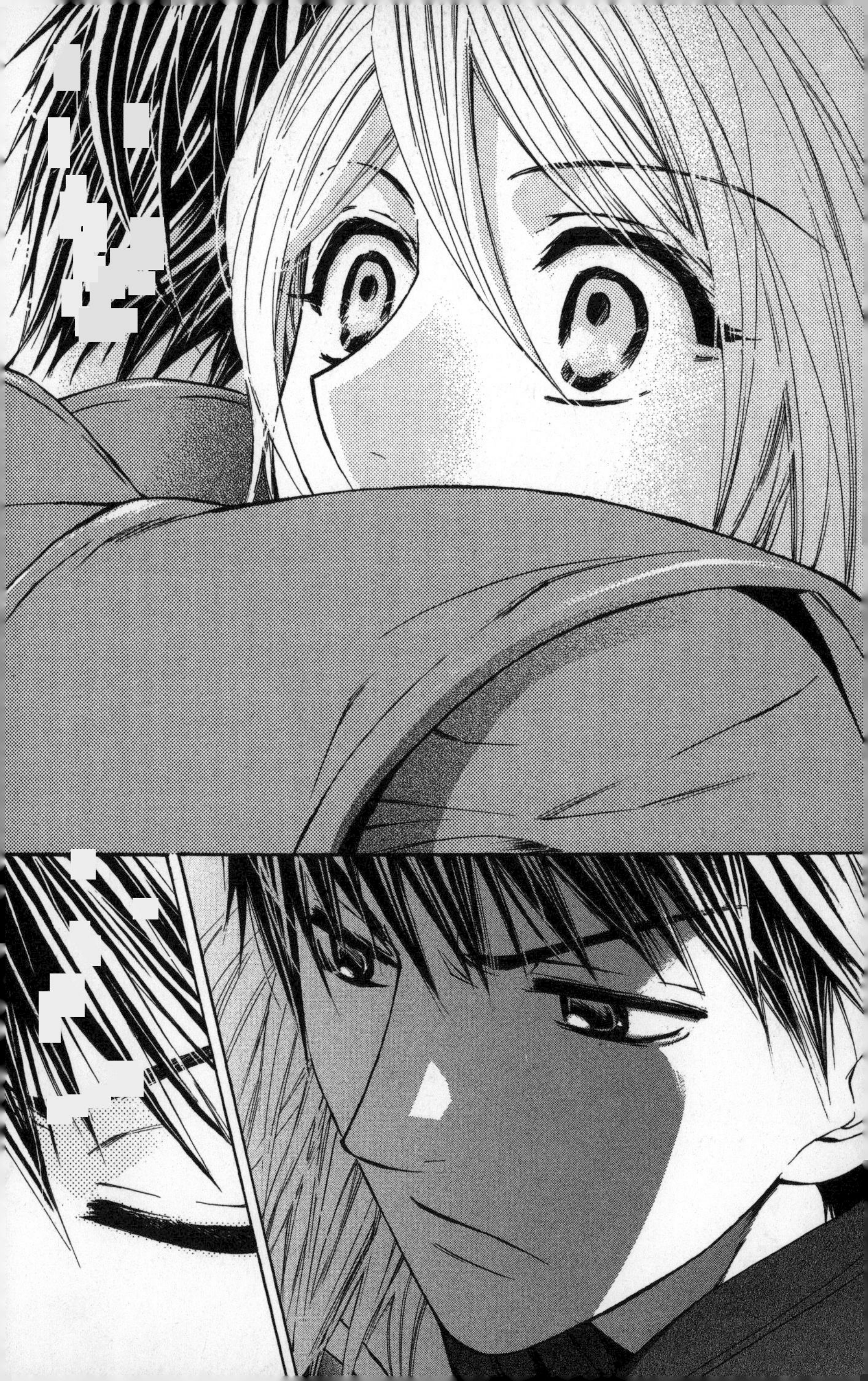

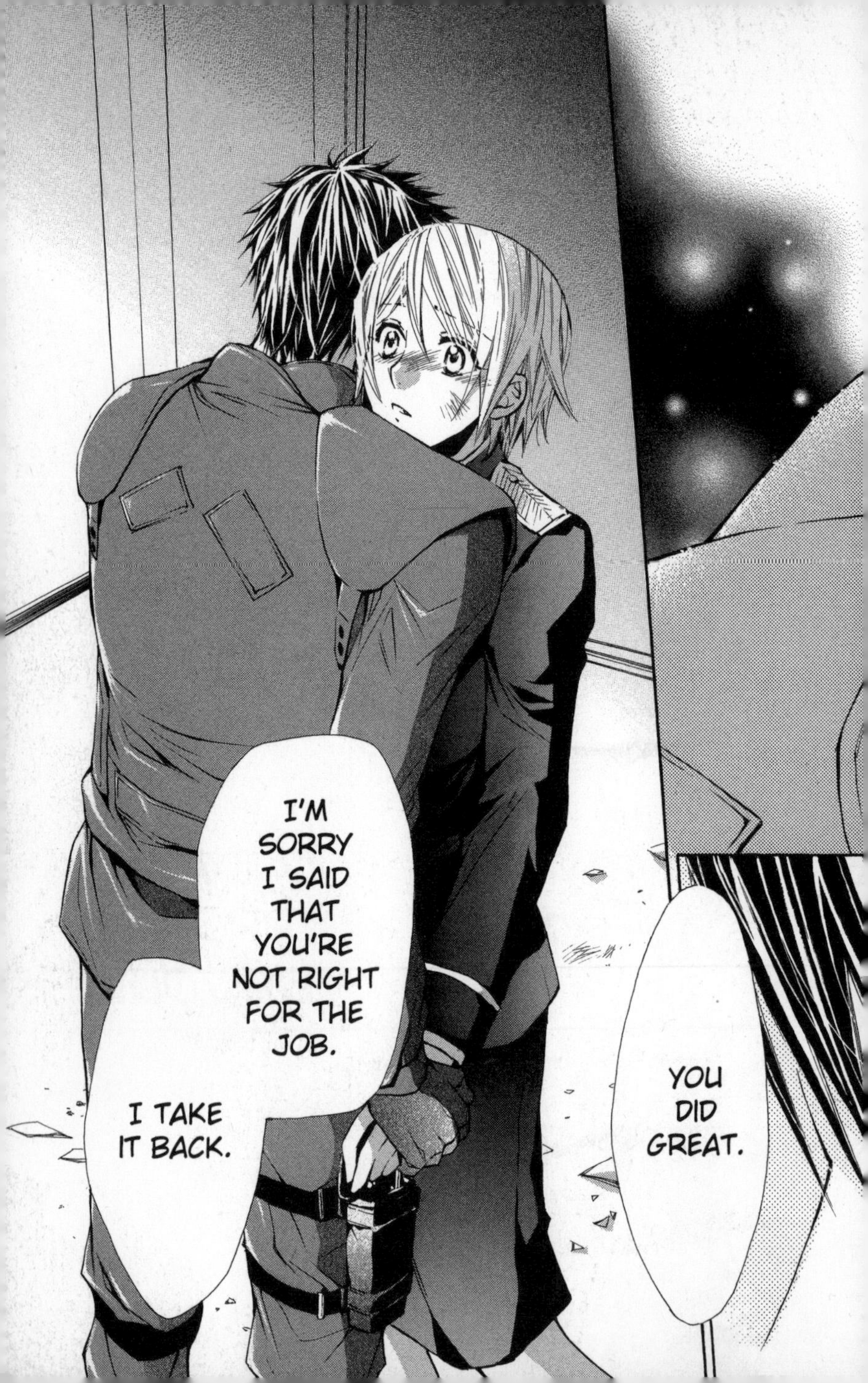
YOU DID GREAT.
I'M SORRY I SAID THAT YOU'RE NOT RIGHT FOR THE JOB.
I TAKE IT BACK.

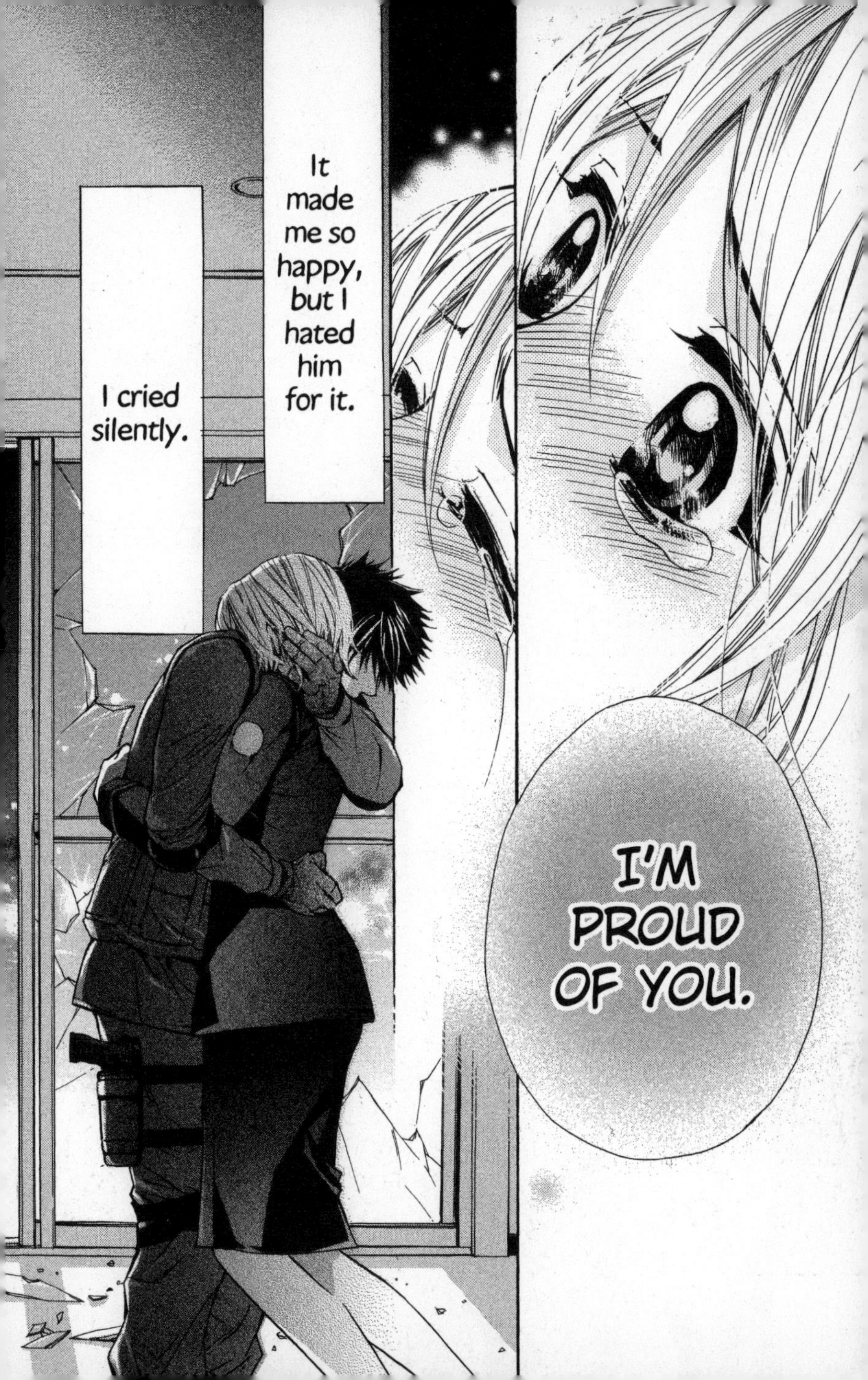
I'M PROUD OF YOU.
It made me so happy, but I hated him for it.
I cried silently.

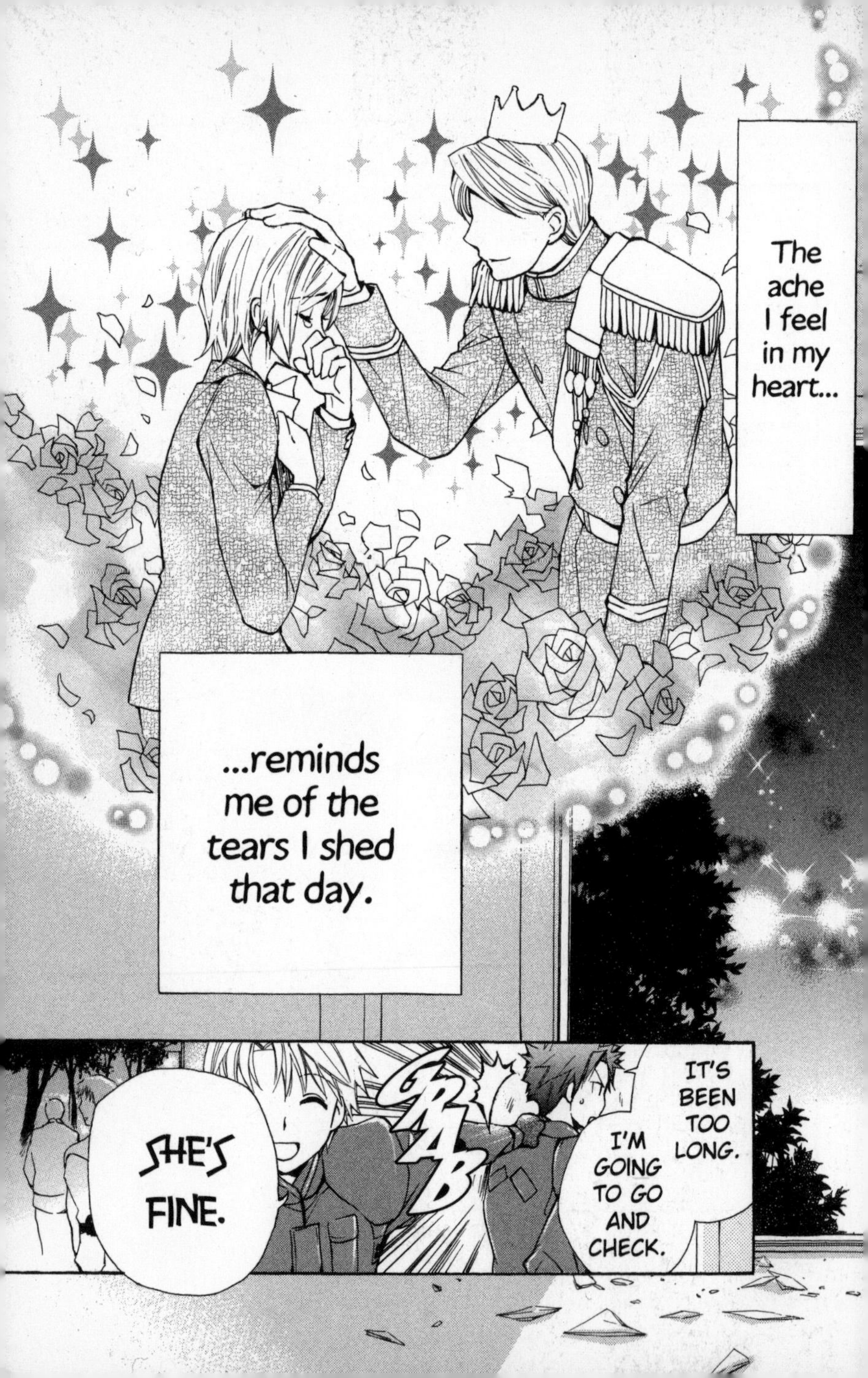
The ache I feel in my heart...
...reminds me of the tears I shed that day.
IT'S BEEN TOO LONG.
I'M GOING TO GO AND CHECK.
GRAB
SHE'S FINE.

Secret Admirer part 3.

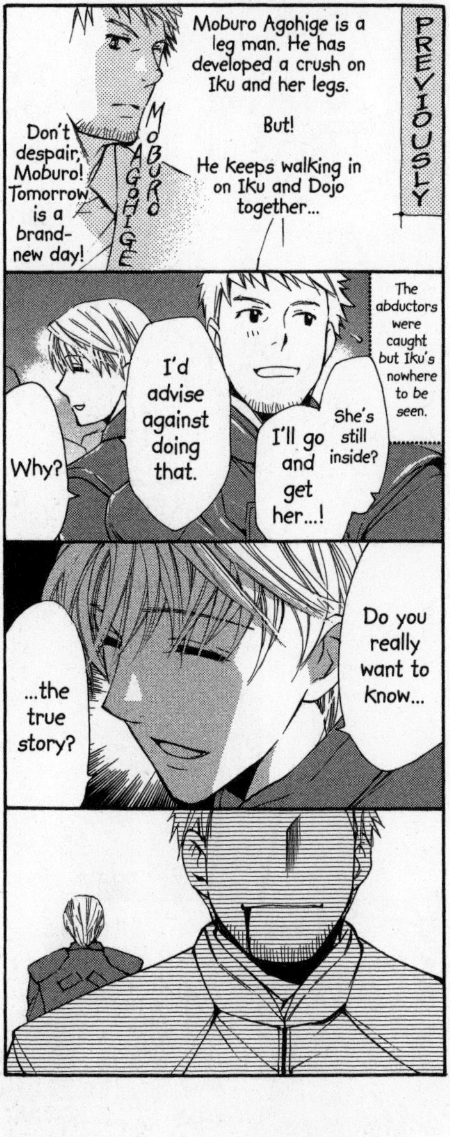

PREVIOUSLY
Moburo Agohige is a leg man. He has developed a crush on Iku and her legs.
But!
He keeps walking in on Iku and Dojo together...
MOBURO AGOHIGE
Don't despair, Moburo! Tomorrow is a brand-new day!
The abductors were caught but Iku's nowhere to be seen.
She's still inside?
I'll go and get her...!
I'd advise against doing that.
Why?
Do you really want to know...
...the true story?

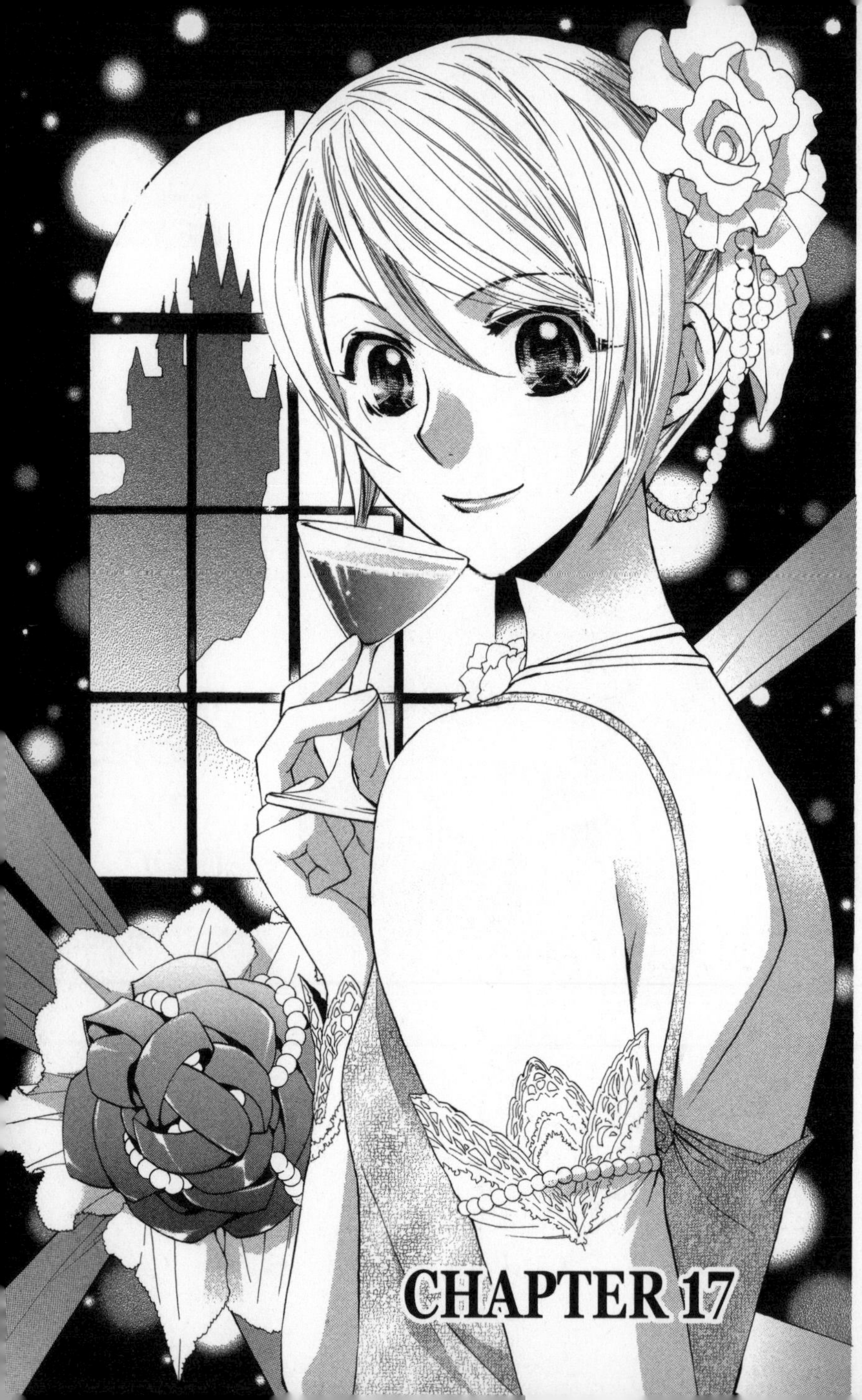
CHAPTER 17

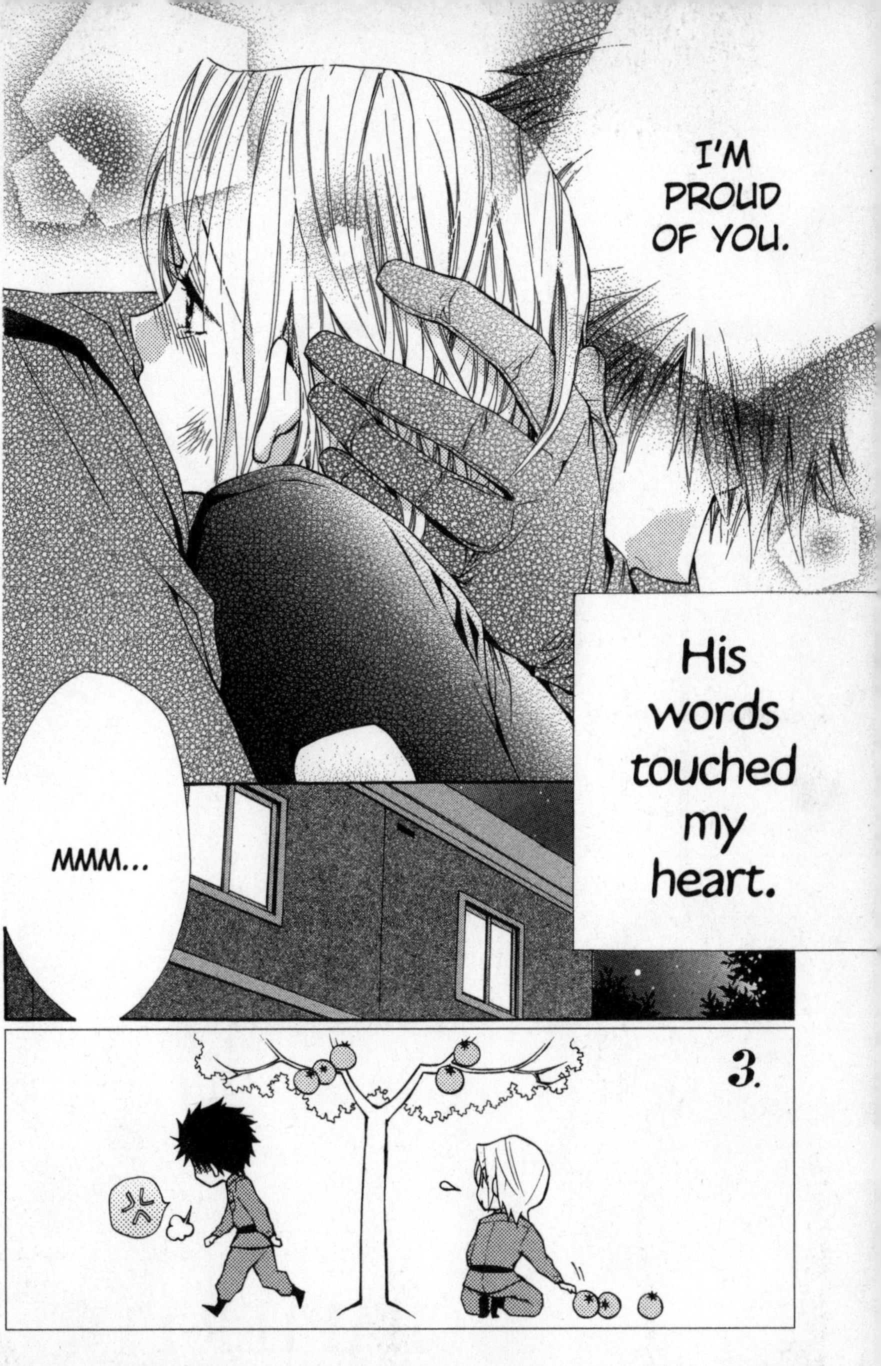
I'M PROUD OF YOU.
His words touched my heart.
MMM...
3.

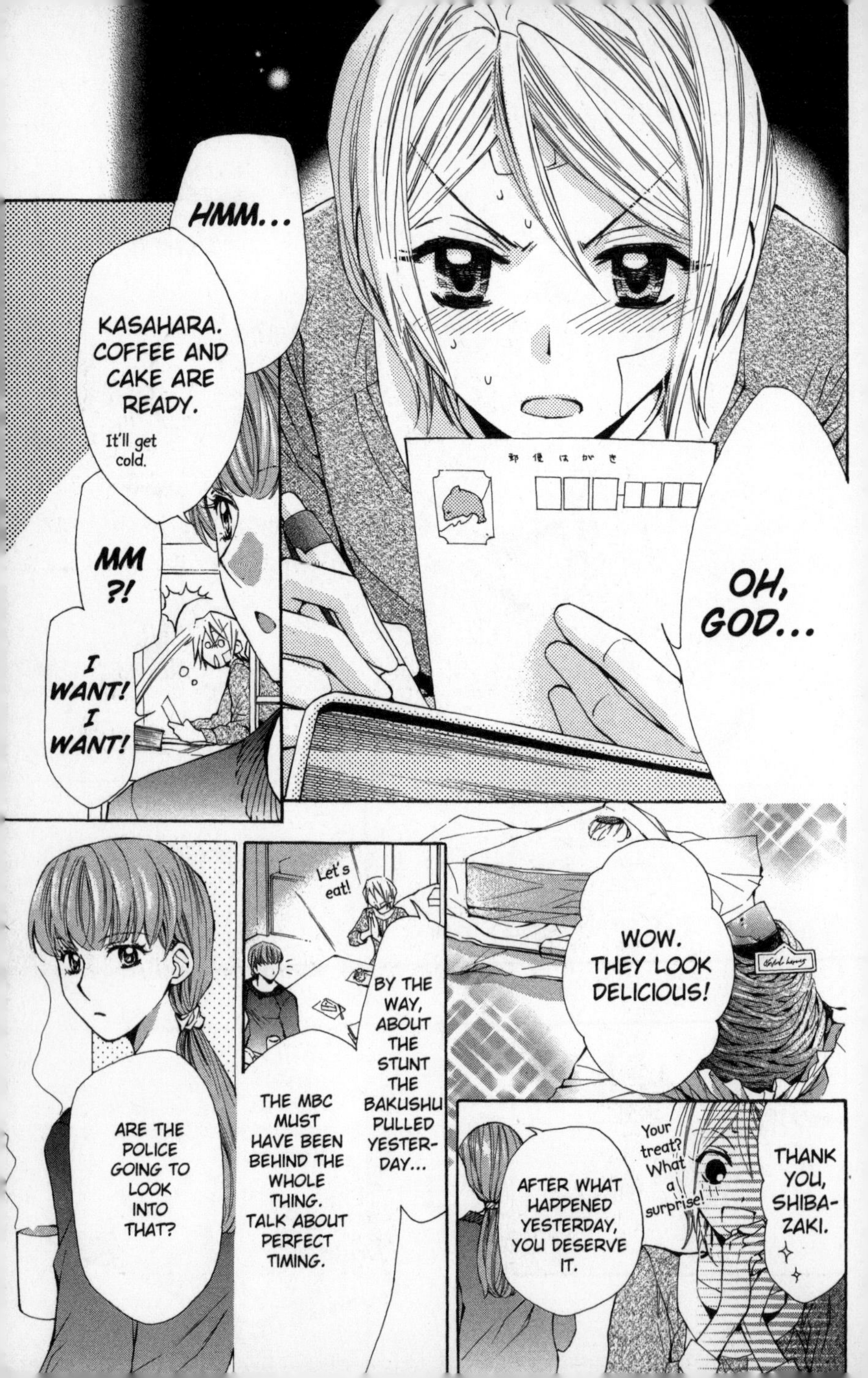
HMM...
郵便はがき
OH, GOD...
KASAHARA. COFFEE AND CAKE ARE READY.
It'll get cold.
MM ?!
I WANT! I WANT!
WOW. THEY LOOK DELICIOUS!
THANK YOU, SHIBA-ZAKI.
Your treat? What a surprise!
AFTER WHAT HAPPENED YESTERDAY, YOU DESERVE IT.
Let's eat!
BY THE WAY, ABOUT THE STUNT THE BAKUSHU PULLED YESTER-DAY...
THE MBC MUST HAVE BEEN BEHIND THE WHOLE THING. TALK ABOUT PERFECT TIMING.
ARE THE POLICE GOING TO LOOK INTO THAT?

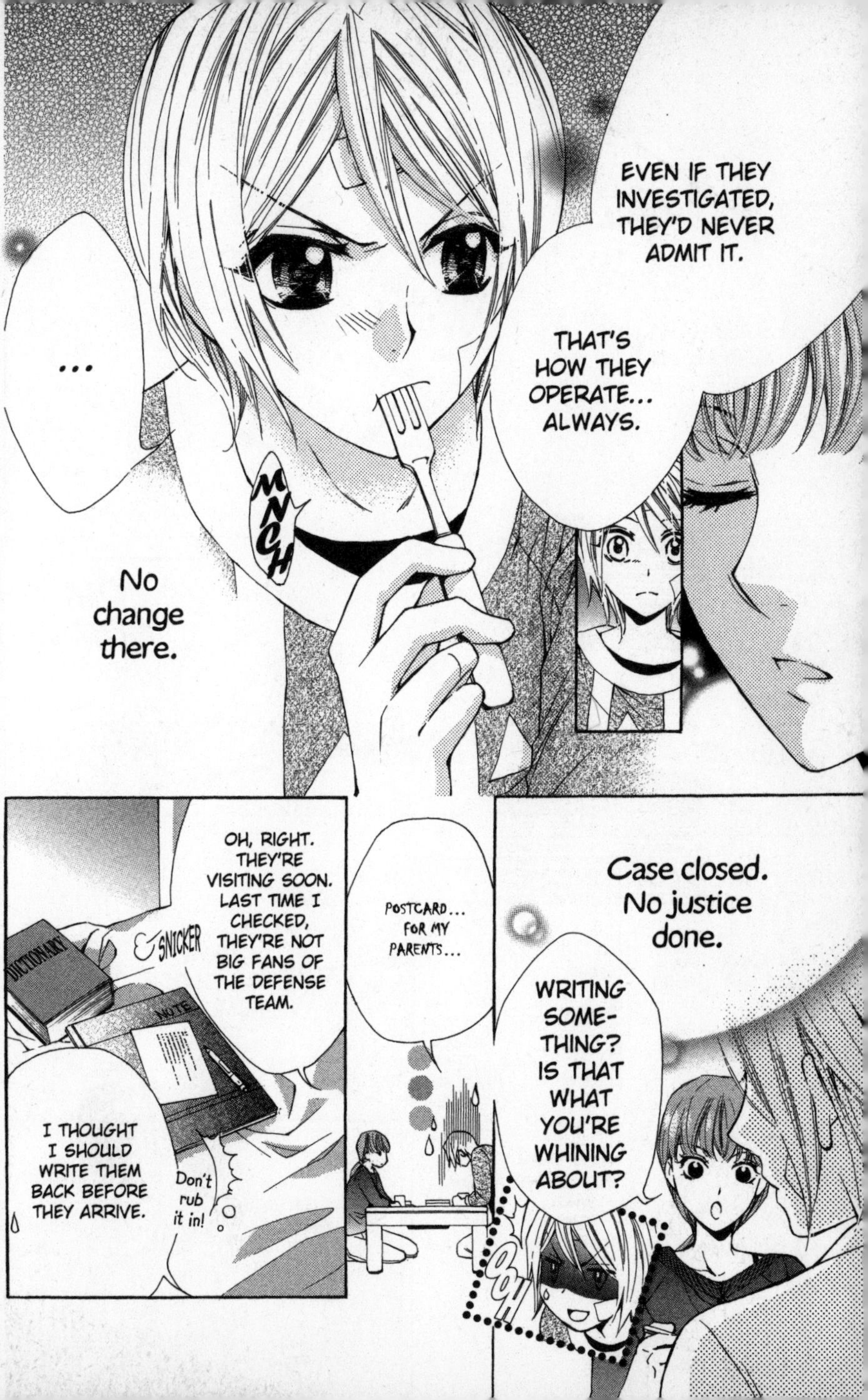
EVEN IF THEY INVESTIGATED, THEY'D NEVER ADMIT IT.
THAT'S HOW THEY OPERATE... ALWAYS.
MNCH
...
No change there.
Case closed. No justice done.
WRITING SOME-THING? IS THAT WHAT YOU'RE WHINING ABOUT?
OOH
POSTCARD... FOR MY PARENTS...
OH, RIGHT. THEY'RE VISITING SOON. LAST TIME I CHECKED, THEY'RE NOT BIG FANS OF THE DEFENSE TEAM.
SNICKER
DICTIONARY
NOTE
I THOUGHT I SHOULD WRITE THEM BACK BEFORE THEY ARRIVE.
Don't rub it in!

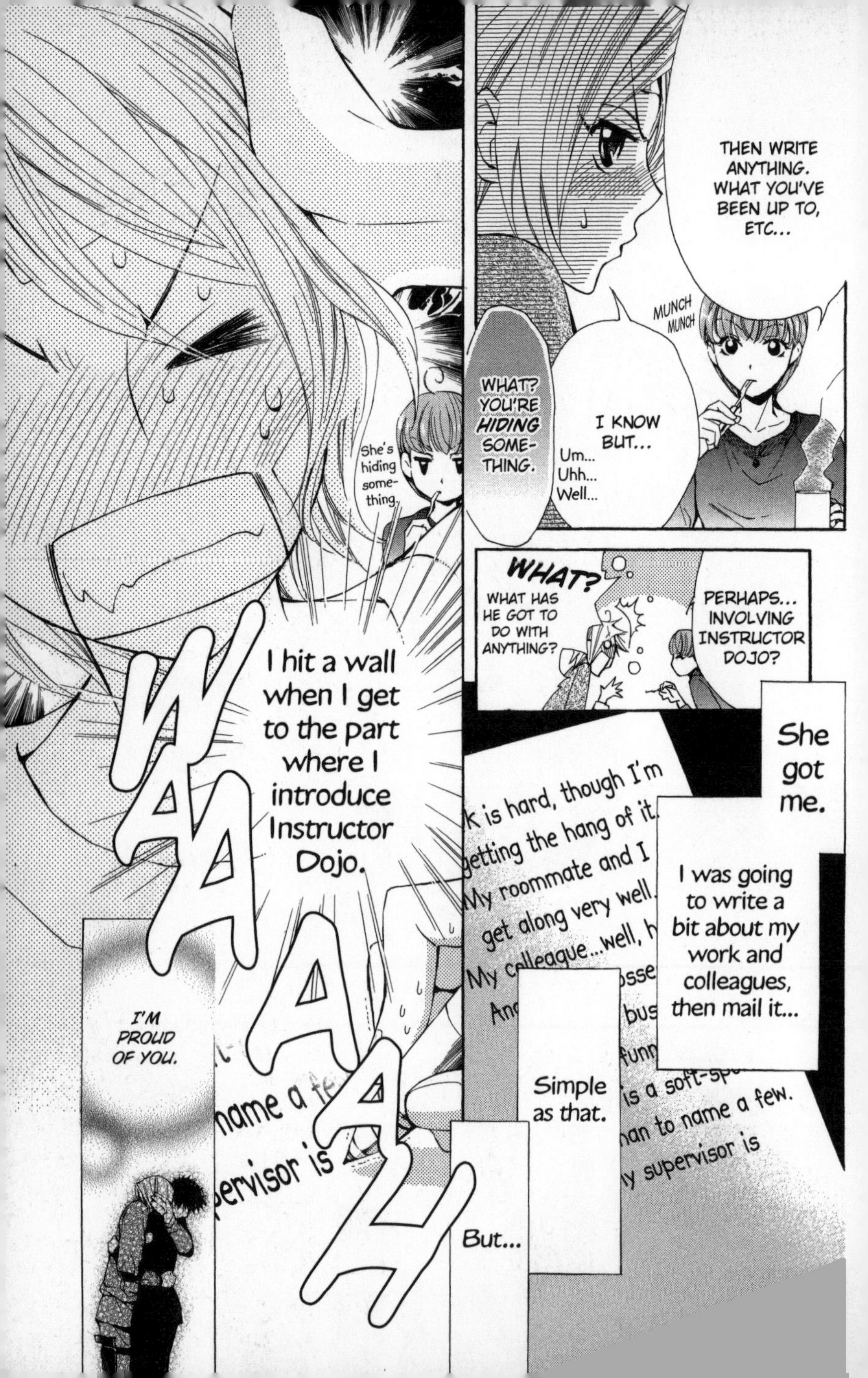
THEN WRITE ANYTHING. WHAT YOU'VE BEEN UP TO, ETC...
MUNCH MUNCH
I KNOW BUT...
Um... Uhh... Well...
WHAT? YOU'RE HIDING SOMETHING.
PERHAPS... INVOLVING INSTRUCTOR DOJO?
WHAT?
WHAT HAS HE GOT TO DO WITH ANYTHING?
She got me.
I was going to write a bit about my work and colleagues, then mail it...
k is hard, though I'm getting the hang of it. My roommate and I get along very well. My colleague...well, h
An bus funn is a soft-sp han to name a few. y supervisor is
Simple as that.
But...
She's hiding something.
I hit a wall when I get to the part where I introduce Instructor Dojo.
WAAAAH
name a fe
pervisor is
I'M PROUD OF YOU.

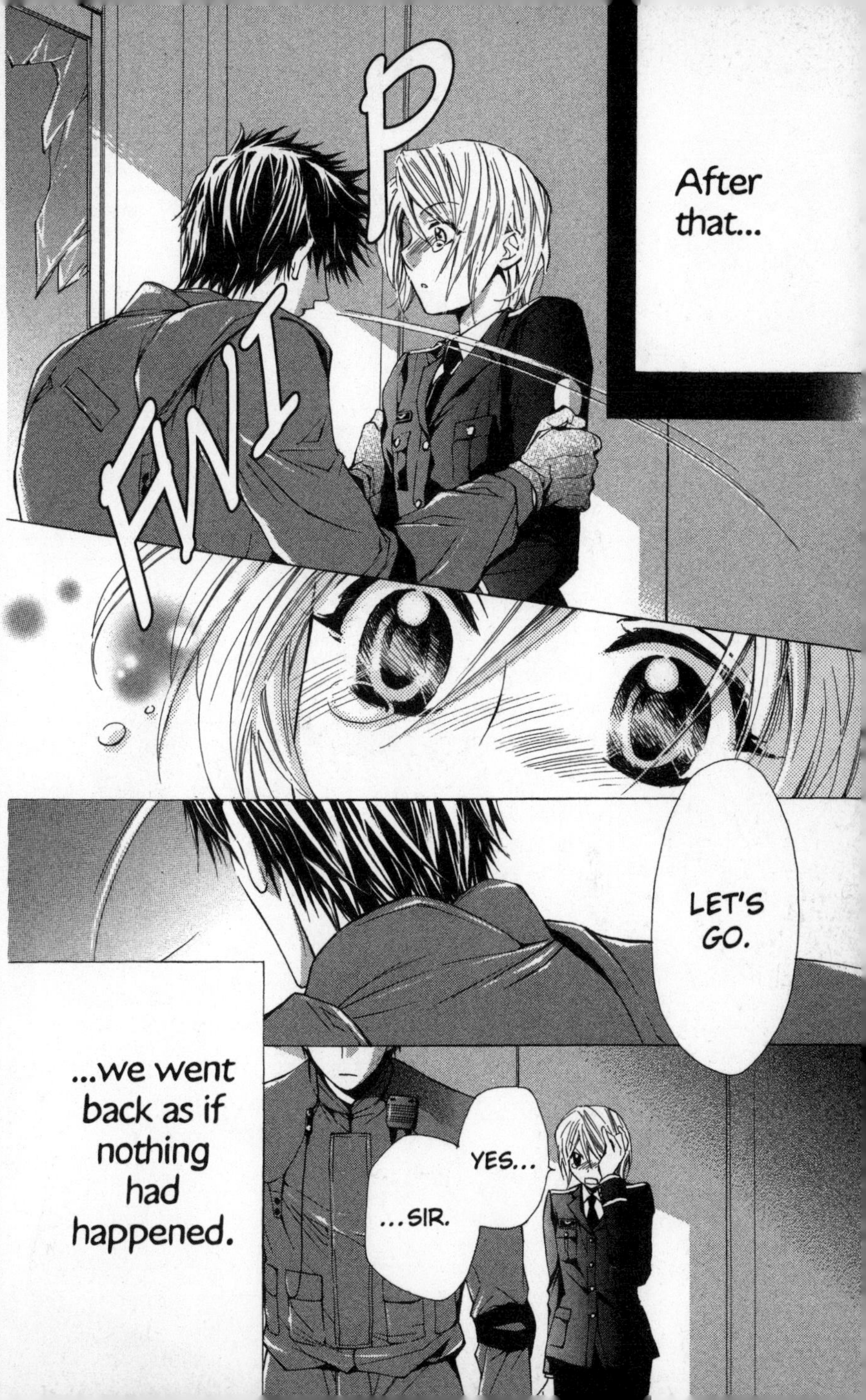
After that...
FWIP
LET'S GO.
YES...
...SIR.
...we went back as if nothing had happened.

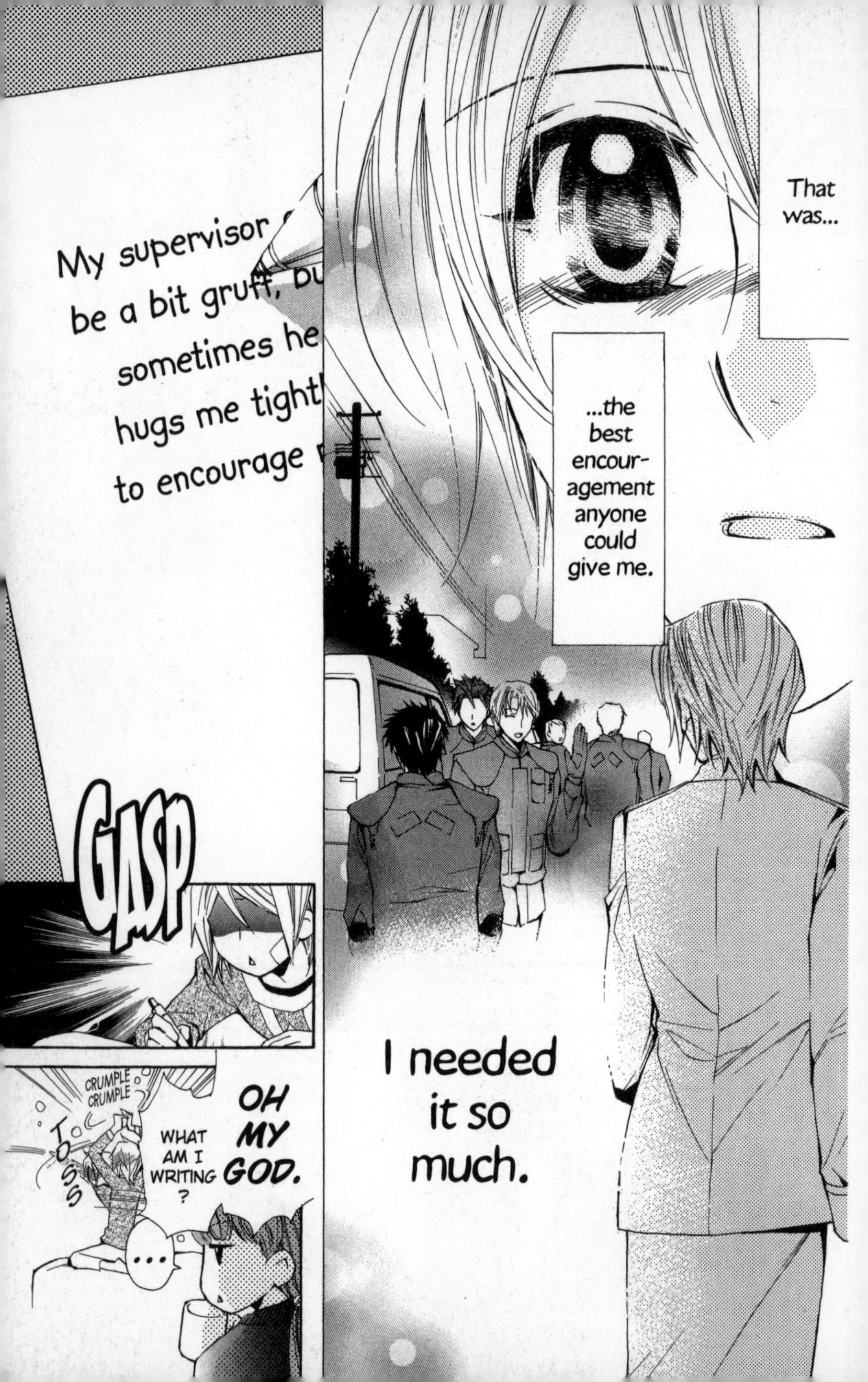
That was...
...the best encour-agement anyone could give me.
I needed it so much.
My supervisor
be a bit gruff, bu
sometimes he
hugs me tight
to encourage
GASP
OH MY GOD.
CRUMPLE CRUMPLE
WHAT AM I WRITING?
TOSS
...

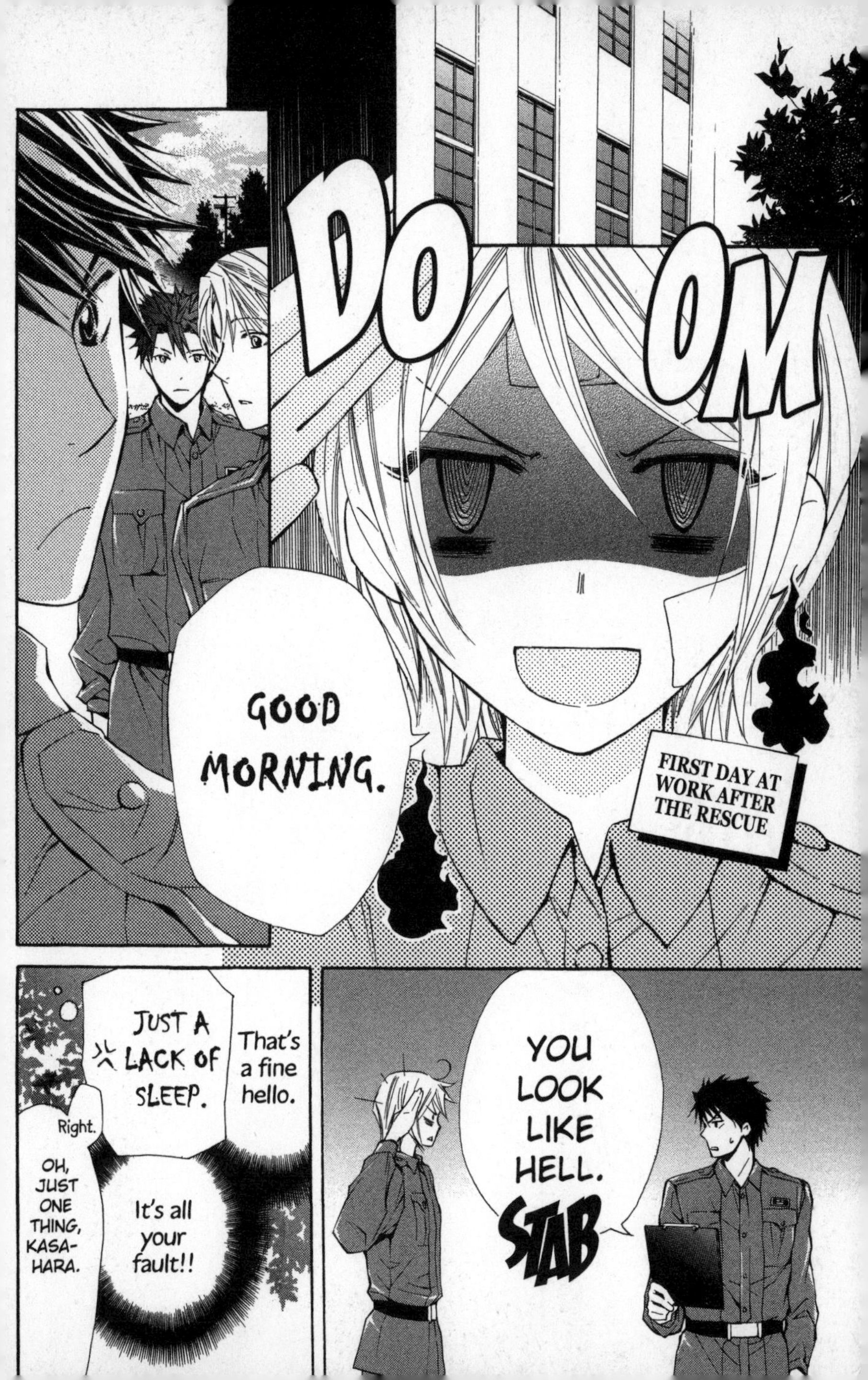
DOOM
FIRST DAY AT WORK AFTER THE RESCUE
GOOD MORNING.
YOU LOOK LIKE HELL.
STAB
That's a fine hello.
JUST A LACK OF SLEEP.
Right.
It's all your fault!!
OH, JUST ONE THING, KASA-HARA.

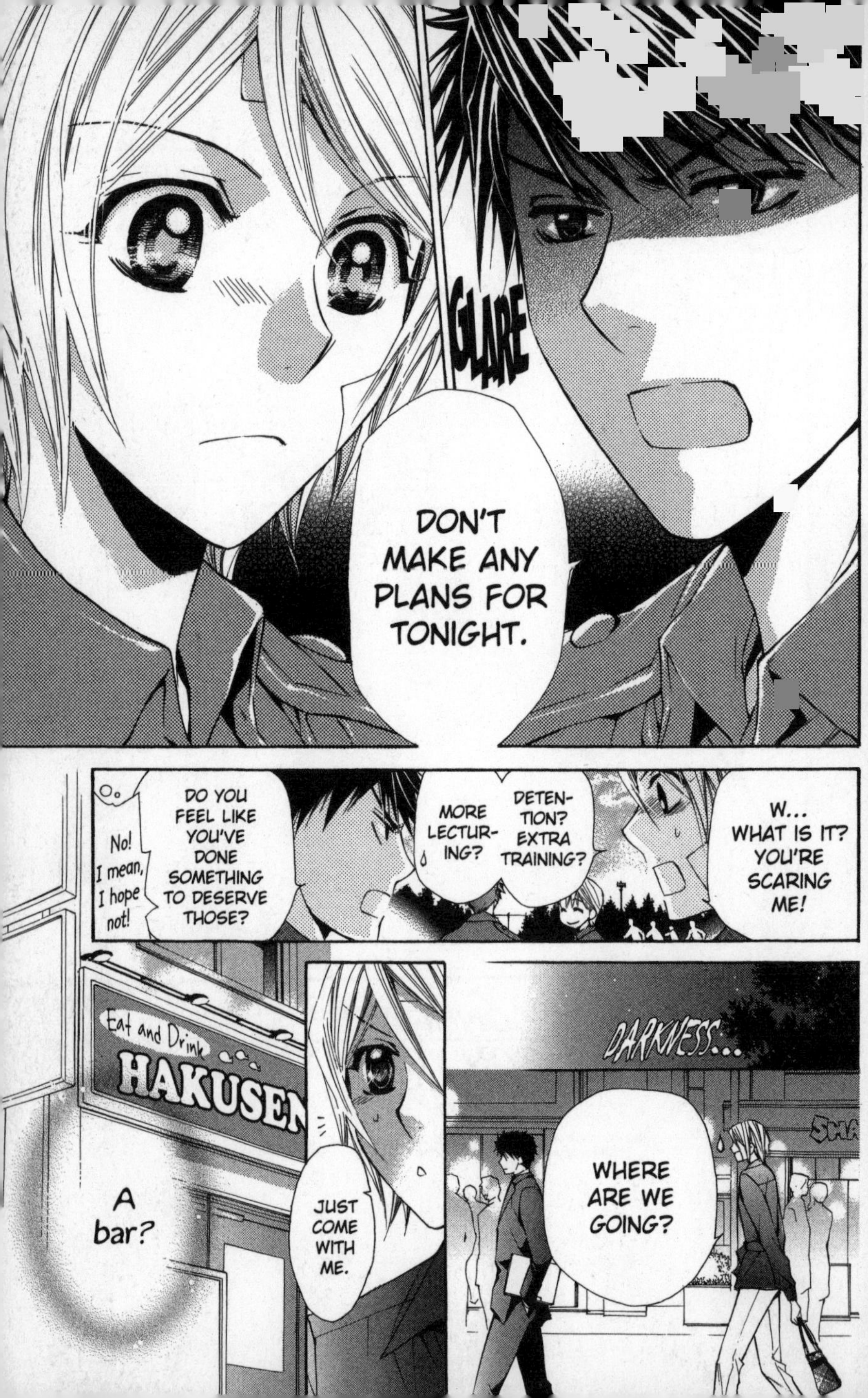
GLARE
DON'T MAKE ANY PLANS FOR TONIGHT.
W... WHAT IS IT? YOU'RE SCARING ME!
DETEN-TION? EXTRA TRAINING?
MORE LECTUR-ING?
DO YOU FEEL LIKE YOU'VE DONE SOMETHING TO DESERVE THOSE?
No! I mean, I hope not!
DARKNESS...
WHERE ARE WE GOING?
JUST COME WITH ME.
Eat and Drink
HAKUSEN
A bar?

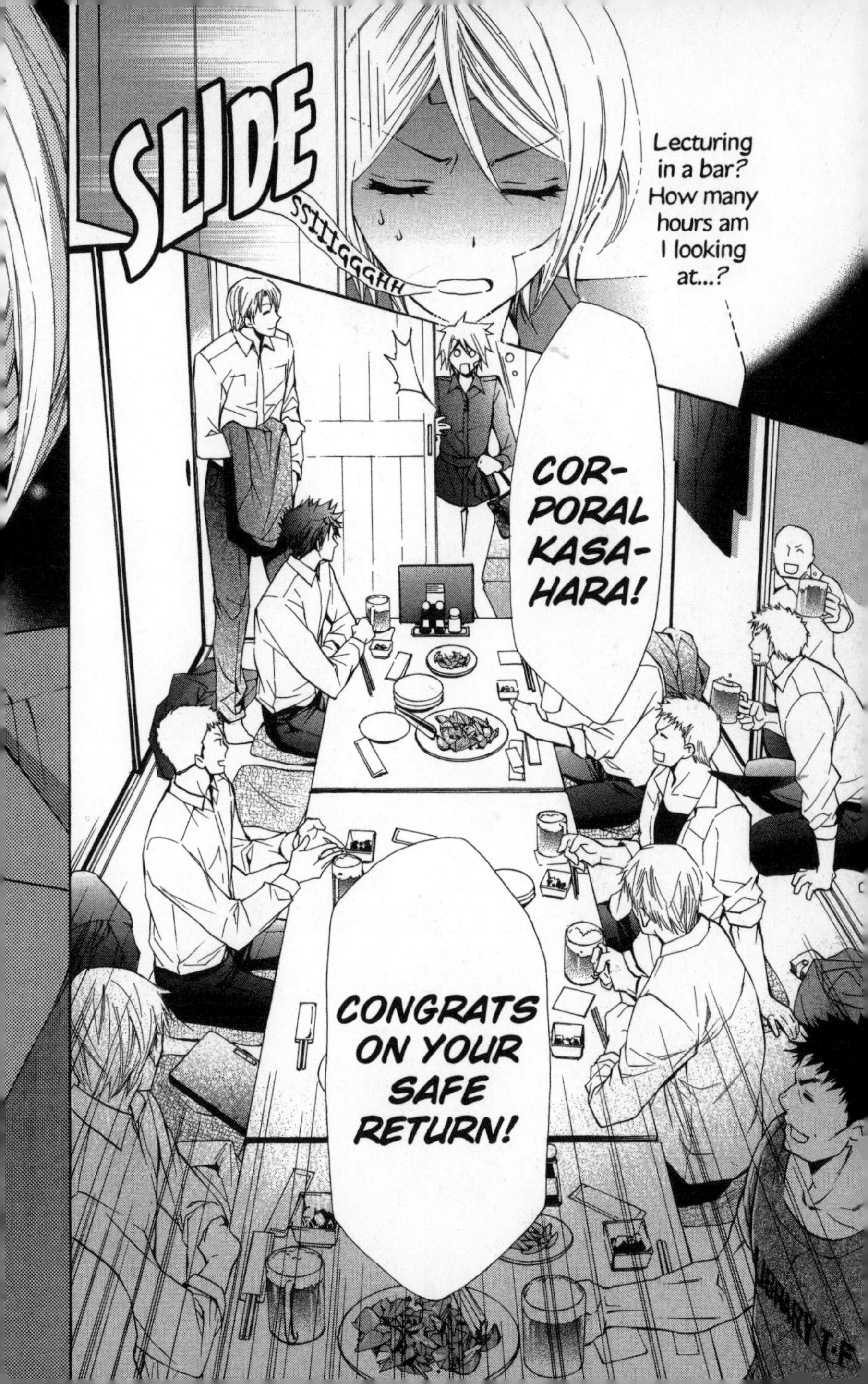
Lecturing in a bar? How many hours am I looking at...?
SLIDE
SSIIIGGGHH
CORPORAL KASAHARA!
CONGRATS ON YOUR SAFE RETURN!
LIBRARY T·F

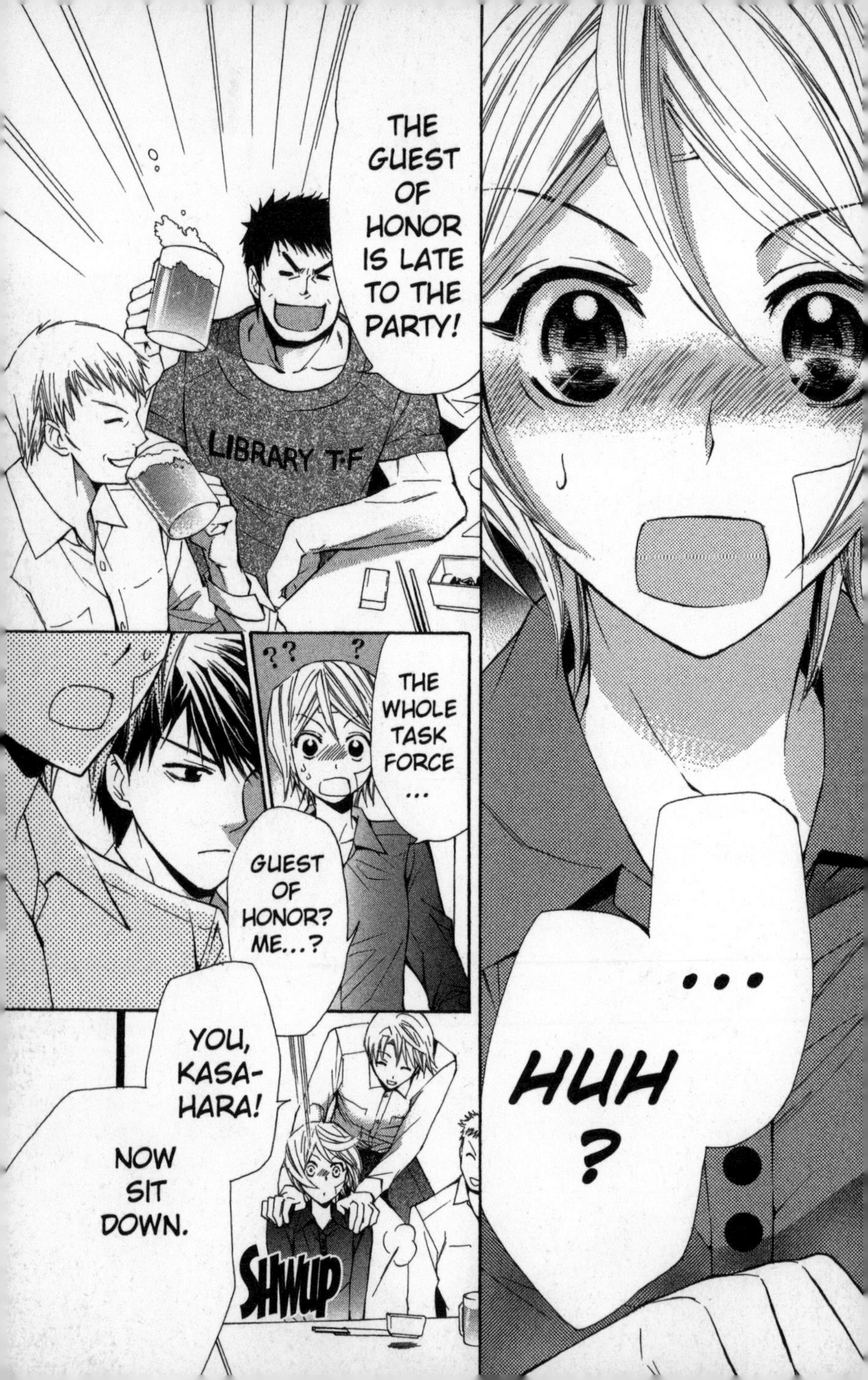

... HUH?
THE GUEST OF HONOR IS LATE TO THE PARTY!
LIBRARY T·F
??
?
THE WHOLE TASK FORCE ...
GUEST OF HONOR? ME...?
YOU, KASA-HARA!
NOW SIT DOWN.
SHWUP

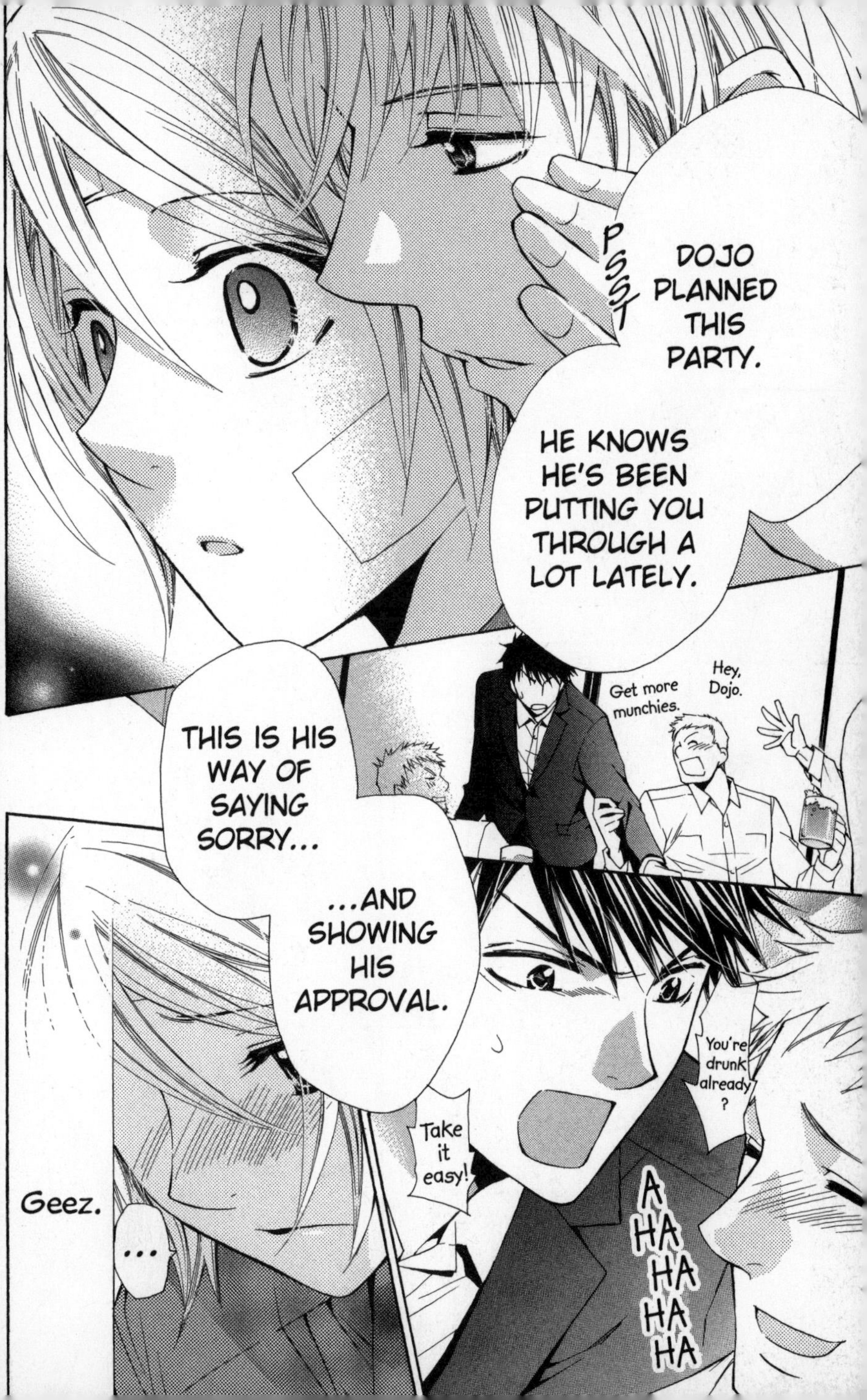
PSST
DOJO PLANNED THIS PARTY.
HE KNOWS HE'S BEEN PUTTING YOU THROUGH A LOT LATELY.
Hey, Dojo.
Get more munchies.
THIS IS HIS WAY OF SAYING SORRY...
...AND SHOWING HIS APPROVAL.
You're drunk already?
Take it easy!
AHAHAHAHAHA
...
Geez.

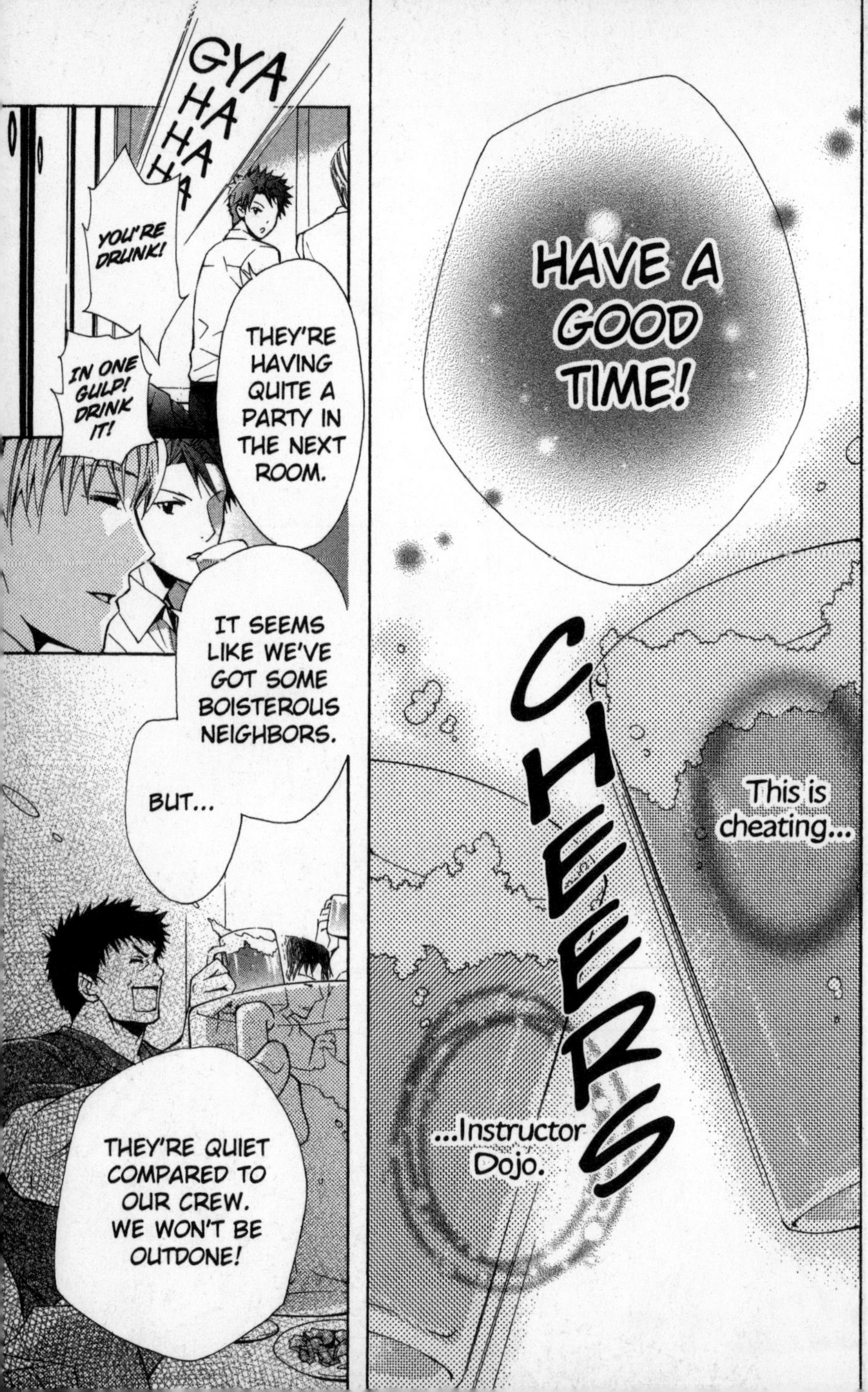
HAVE A GOOD TIME!
CHEERS
This is cheating...
...Instructor Dojo.
GYA HA HA HA HA
YOU'RE DRUNK!
IN ONE GULP! DRINK IT!
THEY'RE HAVING QUITE A PARTY IN THE NEXT ROOM.
IT SEEMS LIKE WE'VE GOT SOME BOISTEROUS NEIGHBORS.
BUT...
THEY'RE QUIET COMPARED TO OUR CREW. WE WON'T BE OUTDONE!

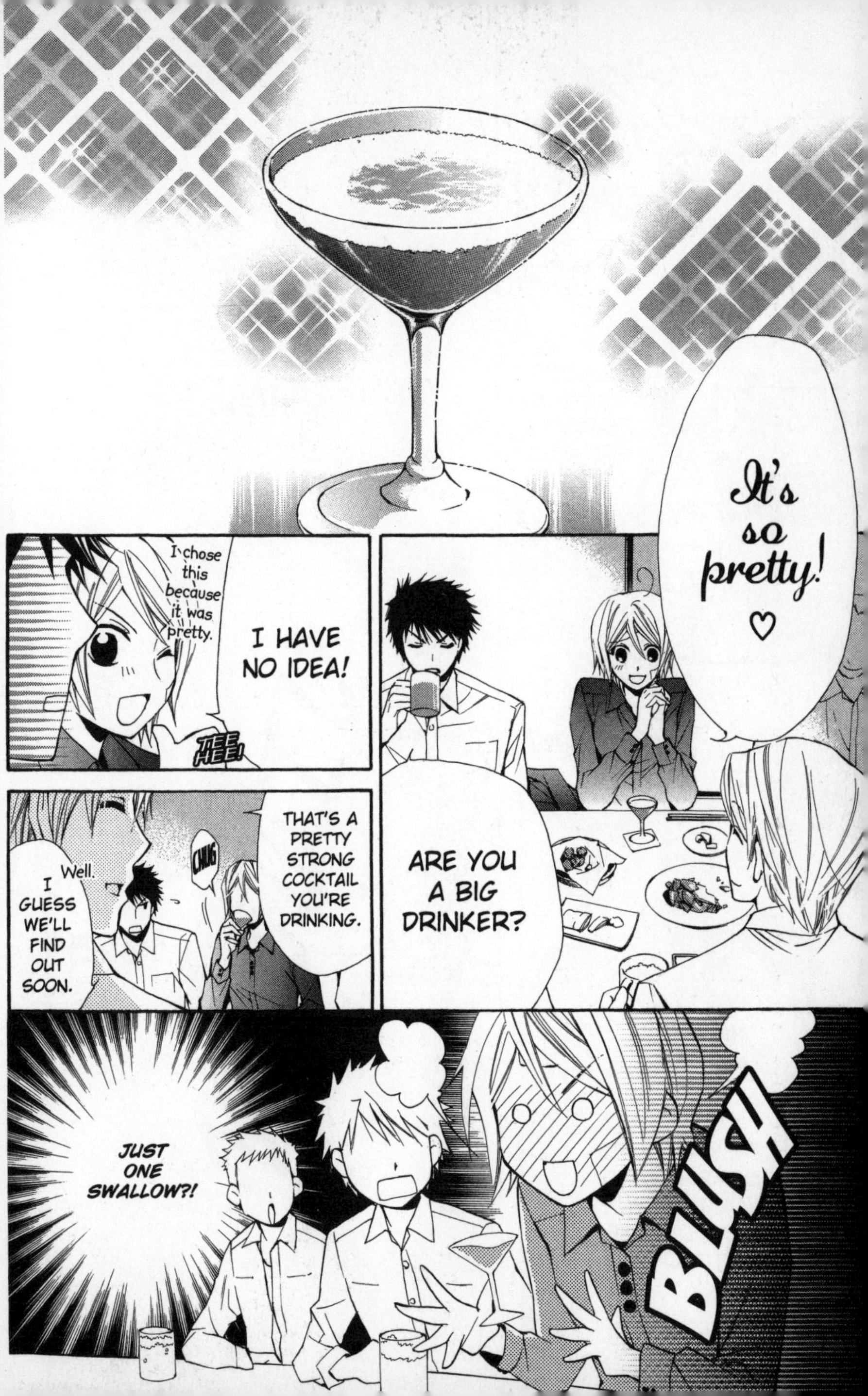
It's so pretty! ♡
ARE YOU A BIG DRINKER?
I HAVE NO IDEA!
I chose this because it was pretty.
TEE HEE!
THAT'S A PRETTY STRONG COCKTAIL YOU'RE DRINKING.
CHUG
Well. I GUESS WE'LL FIND OUT SOON.
BLUSH
JUST ONE SWALLOW?!

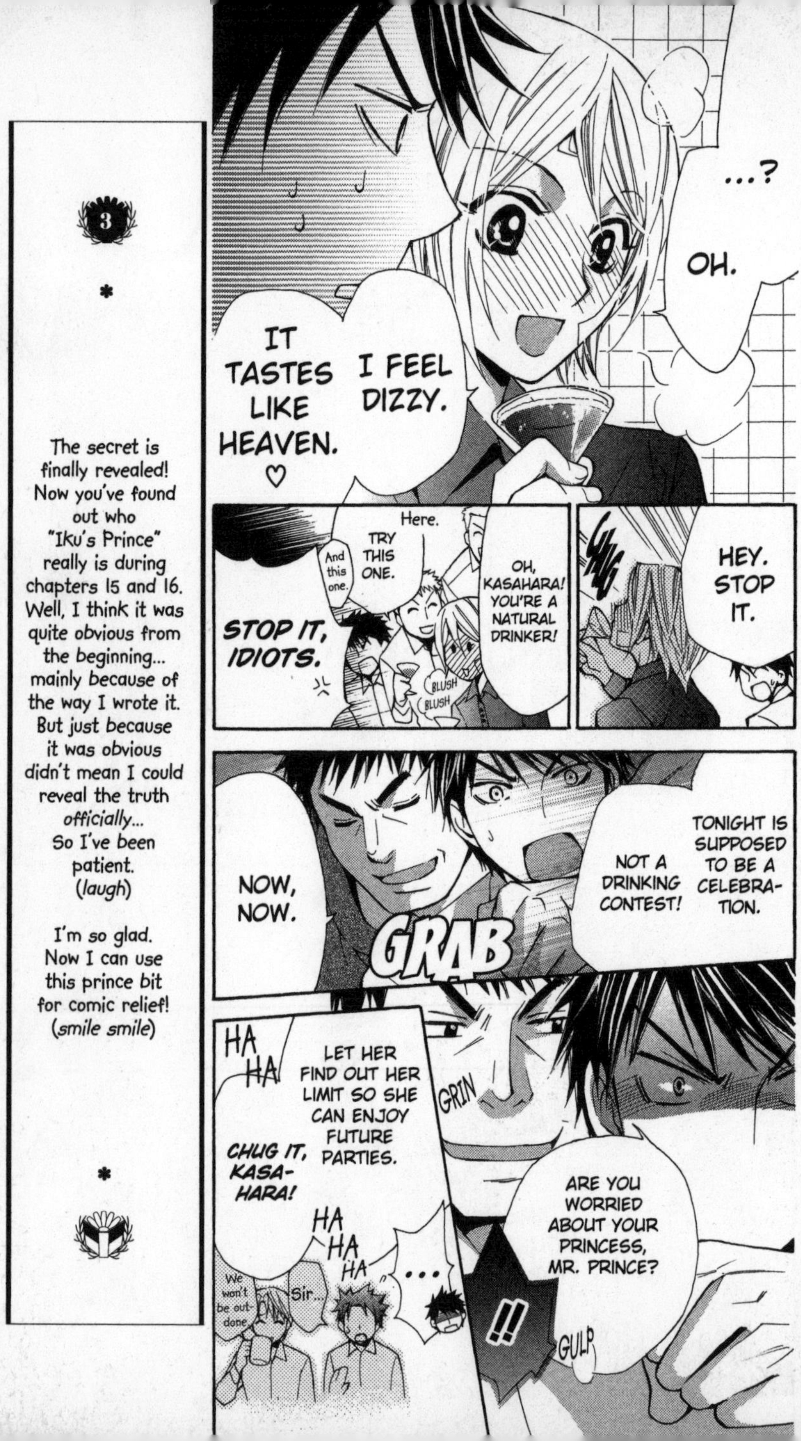
...?
OH.
I FEEL DIZZY.
IT TASTES LIKE HEAVEN. ♡
HEY. STOP IT.
OH, KASAHARA! YOU'RE A NATURAL DRINKER!
Here.
TRY THIS ONE.
And this one.
STOP IT, IDIOTS.
BLUSH BLUSH
TONIGHT IS SUPPOSED TO BE A CELEBRA-TION.
NOT A DRINKING CONTEST!
NOW, NOW.
GRAB
ARE YOU WORRIED ABOUT YOUR PRINCESS, MR. PRINCE?
GRIN
LET HER FIND OUT HER LIMIT SO SHE CAN ENJOY FUTURE PARTIES.
HA HA
CHUG IT, KASA-HARA!
HA HA HA
...
Sir...
We won't be out-done.
!!
GULP

3

*

The secret is finally revealed! Now you've found out who "Iku's Prince" really is during chapters 15 and 16. Well, I think it was quite obvious from the beginning... mainly because of the way I wrote it. But just because it was obvious didn't mean I could reveal the truth *officially*... So I've been patient. (*laugh*)

I'm so glad. Now I can use this prince bit for comic relief! (*smile smile*)

*

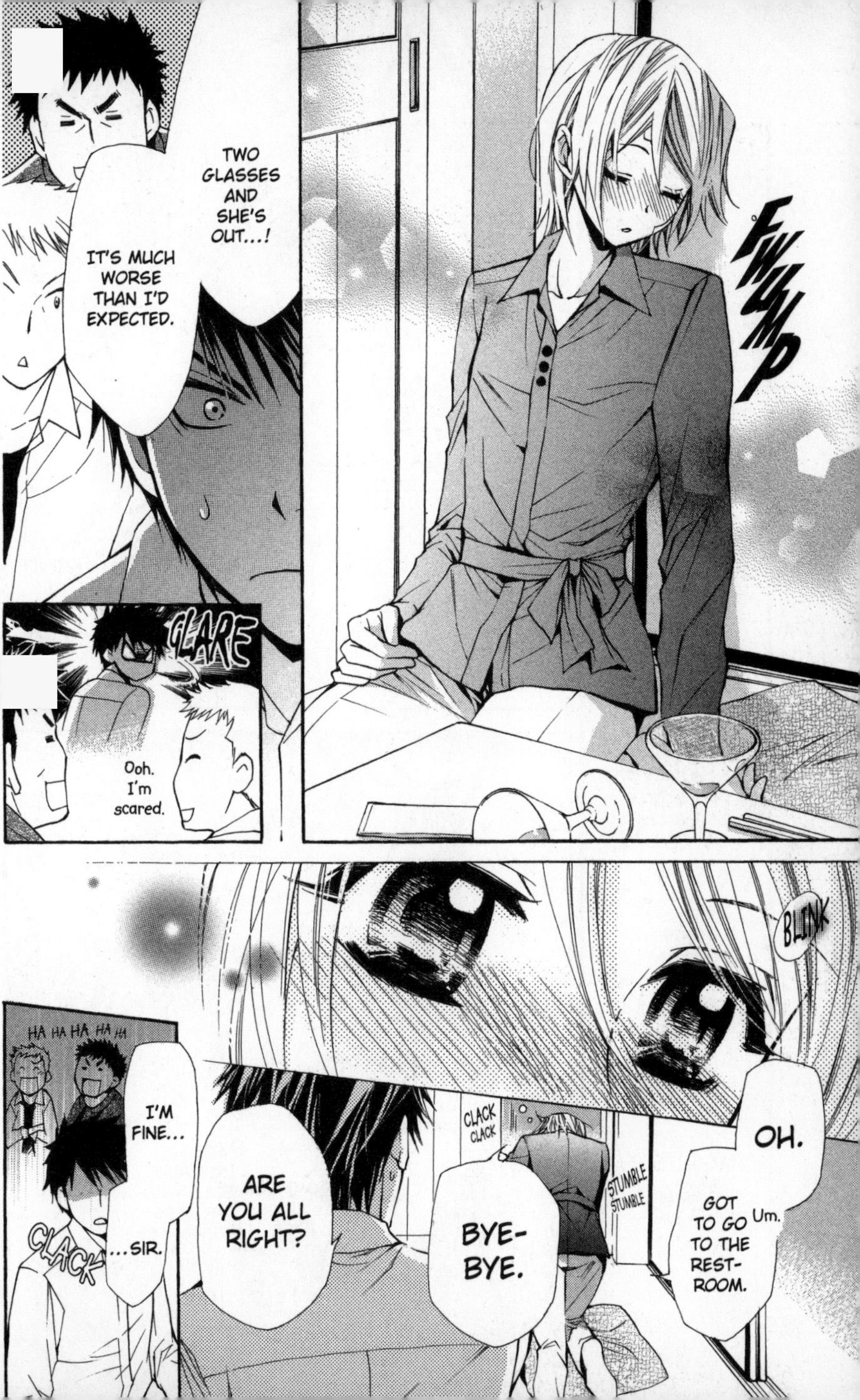
FWUMP
TWO GLASSES AND SHE'S OUT...!
IT'S MUCH WORSE THAN I'D EXPECTED.
GLARE
Ooh. I'm scared.
BLINK
OH.
Um.
GOT TO GO TO THE REST-ROOM.
STUMBLE STUMBLE
BYE-BYE.
CLACK CLACK
ARE YOU ALL RIGHT?
I'M FINE...
...SIR.
CLACK
HA HA HA HA HA

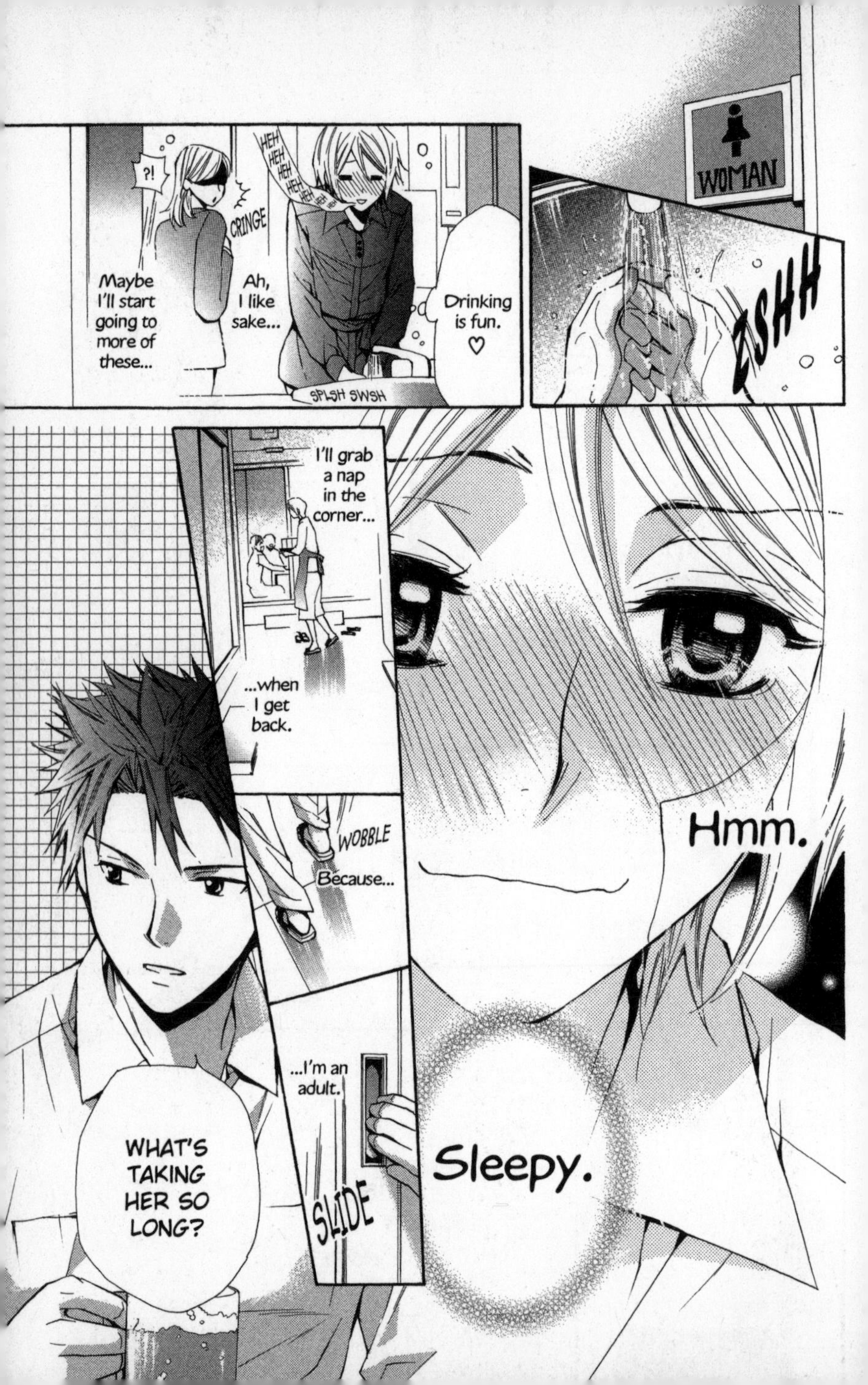
WOMAN
ZSHH
Drinking is fun. ♡
HEH HEH HEH HEH HEH HEH HEH
Ah, I like sake...
CRINGE
?!
Maybe I'll start going to more of these...
SPLSH SWSH
Hmm.
Sleepy.
I'll grab a nap in the corner...
...when I get back.
WOBBLE
Because...
...I'm an adult.
SLIDE
WHAT'S TAKING HER SO LONG?

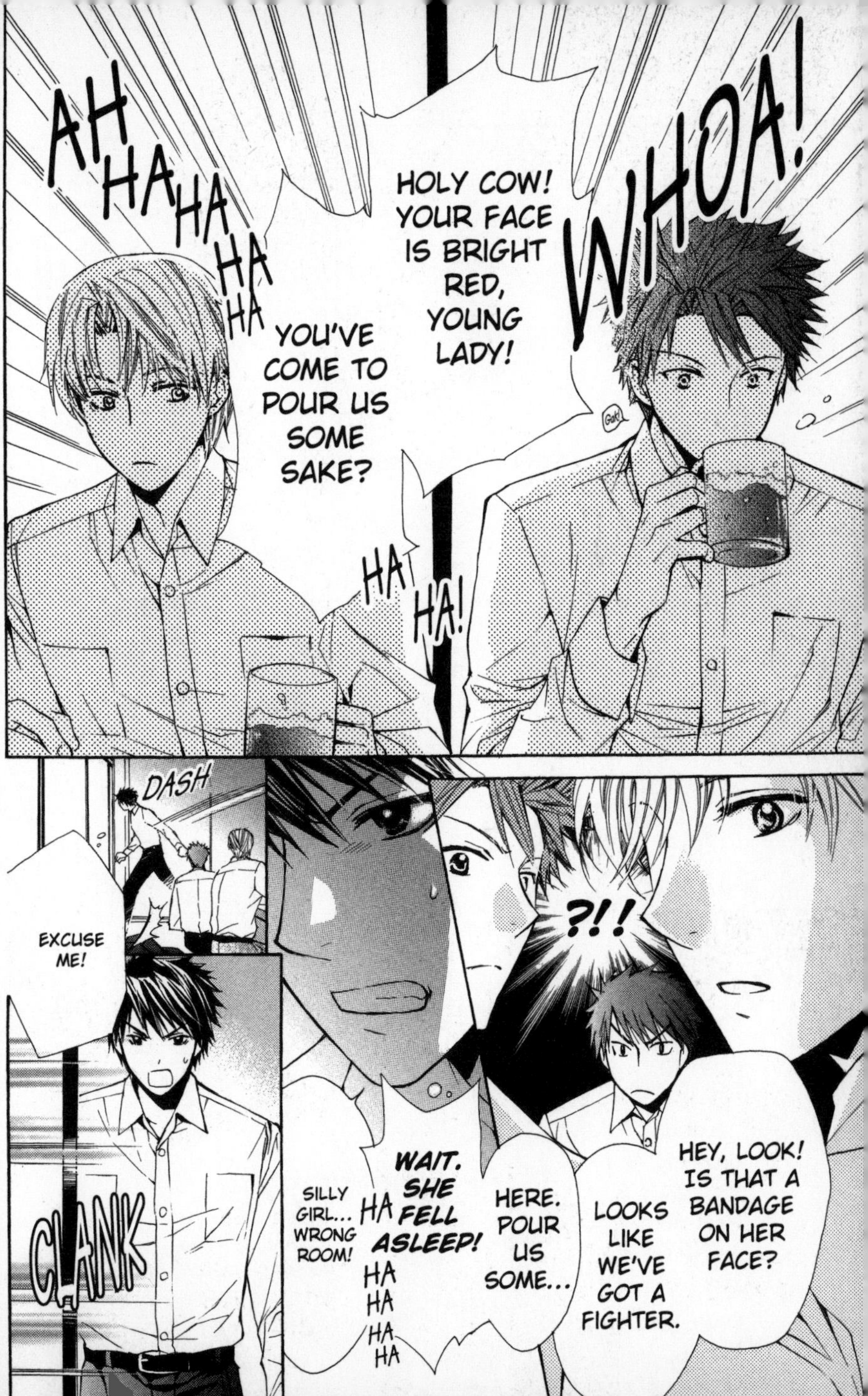
WHOA!
HOLY COW! YOUR FACE IS BRIGHT RED, YOUNG LADY!
AH HA HA HA HA HA
YOU'VE COME TO POUR US SOME SAKE?
HA HA!
?!!
HEY, LOOK! IS THAT A BANDAGE ON HER FACE?
LOOKS LIKE WE'VE GOT A FIGHTER.
HERE. POUR US SOME...
WAIT. SHE FELL ASLEEP!
HA HA HA HA HA HA
SILLY GIRL... WRONG ROOM!
DASH
EXCUSE ME!
CLANK

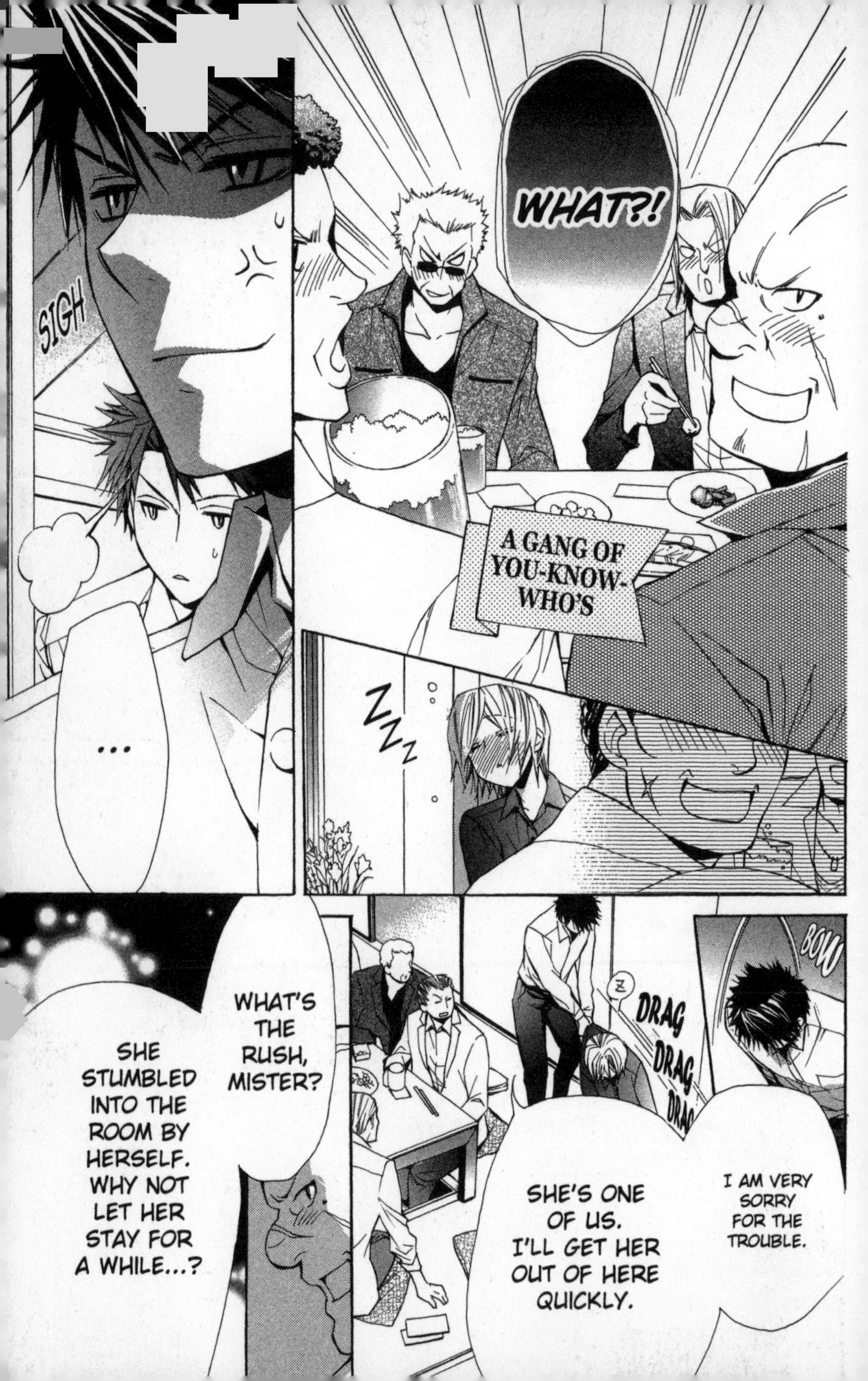
WHAT?!
A GANG OF YOU-KNOW-WHO'S
ZZZ
SIGH
...
BOW
I AM VERY SORRY FOR THE TROUBLE.
DRAG DRAG DRAG
SHE'S ONE OF US. I'LL GET HER OUT OF HERE QUICKLY.
WHAT'S THE RUSH, MISTER?
SHE STUMBLED INTO THE ROOM BY HERSELF. WHY NOT LET HER STAY FOR A WHILE...?

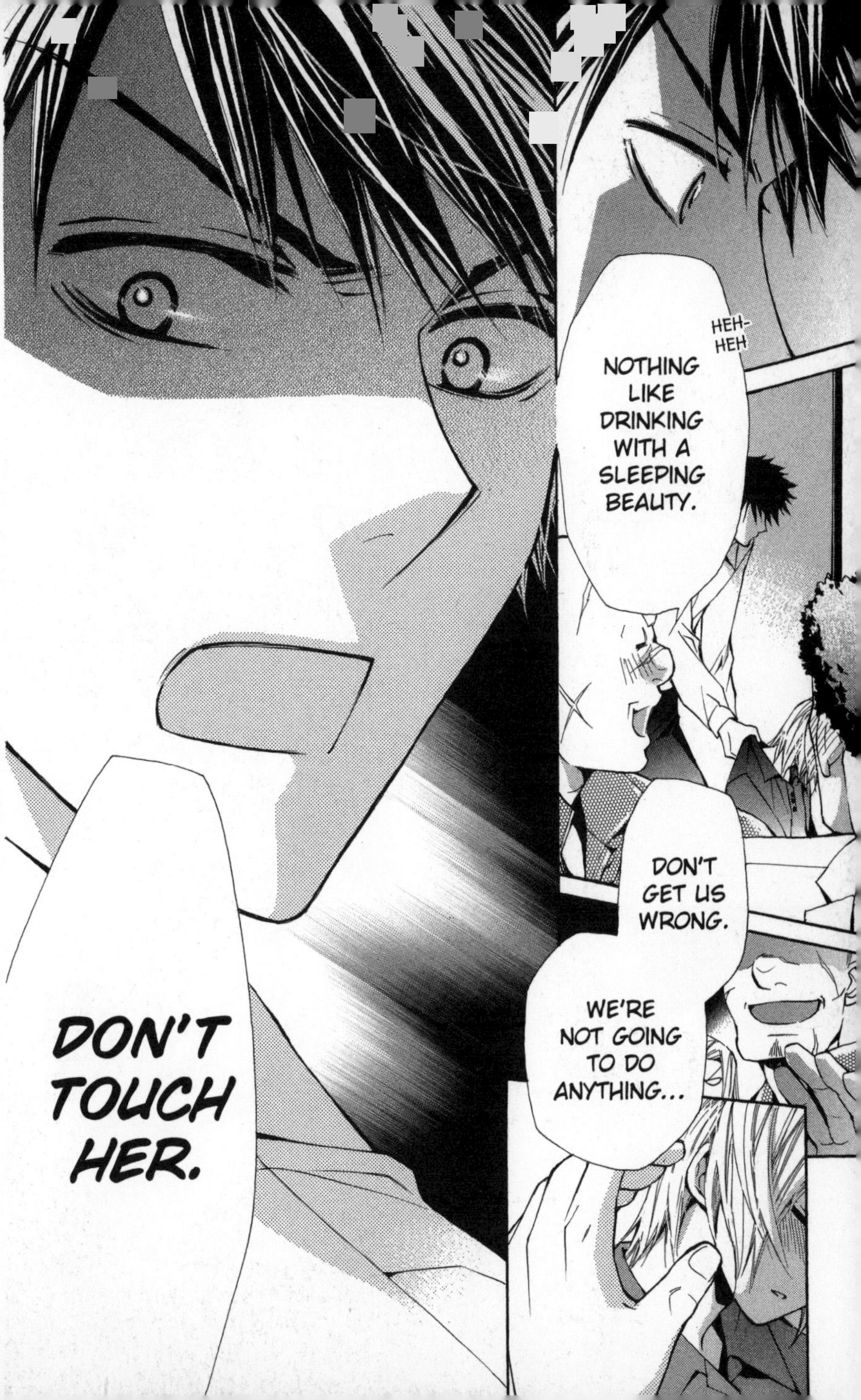
HEH-HEH
NOTHING LIKE DRINKING WITH A SLEEPING BEAUTY.
DON'T GET US WRONG.
WE'RE NOT GOING TO DO ANYTHING...
DON'T TOUCH HER.

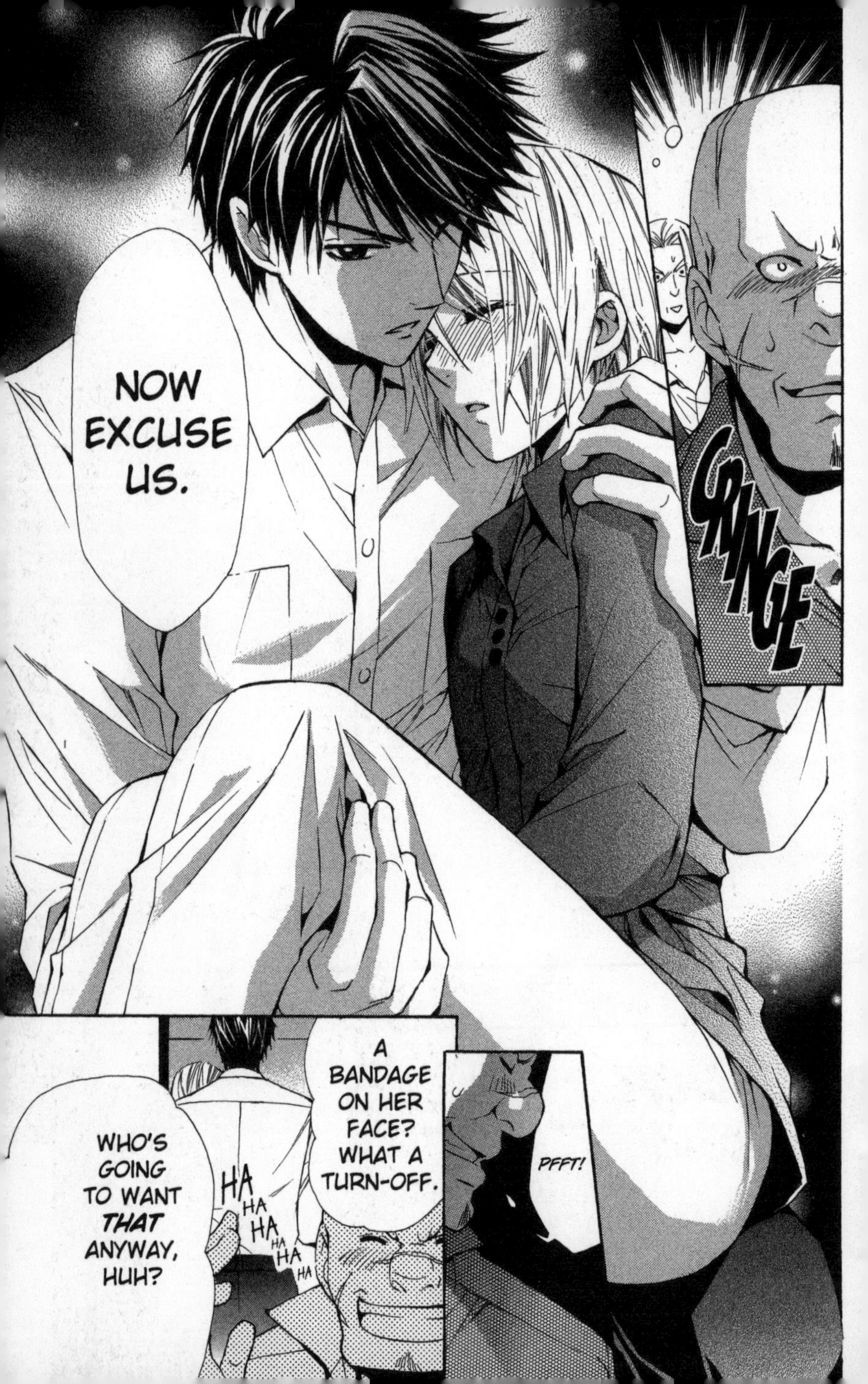
CRINGE
NOW EXCUSE US.
PFFT!
A BANDAGE ON HER FACE? WHAT A TURN-OFF.
HA HA HA HA HA HA
WHO'S GOING TO WANT *THAT* ANYWAY, HUH?

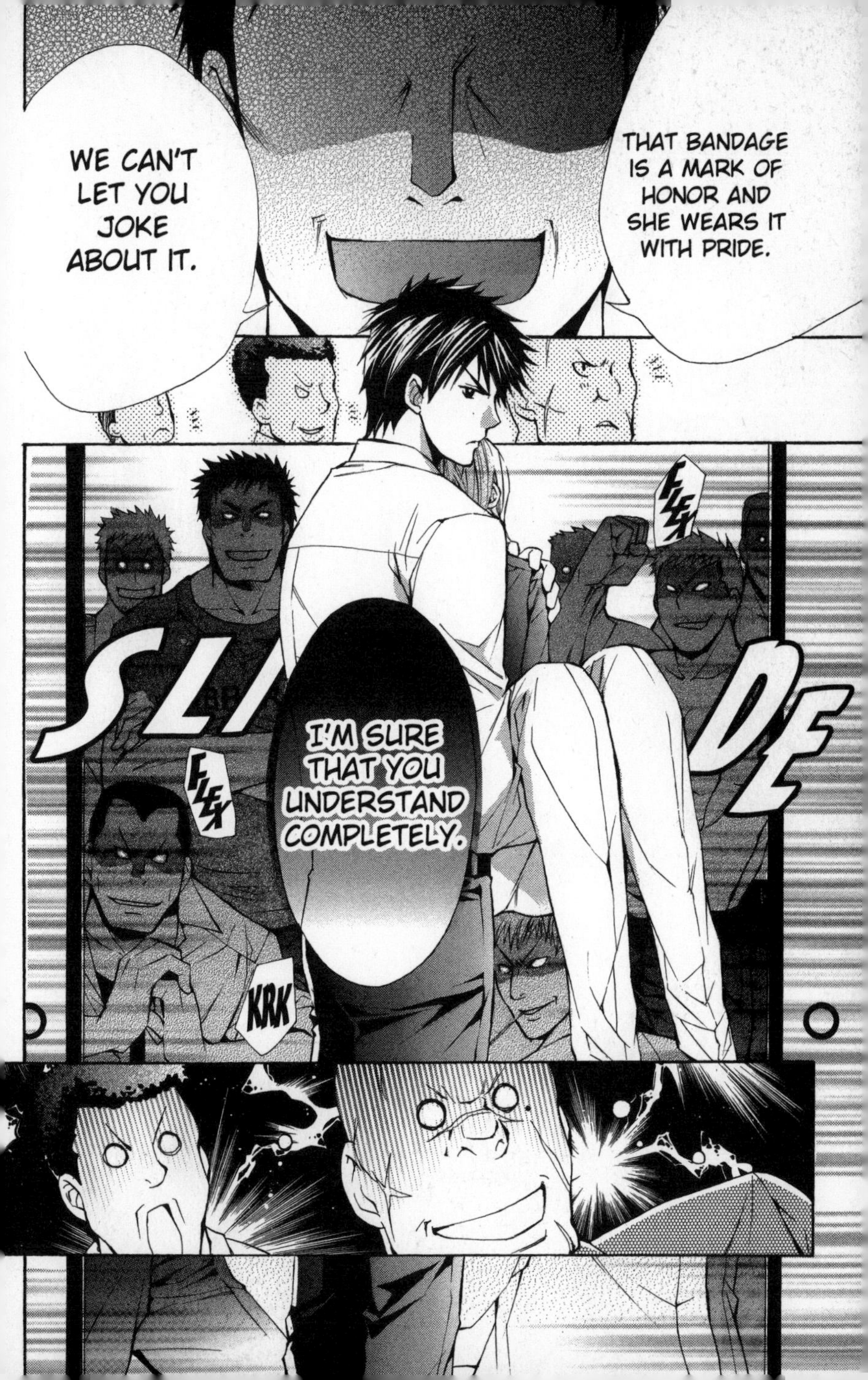
THAT BANDAGE IS A MARK OF HONOR AND SHE WEARS IT WITH PRIDE.
WE CAN'T LET YOU JOKE ABOUT IT.
FLEX
SLI
DE
I'M SURE THAT YOU UNDERSTAND COMPLETELY.
FLEX
KRK

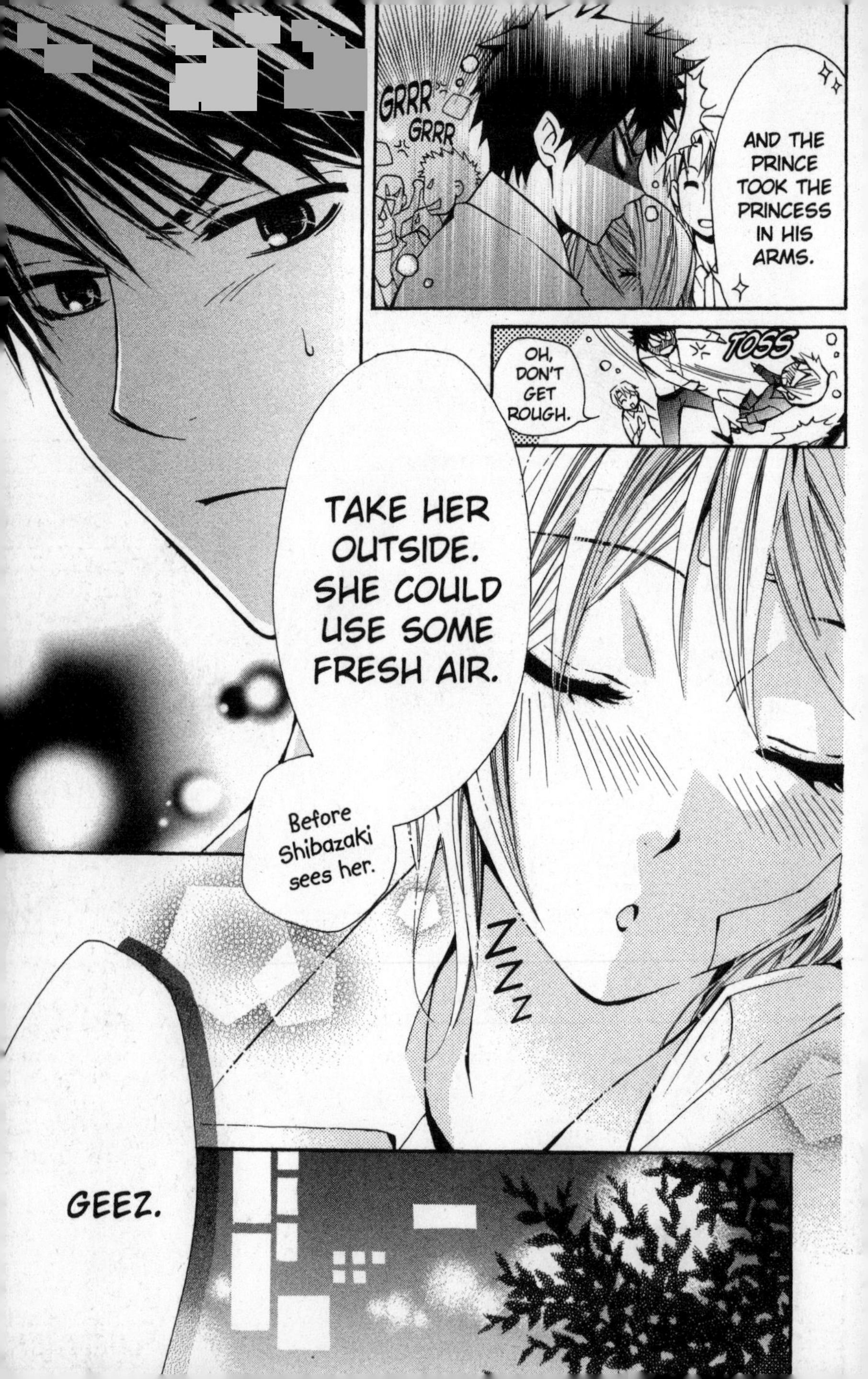
AND THE PRINCE TOOK THE PRINCESS IN HIS ARMS.
GRRR GRRR
OH, DON'T GET ROUGH.
TOSS
TAKE HER OUTSIDE. SHE COULD USE SOME FRESH AIR.
Before Shibazaki sees her.
ZZZ
GEEZ.

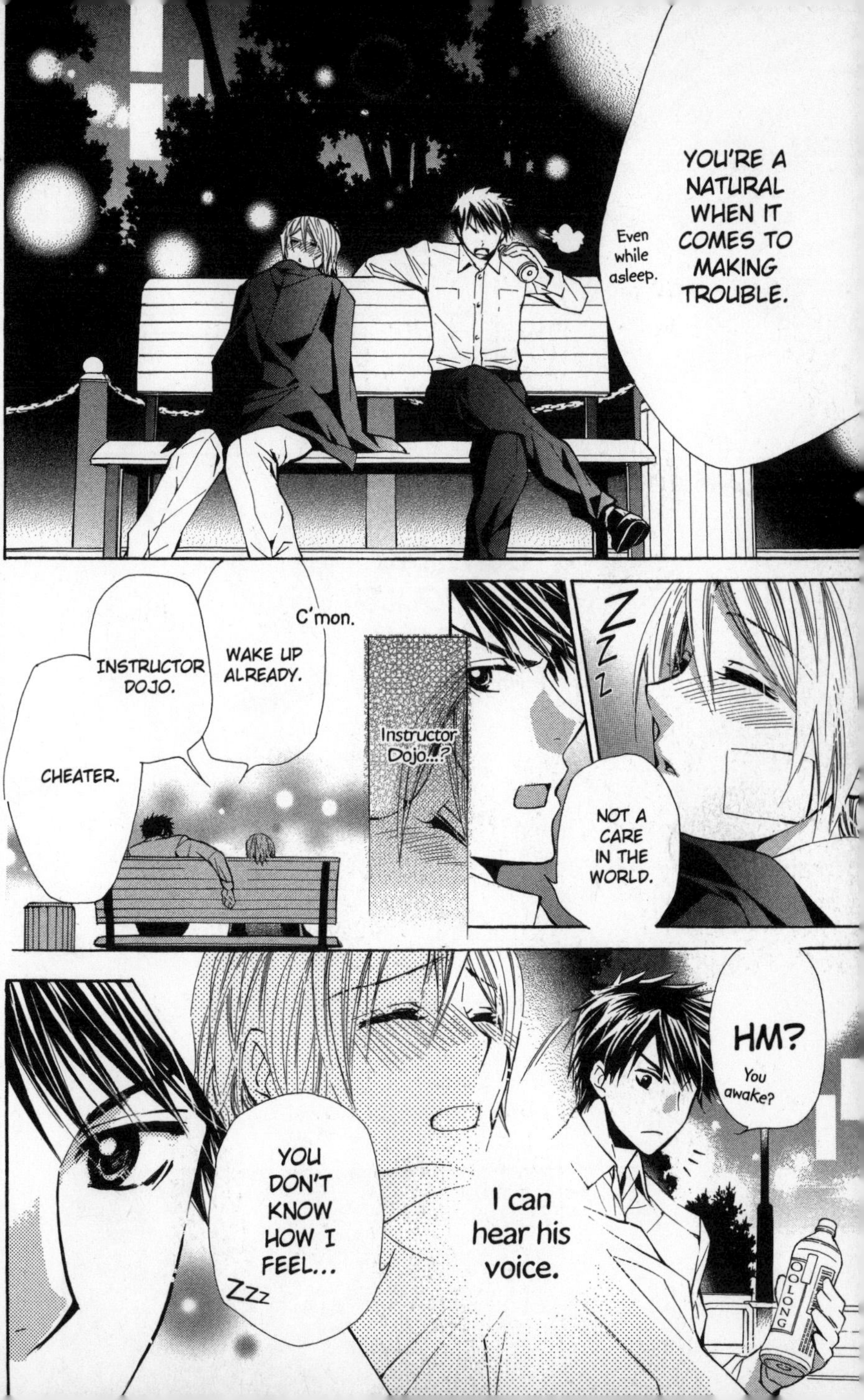
YOU'RE A NATURAL WHEN IT COMES TO MAKING TROUBLE.
Even while asleep.
ZZZ
NOT A CARE IN THE WORLD.
Instructor Dojo...?
C'mon.
WAKE UP ALREADY.
INSTRUCTOR DOJO.
CHEATER.
HM?
You awake?
I can hear his voice.
YOU DON'T KNOW HOW I FEEL...
Zzz
OOLONG

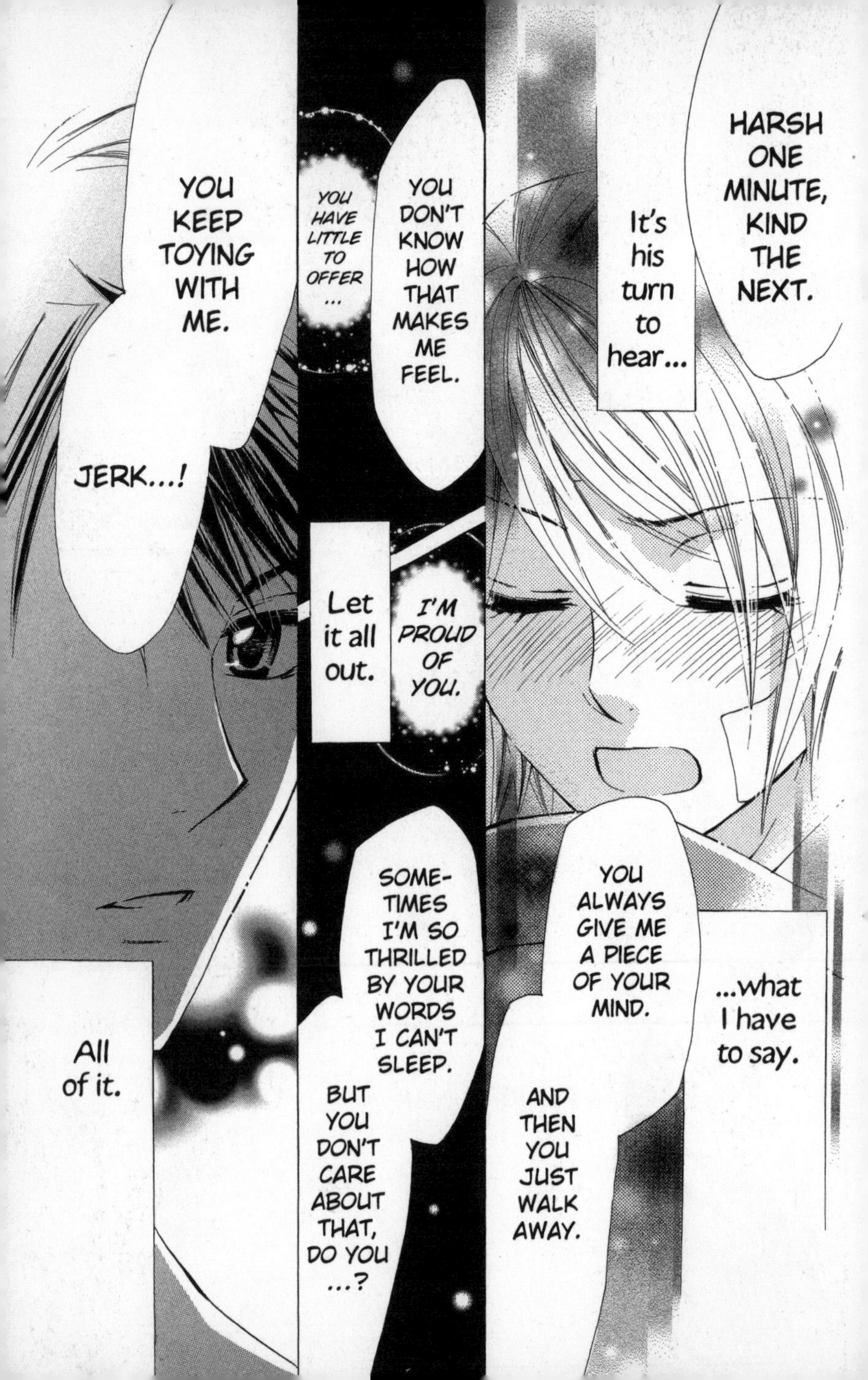
HARSH ONE MINUTE, KIND THE NEXT.
It's his turn to hear...
...what I have to say.
YOU ALWAYS GIVE ME A PIECE OF YOUR MIND.
AND THEN YOU JUST WALK AWAY.
YOU DON'T KNOW HOW THAT MAKES ME FEEL.
YOU HAVE LITTLE TO OFFER...
I'M PROUD OF YOU.
Let it all out.
SOME-TIMES I'M SO THRILLED BY YOUR WORDS I CAN'T SLEEP.
BUT YOU DON'T CARE ABOUT THAT, DO YOU...?
YOU KEEP TOYING WITH ME.
JERK...!
All of it.

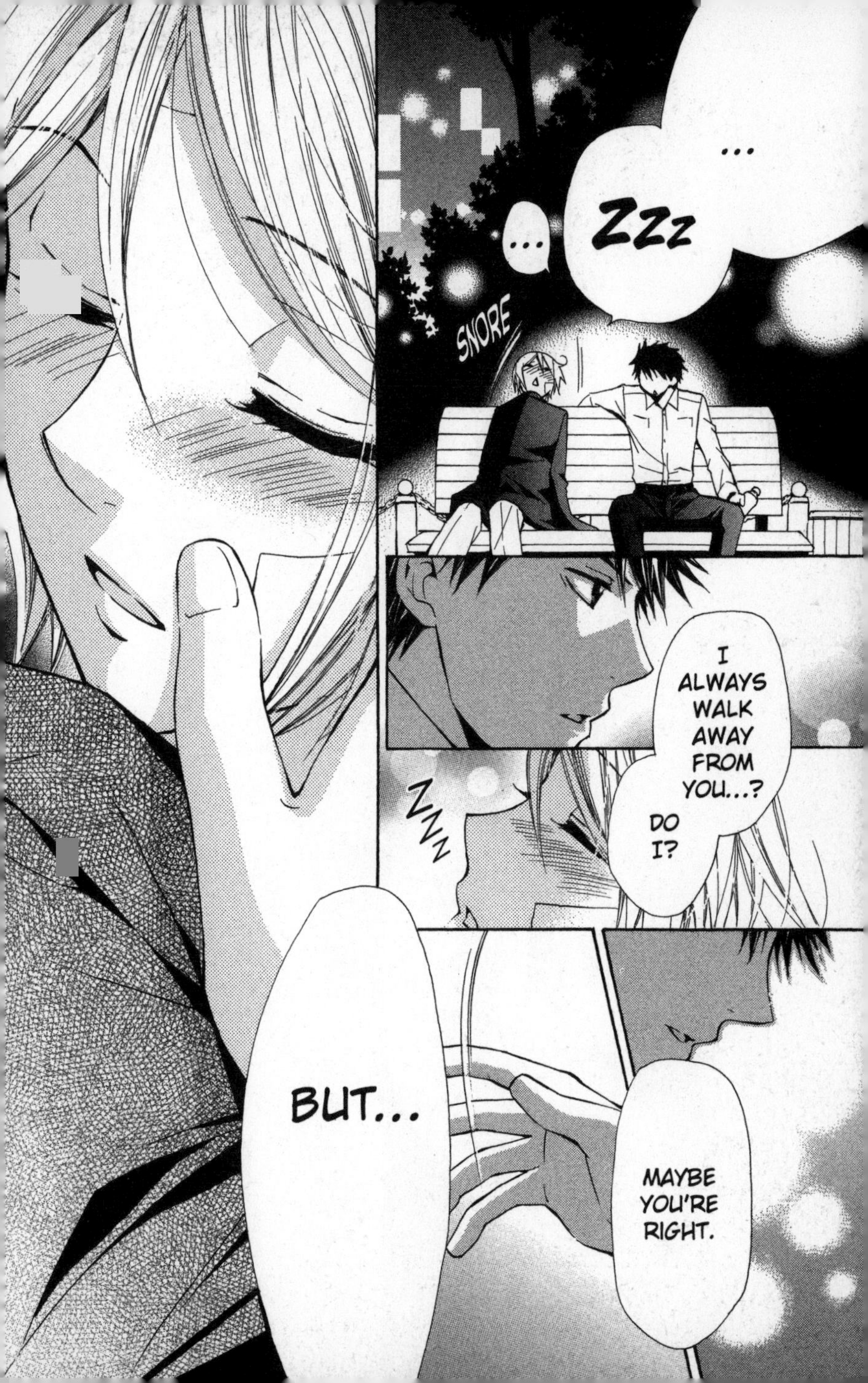
...
ZZz
...
SNORE
I ALWAYS WALK AWAY FROM YOU...?
DO I?
MAYBE YOU'RE RIGHT.
BUT...

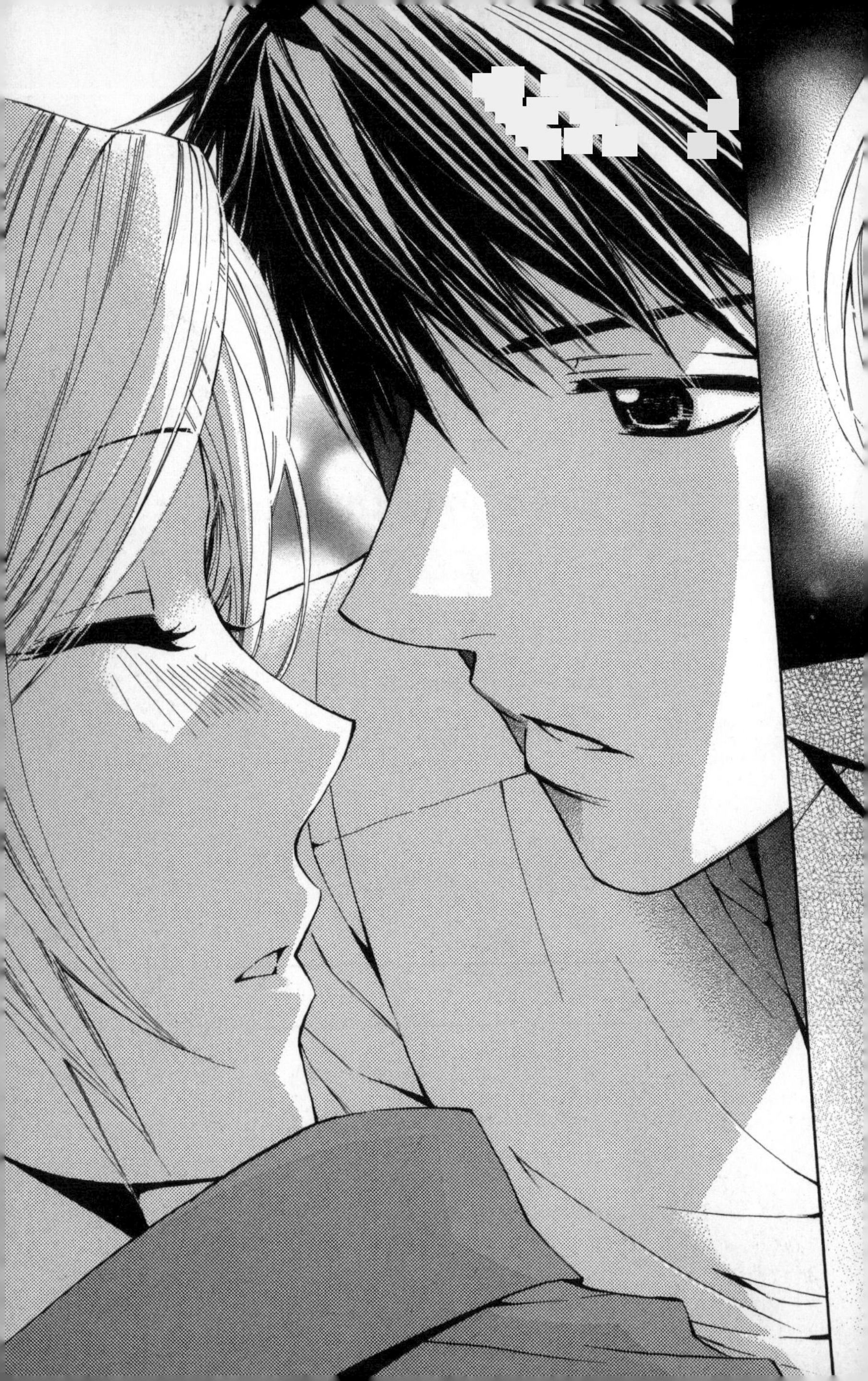

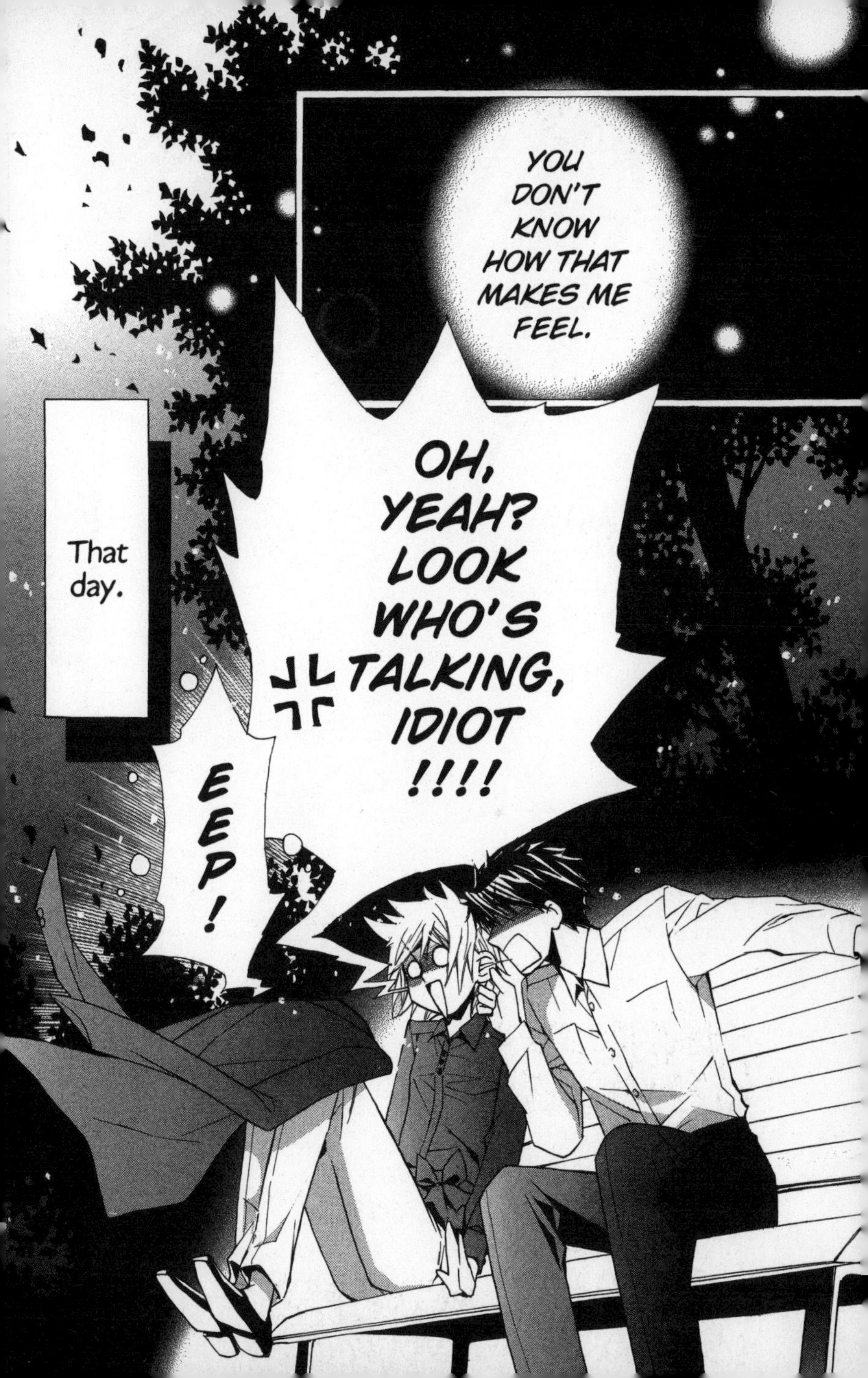
YOU DON'T KNOW HOW THAT MAKES ME FEEL.
OH, YEAH? LOOK WHO'S TALKING, IDIOT!!!!
That day.
EEP!

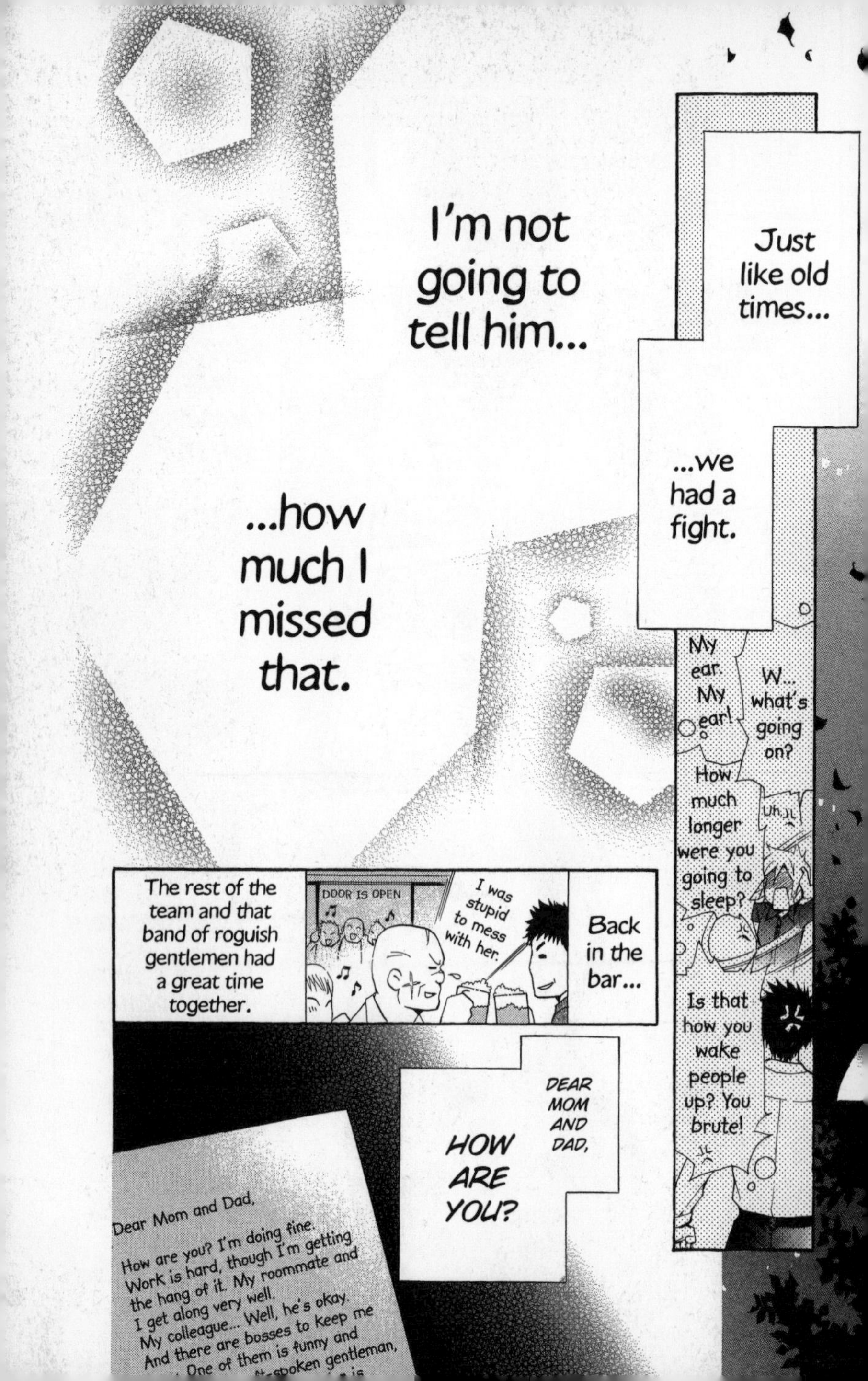

Just like old times...
...we had a fight.
My ear. My ear!
W... what's going on?
How much longer were you going to sleep?
Uh...
Is that how you wake people up? You brute!
I'm not going to tell him...
...how much I missed that.
Back in the bar...
I was stupid to mess with her.
DOOR IS OPEN
The rest of the team and that band of roguish gentlemen had a great time together.
DEAR MOM AND DAD,
HOW ARE YOU?
Dear Mom and Dad,
How are you? I'm doing fine.
Work is hard, though I'm getting
the hang of it. My roommate and
I get along very well.
My colleague... Well, he's okay.
And there are bosses to keep me

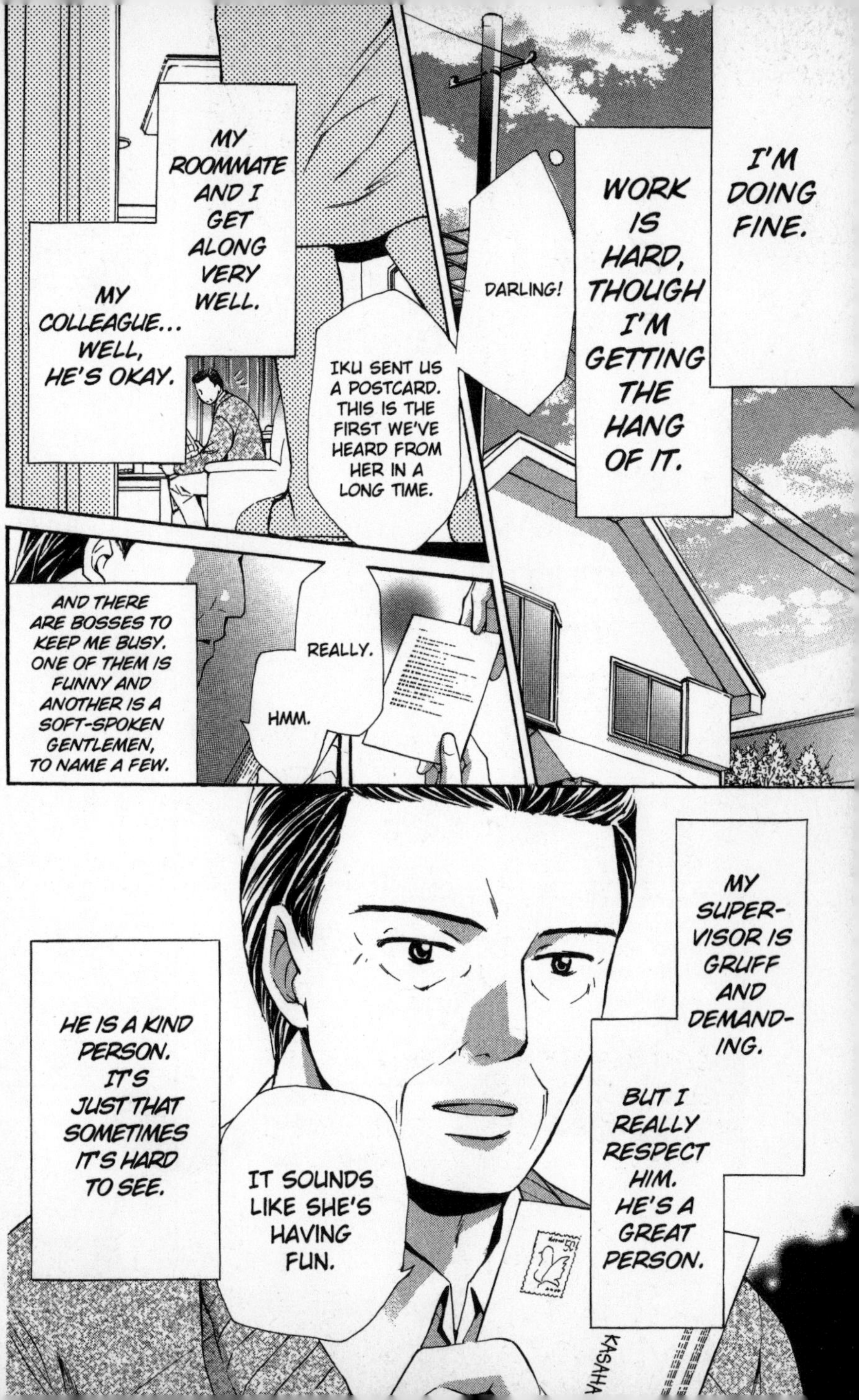
I'M DOING FINE.
WORK IS HARD, THOUGH I'M GETTING THE HANG OF IT.
DARLING!
IKU SENT US A POSTCARD. THIS IS THE FIRST WE'VE HEARD FROM HER IN A LONG TIME.
MY ROOMMATE AND I GET ALONG VERY WELL.
MY COLLEAGUE... WELL, HE'S OKAY.
REALLY.
HMM.
AND THERE ARE BOSSES TO KEEP ME BUSY. ONE OF THEM IS FUNNY AND ANOTHER IS A SOFT-SPOKEN GENTLEMEN, TO NAME A FEW.
MY SUPER-VISOR IS GRUFF AND DEMAND-ING.
BUT I REALLY RESPECT HIM. HE'S A GREAT PERSON.
IT SOUNDS LIKE SHE'S HAVING FUN.
HE IS A KIND PERSON. IT'S JUST THAT SOMETIMES IT'S HARD TO SEE.
KASAHA

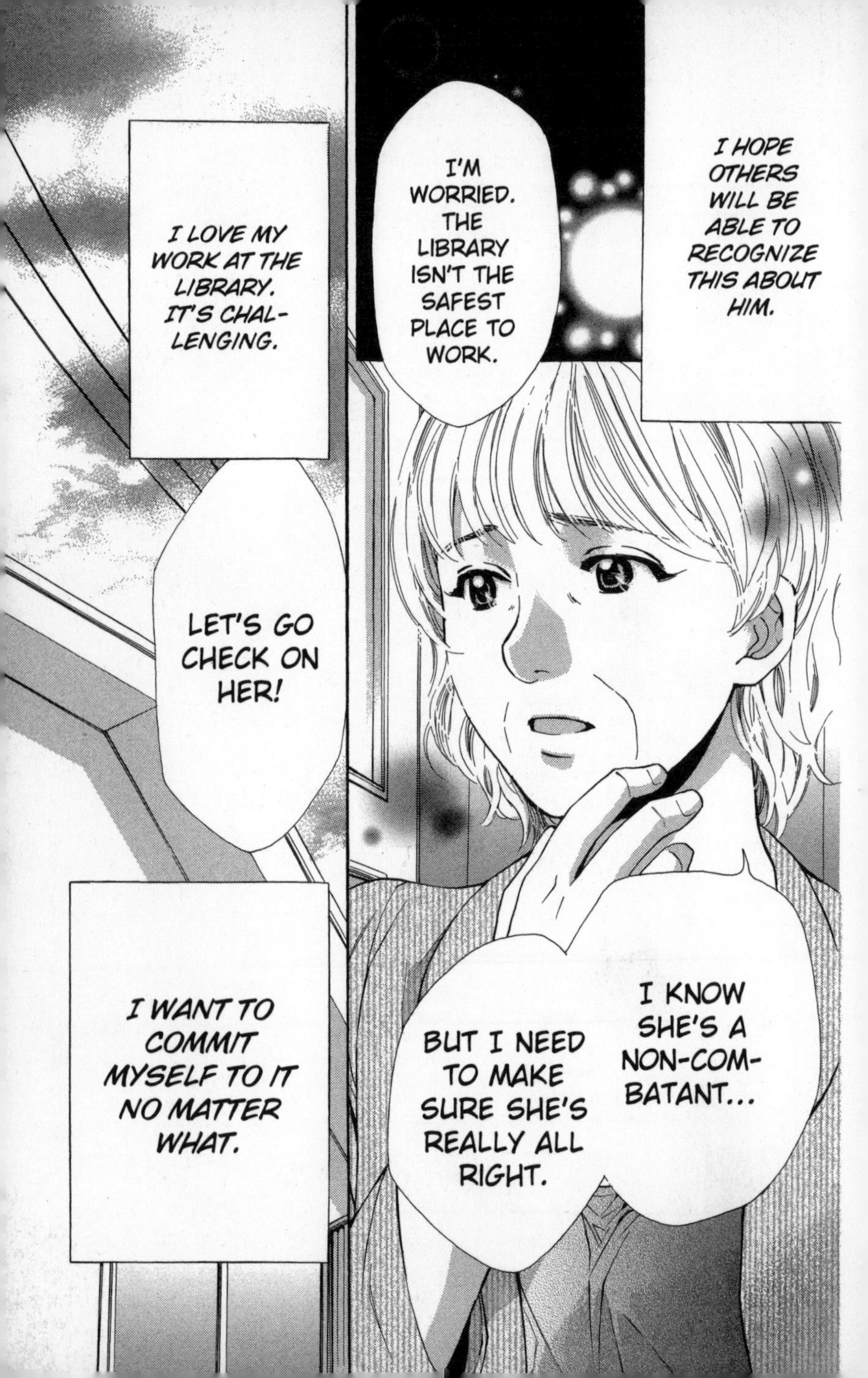
I HOPE OTHERS WILL BE ABLE TO RECOGNIZE THIS ABOUT HIM.
I'M WORRIED. THE LIBRARY ISN'T THE SAFEST PLACE TO WORK.
I KNOW SHE'S A NON-COM-BATANT...
BUT I NEED TO MAKE SURE SHE'S REALLY ALL RIGHT.
I LOVE MY WORK AT THE LIBRARY. IT'S CHAL-LENGING.
LET'S GO CHECK ON HER!
I WANT TO COMMIT MYSELF TO IT NO MATTER WHAT.

Nothing has been going on.

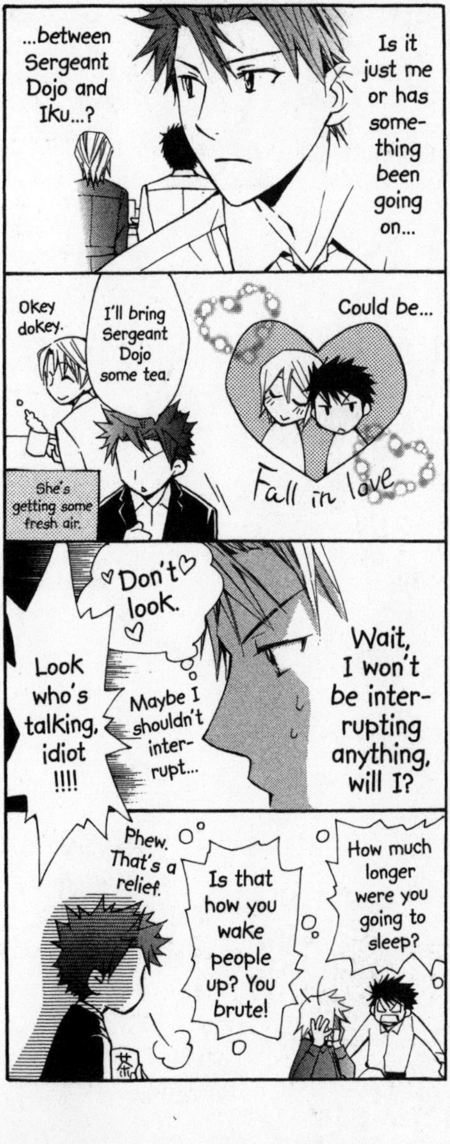
Is it just me or has something been going on...
...between Sergeant Dojo and Iku...?
Could be...
Fall in love
I'll bring Sergeant Dojo some tea.
Okey dokey.
She's getting some fresh air.
Wait, I won't be interrupting anything, will I?
Don't look.
Maybe I shouldn't interrupt...
Look who's talking, idiot!!!!
How much longer were you going to sleep?
Is that how you wake people up? You brute!
Phew. That's a relief.
茶

CHAPTER 18

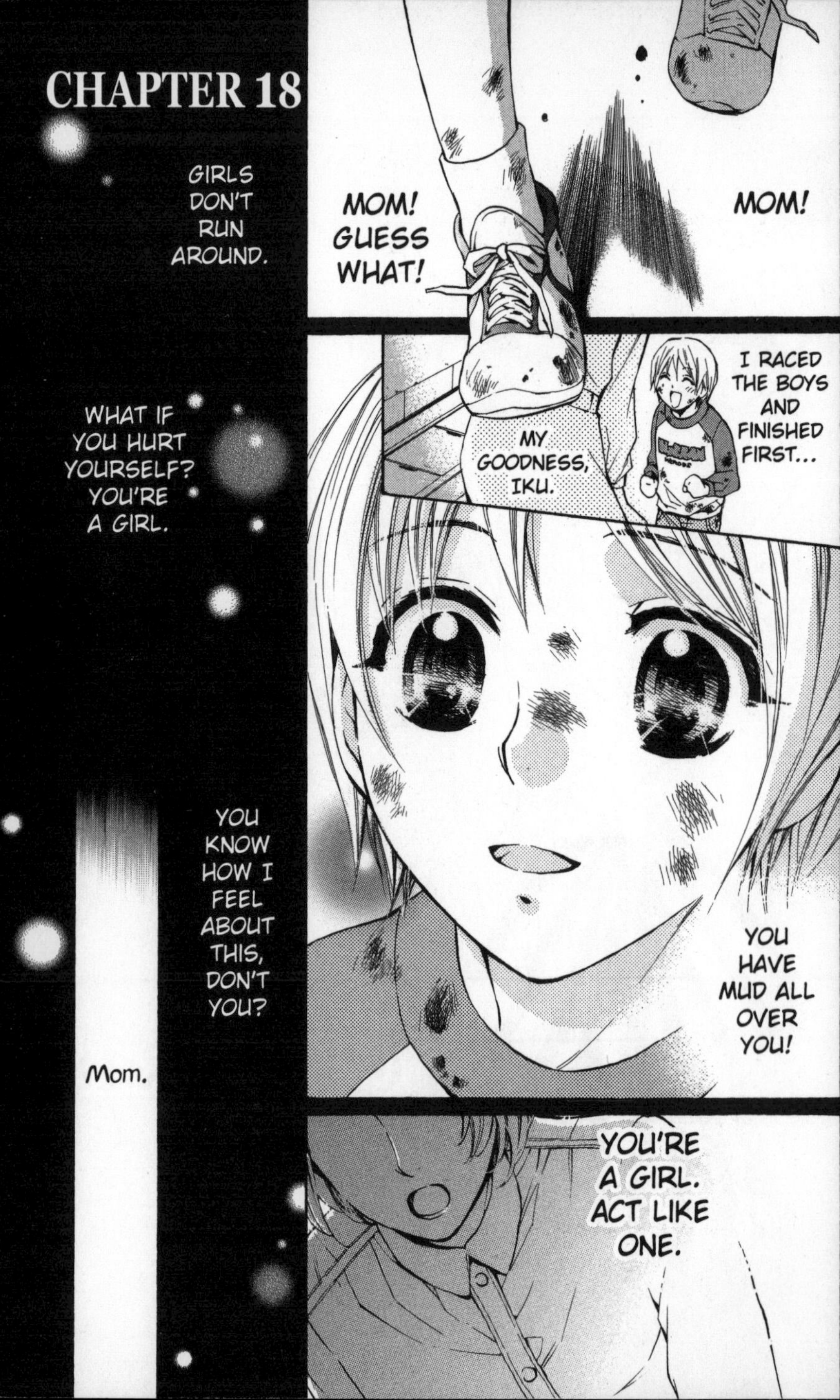

MOM!
MOM! GUESS WHAT!
I RACED THE BOYS AND FINISHED FIRST...
MY GOODNESS, IKU.
YOU HAVE MUD ALL OVER YOU!
YOU'RE A GIRL. ACT LIKE ONE.
GIRLS DON'T RUN AROUND.
WHAT IF YOU HURT YOURSELF? YOU'RE A GIRL.
YOU KNOW HOW I FEEL ABOUT THIS, DON'T YOU?
Mom.

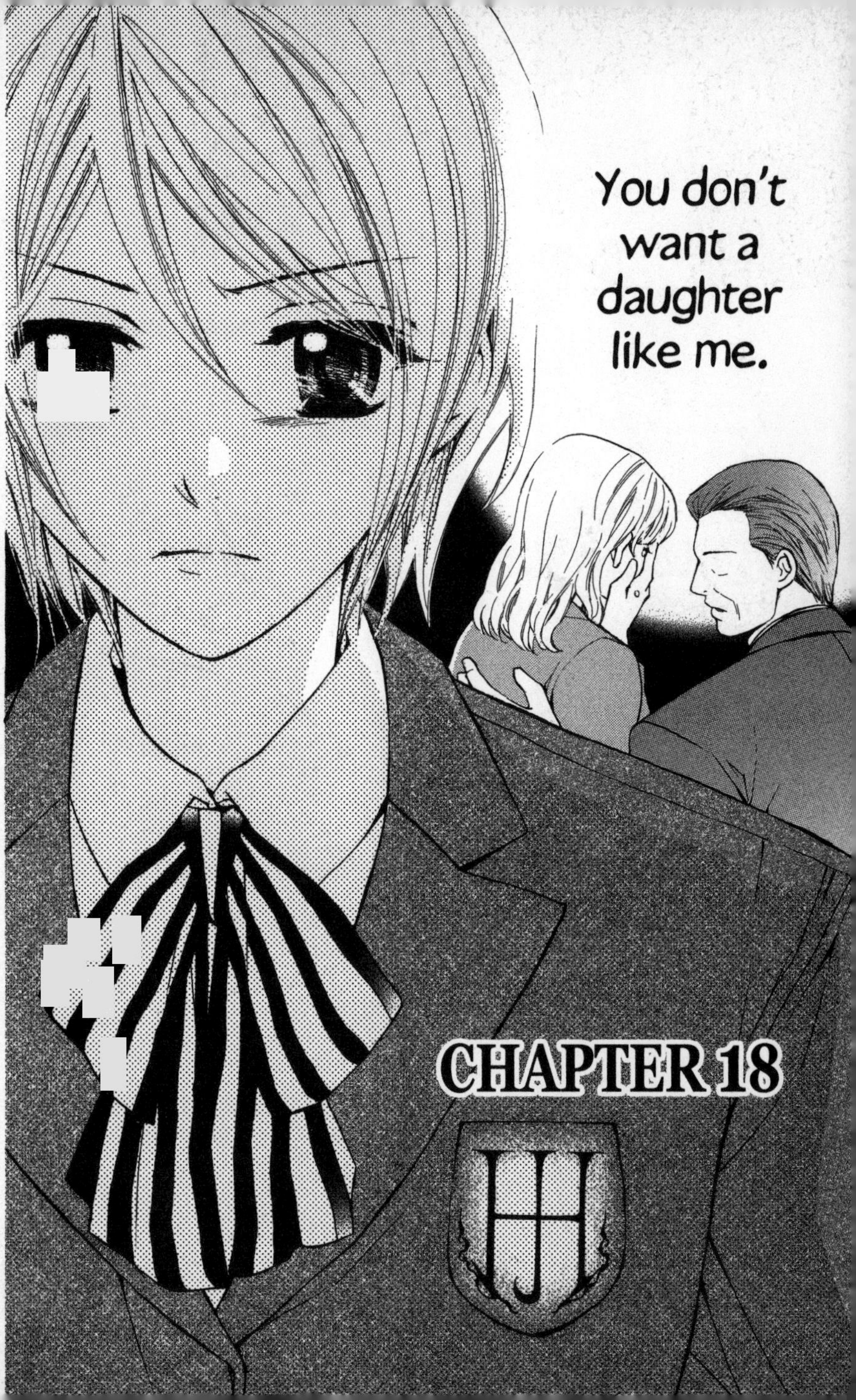
You don't want a daughter like me.
CHAPTER 18

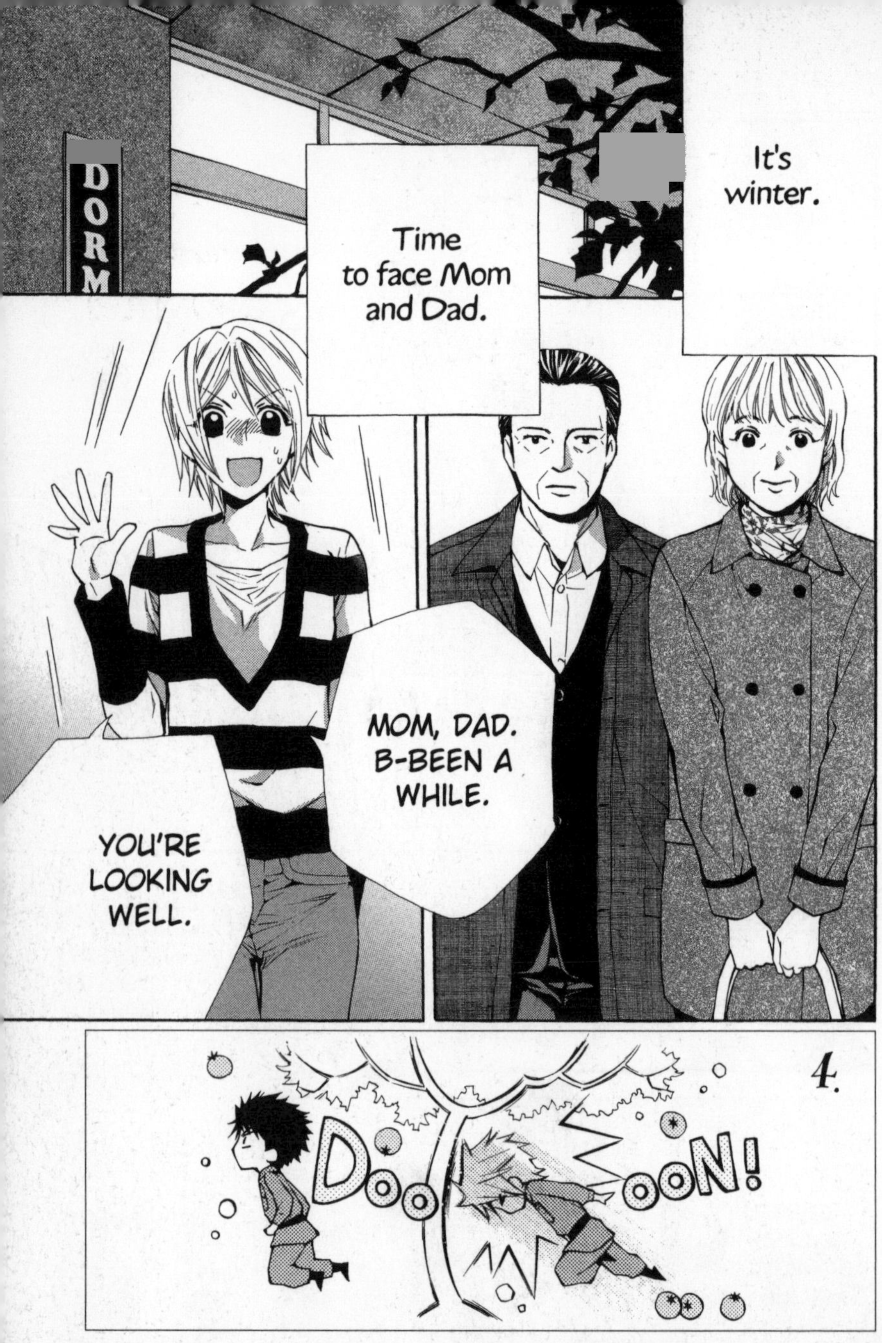
DORM
It's winter.
Time to face Mom and Dad.
MOM, DAD. B-BEEN A WHILE.
YOU'RE LOOKING WELL.
4.
DOOO
OON!

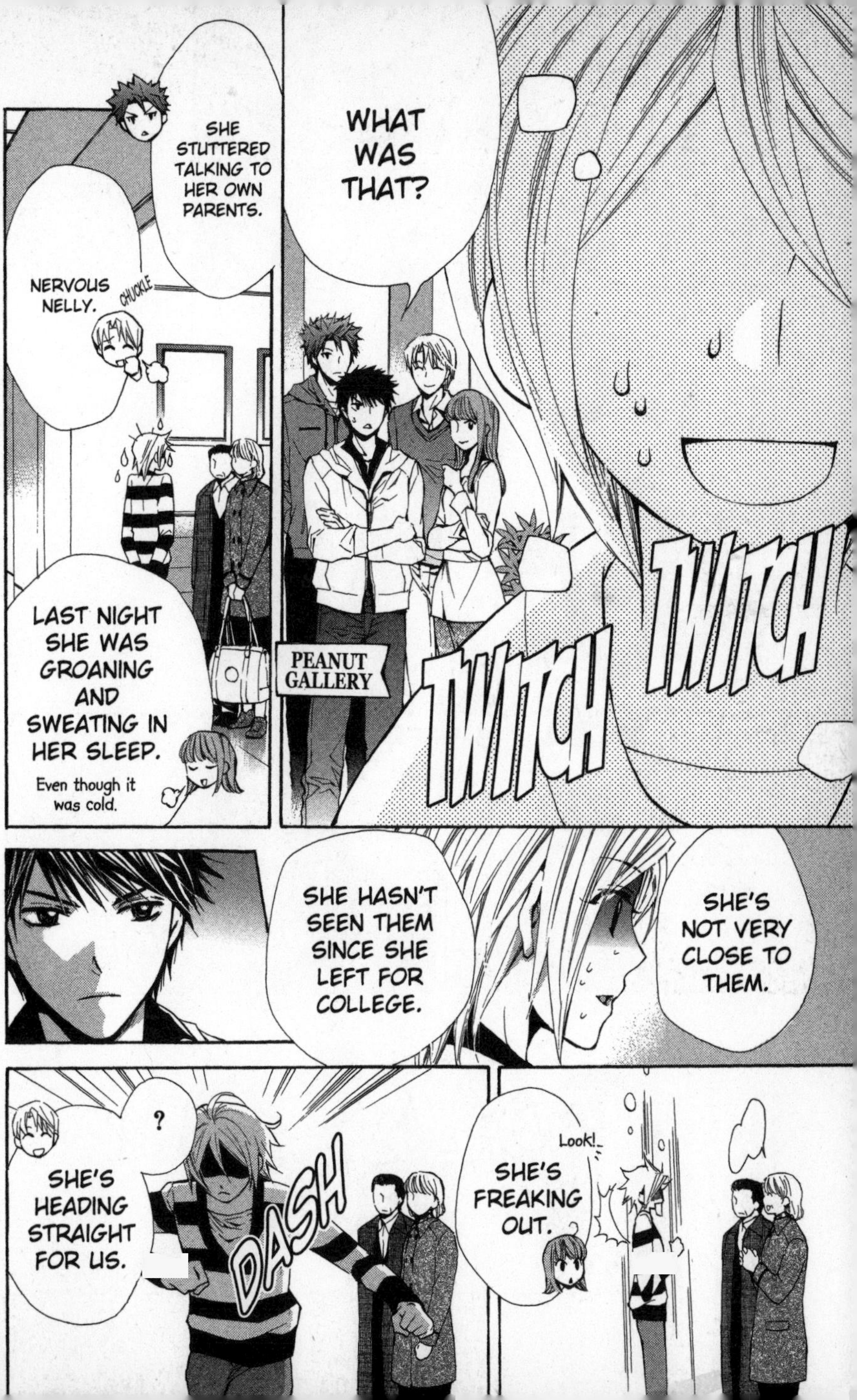
WHAT WAS THAT?
TWITCH
TWITCH
PEANUT GALLERY
SHE STUTTERED TALKING TO HER OWN PARENTS.
NERVOUS NELLY.
CHUCKLE
LAST NIGHT SHE WAS GROANING AND SWEATING IN HER SLEEP.
Even though it was cold.
SHE'S NOT VERY CLOSE TO THEM.
SHE HASN'T SEEN THEM SINCE SHE LEFT FOR COLLEGE.
Look!
SHE'S FREAKING OUT.
?
SHE'S HEADING STRAIGHT FOR US.
DASH

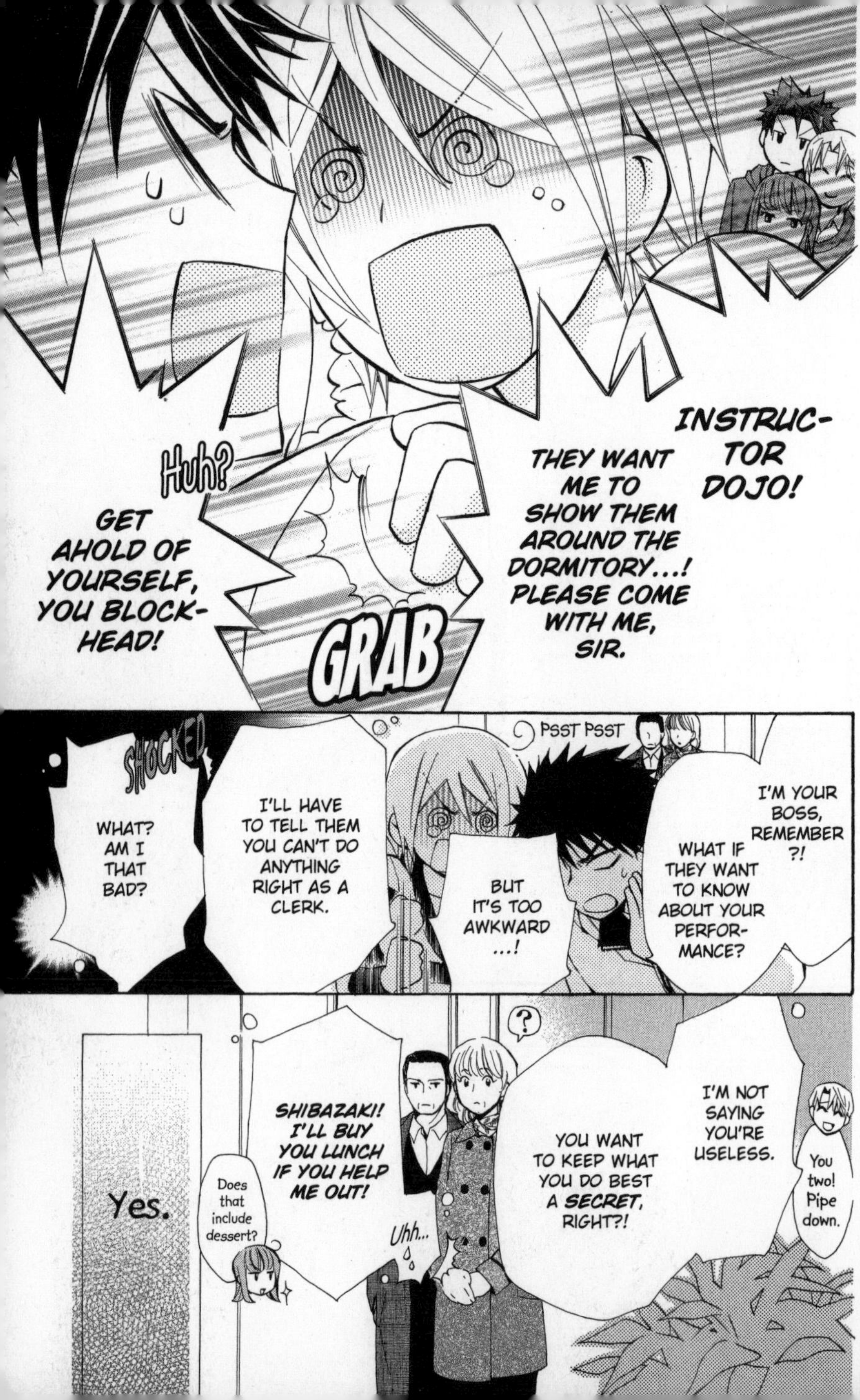
INSTRUCTOR DOJO!
THEY WANT ME TO SHOW THEM AROUND THE DORMITORY...! PLEASE COME WITH ME, SIR.
GRAB
Huh?
GET AHOLD OF YOURSELF, YOU BLOCKHEAD!
I'M YOUR BOSS, REMEMBER?!
WHAT IF THEY WANT TO KNOW ABOUT YOUR PERFORMANCE?
BUT IT'S TOO AWKWARD ...!
PSST PSST
I'LL HAVE TO TELL THEM YOU CAN'T DO ANYTHING RIGHT AS A CLERK.
SHOCKED
WHAT? AM I THAT BAD?
You two! Pipe down.
I'M NOT SAYING YOU'RE USELESS.
YOU WANT TO KEEP WHAT YOU DO BEST A *SECRET*, RIGHT?!
?
SHIBAZAKI! I'LL BUY YOU LUNCH IF YOU HELP ME OUT!
Uhh...
Does that include dessert?
Yes.

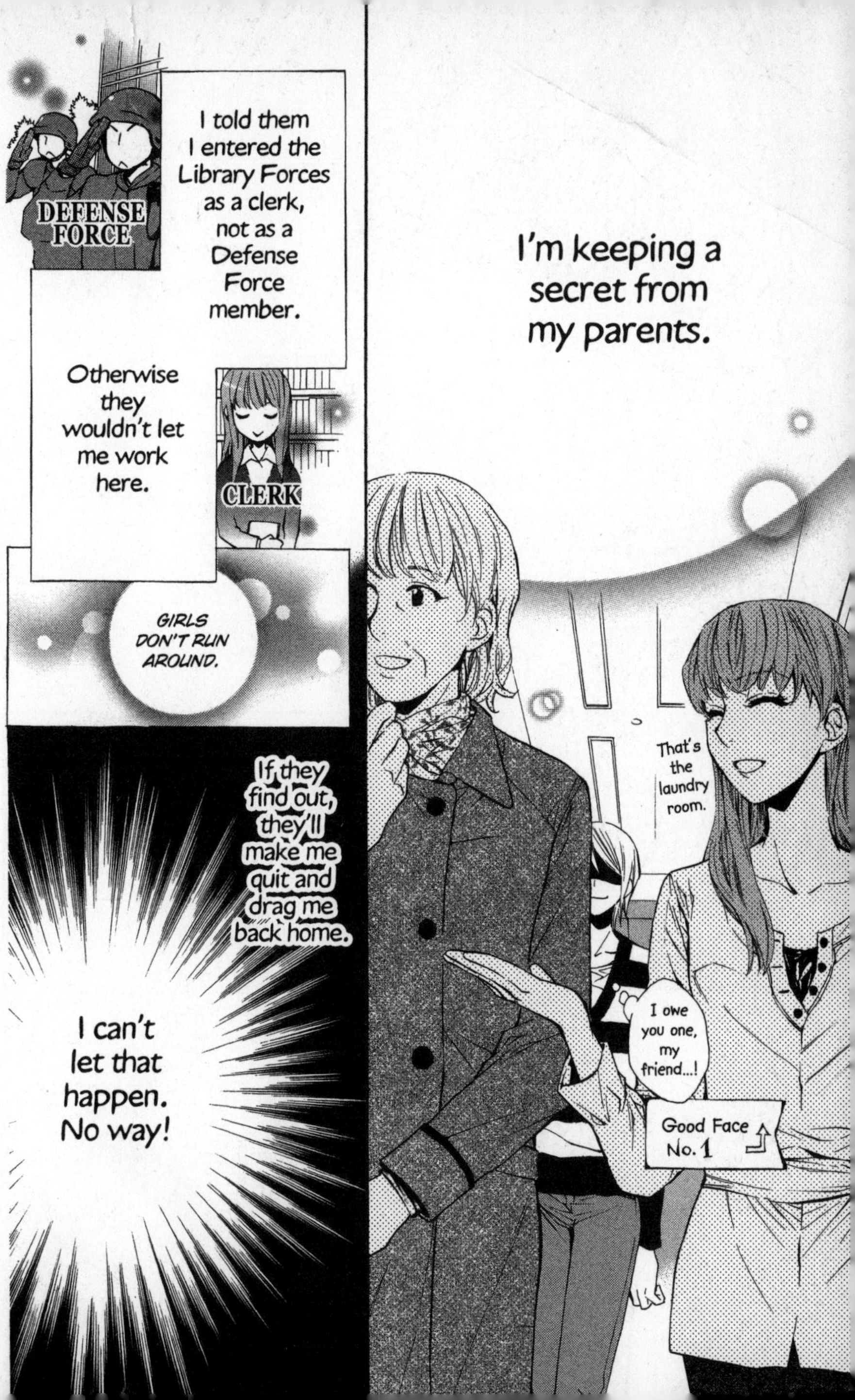
I'm keeping a secret from my parents.
That's the laundry room.
I owe you one, my friend...!
Good Face No. 1
I told them I entered the Library Forces as a clerk, not as a Defense Force member.
DEFENSE FORCE
CLERK
Otherwise they wouldn't let me work here.
GIRLS DON'T RUN AROUND.
If they find out, they'll make me quit and drag me back home.
I can't let that happen. No way!

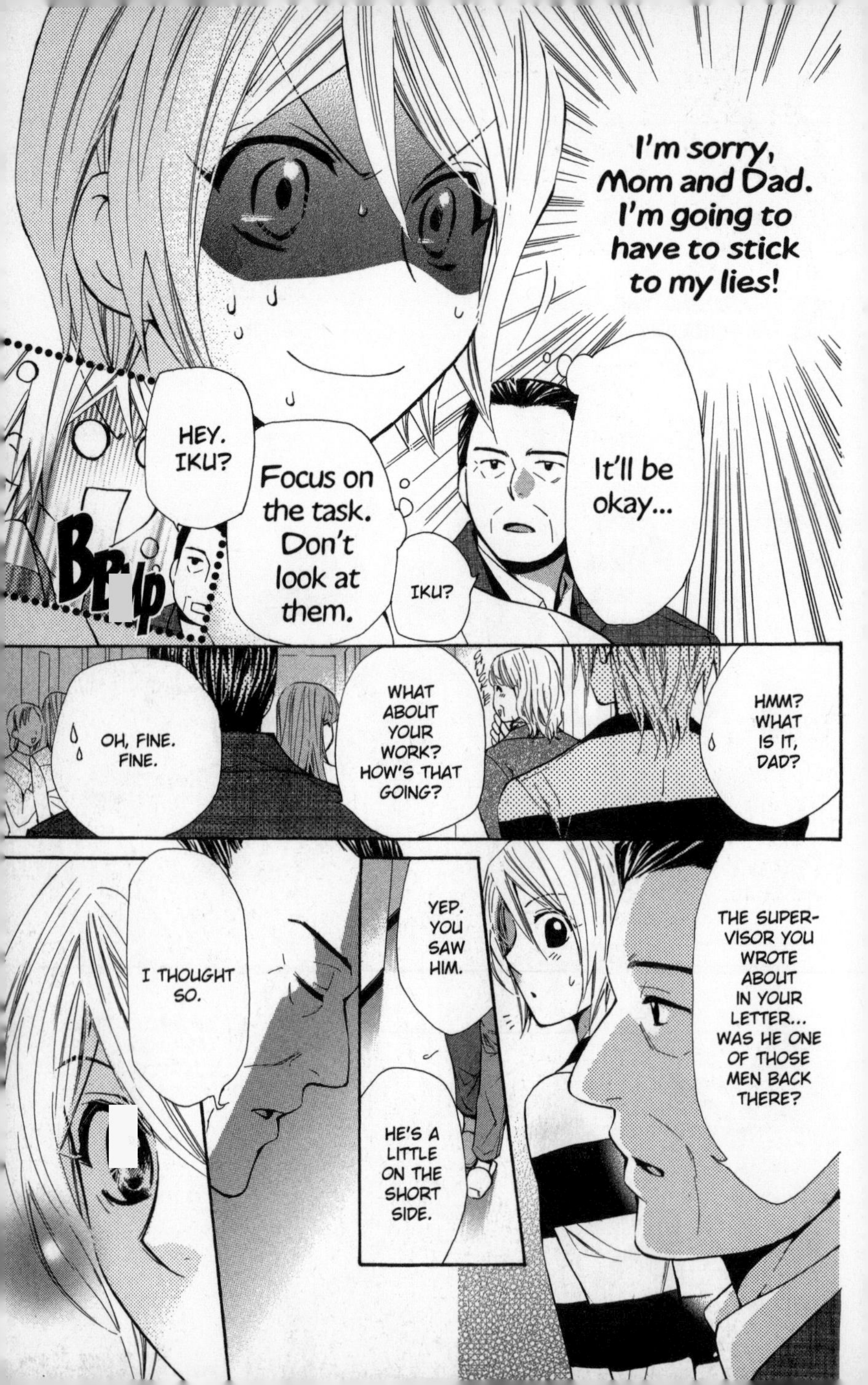
I'm sorry, Mom and Dad. I'm going to have to stick to my lies!
It'll be okay...
IKU?
Focus on the task. Don't look at them.
HEY. IKU?
HMM? WHAT IS IT, DAD?
WHAT ABOUT YOUR WORK? HOW'S THAT GOING?
OH, FINE. FINE.
THE SUPER-VISOR YOU WROTE ABOUT IN YOUR LETTER... WAS HE ONE OF THOSE MEN BACK THERE?
YEP. YOU SAW HIM.
HE'S A LITTLE ON THE SHORT SIDE.
I THOUGHT SO.

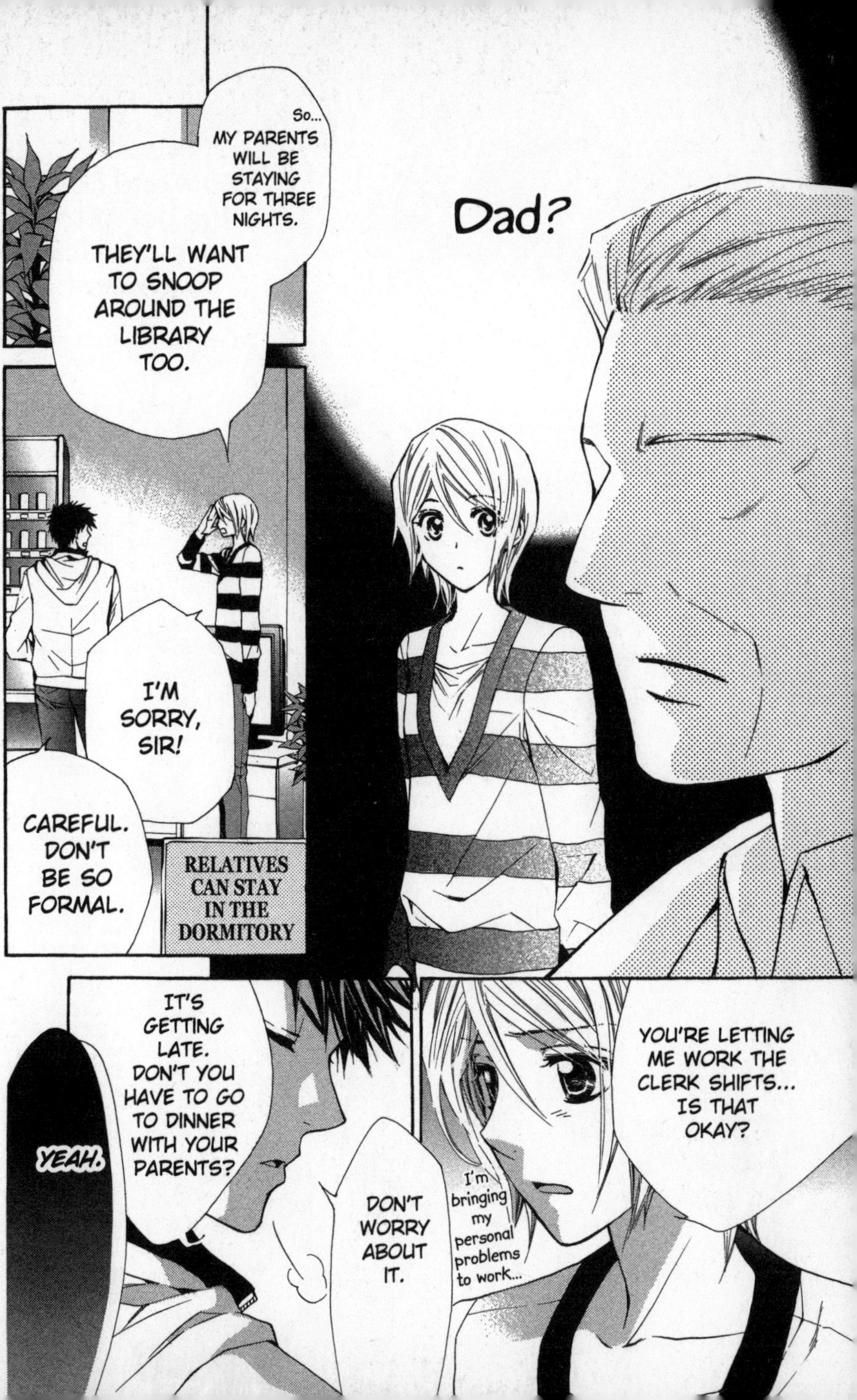
Dad?
So... my parents will be staying for three nights.
They'll want to snoop around the library too.
I'm sorry, sir!
Careful. Don't be so formal.
RELATIVES CAN STAY IN THE DORMITORY
You're letting me work the clerk shifts... is that okay?
I'm bringing my personal problems to work...
Don't worry about it.
It's getting late. Don't you have to go to dinner with your parents?
Yeah.

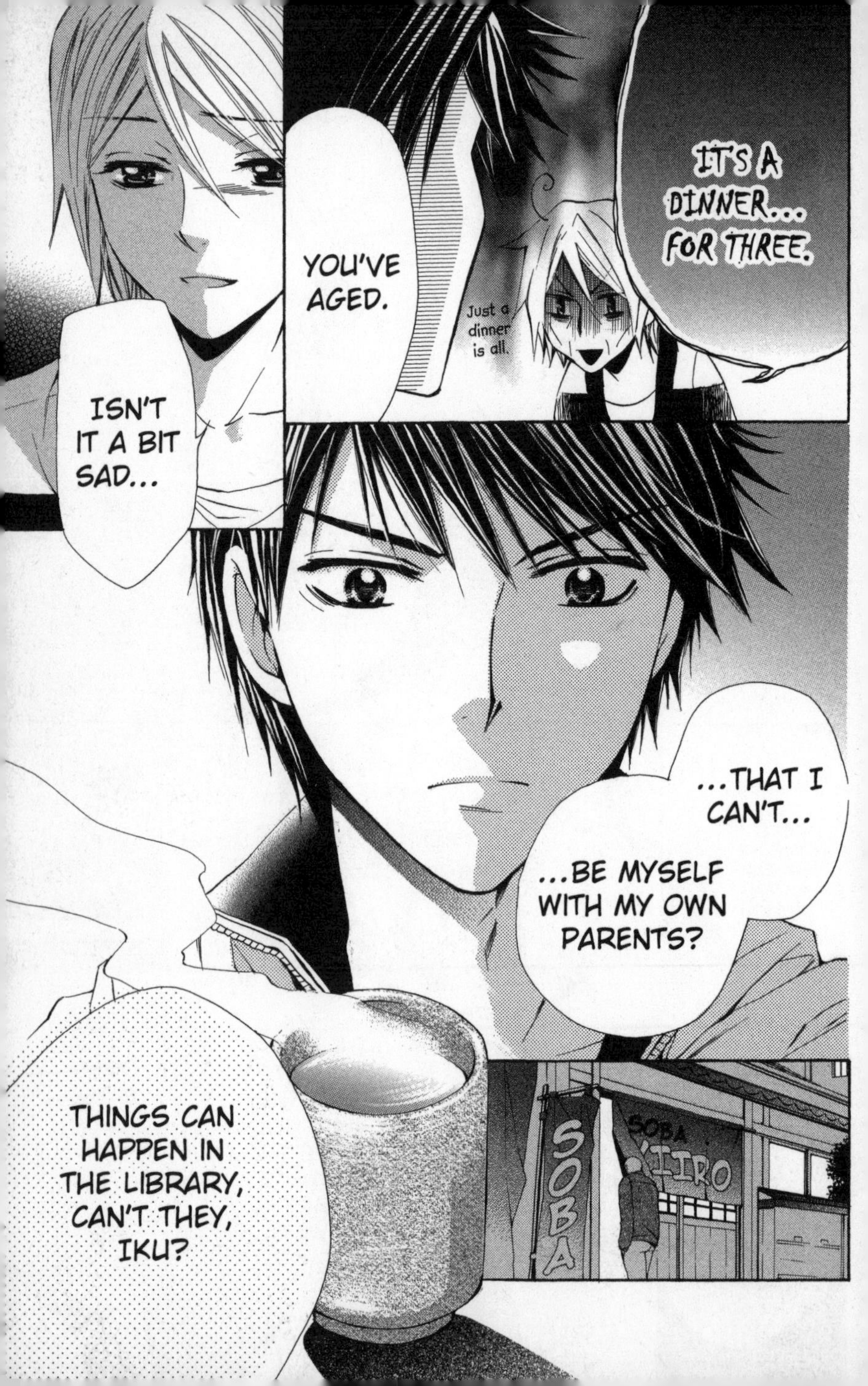
IT'S A DINNER... FOR THREE.
Just a dinner is all.
YOU'VE AGED.
ISN'T IT A BIT SAD...
...THAT I CAN'T...
...BE MYSELF WITH MY OWN PARENTS?
SOBA
SOBA
THINGS CAN HAPPEN IN THE LIBRARY, CAN'T THEY, IKU?

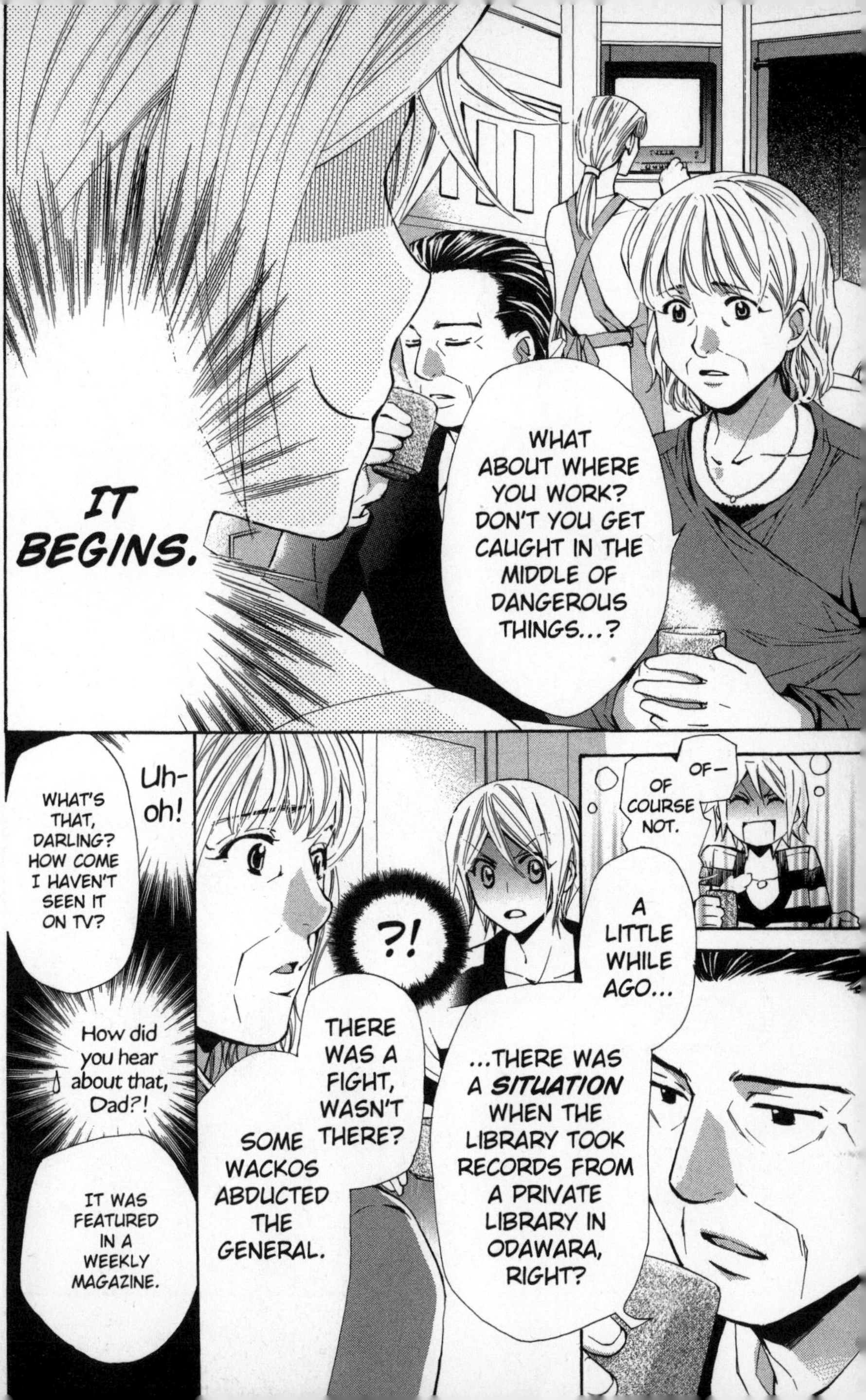
WHAT ABOUT WHERE YOU WORK? DON'T YOU GET CAUGHT IN THE MIDDLE OF DANGEROUS THINGS...?
IT BEGINS.
OF— OF COURSE NOT.
A LITTLE WHILE AGO...
...THERE WAS A SITUATION WHEN THE LIBRARY TOOK RECORDS FROM A PRIVATE LIBRARY IN ODAWARA, RIGHT?
THERE WAS A FIGHT, WASN'T THERE?
SOME WACKOS ABDUCTED THE GENERAL.
?!
Uh-oh!
WHAT'S THAT, DARLING? HOW COME I HAVEN'T SEEN IT ON TV?
How did you hear about that, Dad?!
IT WAS FEATURED IN A WEEKLY MAGAZINE.

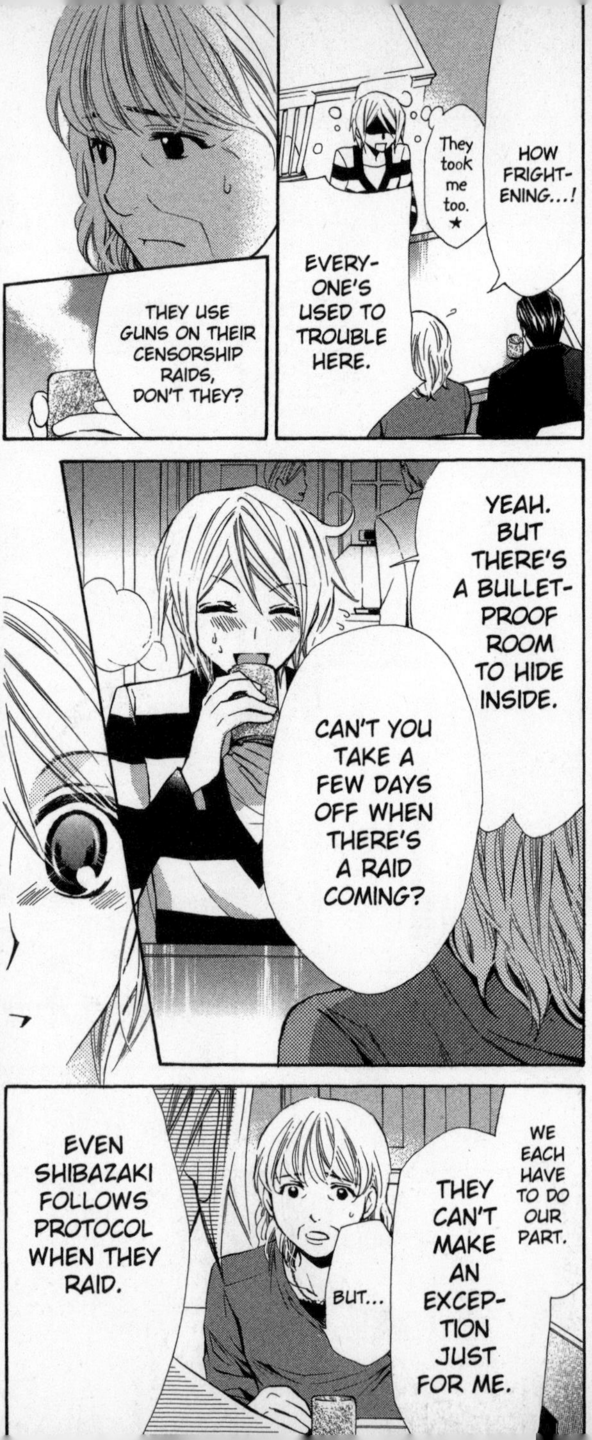
HOW FRIGHTENING...!
They took me too. ★
EVERYONE'S USED TO TROUBLE HERE.
THEY USE GUNS ON THEIR CENSORSHIP RAIDS, DON'T THEY?
YEAH. BUT THERE'S A BULLETPROOF ROOM TO HIDE INSIDE.
CAN'T YOU TAKE A FEW DAYS OFF WHEN THERE'S A RAID COMING?
WE EACH HAVE TO DO OUR PART.
THEY CAN'T MAKE AN EXCEPTION JUST FOR ME.
BUT...
EVEN SHIBAZAKI FOLLOWS PROTOCOL WHEN THEY RAID.

4

*

As you all know, this is a *shojo* manga. I shouldn't be focusing on muscle all the time, should I? I tried to find other entertaining things to explore. Like in chapter 16... I used a certain phrase that made me feel uncomfortably funny... But I didn't use anything that sounds unnatural...so...

It's part of the fun, isn't it? To enjoy overdramatic phrases and take them seriously?

Every day is a new challenge and full of learning...

I keep trying!

*

*

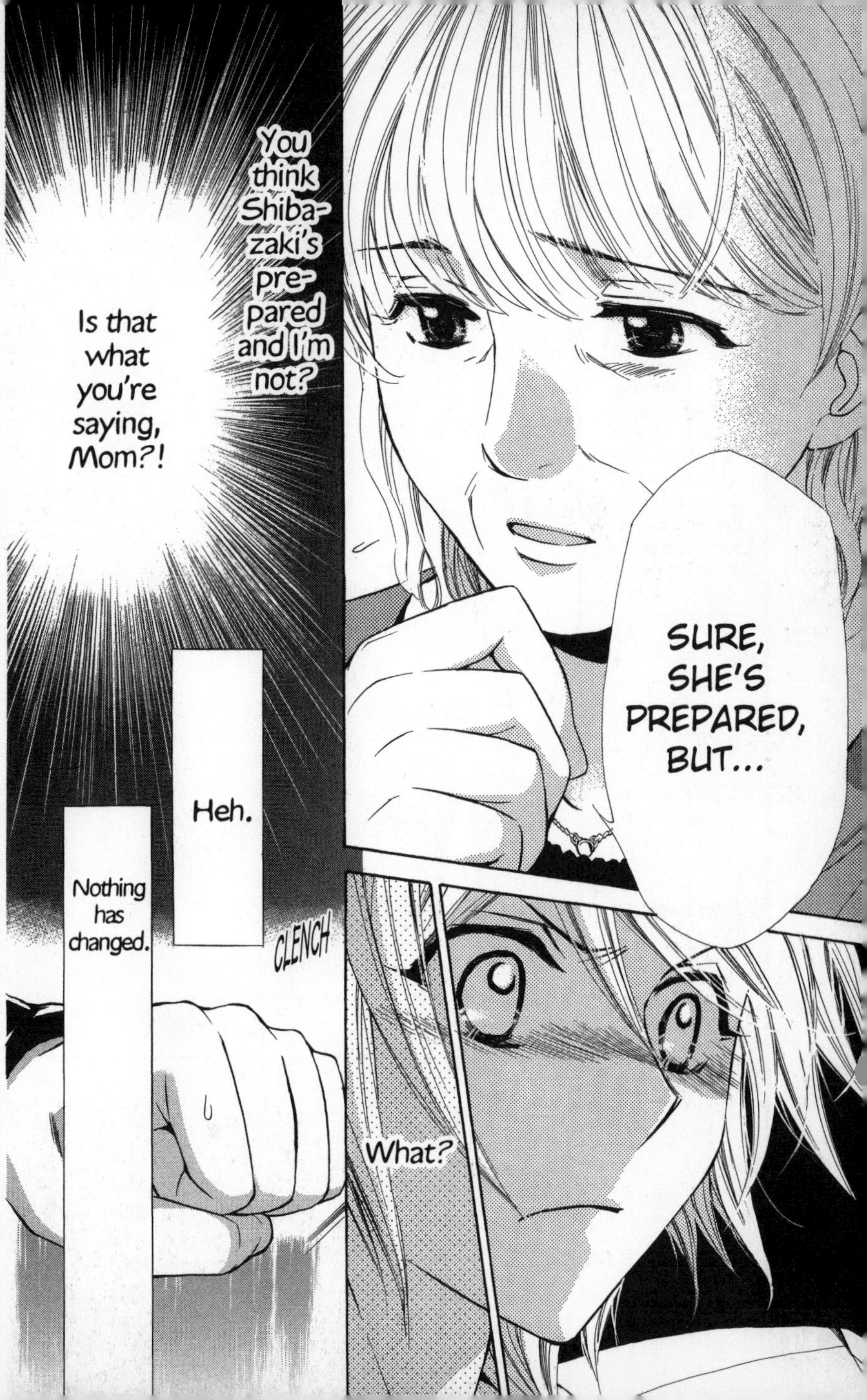
SURE, SHE'S PREPARED, BUT...
What?
You think Shiba-zaki's pre-pared and I'm not?
Is that what you're saying, Mom?!
Heh.
Nothing has changed.
CLENCH

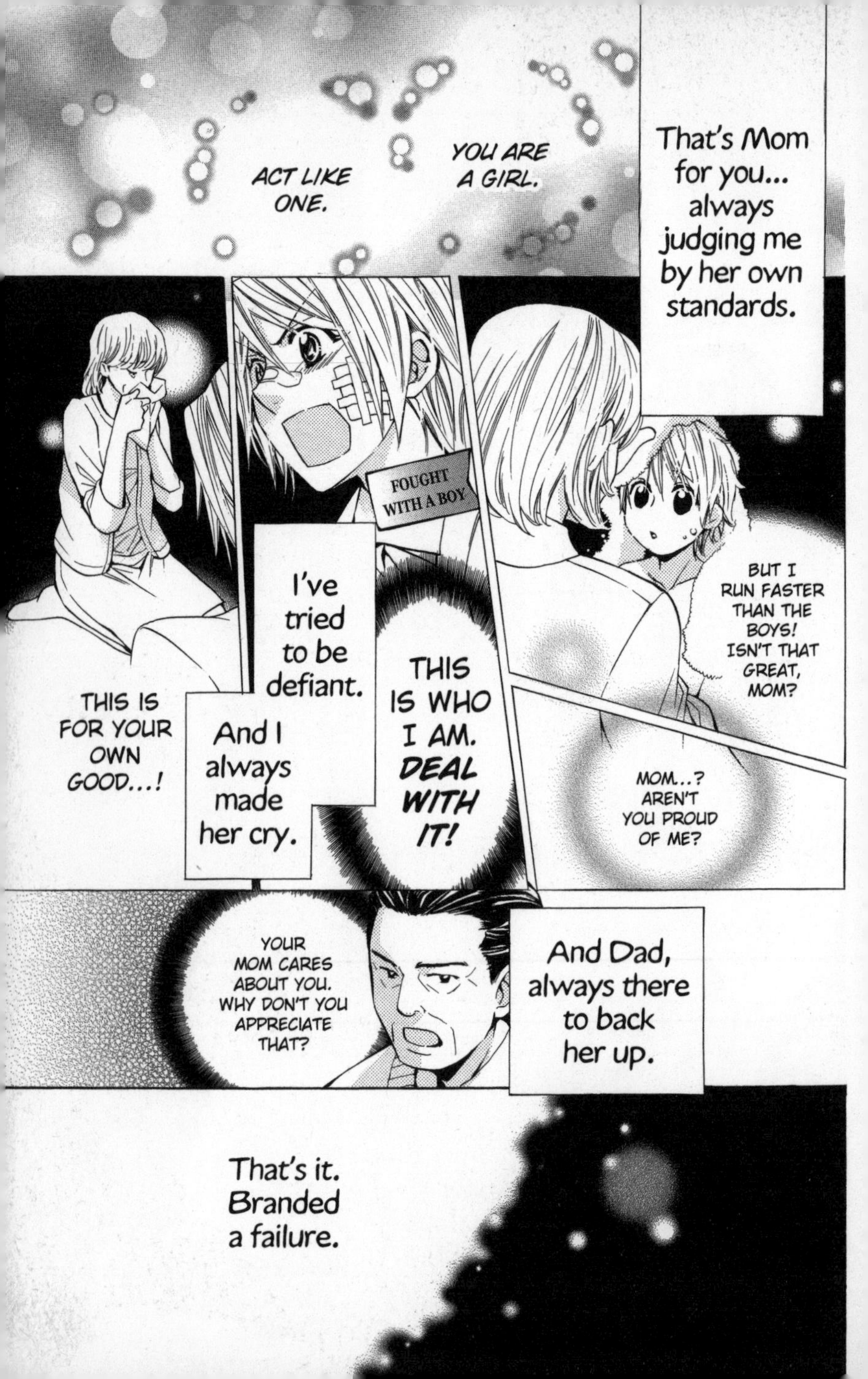
That's Mom for you... always judging me by her own standards.
YOU ARE A GIRL.
ACT LIKE ONE.
BUT I RUN FASTER THAN THE BOYS! ISN'T THAT GREAT, MOM?
MOM...? AREN'T YOU PROUD OF ME?
FOUGHT WITH A BOY
I've tried to be defiant.
THIS IS WHO I AM. DEAL WITH IT!
And I always made her cry.
THIS IS FOR YOUR OWN GOOD...!
And Dad, always there to back her up.
YOUR MOM CARES ABOUT YOU. WHY DON'T YOU APPRECIATE THAT?
That's it. Branded a failure.

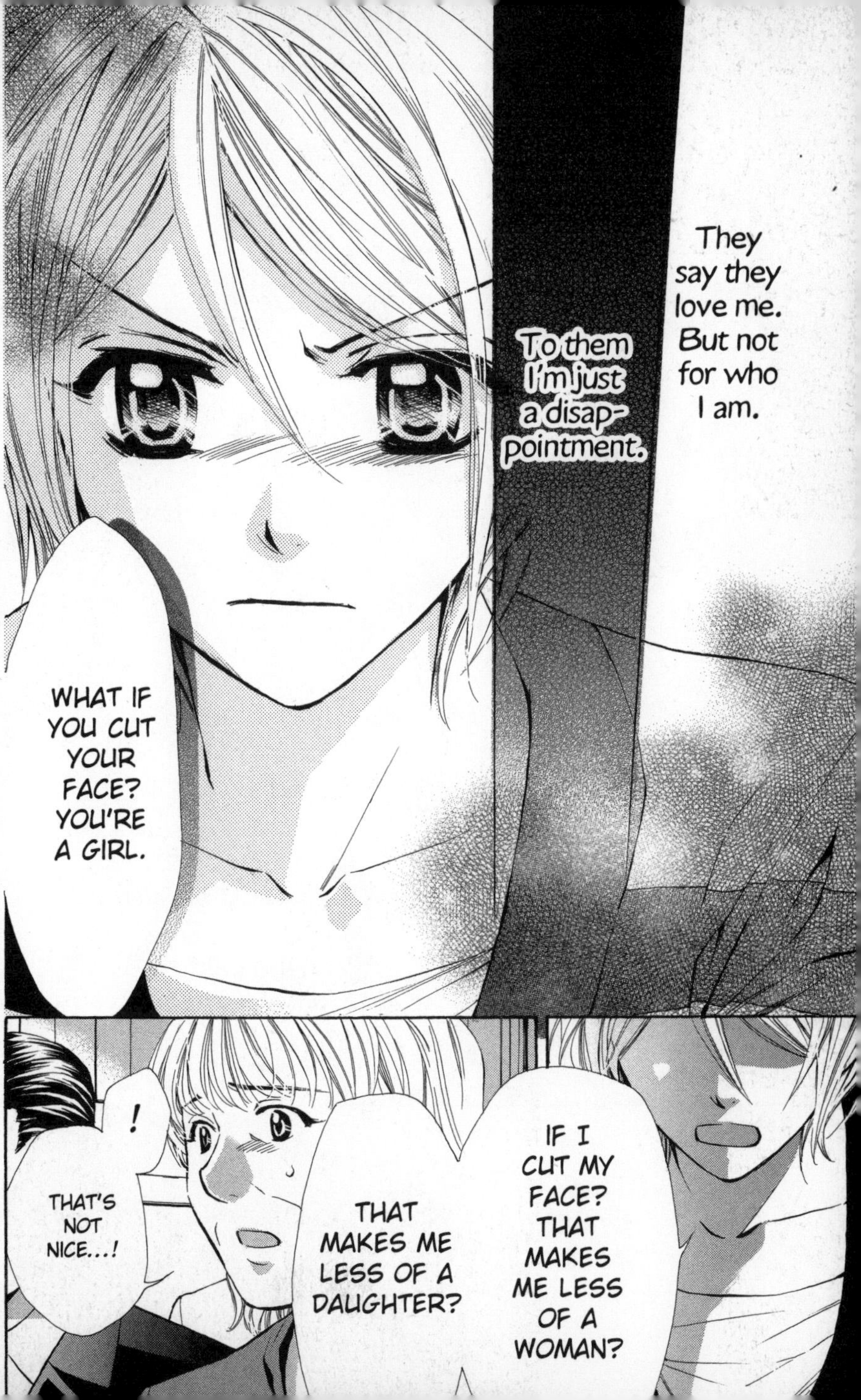
They say they love me. But not for who I am.
To them I'm just a disap-pointment.
WHAT IF YOU CUT YOUR FACE? YOU'RE A GIRL.
IF I CUT MY FACE? THAT MAKES ME LESS OF A WOMAN?
THAT MAKES ME LESS OF A DAUGHTER?
!
THAT'S NOT NICE...!

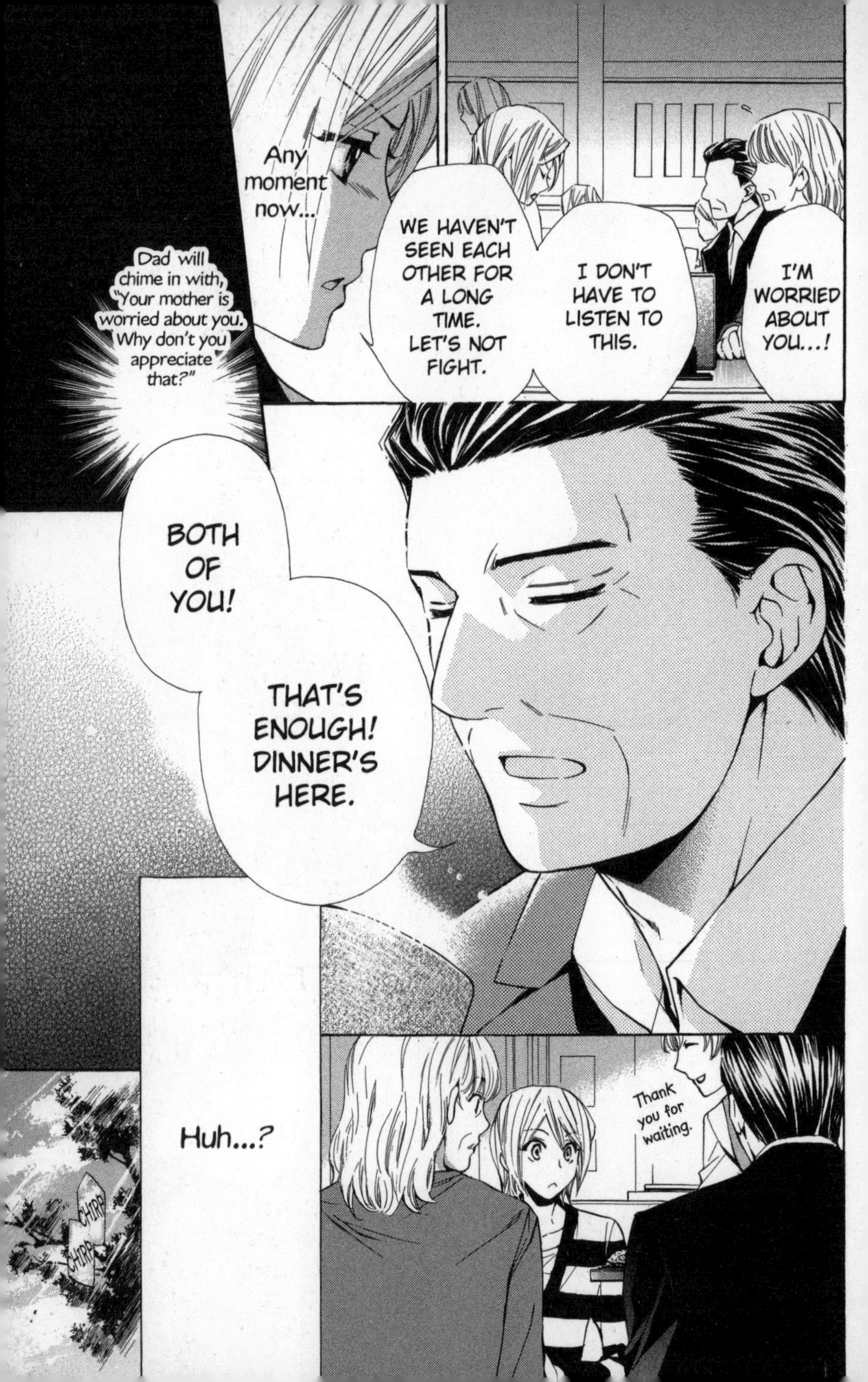
I'M WORRIED ABOUT YOU...!
I DON'T HAVE TO LISTEN TO THIS.
WE HAVEN'T SEEN EACH OTHER FOR A LONG TIME. LET'S NOT FIGHT.
Any moment now...
Dad will chime in with, "Your mother is worried about you. Why don't you appreciate that?"
BOTH OF YOU!
THAT'S ENOUGH! DINNER'S HERE.
Thank you for waiting.
Huh...?
CHIRP
CHIRP

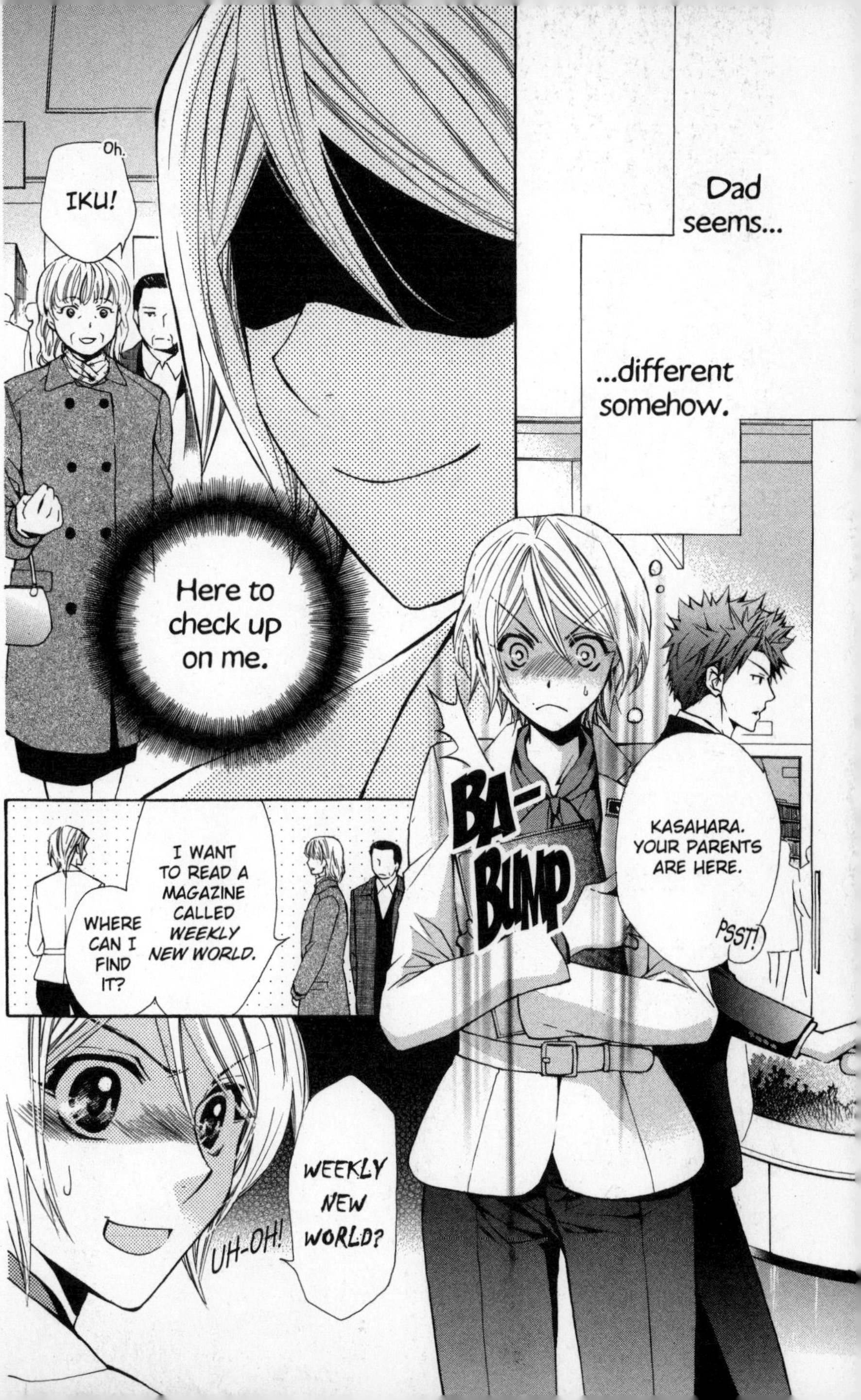
Dad seems...
...different somehow.
Oh.
IKU!
Here to check up on me.
PSST!
KASAHARA. YOUR PARENTS ARE HERE.
BA-BUMP
I WANT TO READ A MAGAZINE CALLED WEEKLY NEW WORLD.
WHERE CAN I FIND IT?
UH-OH!
WEEKLY NEW WORLD?

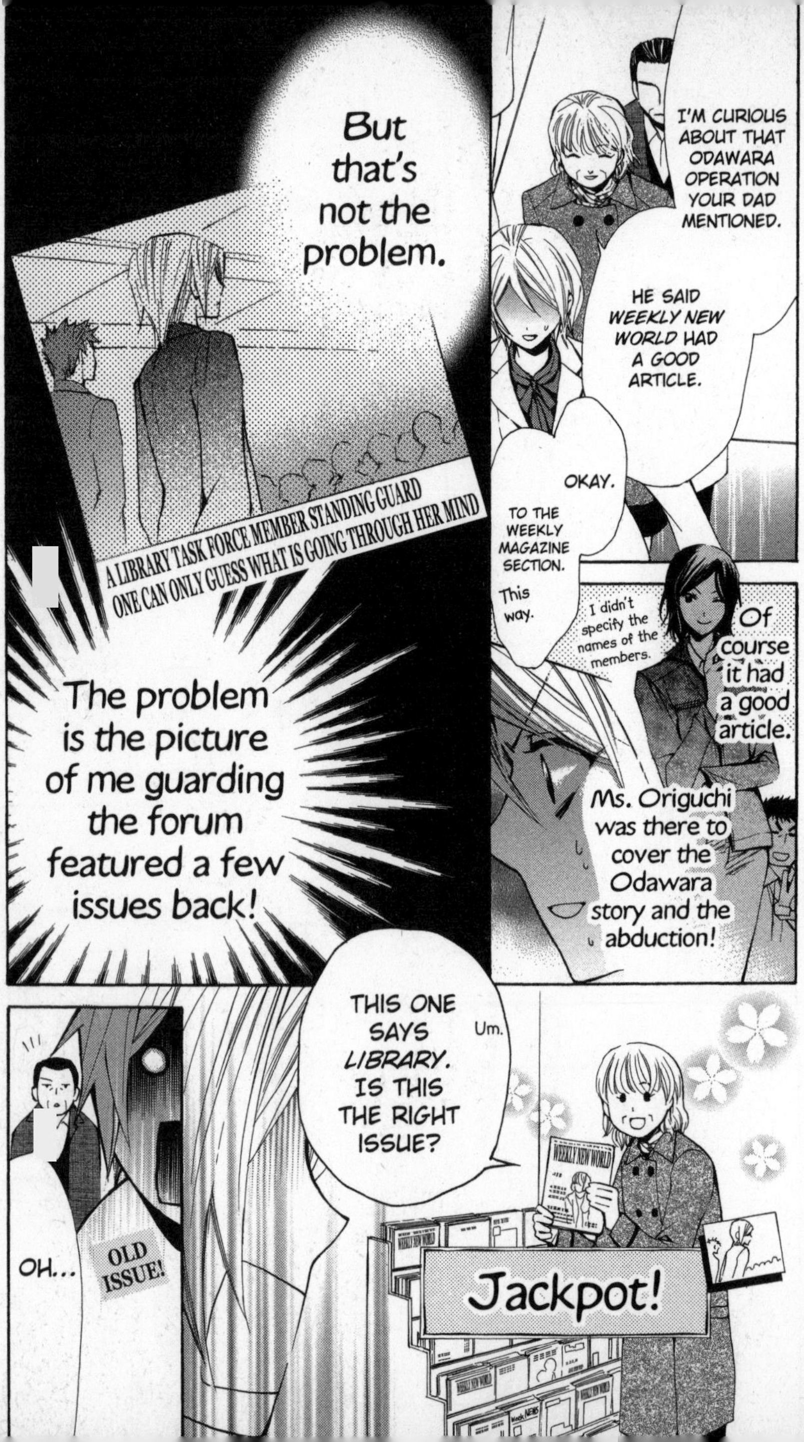

I'M CURIOUS ABOUT THAT ODAWARA OPERATION YOUR DAD MENTIONED.
HE SAID *WEEKLY NEW WORLD* HAD A GOOD ARTICLE.
OKAY.
TO THE WEEKLY MAGAZINE SECTION.
This way.
Of course it had a good article.
I didn't specify the names of the members.
Ms. Origuchi was there to cover the Odawara story and the abduction!
But that's not the problem.
A LIBRARY TASK FORCE MEMBER STANDING GUARD
ONE CAN ONLY GUESS WHAT IS GOING THROUGH HER MIND
The problem is the picture of me guarding the forum featured a few issues back!
Um.
THIS ONE SAYS *LIBRARY*. IS THIS THE RIGHT ISSUE?
WEEKLY NEW WORLD
Jackpot!
OH...
OLD ISSUE!

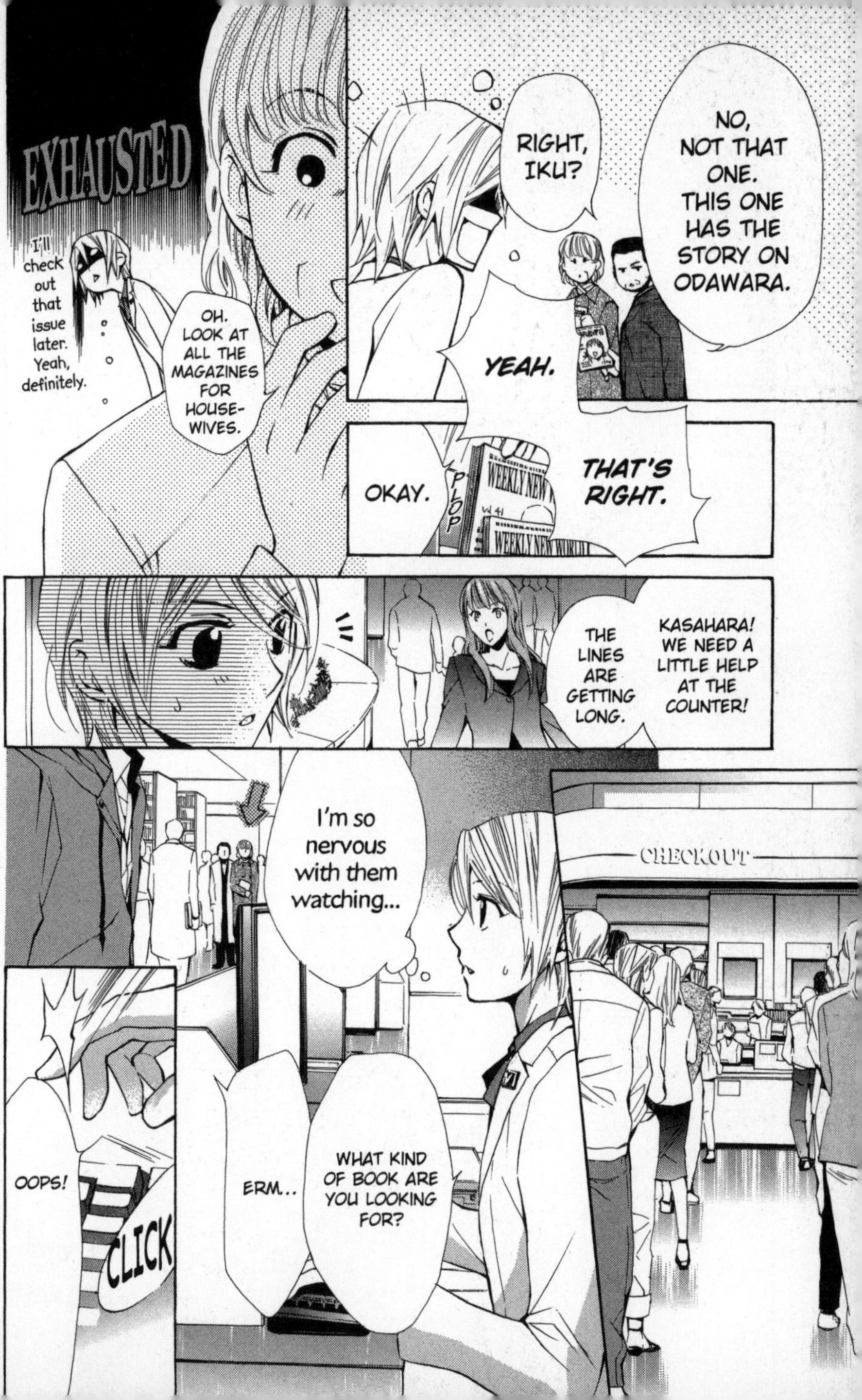
NO, NOT THAT ONE. THIS ONE HAS THE STORY ON ODAWARA.
RIGHT, IKU?
YEAH.
THAT'S RIGHT.
PLOP
OKAY.
OH. LOOK AT ALL THE MAGAZINES FOR HOUSE-WIVES.
EXHAUSTED
I'll check out that issue later. Yeah, definitely.
KASAHARA! WE NEED A LITTLE HELP AT THE COUNTER!
THE LINES ARE GETTING LONG.
I'm so nervous with them watching...
CHECKOUT
WHAT KIND OF BOOK ARE YOU LOOKING FOR?
ERM...
OOPS!
CLICK

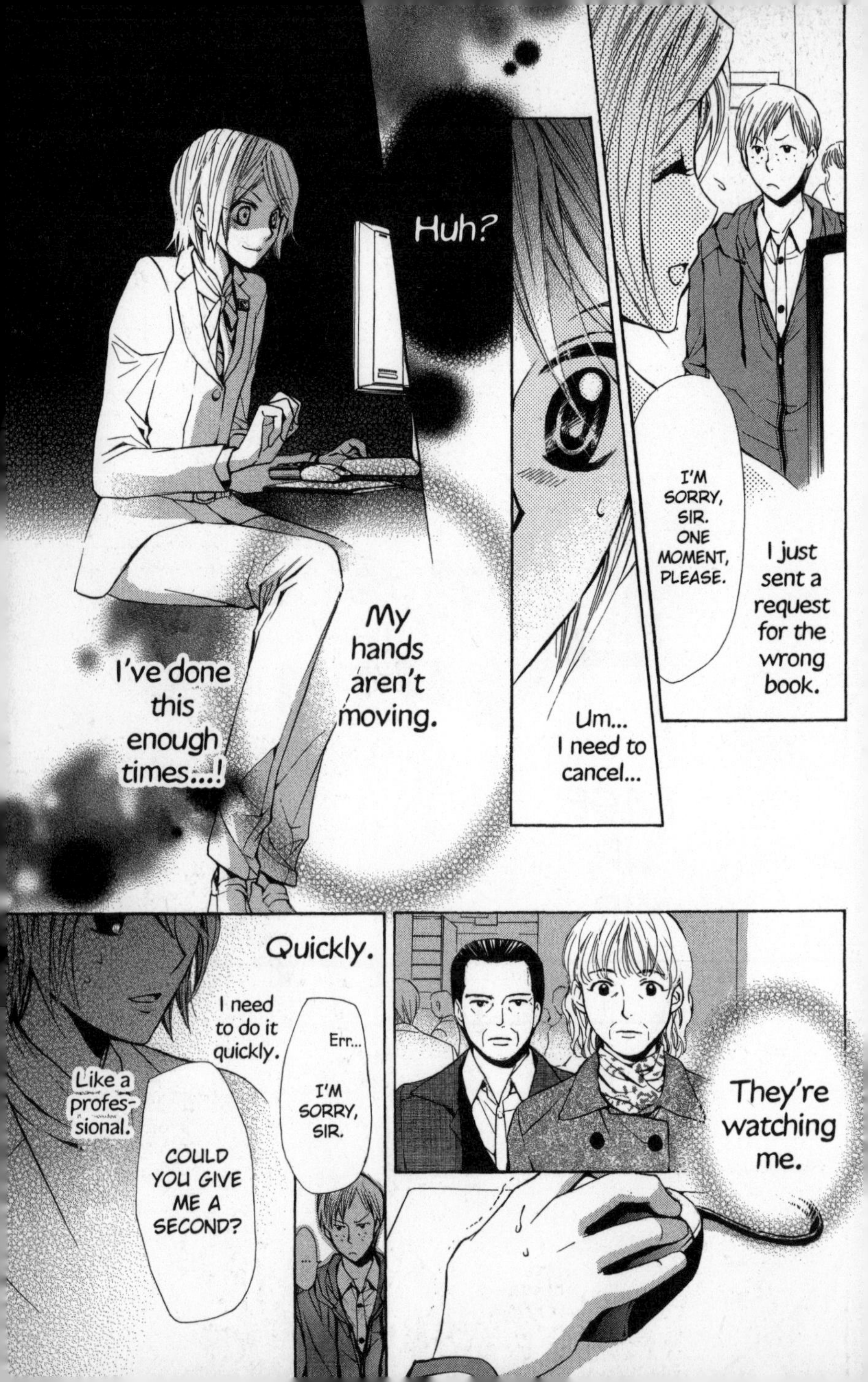
I just sent a request for the wrong book.
I'M SORRY, SIR. ONE MOMENT, PLEASE.
Um... I need to cancel...
Huh?
My hands aren't moving.
I've done this enough times...!
They're watching me.
Quickly.
I need to do it quickly.
Err...
I'M SORRY, SIR.
COULD YOU GIVE ME A SECOND?
Like a profes-sional.

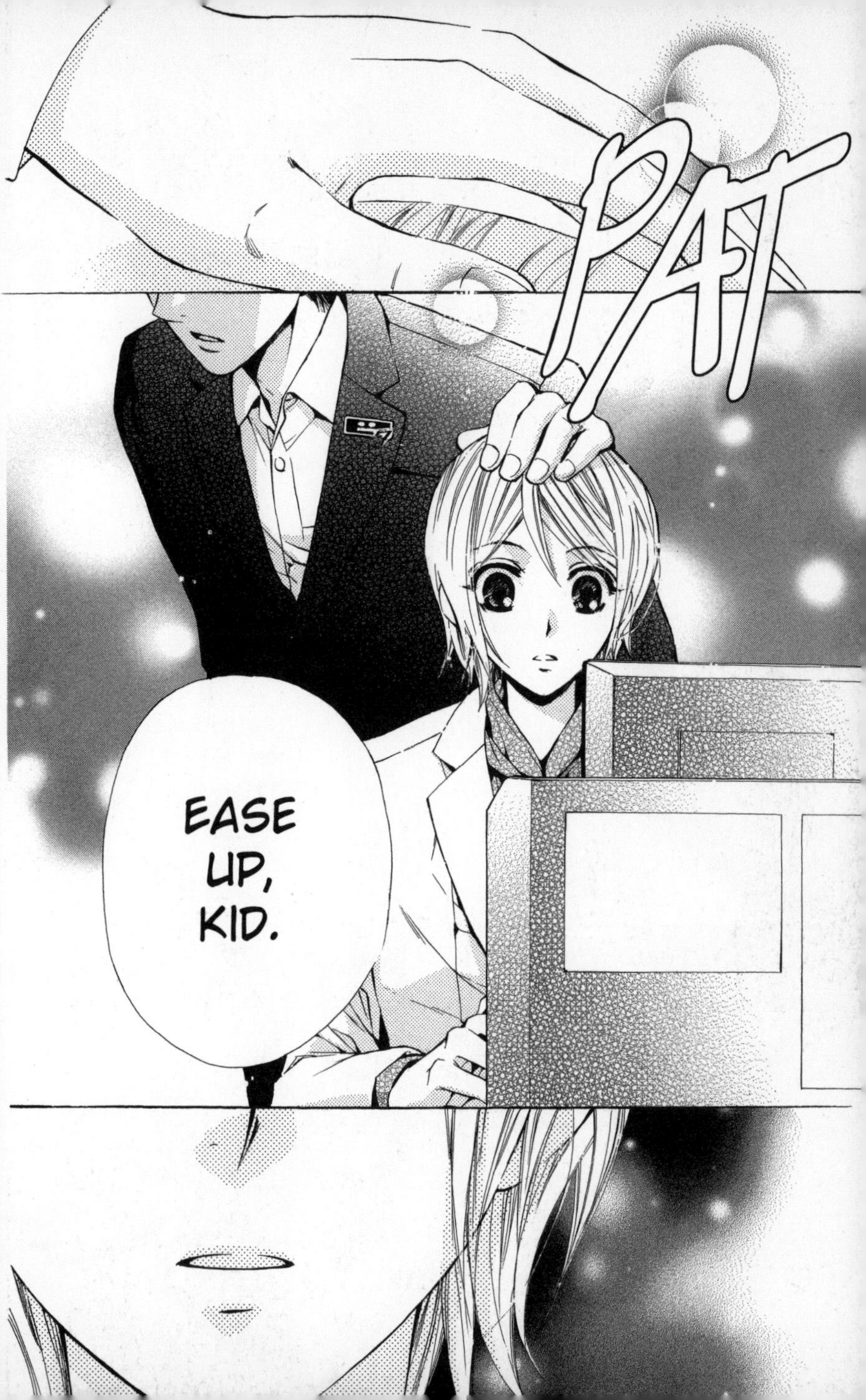
PAT
EASE UP, KID.

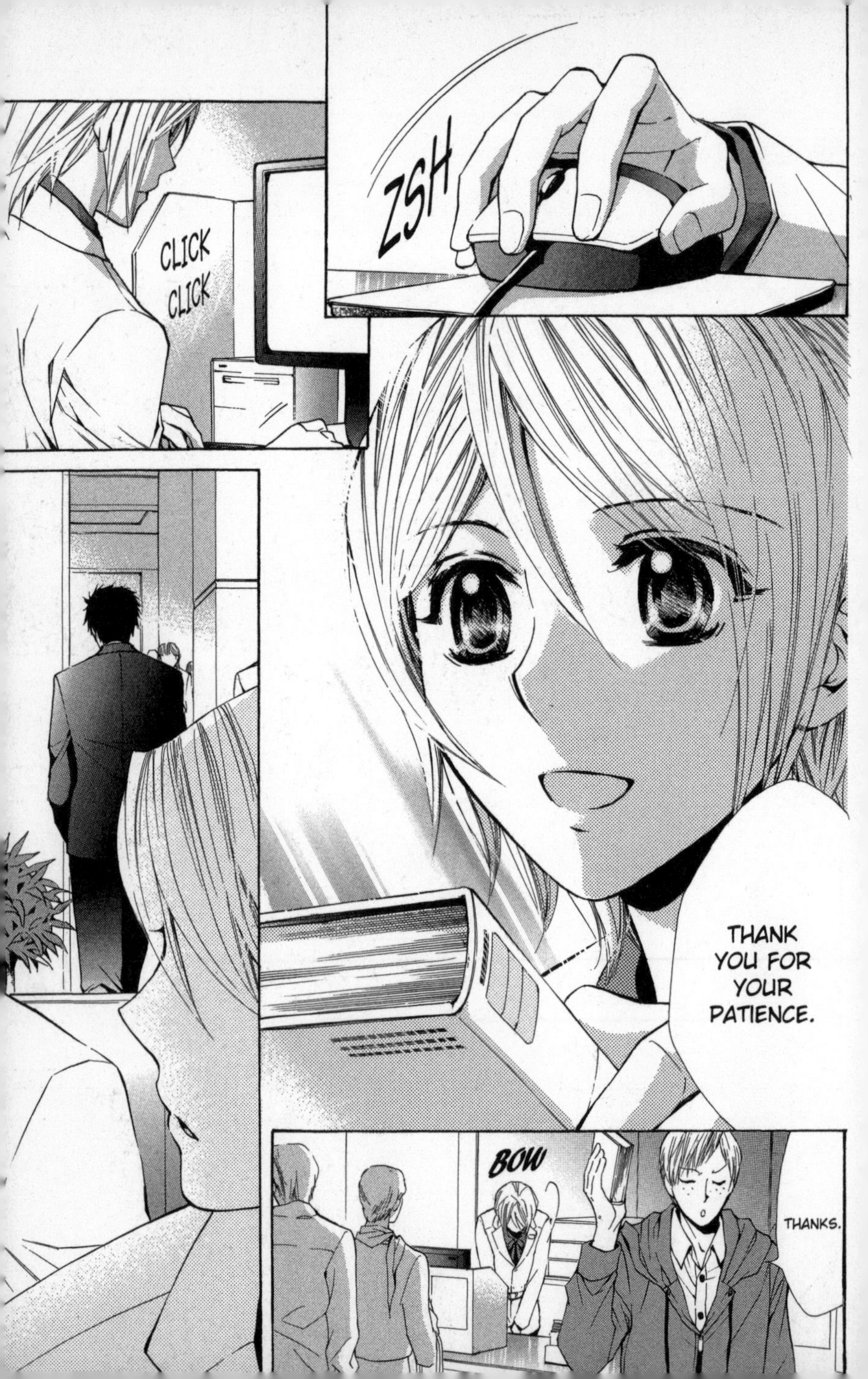
ZSH
CLICK CLICK
THANK YOU FOR YOUR PATIENCE.
BOW
THANKS.

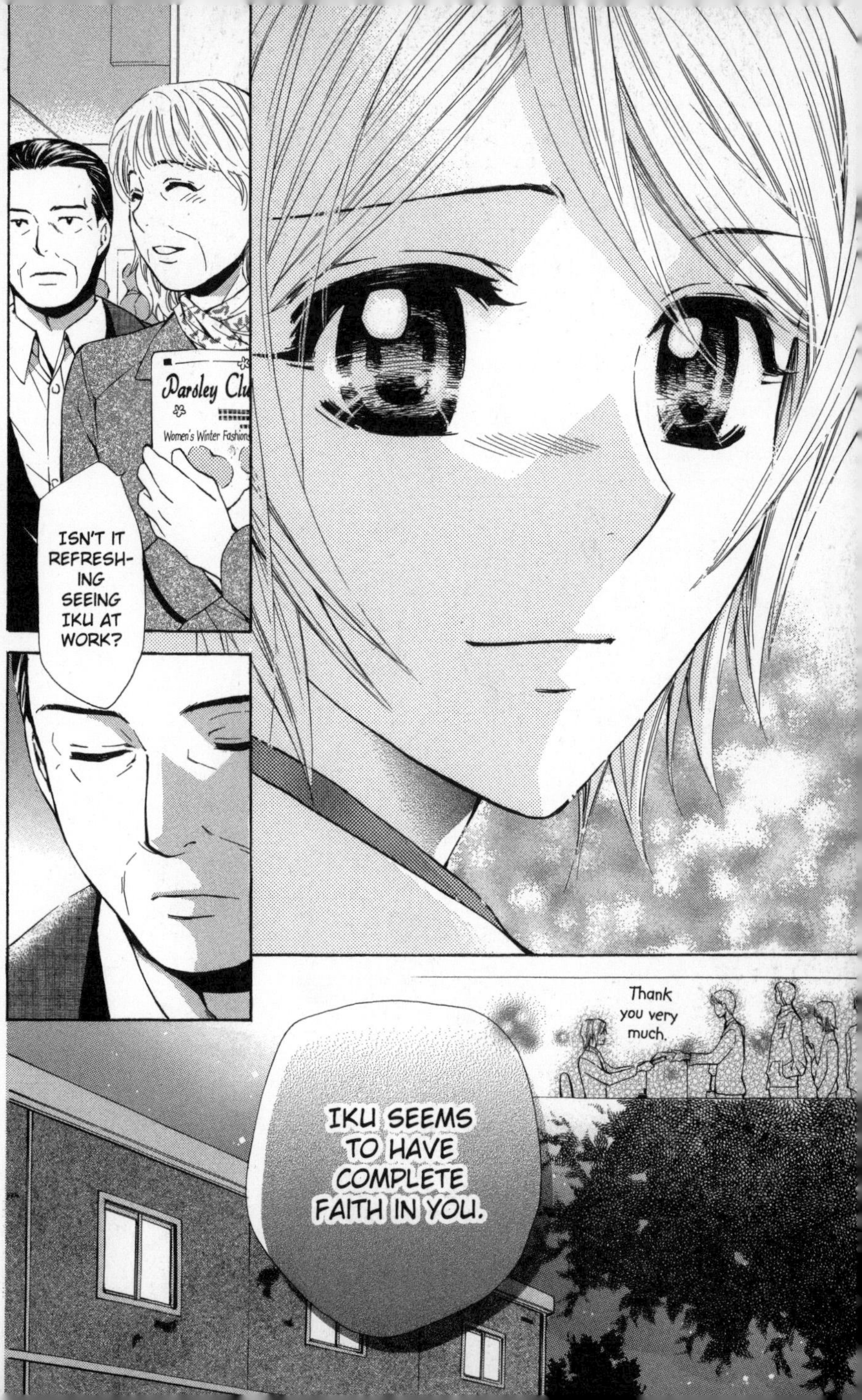
ISN'T IT REFRESHING SEEING IKU AT WORK?
Thank you very much.
IKU SEEMS TO HAVE COMPLETE FAITH IN YOU.

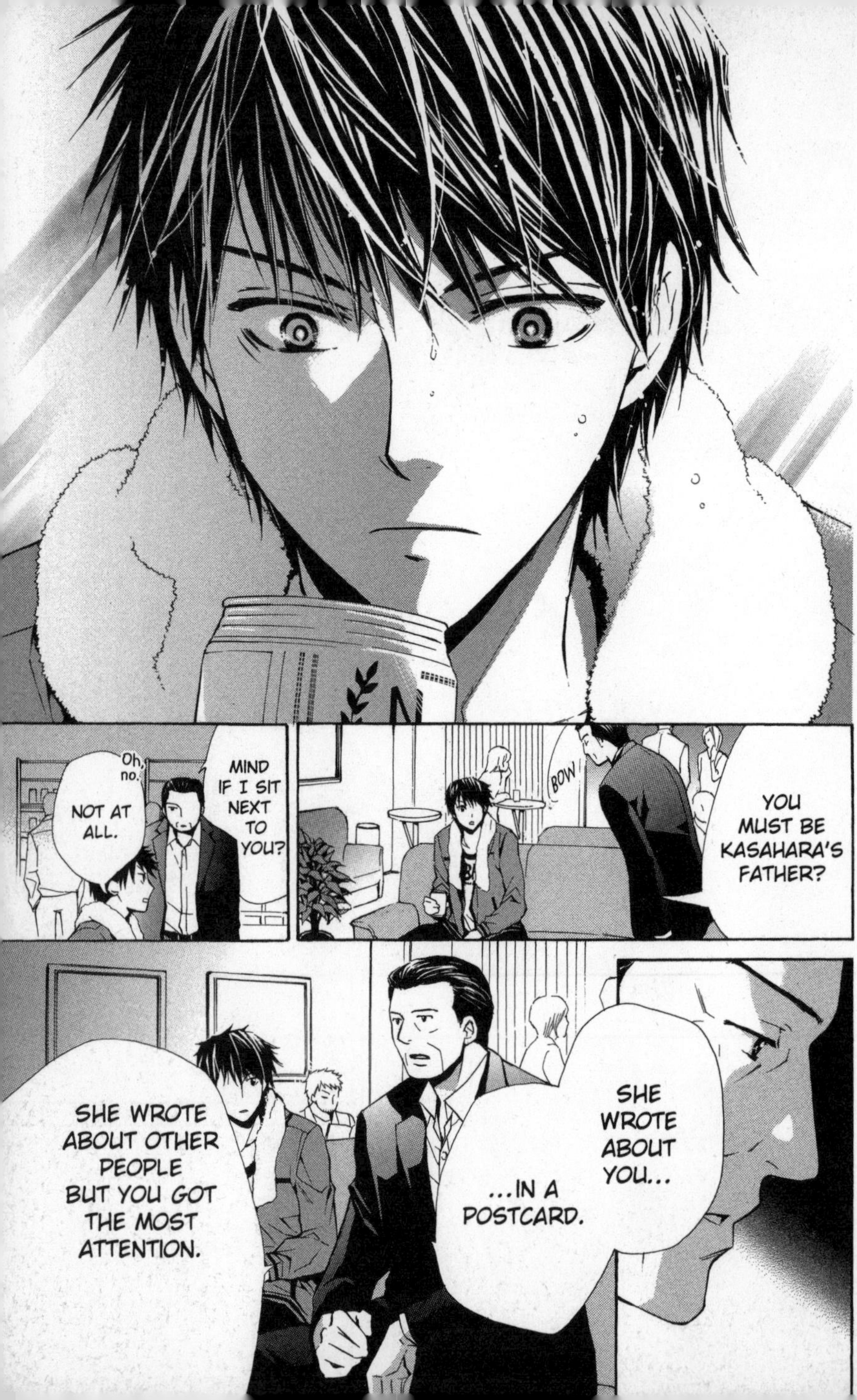
YOU MUST BE KASAHARA'S FATHER?
BOW
MIND IF I SIT NEXT TO YOU?
Oh, no.
NOT AT ALL.
SHE WROTE ABOUT YOU...
...IN A POSTCARD.
SHE WROTE ABOUT OTHER PEOPLE BUT YOU GOT THE MOST ATTENTION.

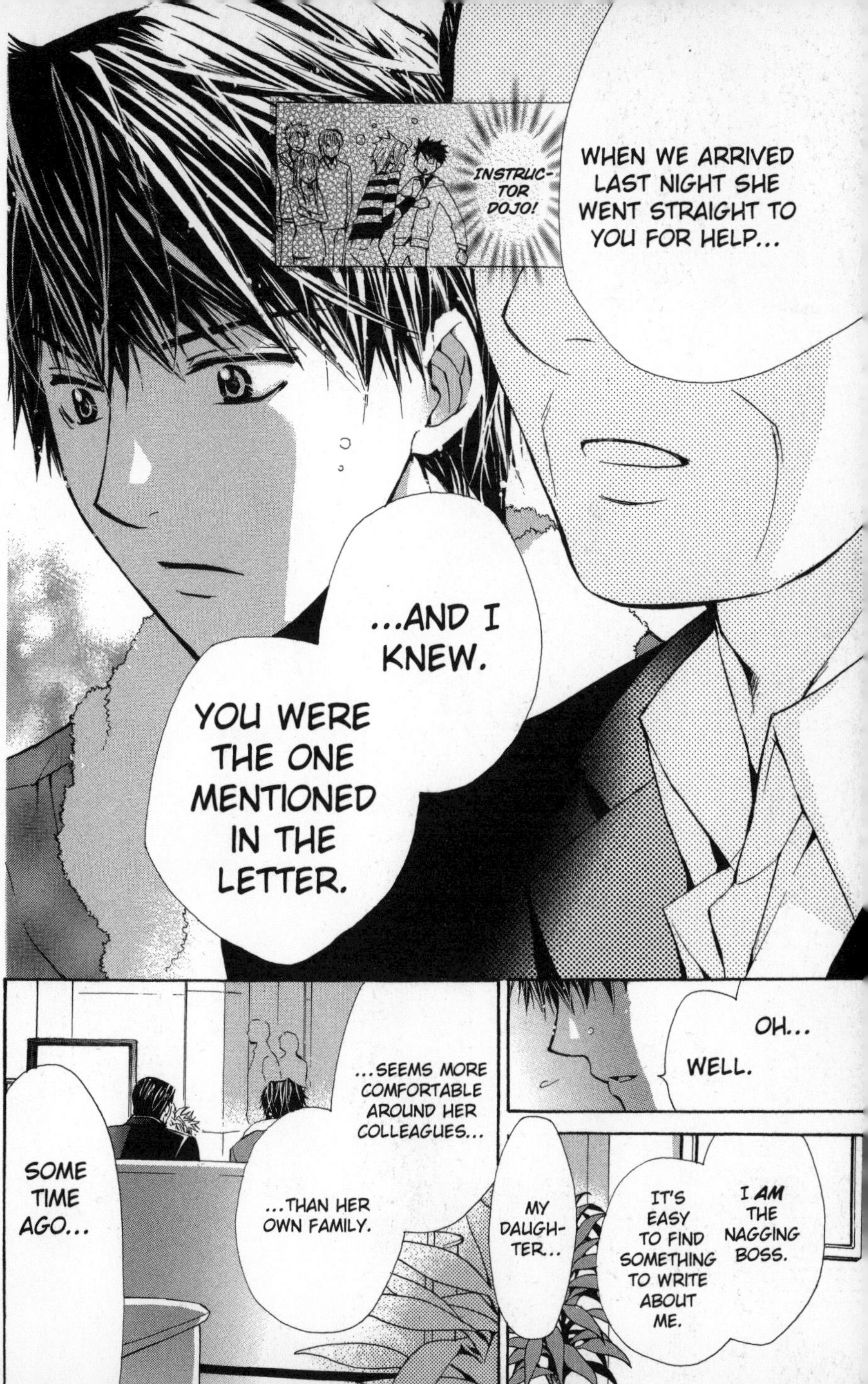
WHEN WE ARRIVED LAST NIGHT SHE WENT STRAIGHT TO YOU FOR HELP...
INSTRUCTOR DOJO!
...AND I KNEW.
YOU WERE THE ONE MENTIONED IN THE LETTER.
OH... WELL.
I *AM* THE NAGGING BOSS.
IT'S EASY TO FIND SOMETHING TO WRITE ABOUT ME.
MY DAUGHTER...
...SEEMS MORE COMFORTABLE AROUND HER COLLEAGUES...
...THAN HER OWN FAMILY.
SOME TIME AGO...

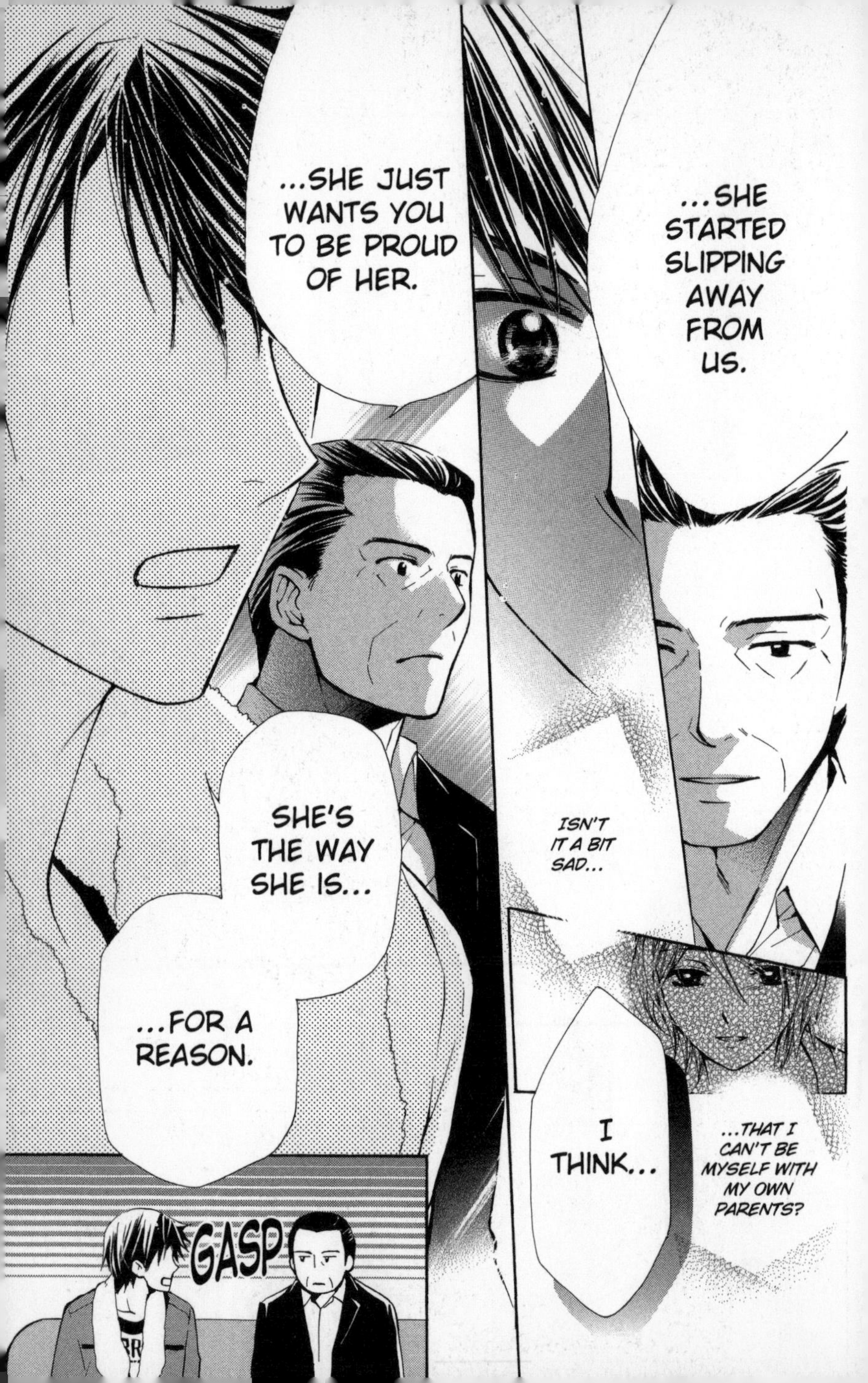
...SHE STARTED SLIPPING AWAY FROM US.
ISN'T IT A BIT SAD...
...THAT I CAN'T BE MYSELF WITH MY OWN PARENTS?
I THINK...
...SHE JUST WANTS YOU TO BE PROUD OF HER.
SHE'S THE WAY SHE IS...
...FOR A REASON.
GASP

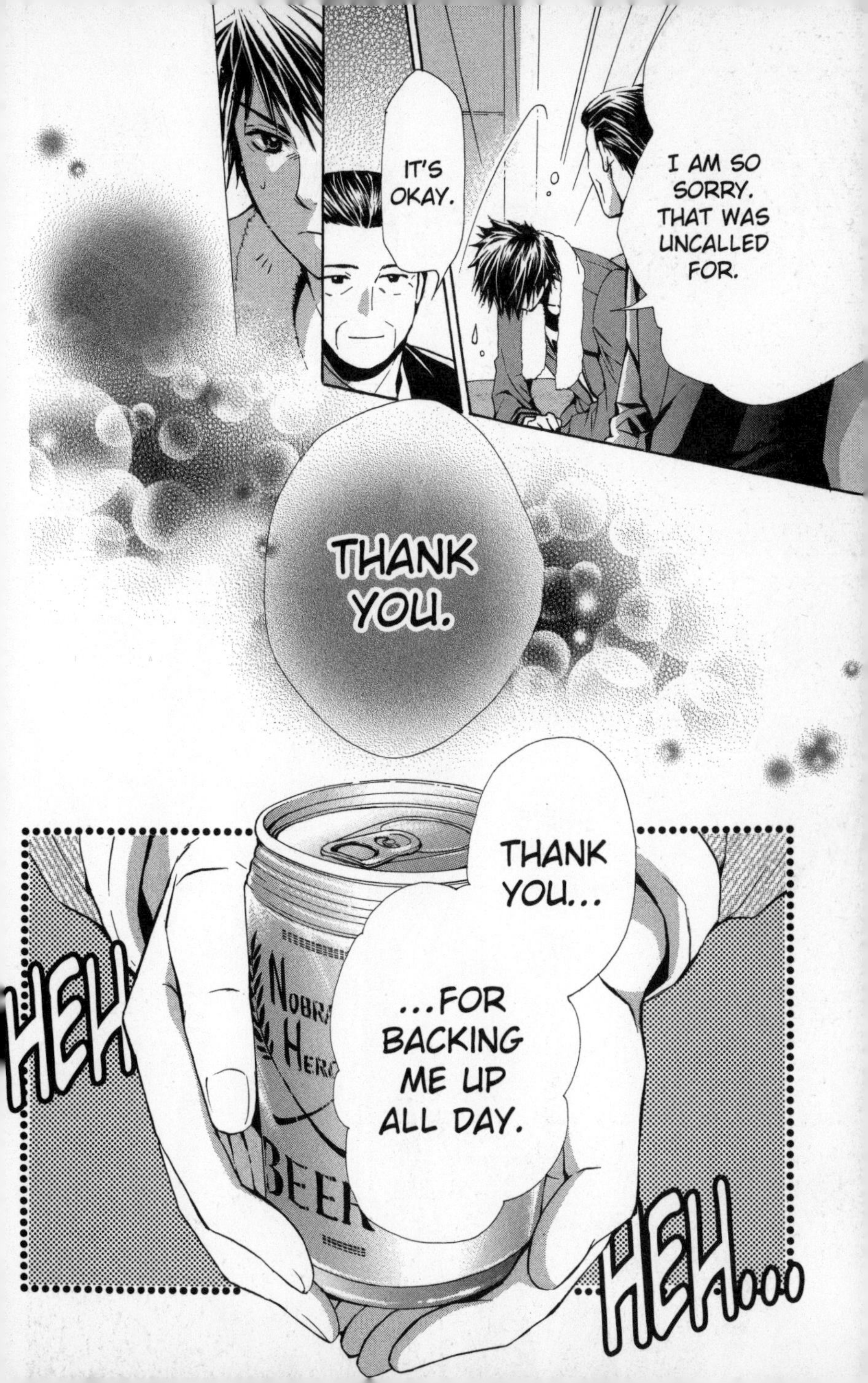
I AM SO SORRY. THAT WAS UNCALLED FOR.
IT'S OKAY.
THANK YOU.
THANK YOU...
...FOR BACKING ME UP ALL DAY.
HEH
HEH...

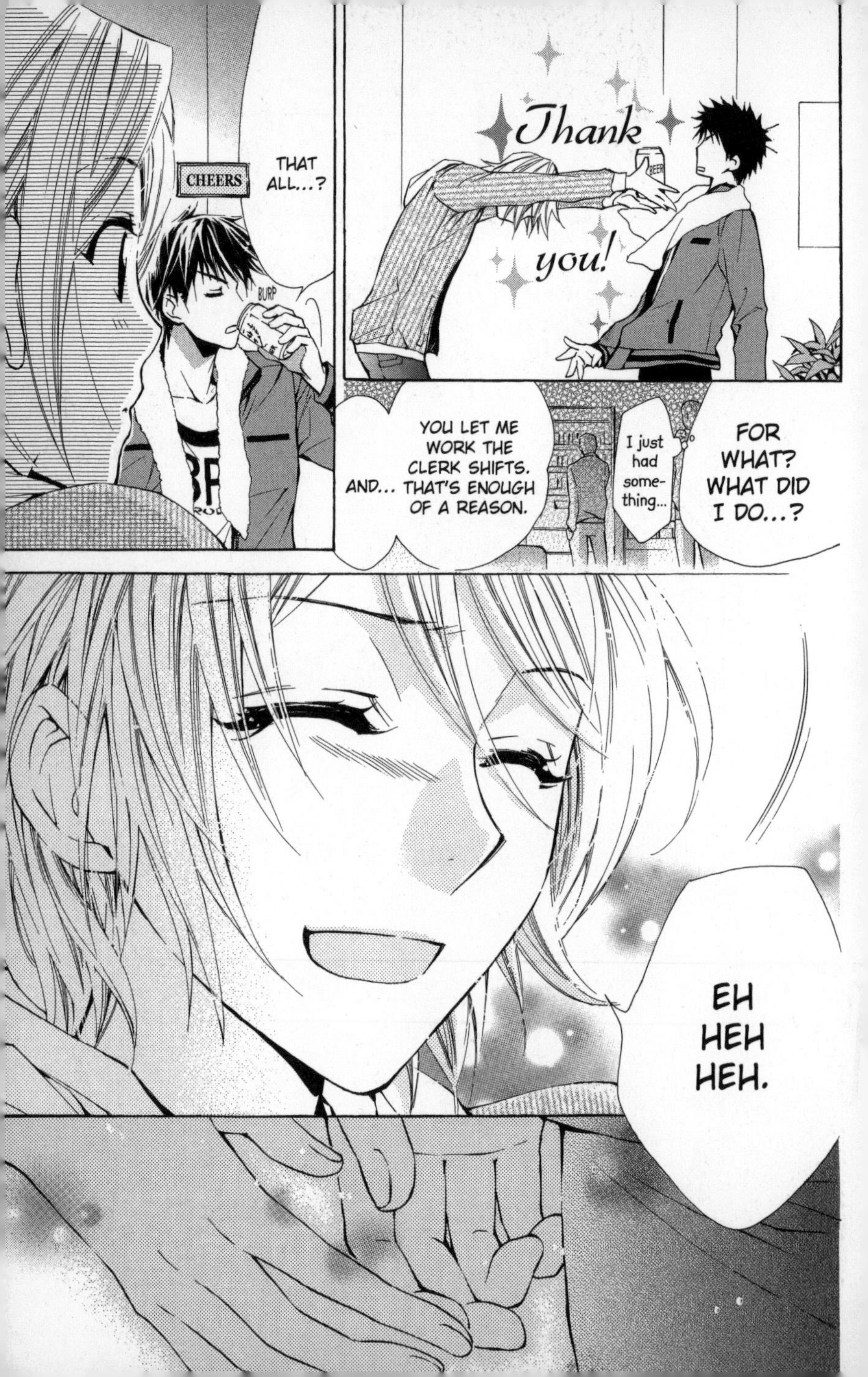
Thank you!
BEER
FOR WHAT? WHAT DID I DO...?
I just had something...
YOU LET ME WORK THE CLERK SHIFTS. AND... THAT'S ENOUGH OF A REASON.
CHEERS
THAT ALL...?
BURP
EH HEH HEH.

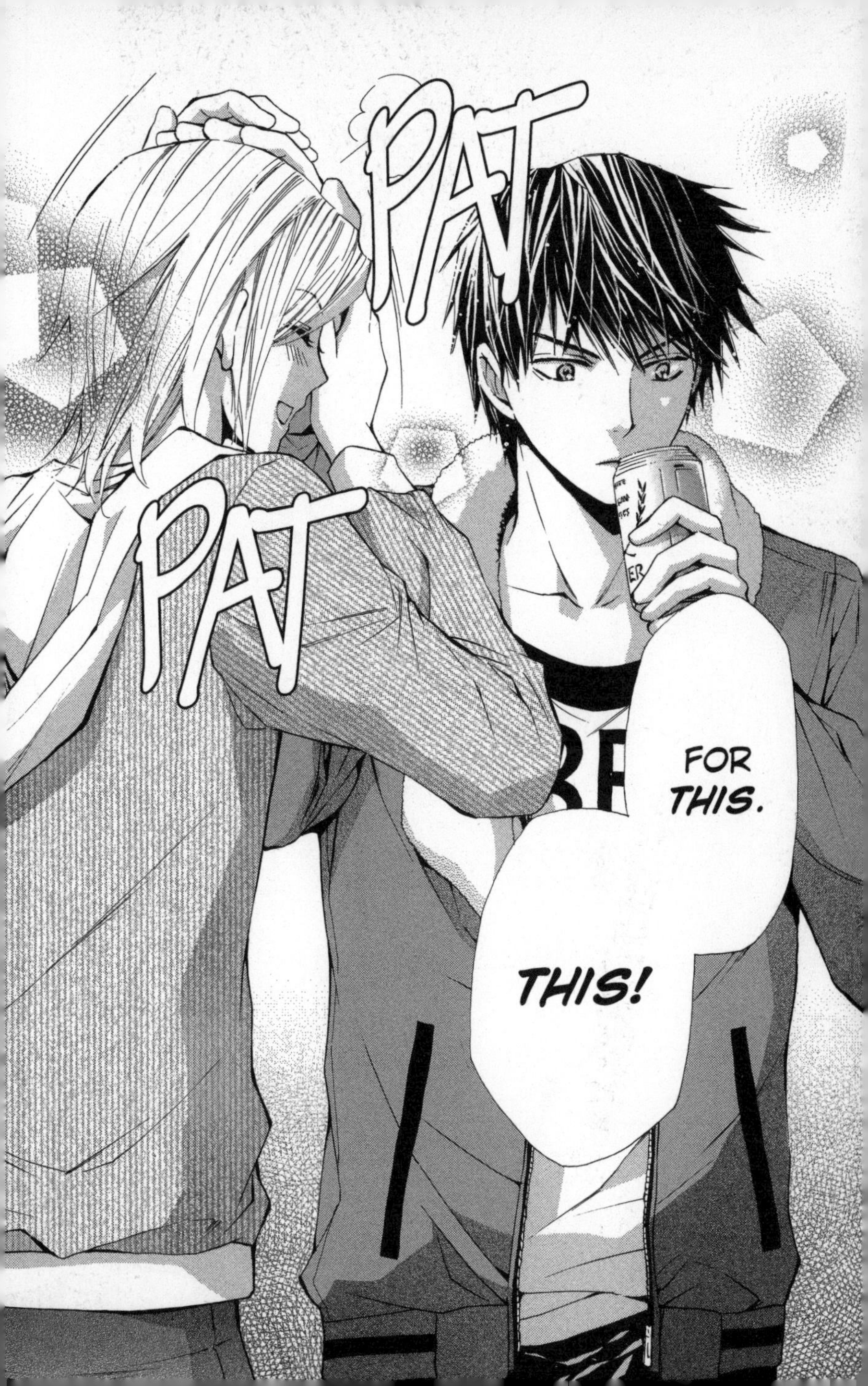
PAT
PAT
FOR THIS.
THIS!

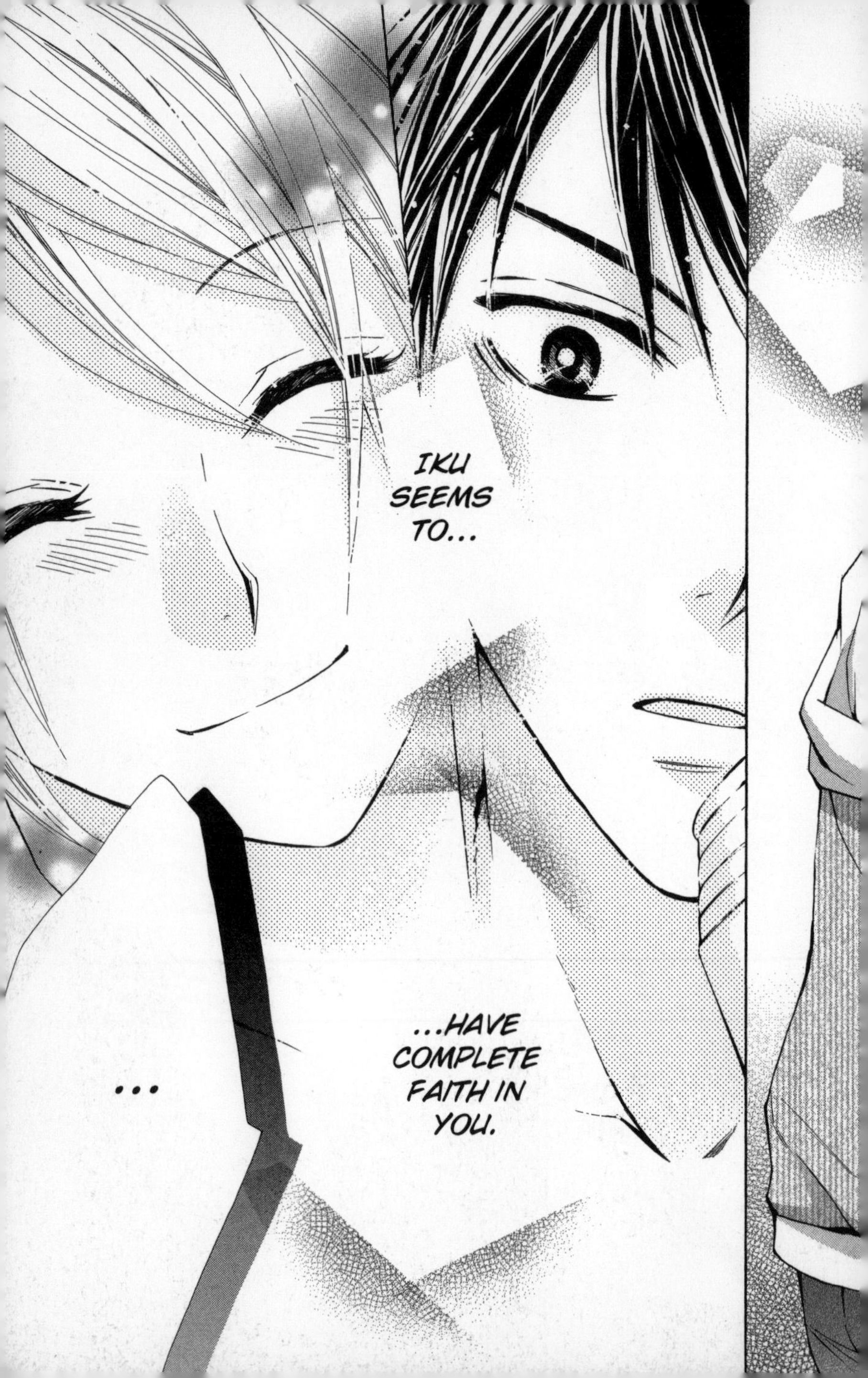
IKU SEEMS TO...
...HAVE COMPLETE FAITH IN YOU.
...

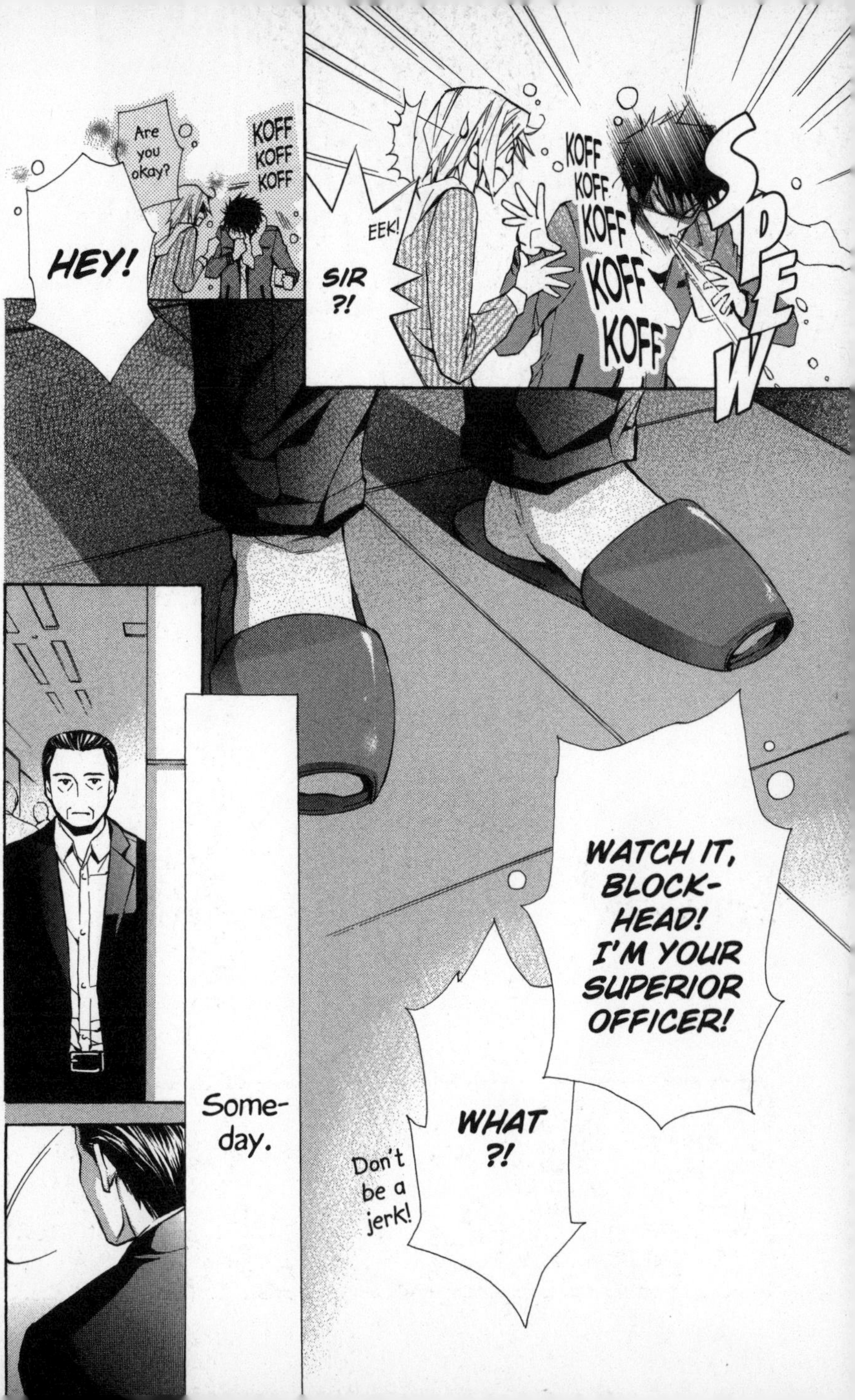
SPEW
KOFF KOFF KOFF KOFF KOFF
EEK!
SIR ?!
KOFF KOFF KOFF
Are you okay?
HEY!
WATCH IT, BLOCK-HEAD! I'M YOUR SUPERIOR OFFICER!
WHAT ?!
Don't be a jerk!
Some-day.

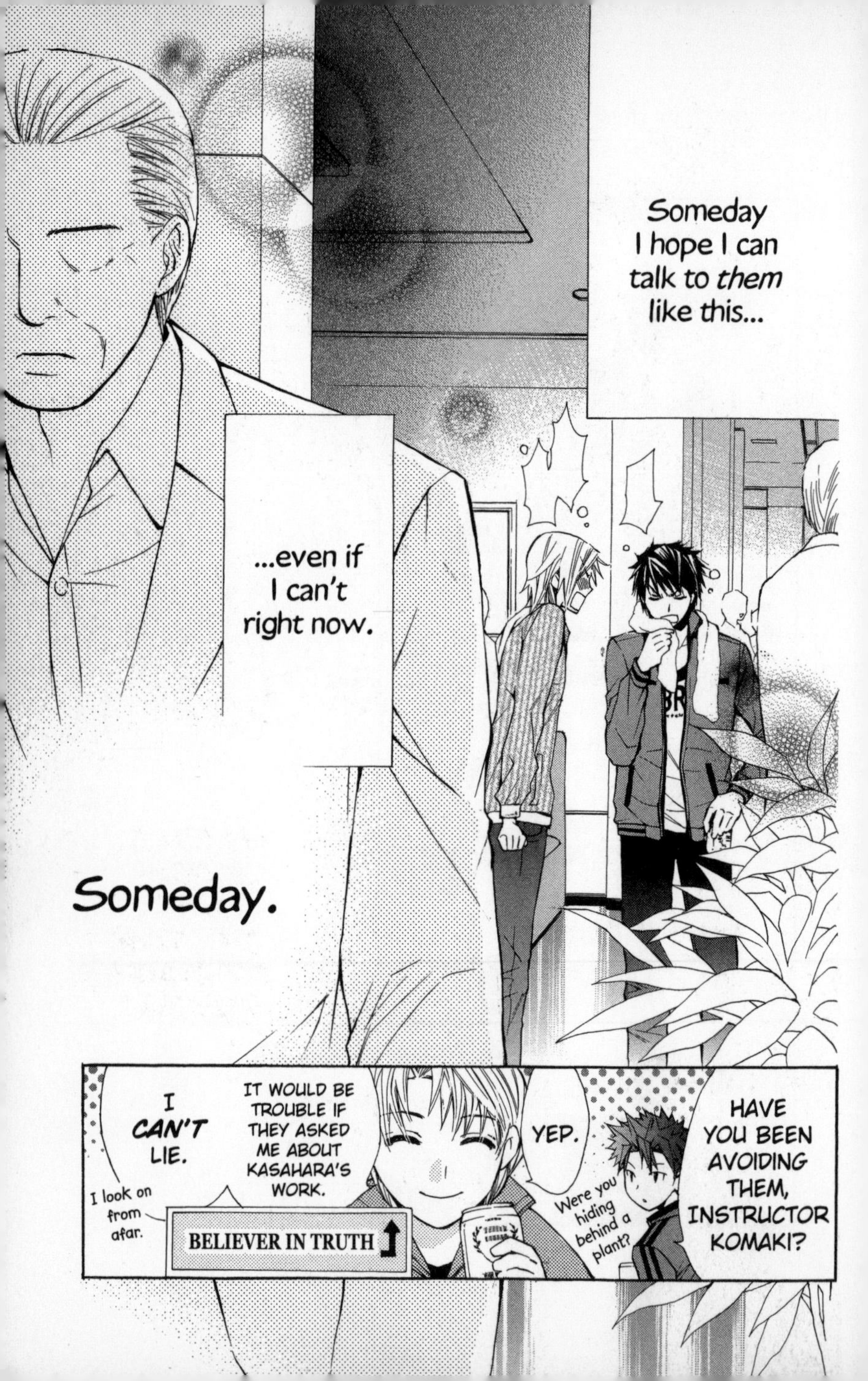
Someday I hope I can talk to *them* like this...
...even if I can't right now.
Someday.
HAVE YOU BEEN AVOIDING THEM, INSTRUCTOR KOMAKI?
Were you hiding behind a plant?
YEP.
IT WOULD BE TROUBLE IF THEY ASKED ME ABOUT KASAHARA'S WORK.
I **CAN'T** LIE.
I look on from afar.
BELIEVER IN TRUTH

Festival of Nicknames

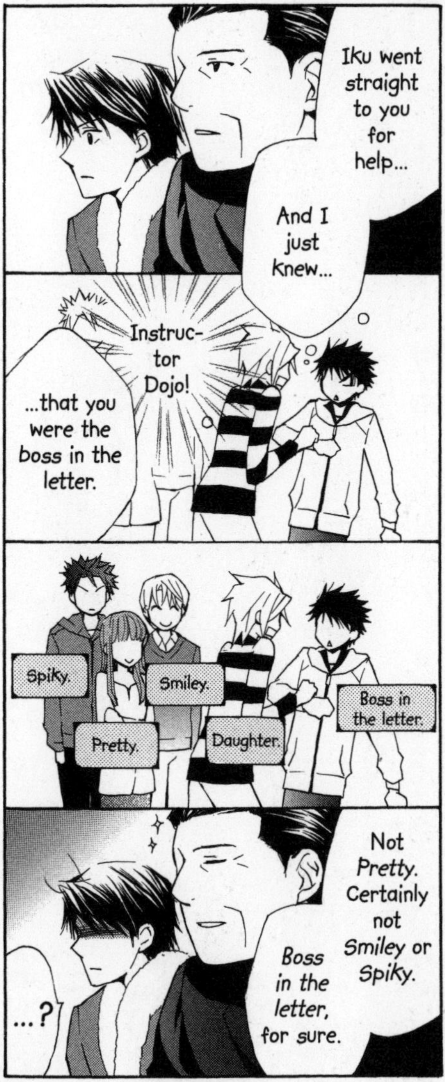
Iku went straight to you for help...
And I just knew...
Instructor Dojo!
...that you were the boss in the letter.
Boss in the letter.
Daughter.
Smiley.
Pretty.
Spiky.
Not Pretty. Certainly not Smiley or Spiky.
Boss in the letter, for sure.
...?

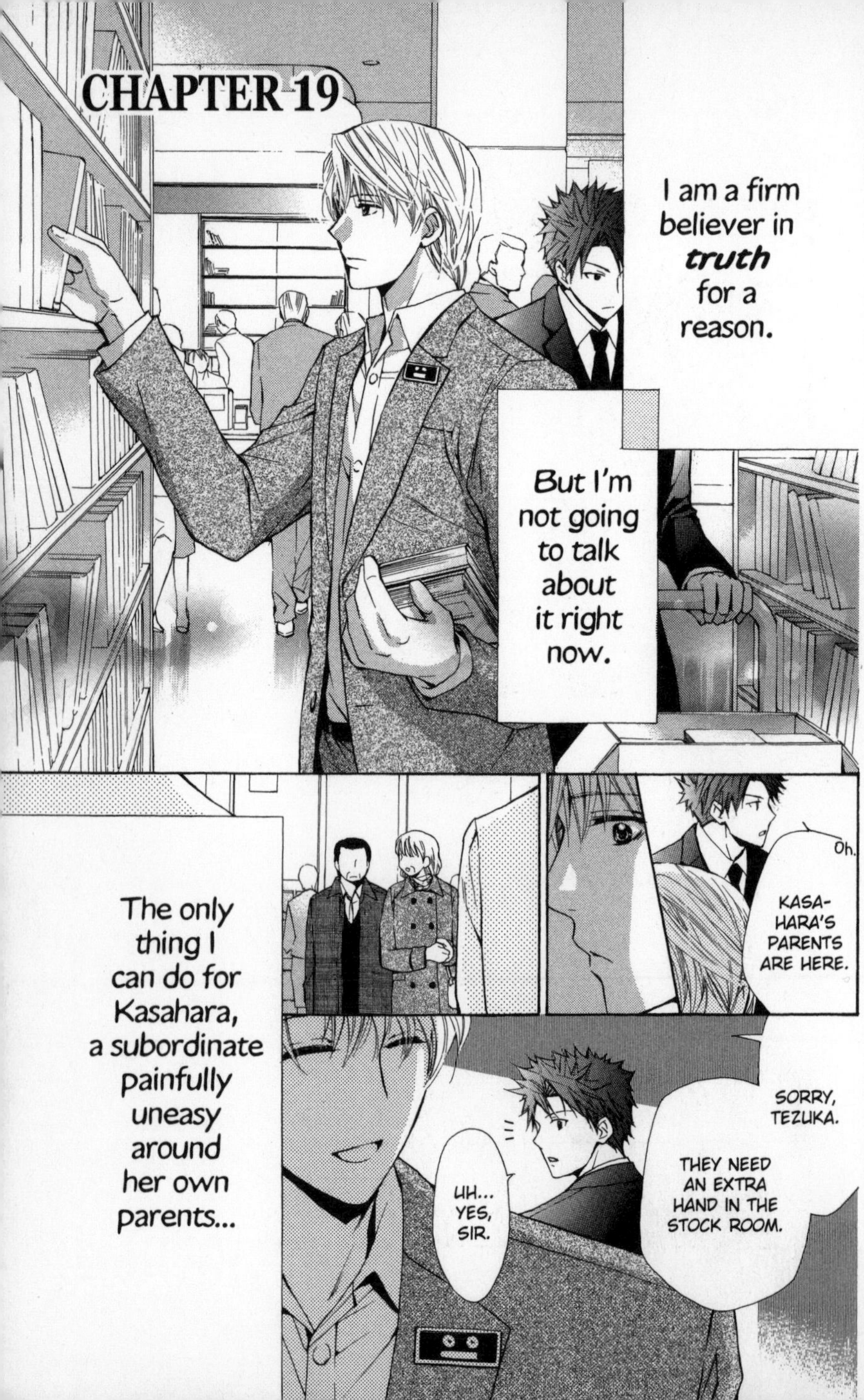
CHAPTER 19
I am a firm believer in truth for a reason.
But I'm not going to talk about it right now.
Oh.
KASA-HARA'S PARENTS ARE HERE.
The only thing I can do for Kasahara, a subordinate painfully uneasy around her own parents...
SORRY, TEZUKA.
THEY NEED AN EXTRA HAND IN THE STOCK ROOM.
UH... YES, SIR.

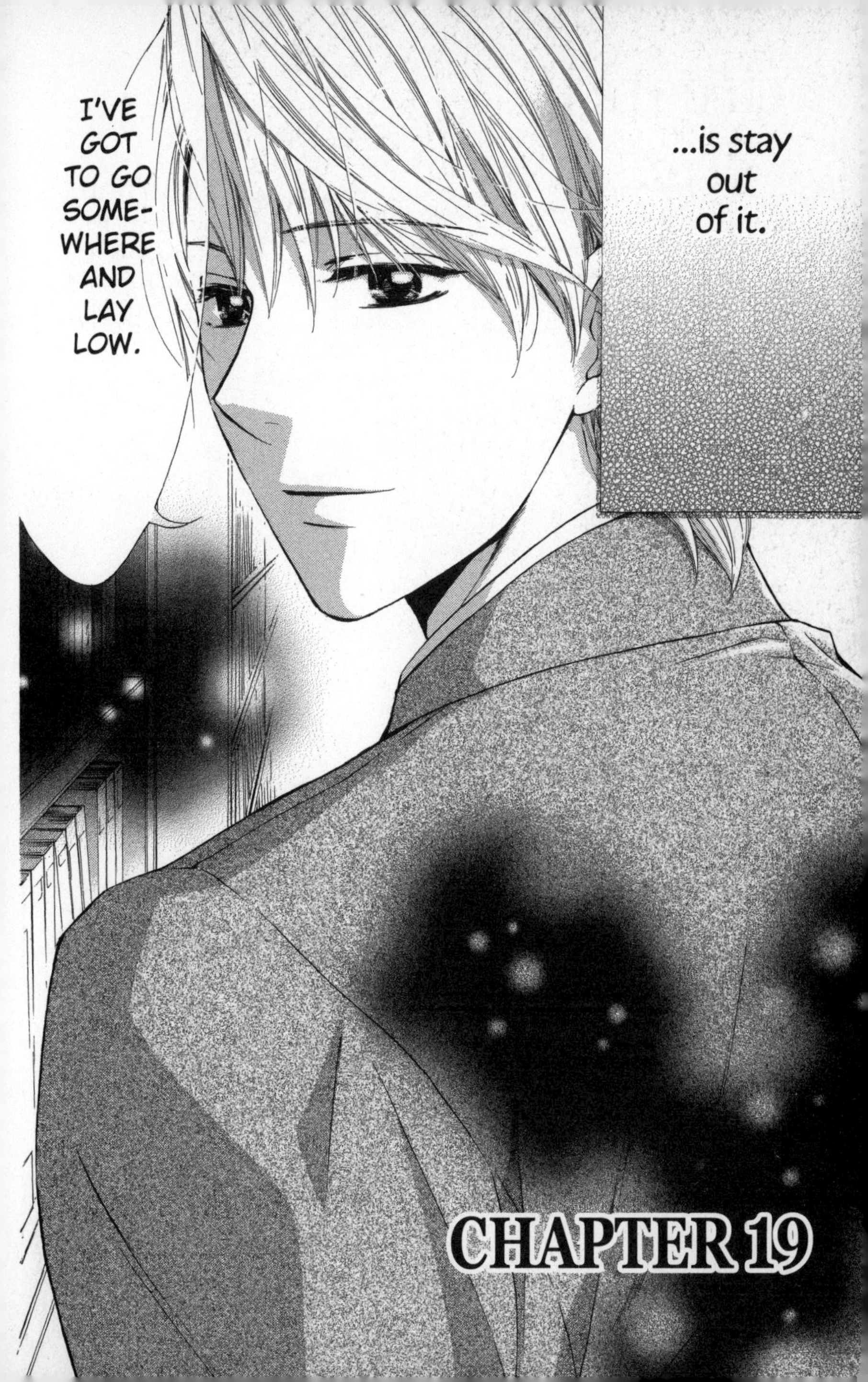
...is stay out of it.
I'VE GOT TO GO SOME-WHERE AND LAY LOW.
CHAPTER 19

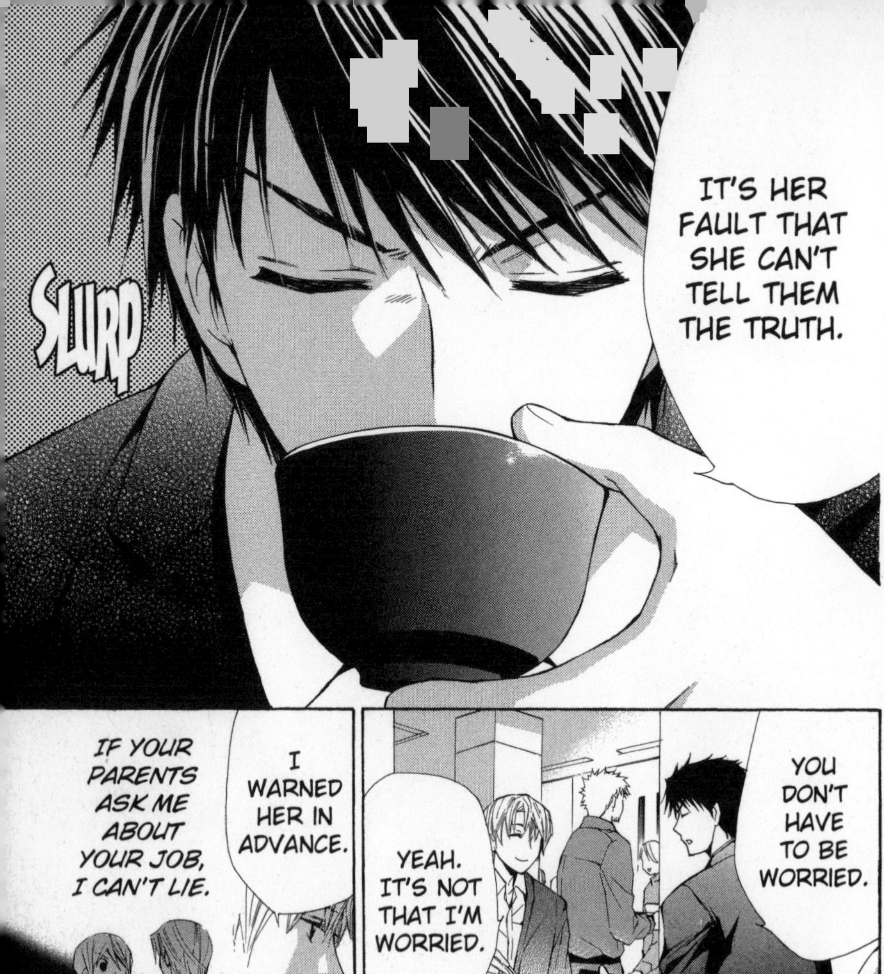
IT'S HER FAULT THAT SHE CAN'T TELL THEM THE TRUTH.
SLURP
YOU DON'T HAVE TO BE WORRIED.
YEAH. IT'S NOT THAT I'M WORRIED.
I WARNED HER IN ADVANCE.
IF YOUR PARENTS ASK ME ABOUT YOUR JOB, I CAN'T LIE.

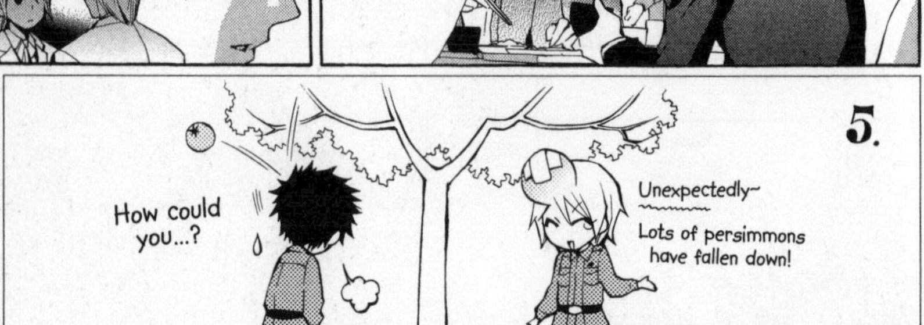
5.
Unexpectedly~
Lots of persimmons have fallen down!
How could you...?

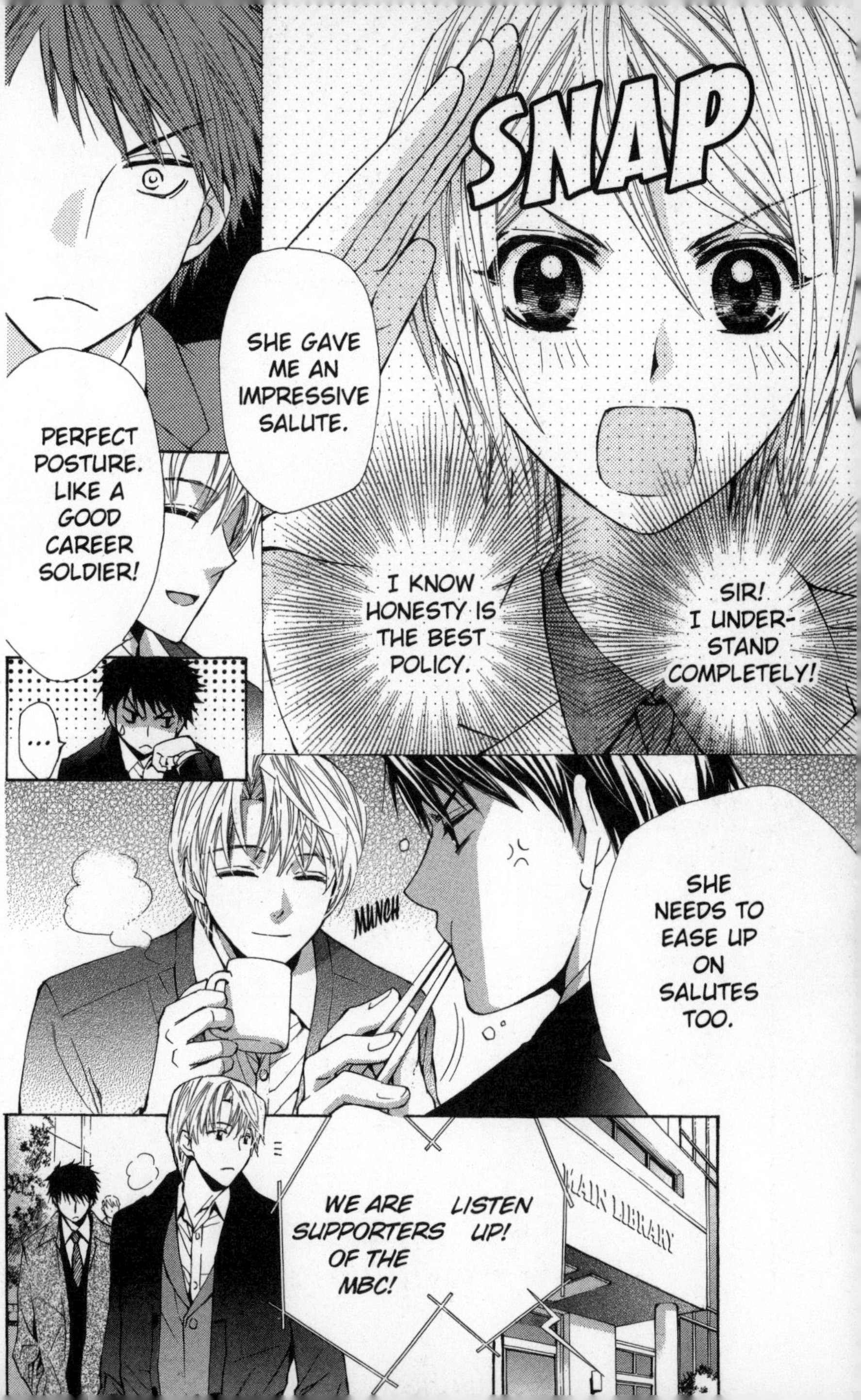
SNAP
SIR! I UNDERSTAND COMPLETELY!
I KNOW HONESTY IS THE BEST POLICY.
SHE GAVE ME AN IMPRESSIVE SALUTE.
PERFECT POSTURE. LIKE A GOOD CAREER SOLDIER!
...
SHE NEEDS TO EASE UP ON SALUTES TOO.
MUNCH
LISTEN UP!
WE ARE SUPPORTERS OF THE MBC!
MAIN LIBRARY

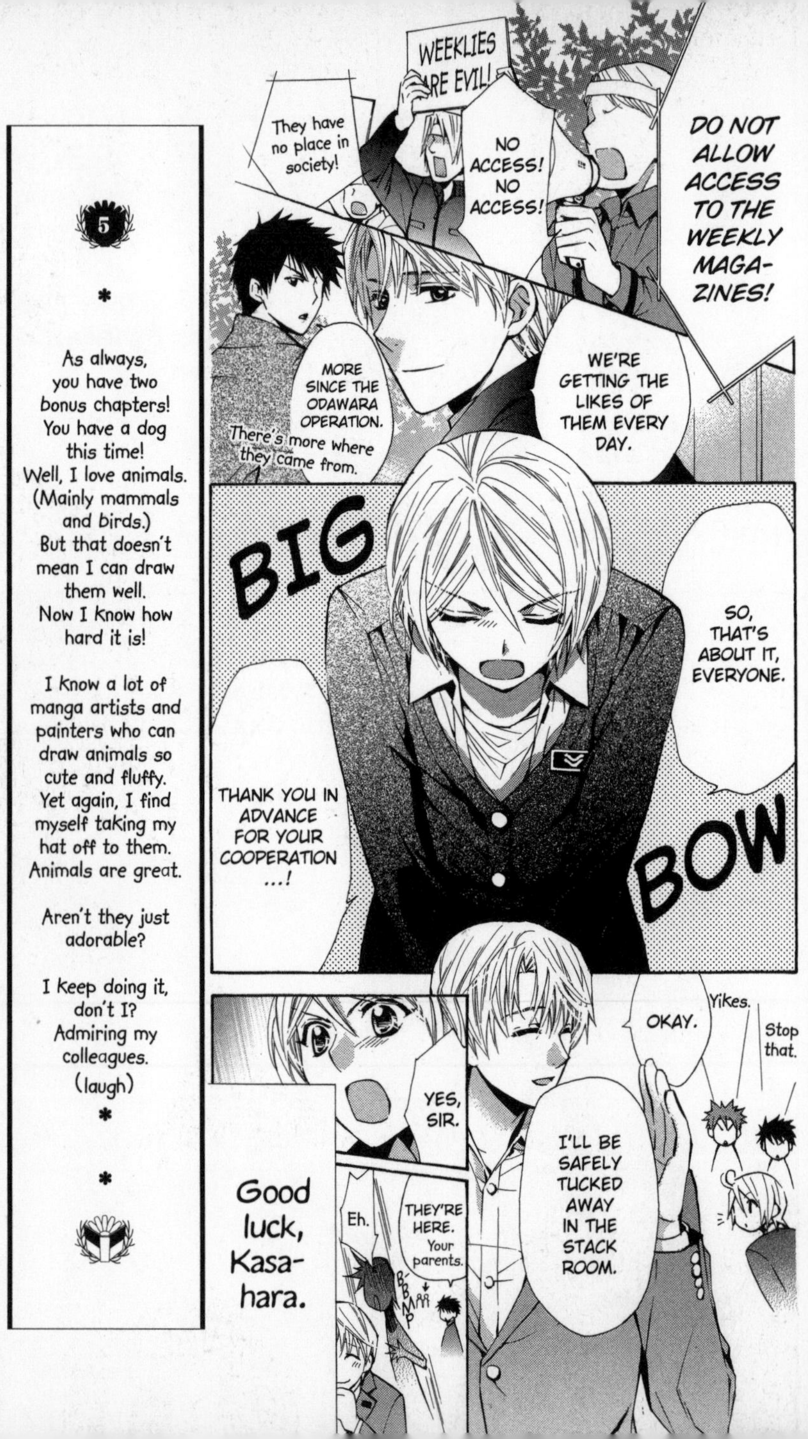
DO NOT ALLOW ACCESS TO THE WEEKLY MAGAZINES!
NO ACCESS! NO ACCESS!
WEEKLIES ARE EVIL!
They have no place in society!
WE'RE GETTING THE LIKES OF THEM EVERY DAY.
MORE SINCE THE ODAWARA OPERATION.
There's more where they came from.
SO, THAT'S ABOUT IT, EVERYONE.
BIG BOW
THANK YOU IN ADVANCE FOR YOUR COOPERATION ...!
Stop that.
Yikes.
OKAY.
I'LL BE SAFELY TUCKED AWAY IN THE STACK ROOM.
YES, SIR.
THEY'RE HERE.
Your parents.
Eh.
Good luck, Kasahara.

5

*

As always, you have two bonus chapters! You have a dog this time! Well, I love animals. (Mainly mammals and birds.) But that doesn't mean I can draw them well. Now I know how hard it is!

I know a lot of manga artists and painters who can draw animals so cute and fluffy. Yet again, I find myself taking my hat off to them. Animals are great.

Aren't they just adorable?

I keep doing it, don't I? Admiring my colleagues. (laugh)

*

*

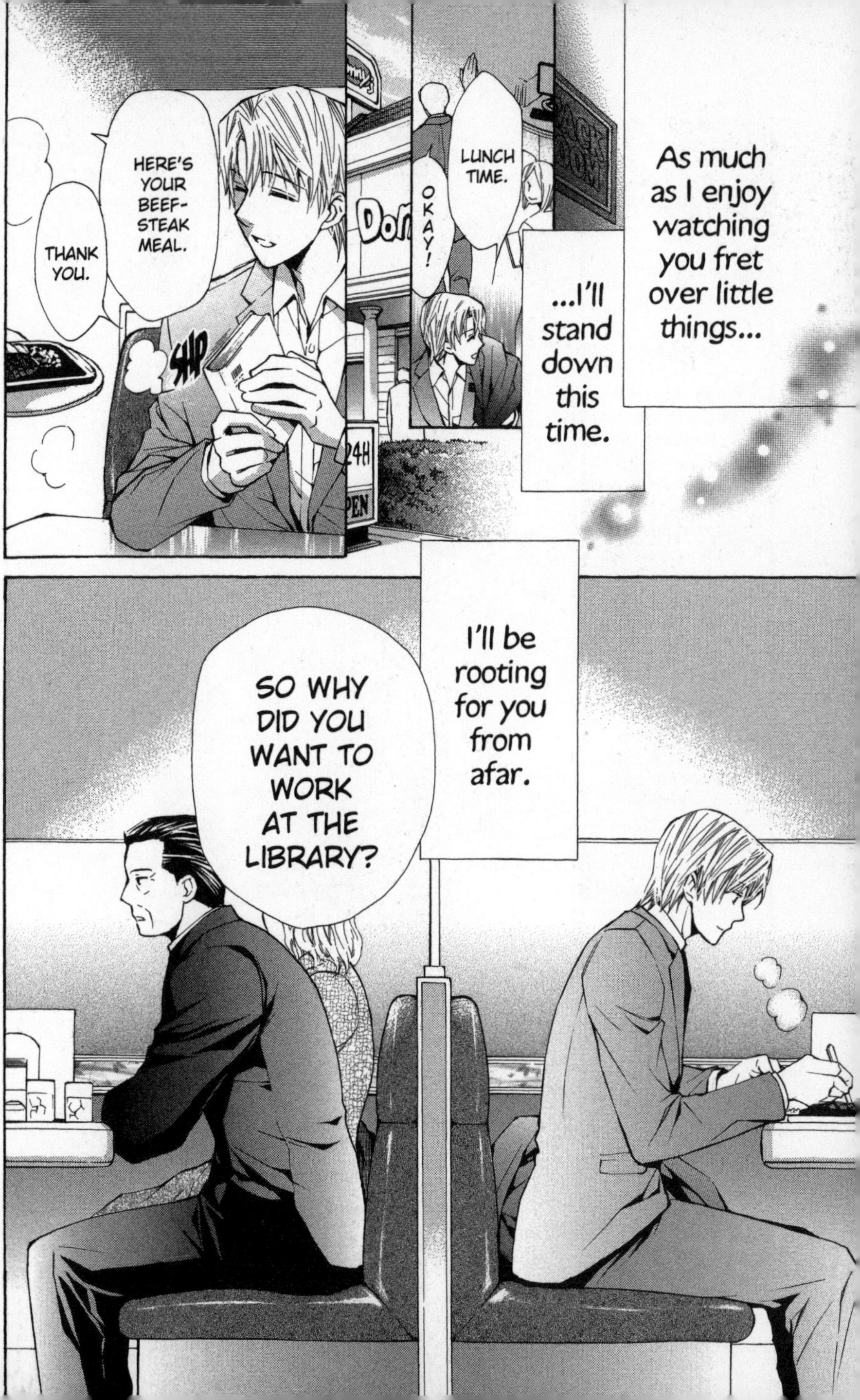

As much as I enjoy watching you fret over little things...
...I'll stand down this time.
LUNCH TIME.
OKAY!
24H
HERE'S YOUR BEEF-STEAK MEAL.
THANK YOU.
SHP
I'll be rooting for you from afar.
SO WHY DID YOU WANT TO WORK AT THE LIBRARY?

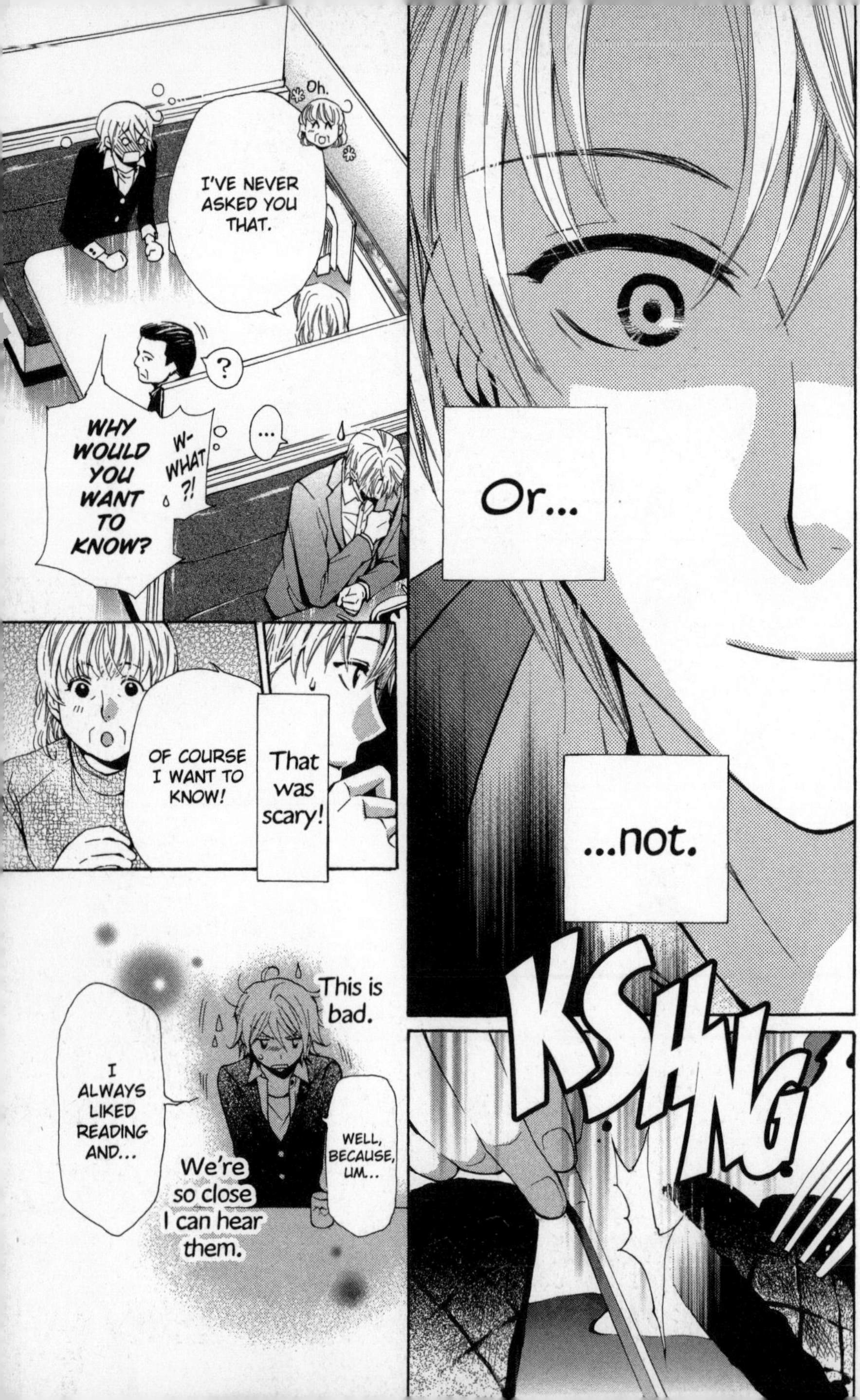
Or...
...not.
KSHNG
Oh.
I'VE NEVER ASKED YOU THAT.
?
...
W-WHAT?!
WHY WOULD YOU WANT TO KNOW?
That was scary!
OF COURSE I WANT TO KNOW!
This is bad.
WELL, BECAUSE, UM...
We're so close I can hear them.
I ALWAYS LIKED READING AND...

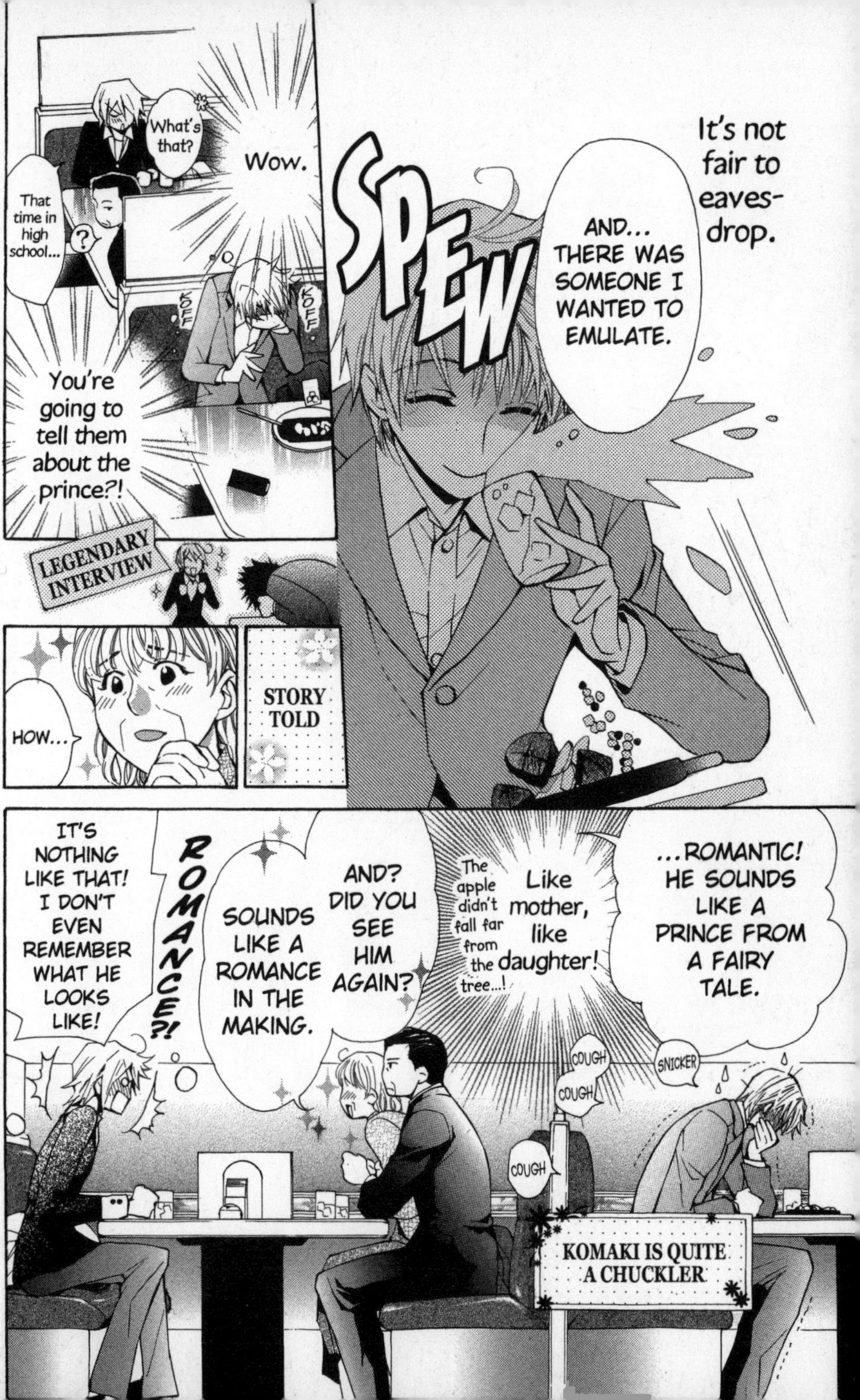

AND... THERE WAS SOMEONE I WANTED TO EMULATE.
It's not fair to eaves-drop.
SPEW
What's that?
Wow.
That time in high school...
?
KOFF
KOFF
You're going to tell them about the prince?!
LEGENDARY INTERVIEW
STORY TOLD
HOW...
...ROMANTIC! HE SOUNDS LIKE A PRINCE FROM A FAIRY TALE.
Like mother, like daughter!
The apple didn't fall far from the tree...!
AND? DID YOU SEE HIM AGAIN?
SOUNDS LIKE A ROMANCE IN THE MAKING.
ROMANCE?!
IT'S NOTHING LIKE THAT! I DON'T EVEN REMEMBER WHAT HE LOOKS LIKE!
SNICKER
COUGH
COUGH
COUGH
KOMAKI IS QUITE A CHUCKLER

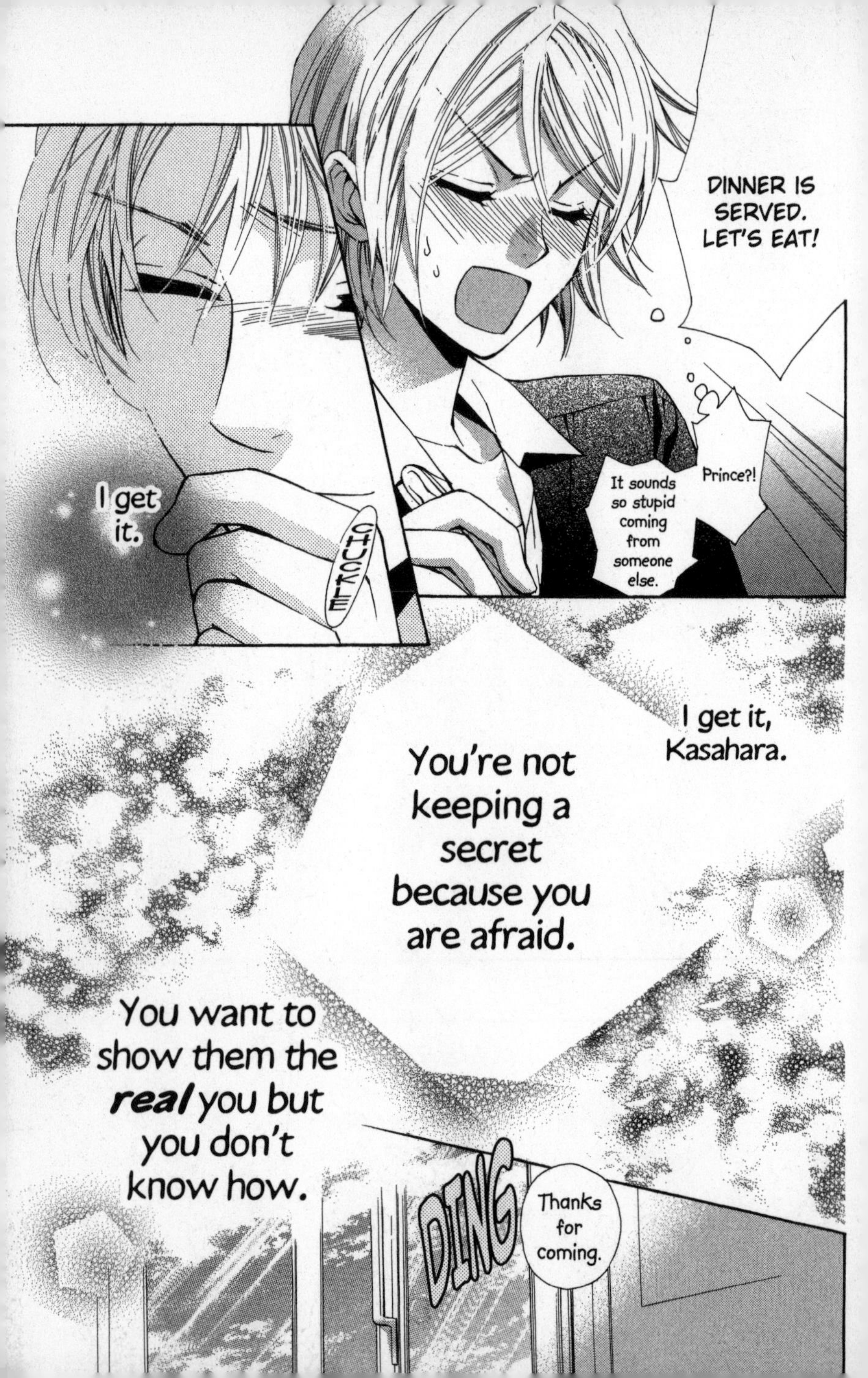
DINNER IS SERVED. LET'S EAT!
Prince?!
It sounds so stupid coming from someone else.
CHUCKLE
I get it.
I get it, Kasahara.
You're not keeping a secret because you are afraid.
You want to show them the *real* you but you don't know how.
DING
Thanks for coming.

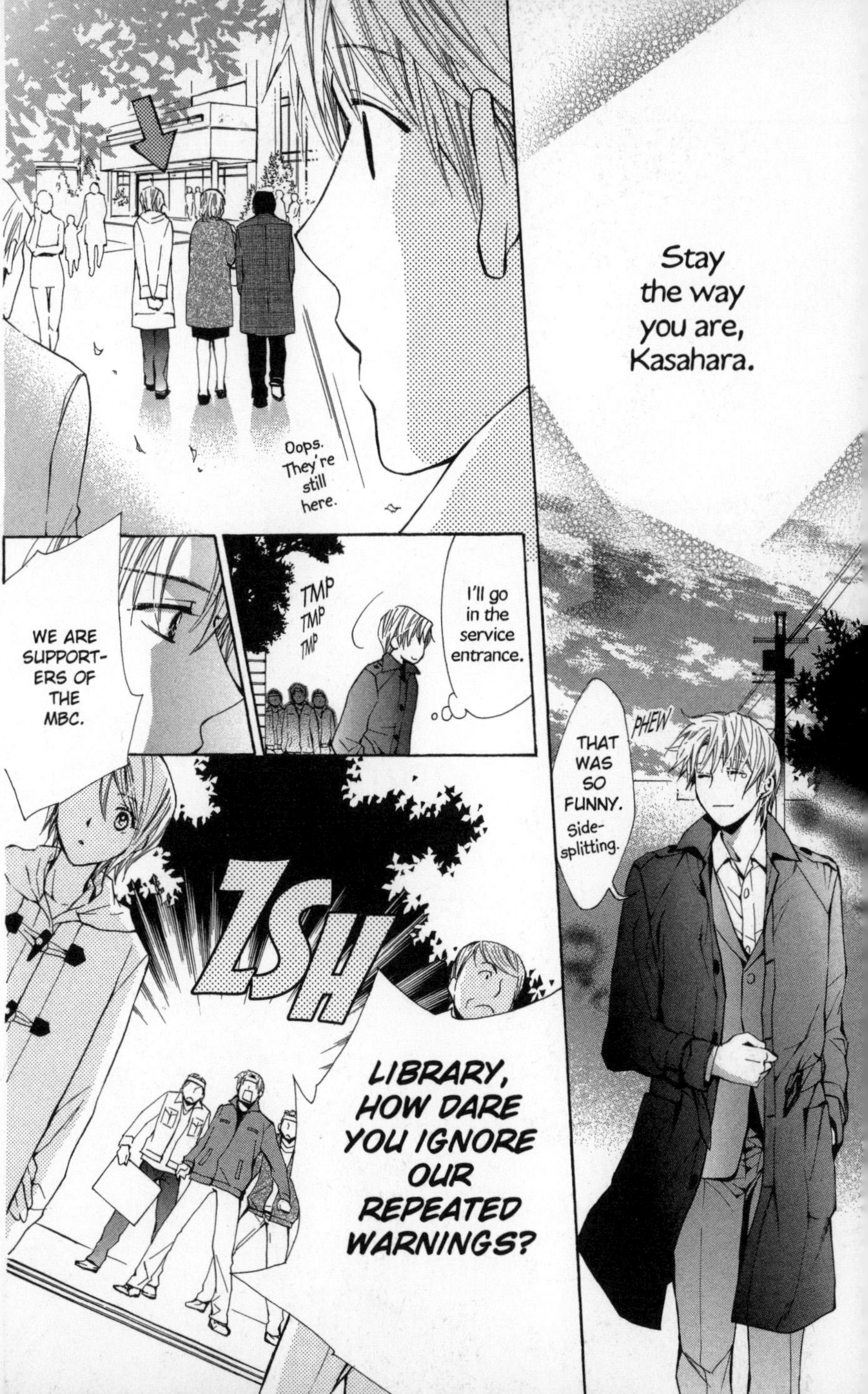
Stay the way you are, Kasahara.
PHEW
THAT WAS SO FUNNY. Side-splitting.
Oops. They're still here.
I'll go in the service entrance.
TMP TMP TMP
WE ARE SUPPORTERS OF THE MBC.
ZSH
LIBRARY, HOW DARE YOU IGNORE OUR REPEATED WARNINGS?

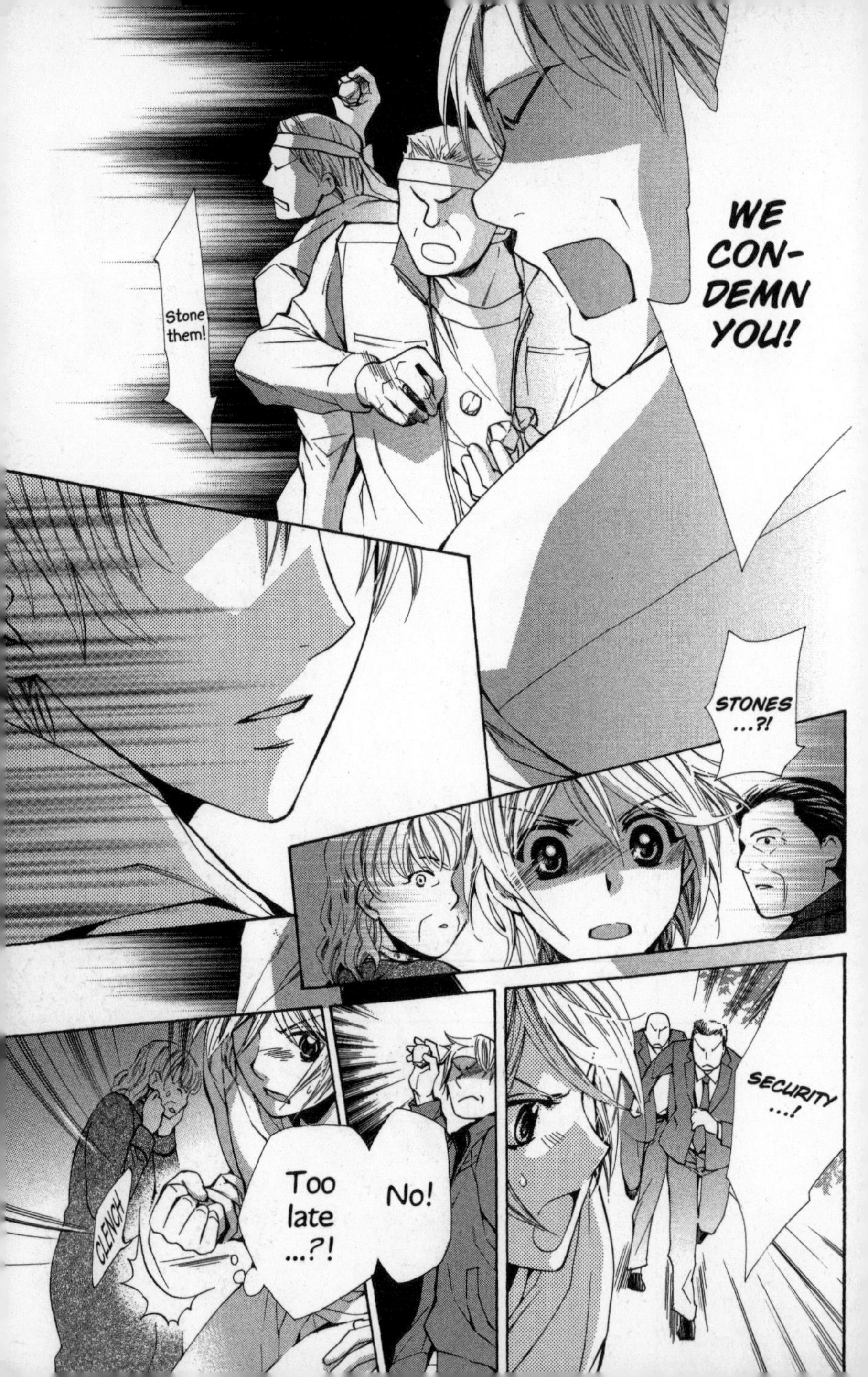
WE CON-DEMN YOU!
Stone them!
STONES ...?!
SECURITY ...!
No!
Too late ...?!
CLENCH

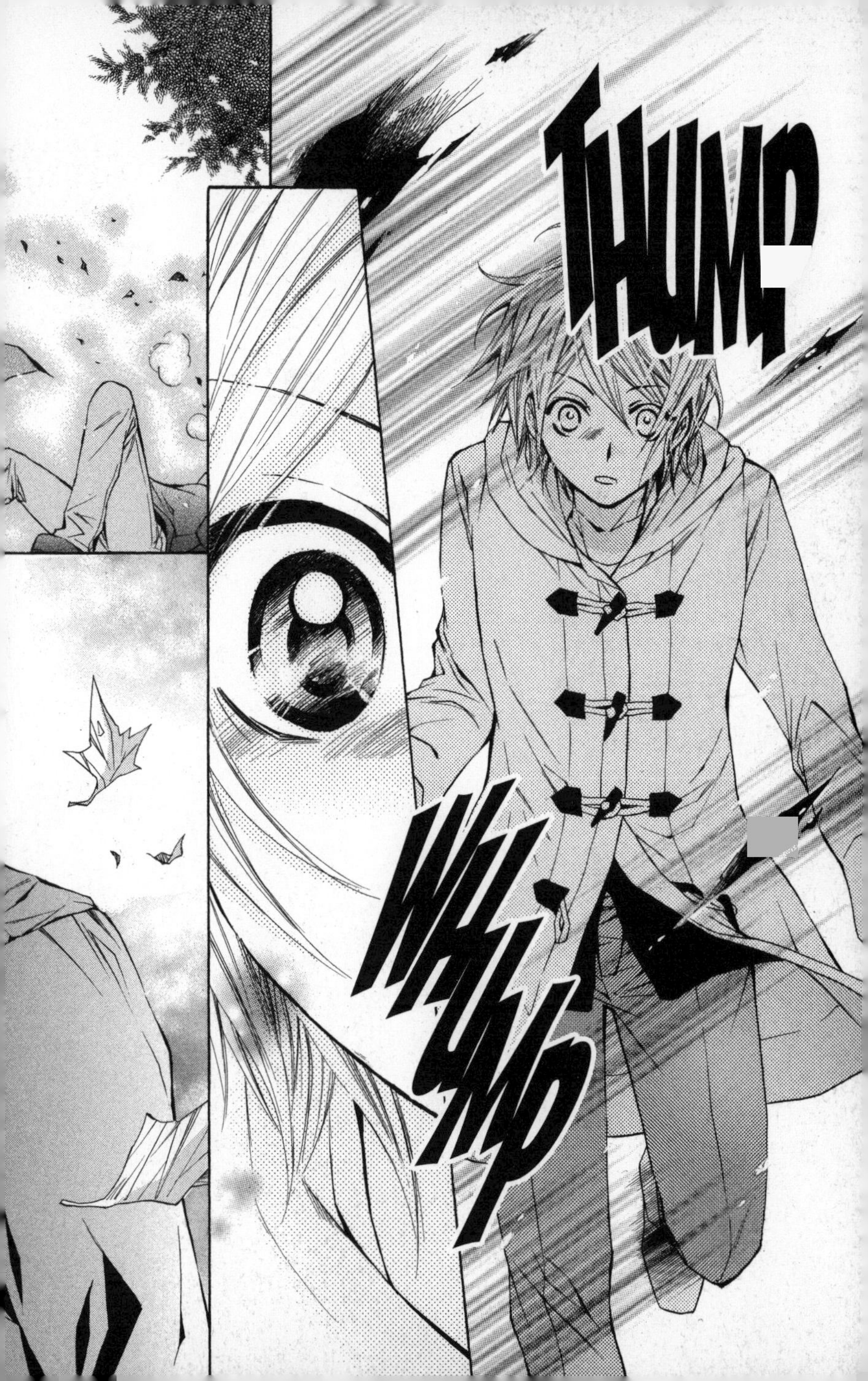
THUMP
WHUMP

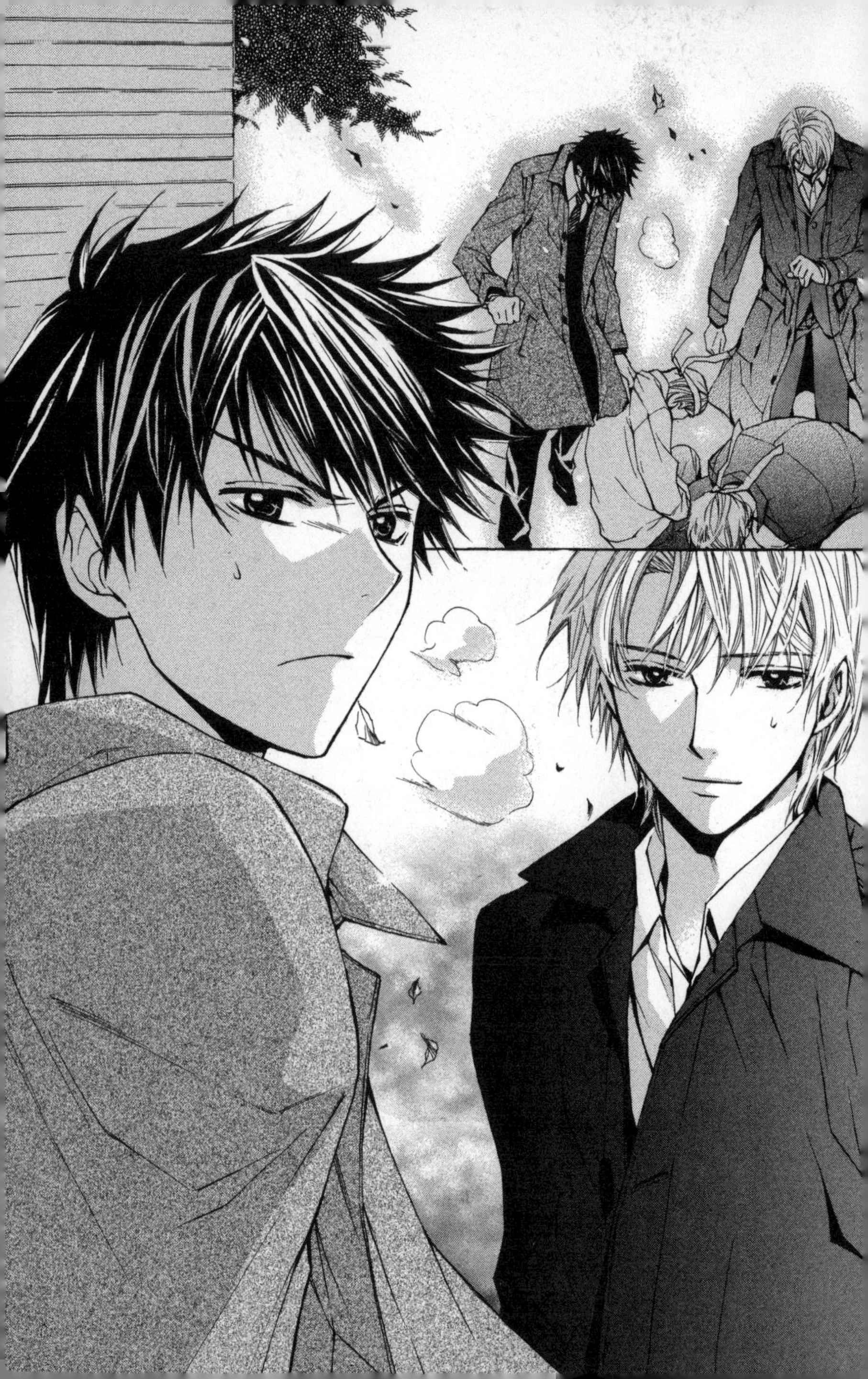

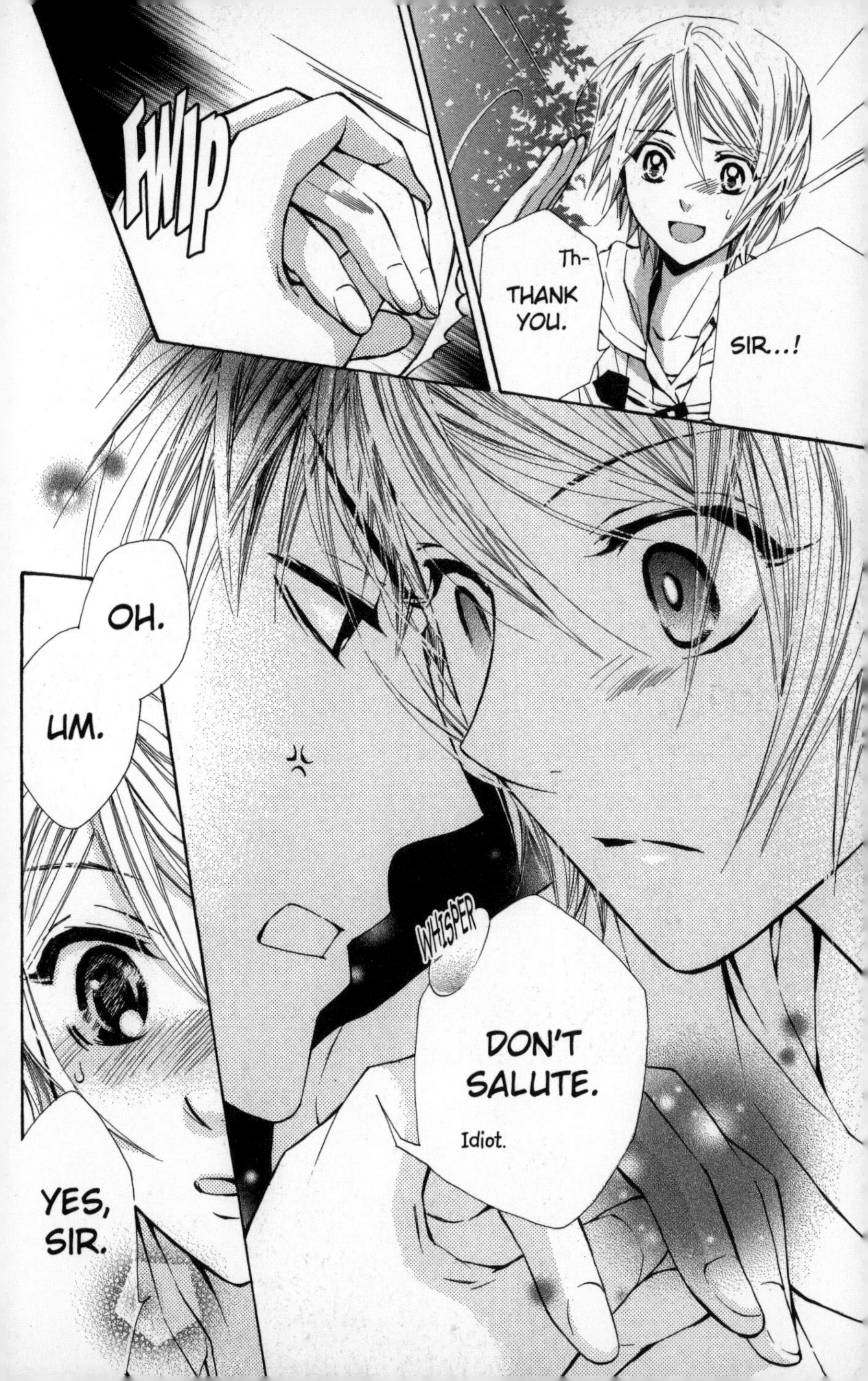
Th-
THANK YOU.
SIR...!
WHIP
WHISPER
DON'T SALUTE.
Idiot.
OH.
UM.
YES, SIR.

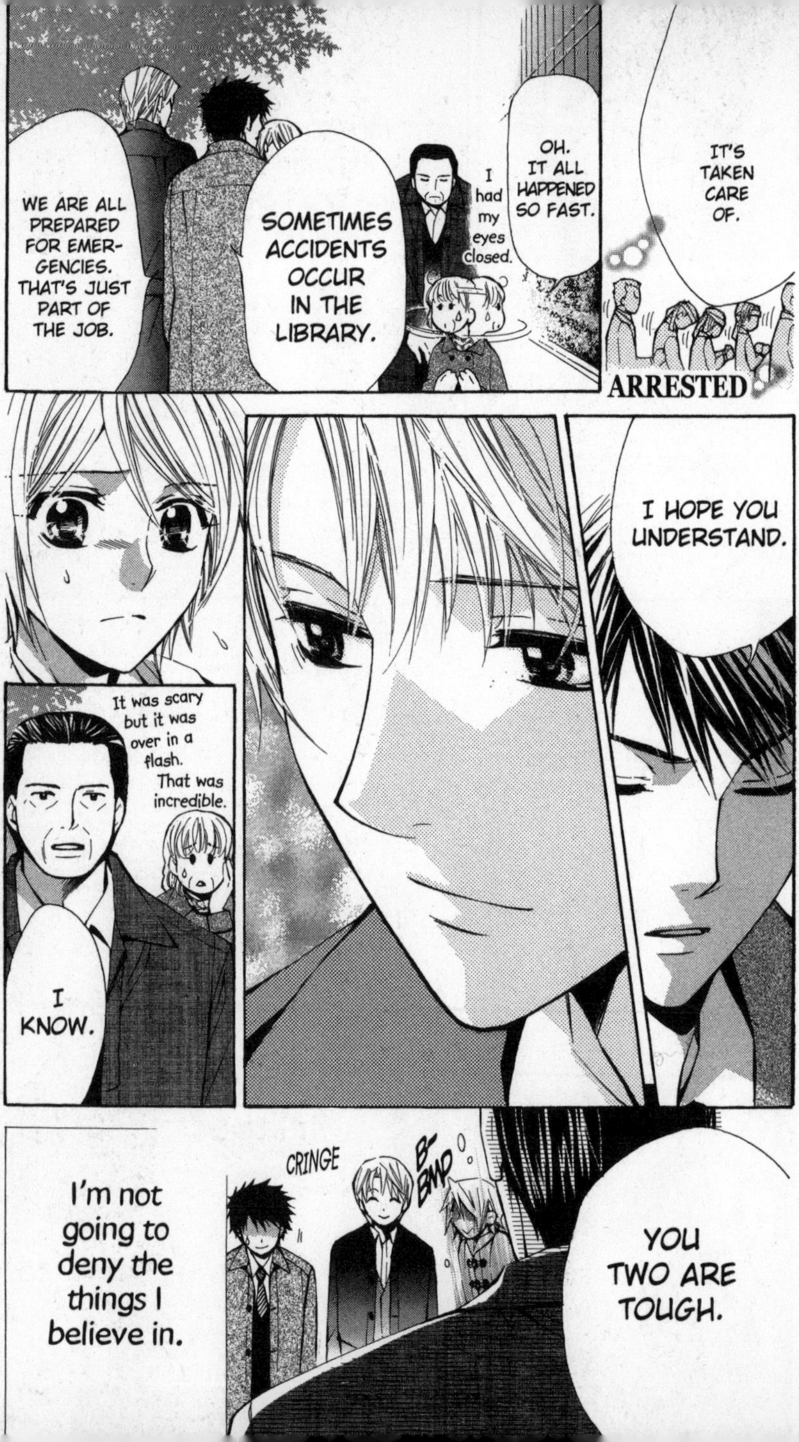
IT'S TAKEN CARE OF.
ARRESTED
OH. IT ALL HAPPENED SO FAST.
I had my eyes closed.
SOMETIMES ACCIDENTS OCCUR IN THE LIBRARY.
WE ARE ALL PREPARED FOR EMER-GENCIES. THAT'S JUST PART OF THE JOB.
I HOPE YOU UNDERSTAND.
It was scary but it was over in a flash.
That was incredible.
I KNOW.
YOU TWO ARE TOUGH.
B-BMP
CRINGE
I'm not going to deny the things I believe in.

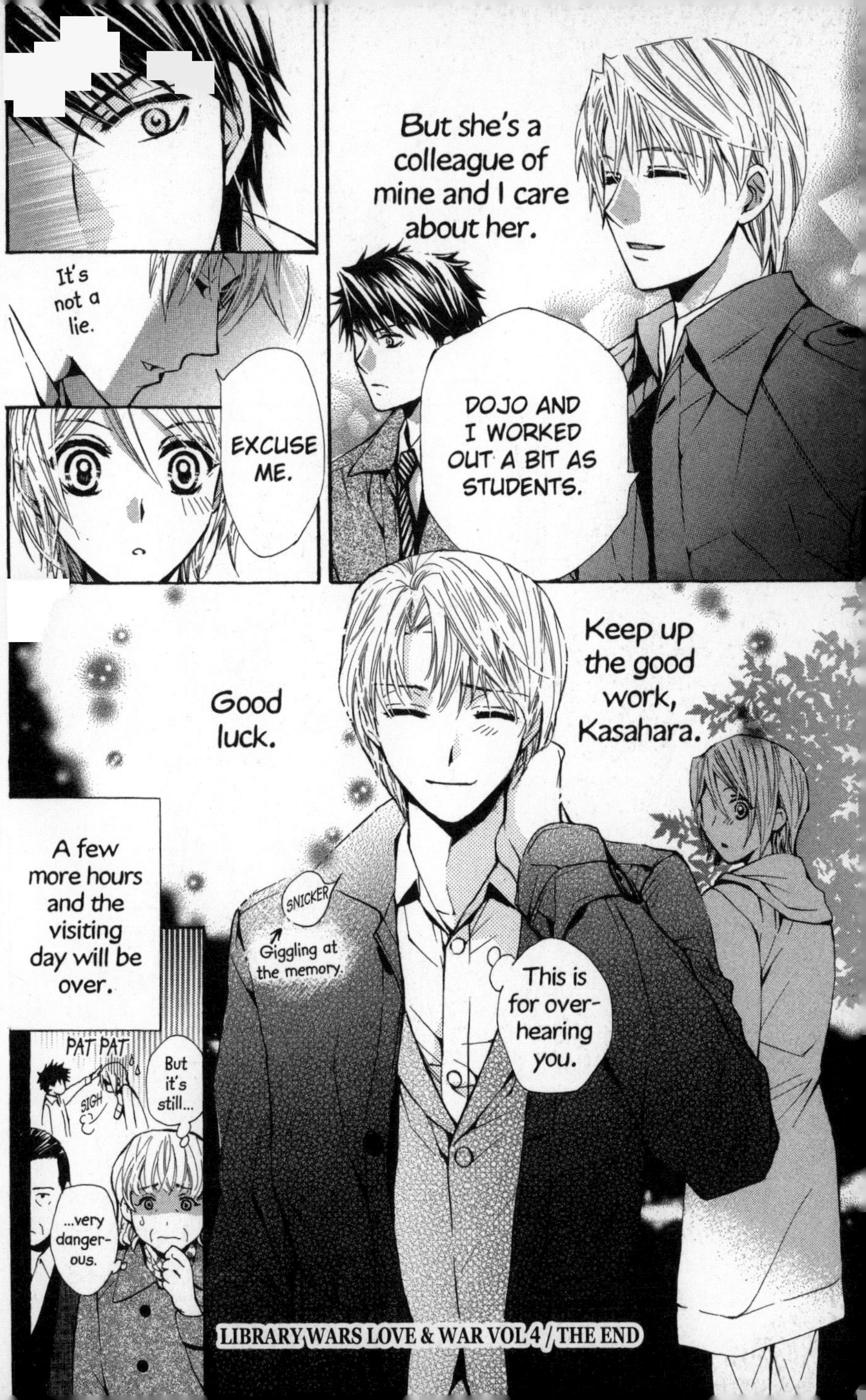
But she's a colleague of mine and I care about her.
DOJO AND I WORKED OUT A BIT AS STUDENTS.
It's not a lie.
EXCUSE ME.
Keep up the good work, Kasahara.
Good luck.
This is for over-hearing you.
SNICKER
Giggling at the memory.
A few more hours and the visiting day will be over.
PAT PAT
SIGH
But it's still...
...very danger-ous.
LIBRARY WARS LOVE & WAR VOL 4 / THE END

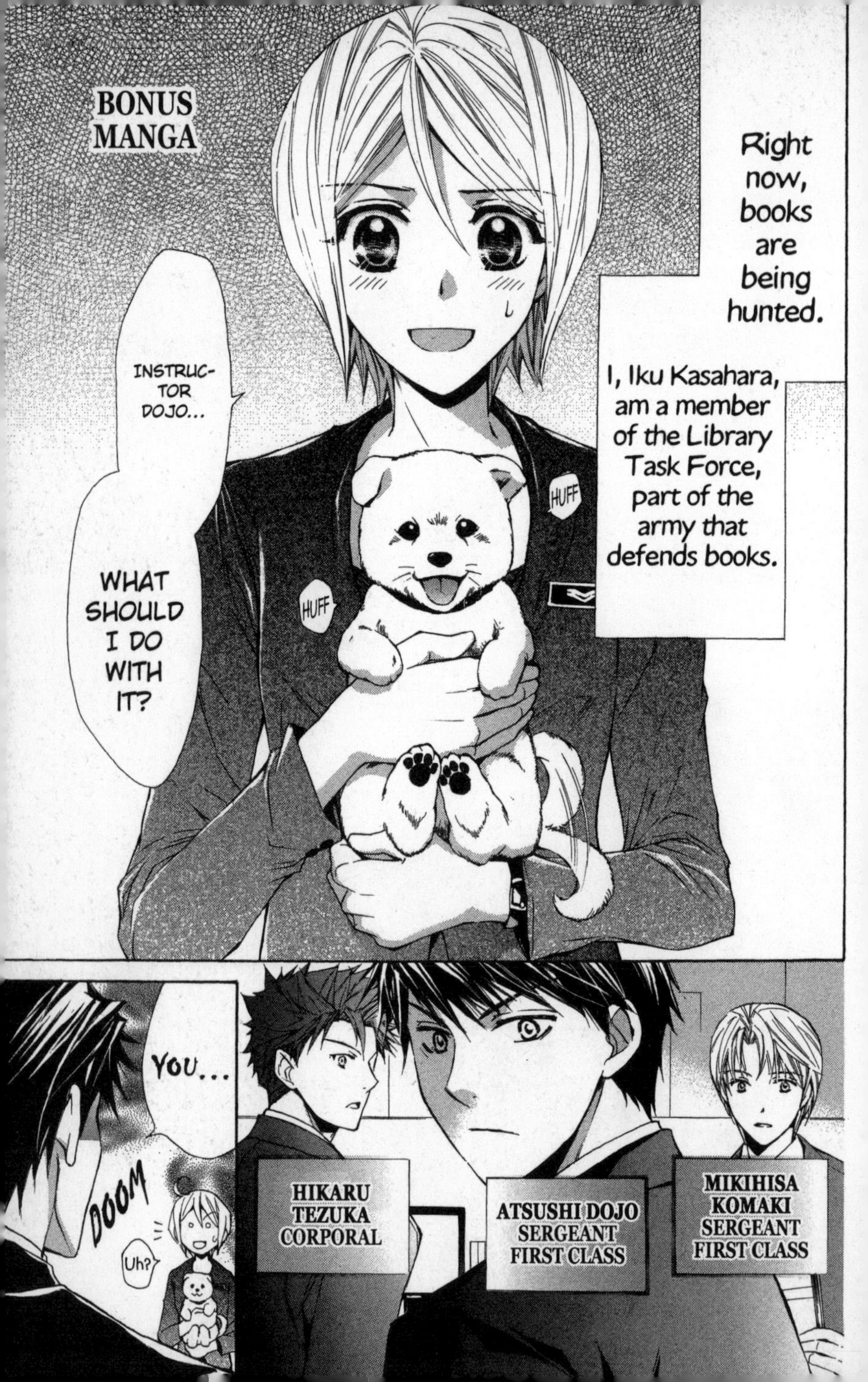
BONUS MANGA
Right now, books are being hunted.
I, Iku Kasahara, am a member of the Library Task Force, part of the army that defends books.
HUFF
HUFF
INSTRUCTOR DOJO...
WHAT SHOULD I DO WITH IT?
MIKIHISA KOMAKI SERGEANT FIRST CLASS
ATSUSHI DOJO SERGEANT FIRST CLASS
HIKARU TEZUKA CORPORAL
YOU...
DOOM
Uh?

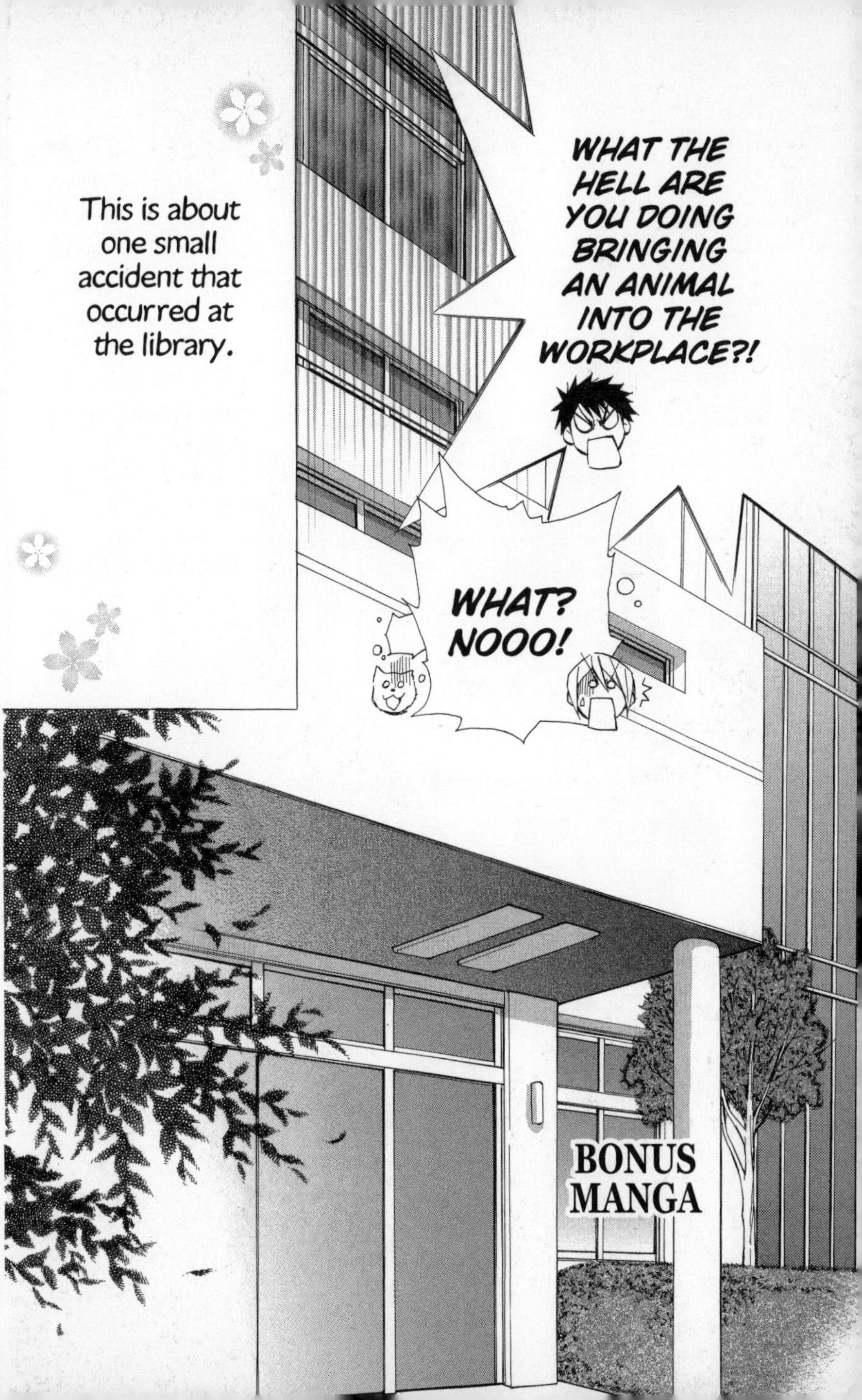
WHAT THE HELL ARE YOU DOING BRINGING AN ANIMAL INTO THE WORKPLACE?!
WHAT? NOOO!
This is about one small accident that occurred at the library.
BONUS MANGA

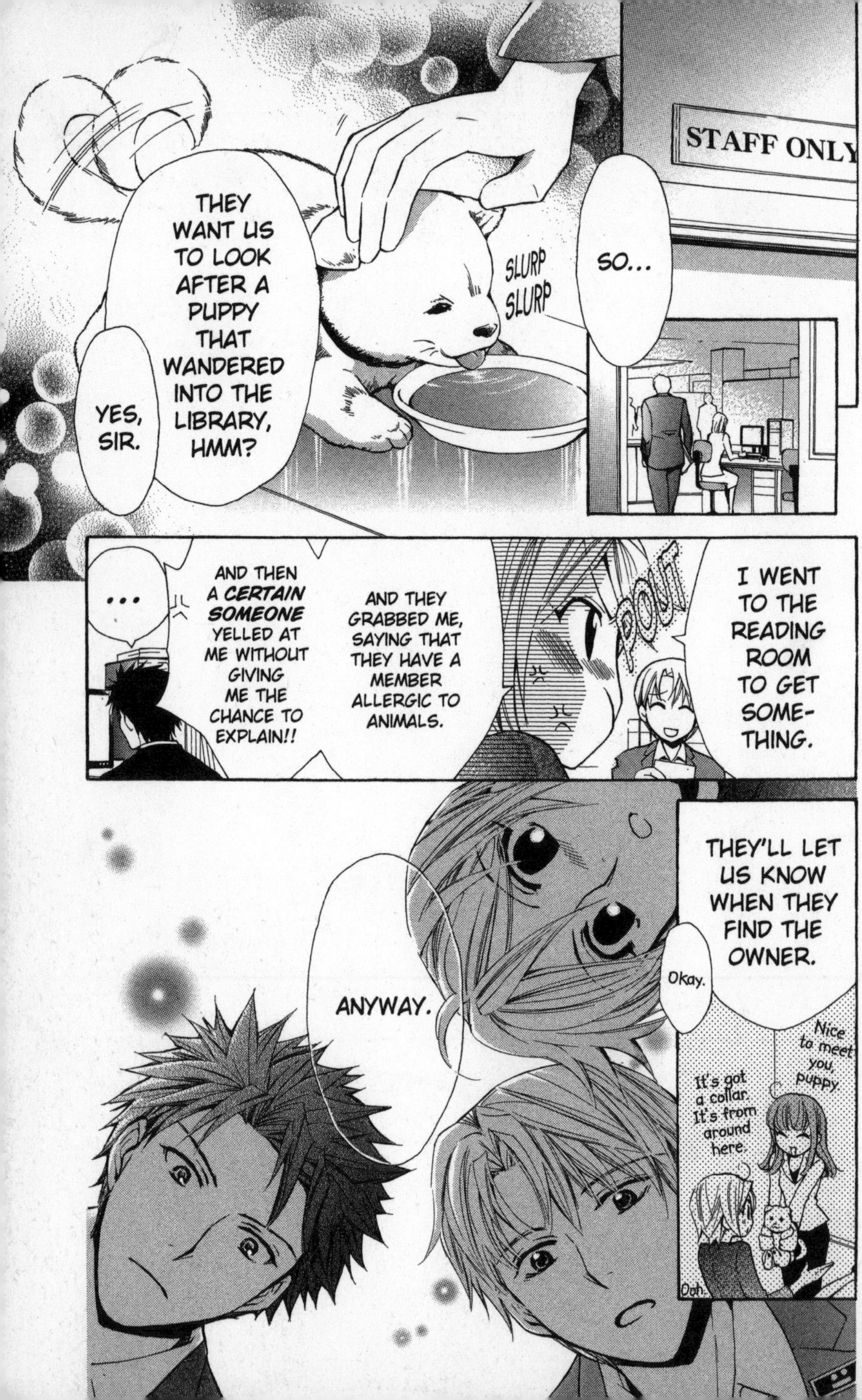
STAFF ONLY
SO...
SLURP SLURP
THEY WANT US TO LOOK AFTER A PUPPY THAT WANDERED INTO THE LIBRARY, HMM?
YES, SIR.
I WENT TO THE READING ROOM TO GET SOME-THING.
POUT
AND THEY GRABBED ME, SAYING THAT THEY HAVE A MEMBER ALLERGIC TO ANIMALS.
AND THEN A CERTAIN SOMEONE YELLED AT ME WITHOUT GIVING ME THE CHANCE TO EXPLAIN!!
...
THEY'LL LET US KNOW WHEN THEY FIND THE OWNER.
Okay.
Nice to meet you, puppy.
It's got a collar. It's from around here.
Ooh.
ANYWAY.

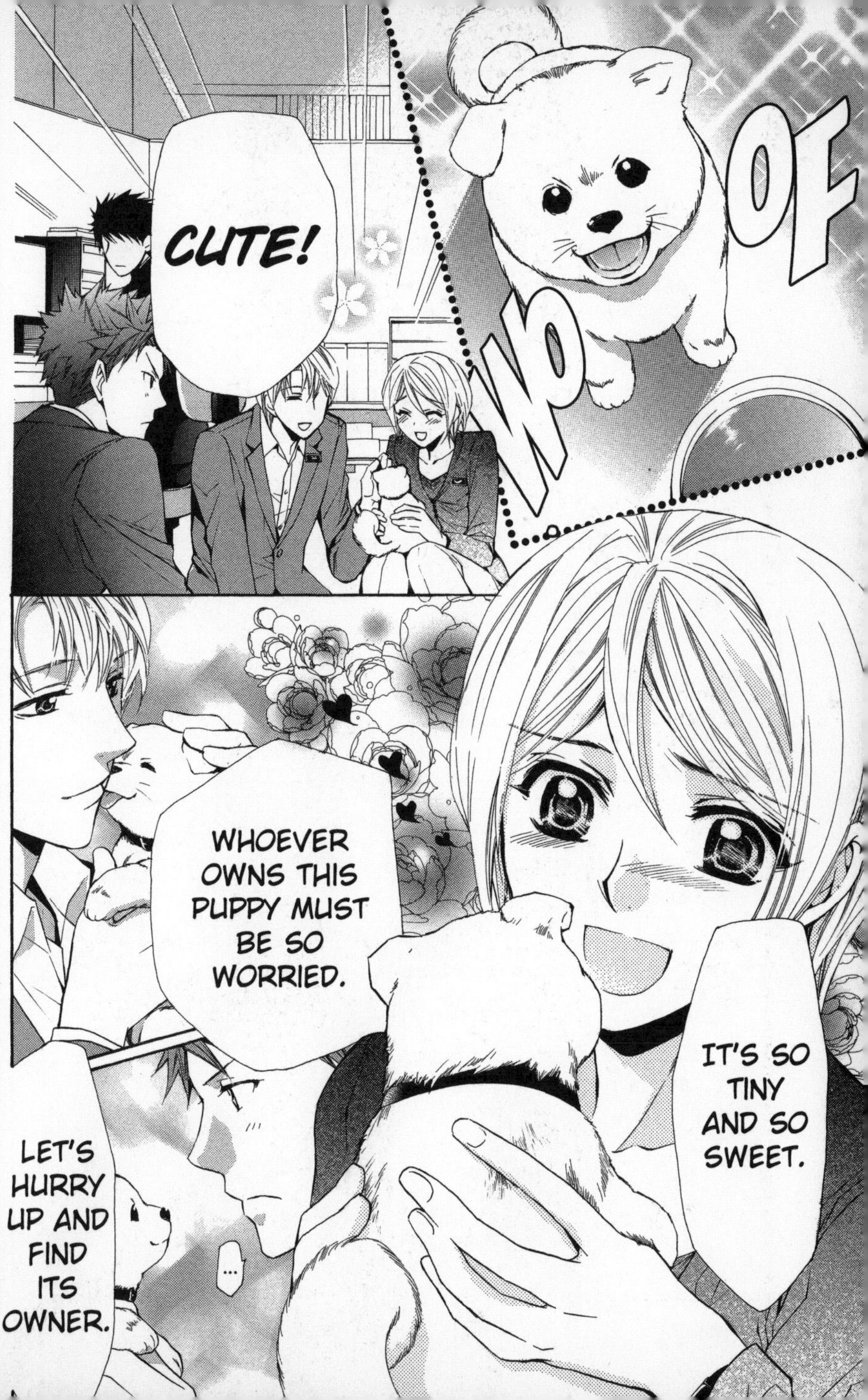
WOOF
CUTE!
IT'S SO TINY AND SO SWEET.
WHOEVER OWNS THIS PUPPY MUST BE SO WORRIED.
...
LET'S HURRY UP AND FIND ITS OWNER.

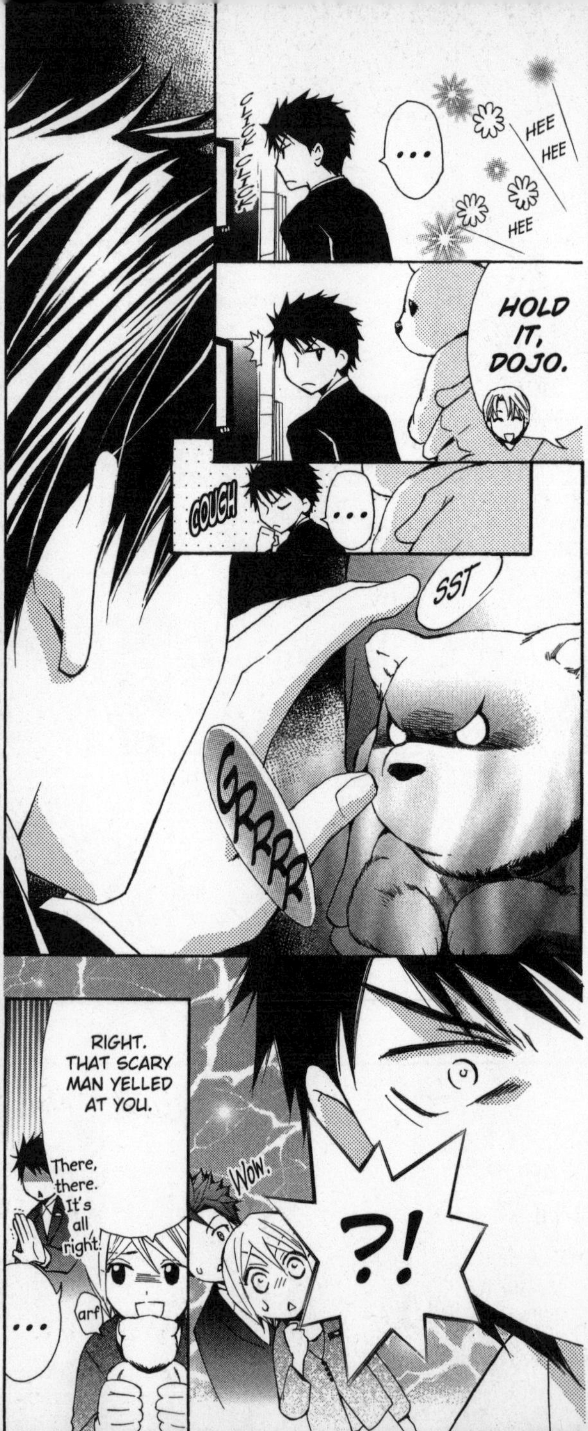
HEE
HEE
HEE
...
CLICK CLICK
HOLD IT, DOJO.
COUGH
...
SST
GRRRR
?!
Wow.
RIGHT. THAT SCARY MAN YELLED AT YOU.
There, there. It's all right!
arf
...

6

*

This is the last of it. Thank you for reading this far.

Parents Visiting Day is the start of the second volume of the original novel. I'm so thrilled!

I'm going to work hard and keep this interesting story active as long as I can!

Thank you very much for supporting me.

Bye for now!

Special Thanks at the end of the graphic novel.

Kiiro Yumi
弓きいろ

*

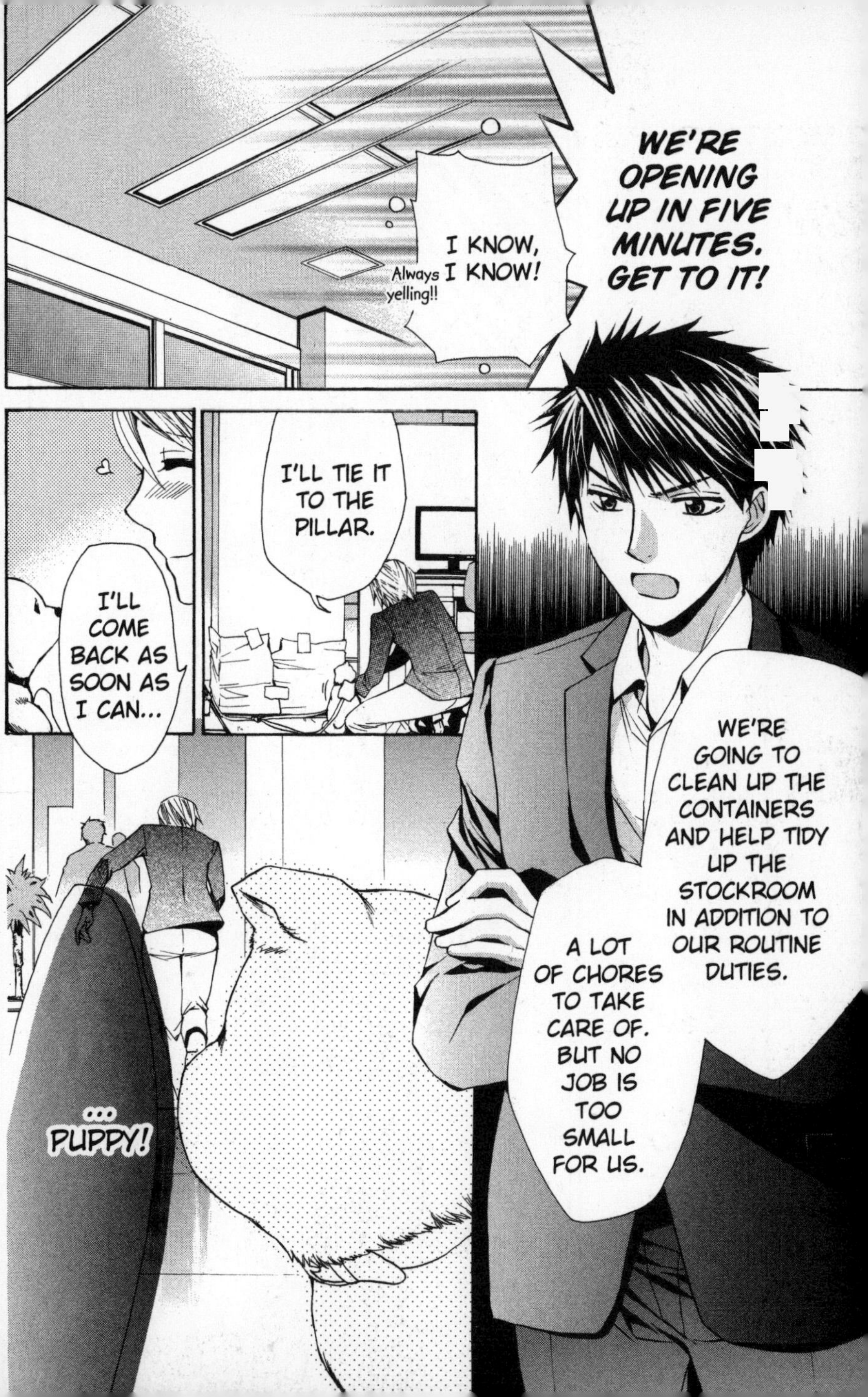
WE'RE OPENING UP IN FIVE MINUTES. GET TO IT!
I KNOW, I KNOW!
Always yelling!!
WE'RE GOING TO CLEAN UP THE CONTAINERS AND HELP TIDY UP THE STOCKROOM IN ADDITION TO OUR ROUTINE DUTIES.
A LOT OF CHORES TO TAKE CARE OF. BUT NO JOB IS TOO SMALL FOR US.
I'LL TIE IT TO THE PILLAR.
I'LL COME BACK AS SOON AS I CAN...
...PUPPY!

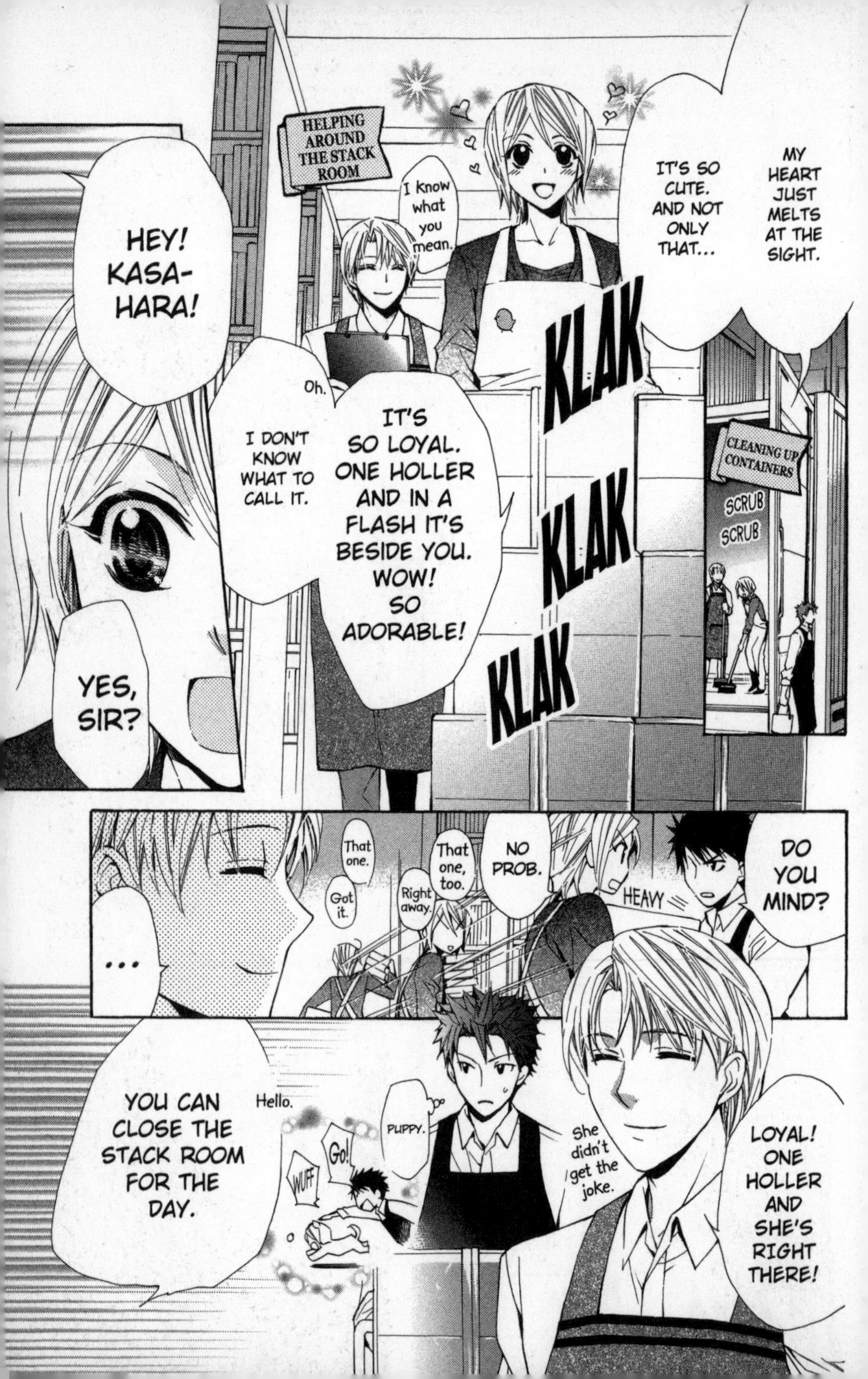
HELPING AROUND THE STACK ROOM
MY HEART JUST MELTS AT THE SIGHT.
IT'S SO CUTE. AND NOT ONLY THAT...
I know what you mean.
HEY! KASAHARA!
YES, SIR?
KLAK KLAK KLAK
CLEANING UP CONTAINERS
SCRUB SCRUB
IT'S SO LOYAL. ONE HOLLER AND IN A FLASH IT'S BESIDE YOU. WOW! SO ADORABLE!
Oh.
I DON'T KNOW WHAT TO CALL IT.
DO YOU MIND?
HEAVY
NO PROB.
That one, too.
Right away.
That one.
Got it.
...
LOYAL! ONE HOLLER AND SHE'S RIGHT THERE!
She didn't get the joke.
PUPPY.
Go!
WUFF
Hello.
YOU CAN CLOSE THE STACK ROOM FOR THE DAY.

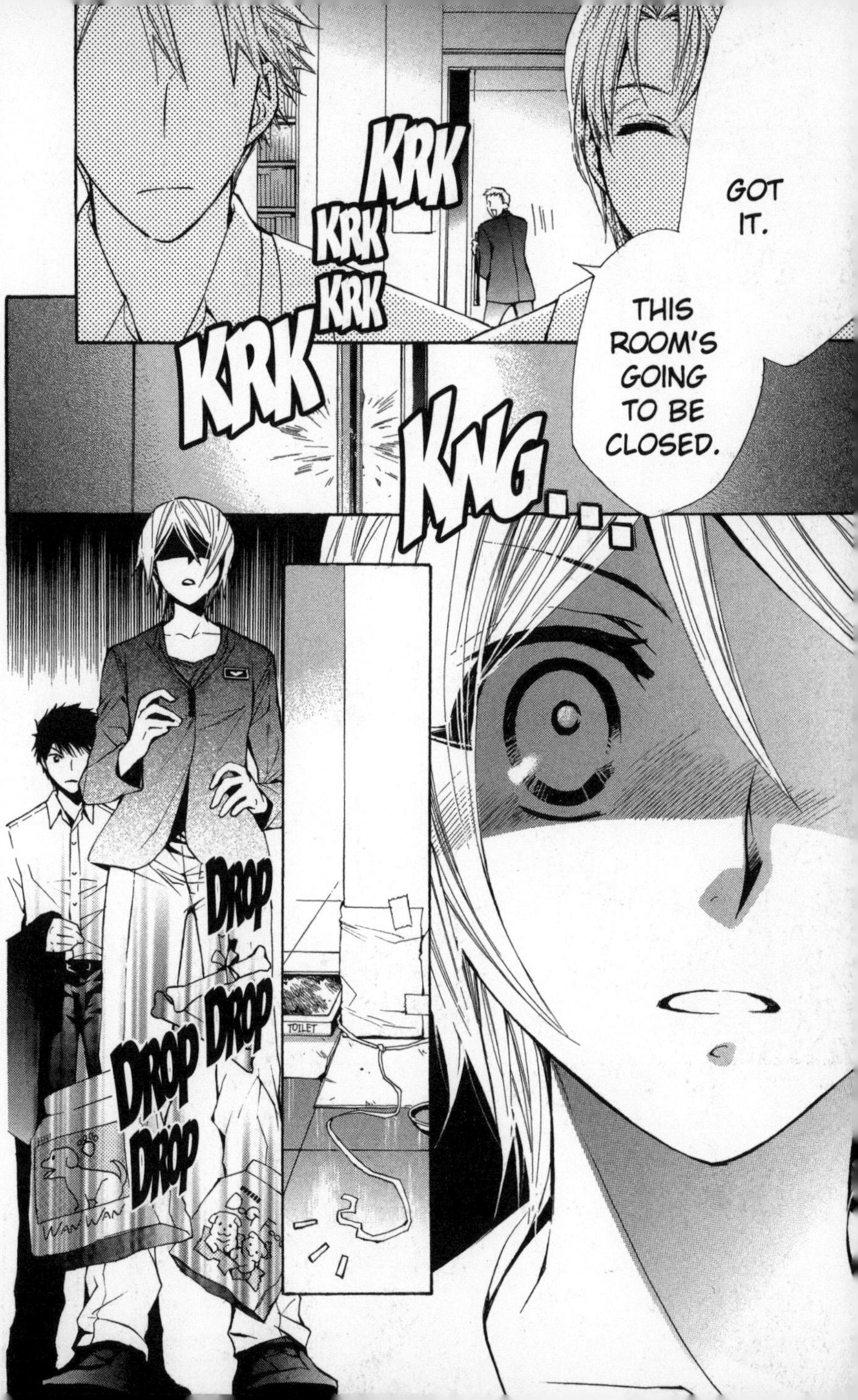
GOT IT.
THIS ROOM'S GOING TO BE CLOSED.
KRK
KRK
KRK
KRK
KNG...
TOILET
DROP
DROP
DROP
DROP
WAN WAN

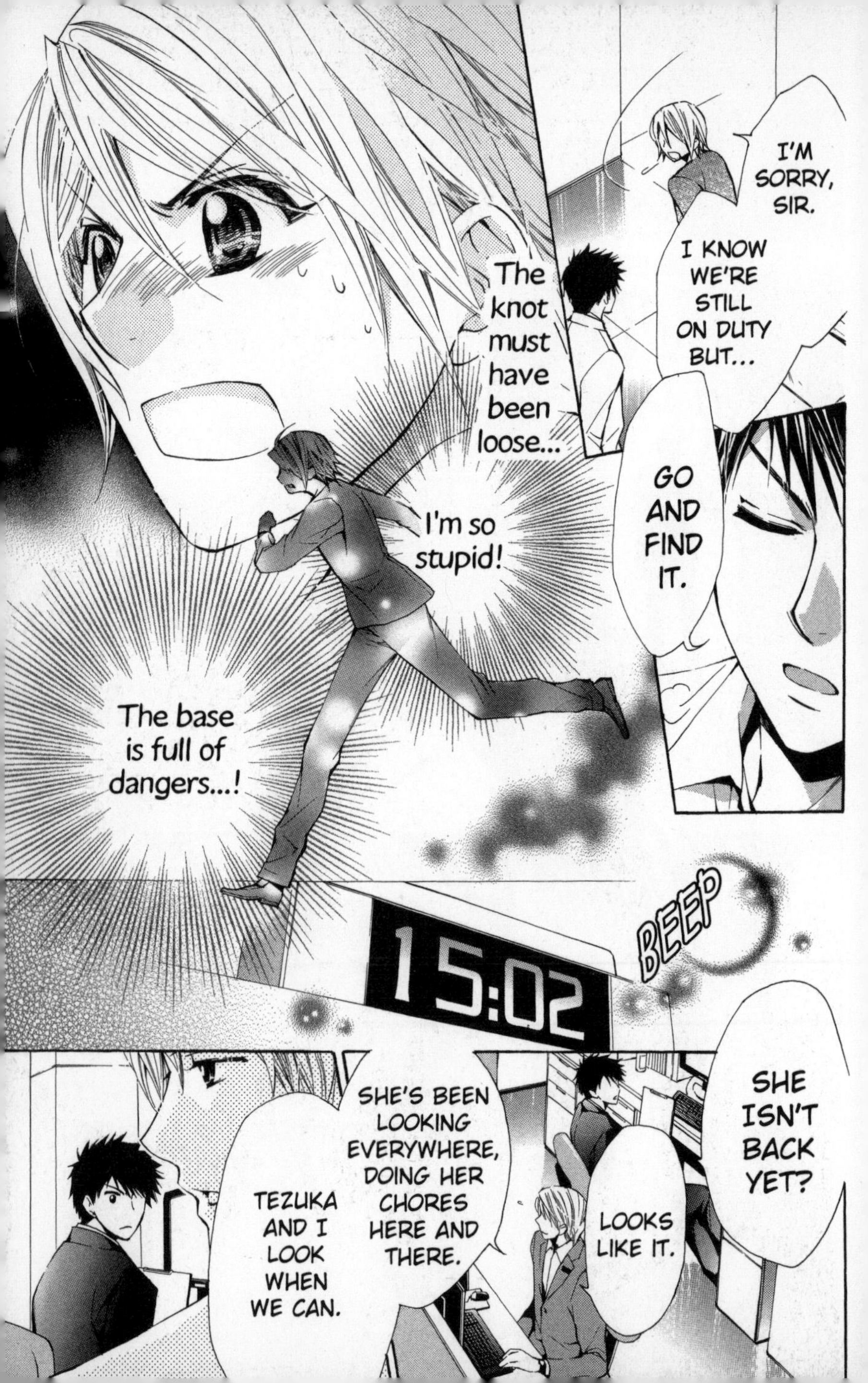
I'M SORRY, SIR.
I KNOW WE'RE STILL ON DUTY BUT...
GO AND FIND IT.
The knot must have been loose...
I'm so stupid!
The base is full of dangers...!
BEEP
15:02
SHE ISN'T BACK YET?
LOOKS LIKE IT.
SHE'S BEEN LOOKING EVERYWHERE, DOING HER CHORES HERE AND THERE.
TEZUKA AND I LOOK WHEN WE CAN.

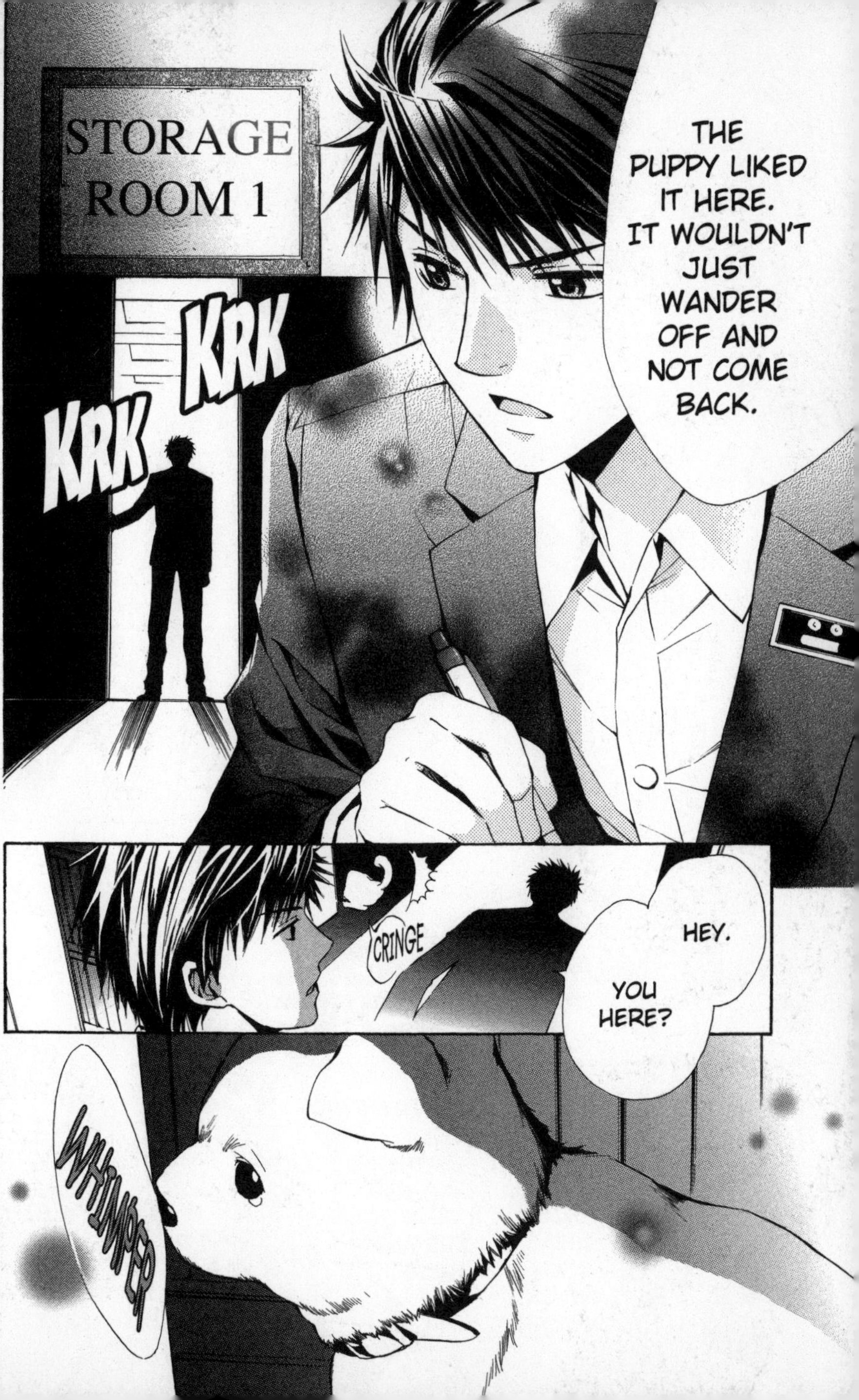
THE PUPPY LIKED IT HERE. IT WOULDN'T JUST WANDER OFF AND NOT COME BACK.
STORAGE ROOM 1
KRK
KRK
HEY.
YOU HERE?
CRINGE
WHIMPER

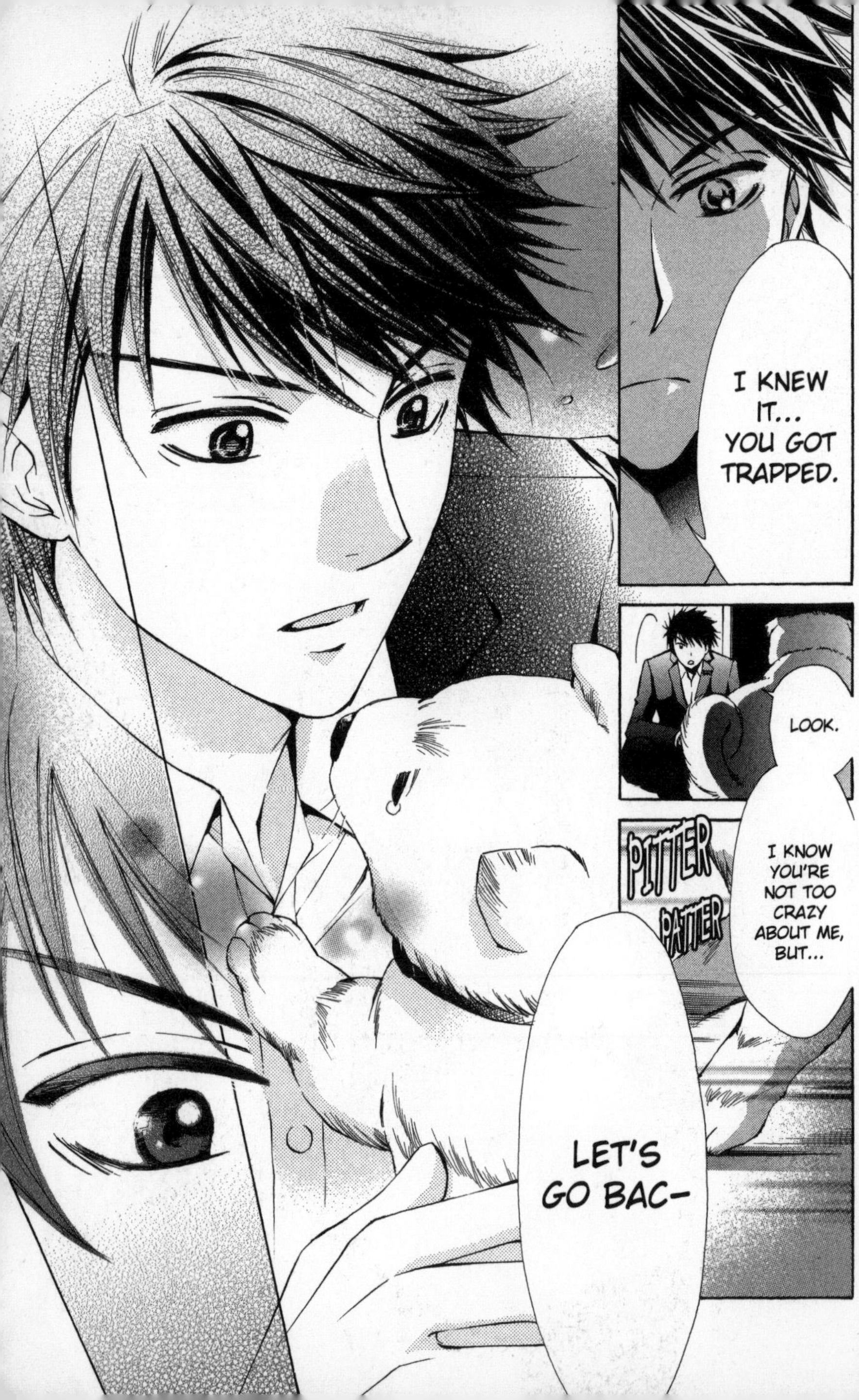
I KNEW IT... YOU GOT TRAPPED.
LOOK.
PITTER PATTER
I KNOW YOU'RE NOT TOO CRAZY ABOUT ME, BUT...
LET'S GO BAC-

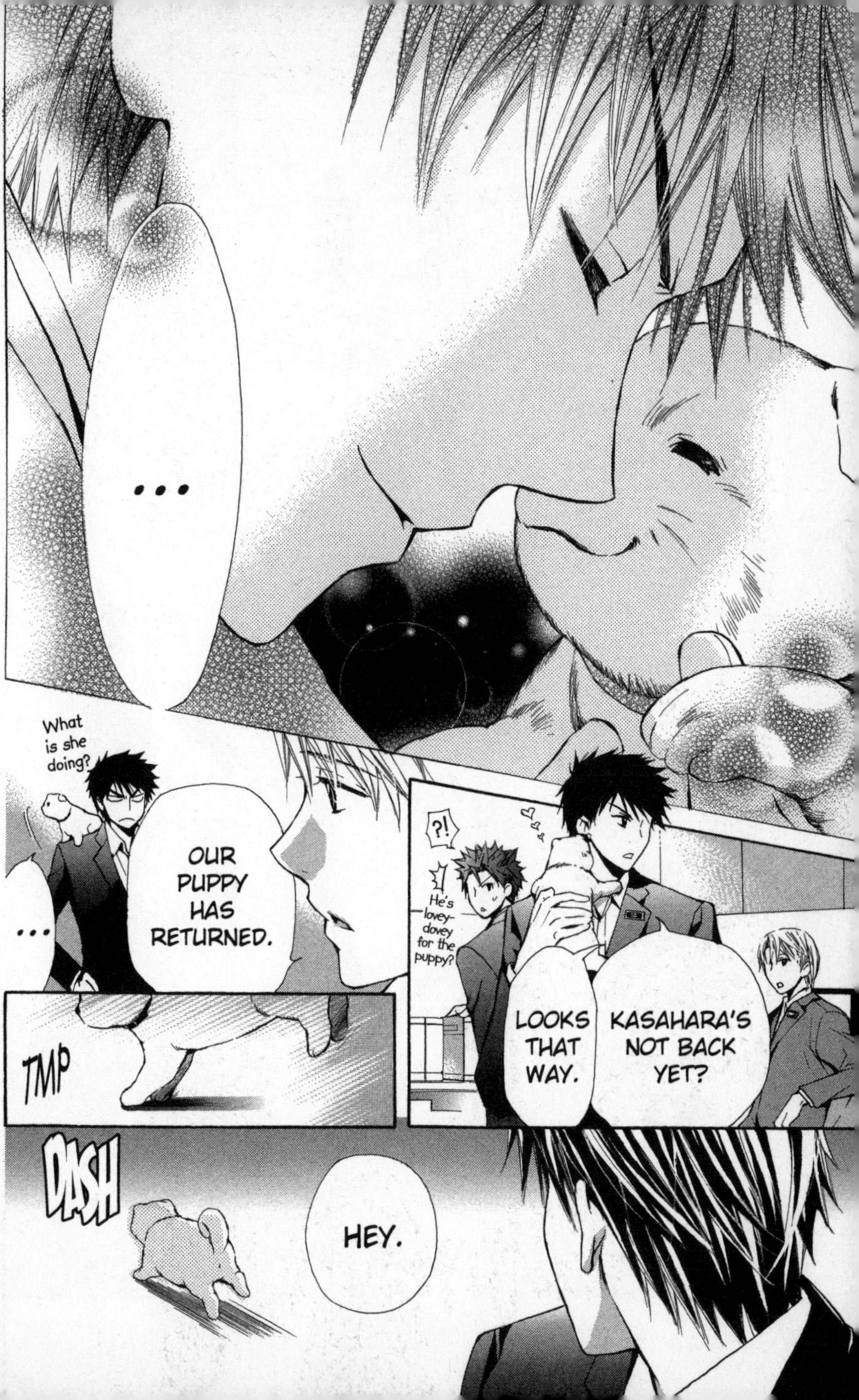
...
?!
He's lovey-dovey for the puppy?
KASAHARA'S NOT BACK YET?
LOOKS THAT WAY.
OUR PUPPY HAS RETURNED.
What is she doing?
...
TMP
HEY.
DASH

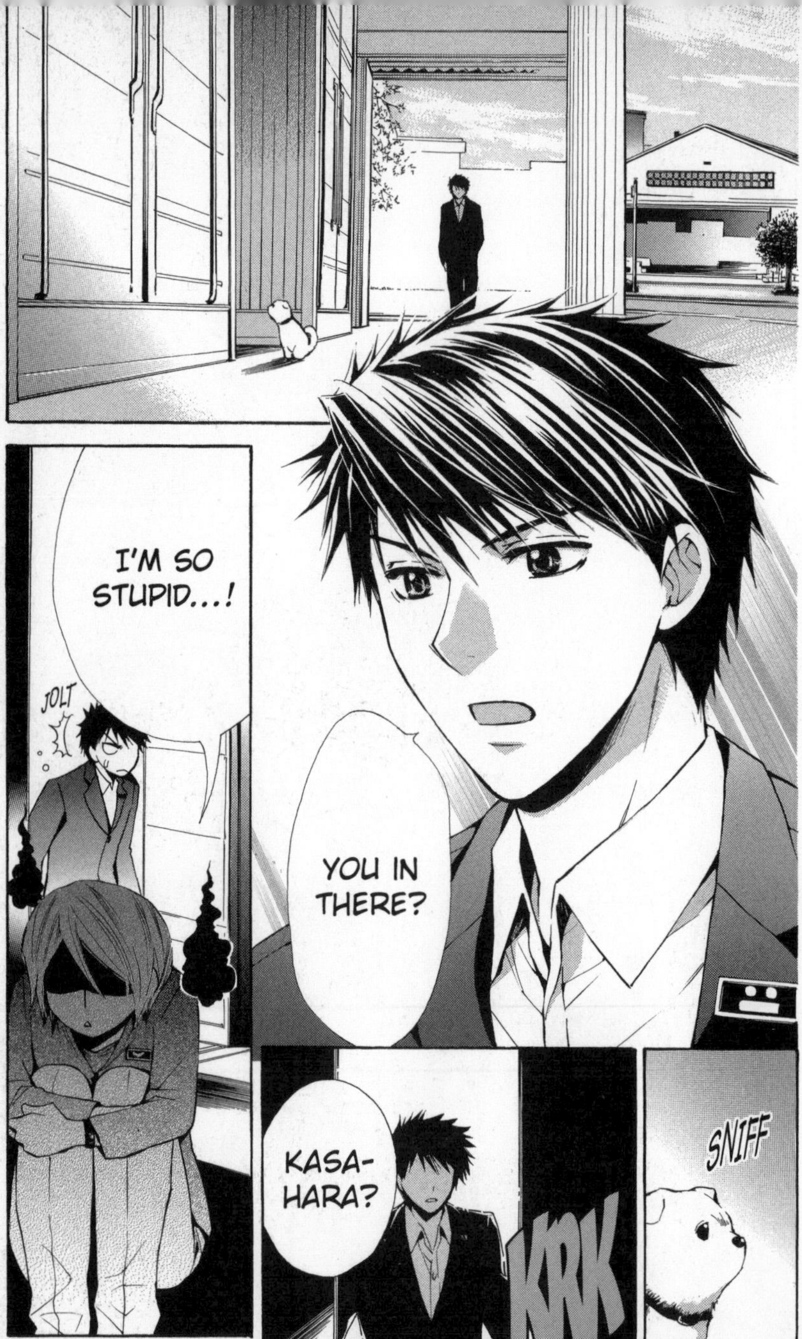
YOU IN THERE?
SNIFF
KRK
KASA-HARA?
I'M SO STUPID...!
JOLT

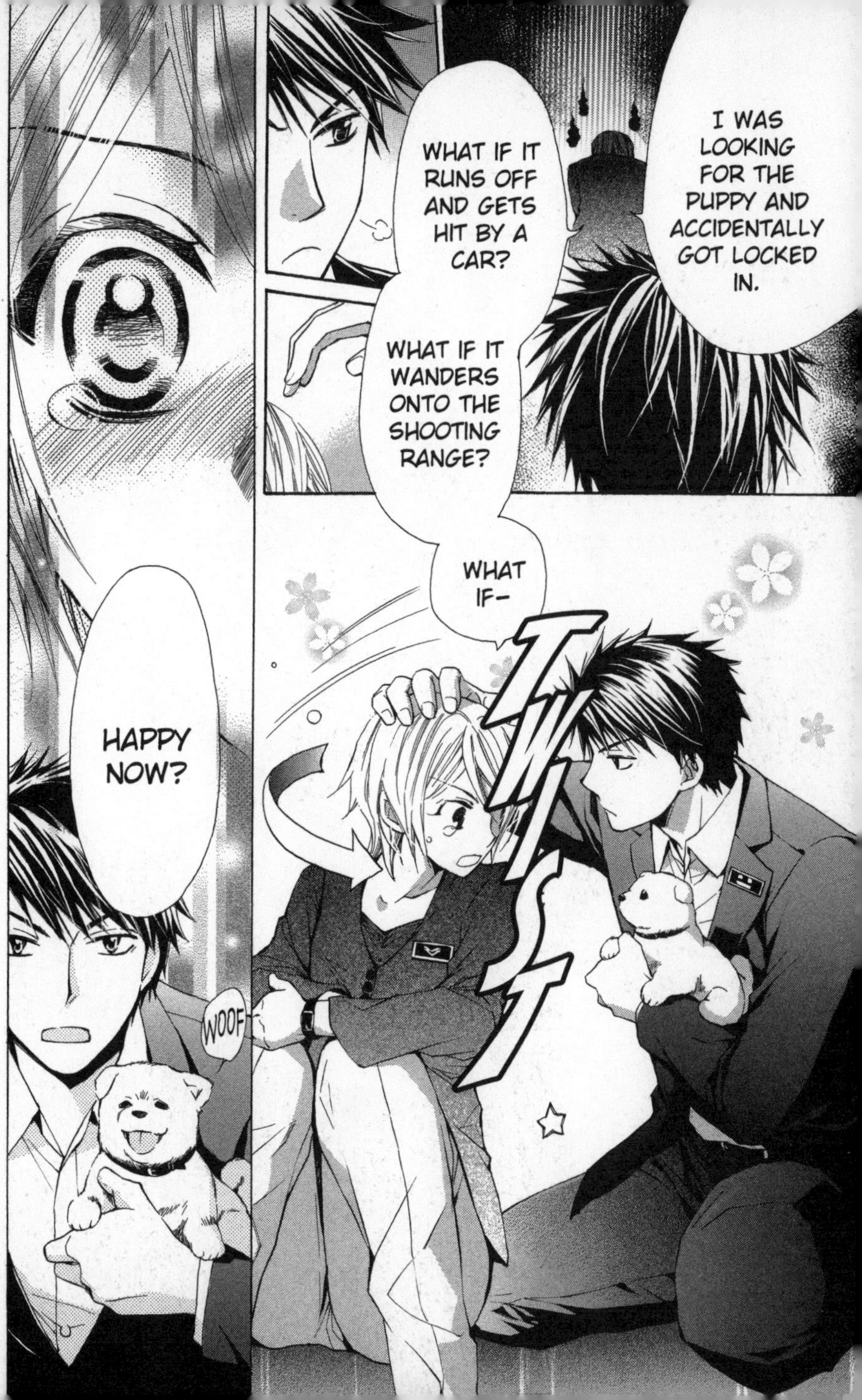
I WAS LOOKING FOR THE PUPPY AND ACCIDENTALLY GOT LOCKED IN.
WHAT IF IT RUNS OFF AND GETS HIT BY A CAR?
WHAT IF IT WANDERS ONTO THE SHOOTING RANGE?
WHAT IF-
HAPPY NOW?
WOOF

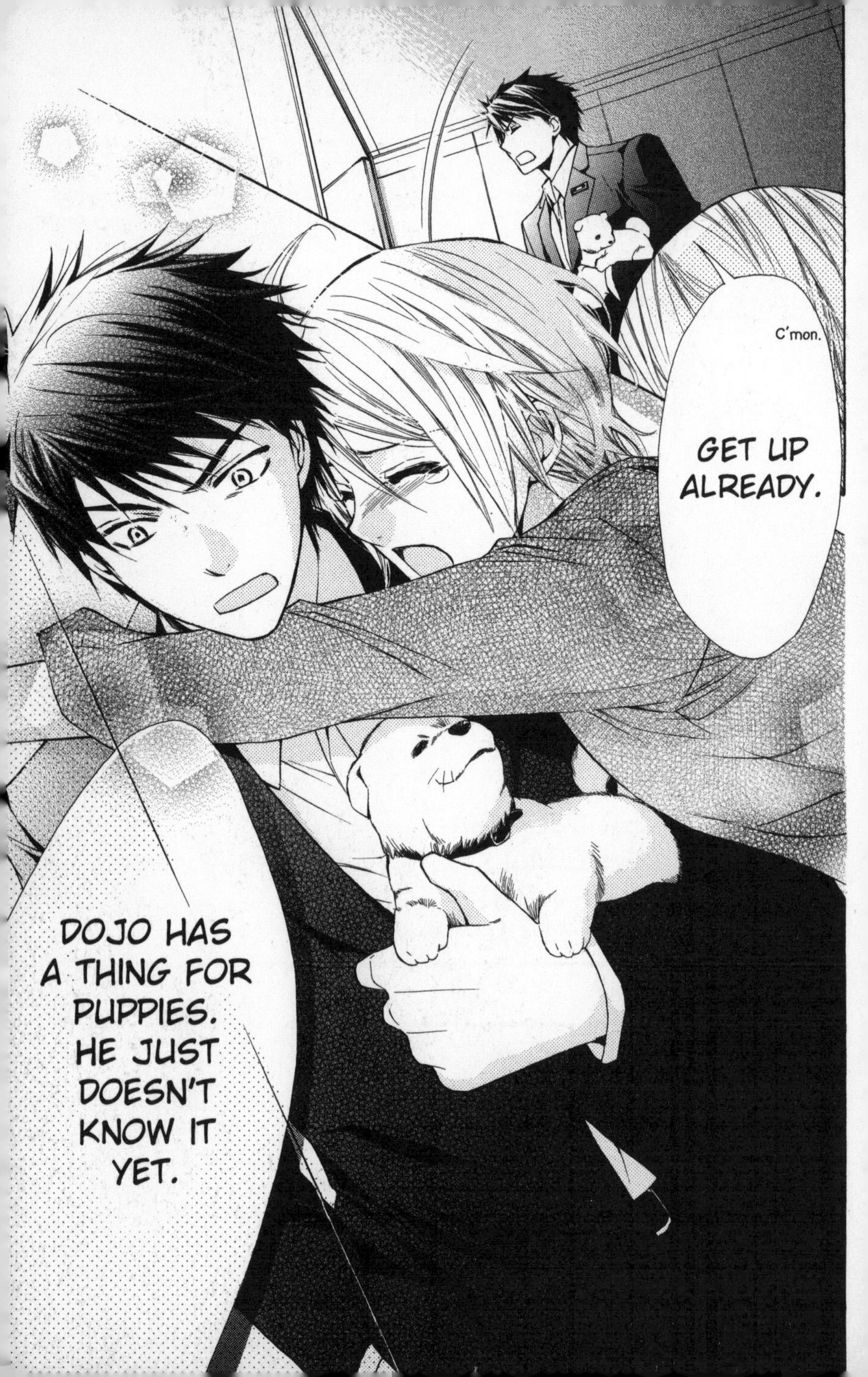
C'mon.
GET UP ALREADY.
DOJO HAS A THING FOR PUPPIES. HE JUST DOESN'T KNOW IT YET.

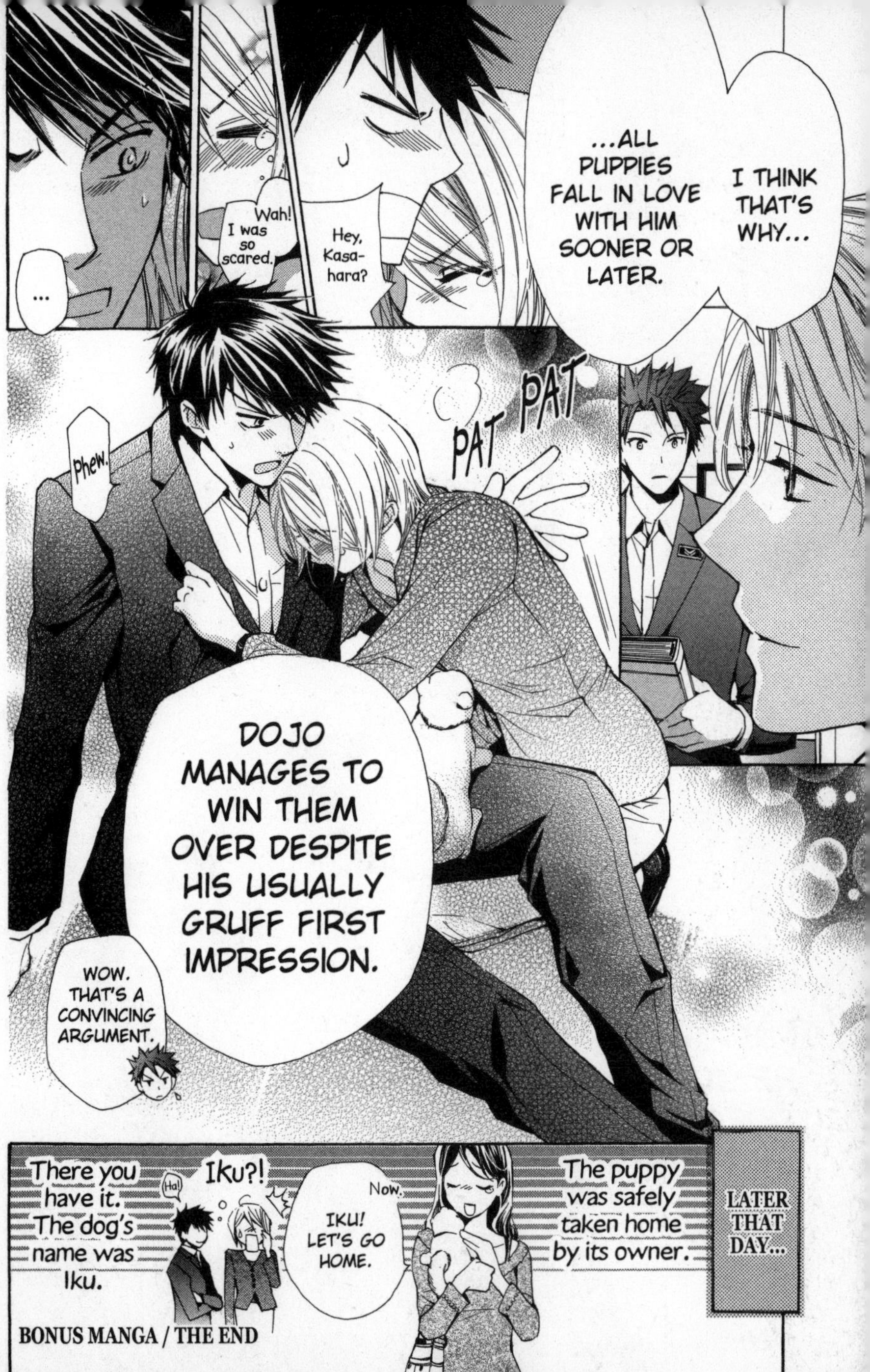
I THINK THAT'S WHY...
...ALL PUPPIES FALL IN LOVE WITH HIM SOONER OR LATER.
Hey, Kasa-hara?
Wah! I was so scared.
...
PAT PAT
Phew.
DOJO MANAGES TO WIN THEM OVER DESPITE HIS USUALLY GRUFF FIRST IMPRESSION.
WOW. THAT'S A CONVINCING ARGUMENT.
LATER THAT DAY...
The puppy was safely taken home by its owner.
Now.
IKU! LET'S GO HOME.
Iku?!
Ha!
There you have it. The dog's name was Iku.
BONUS MANGA / THE END

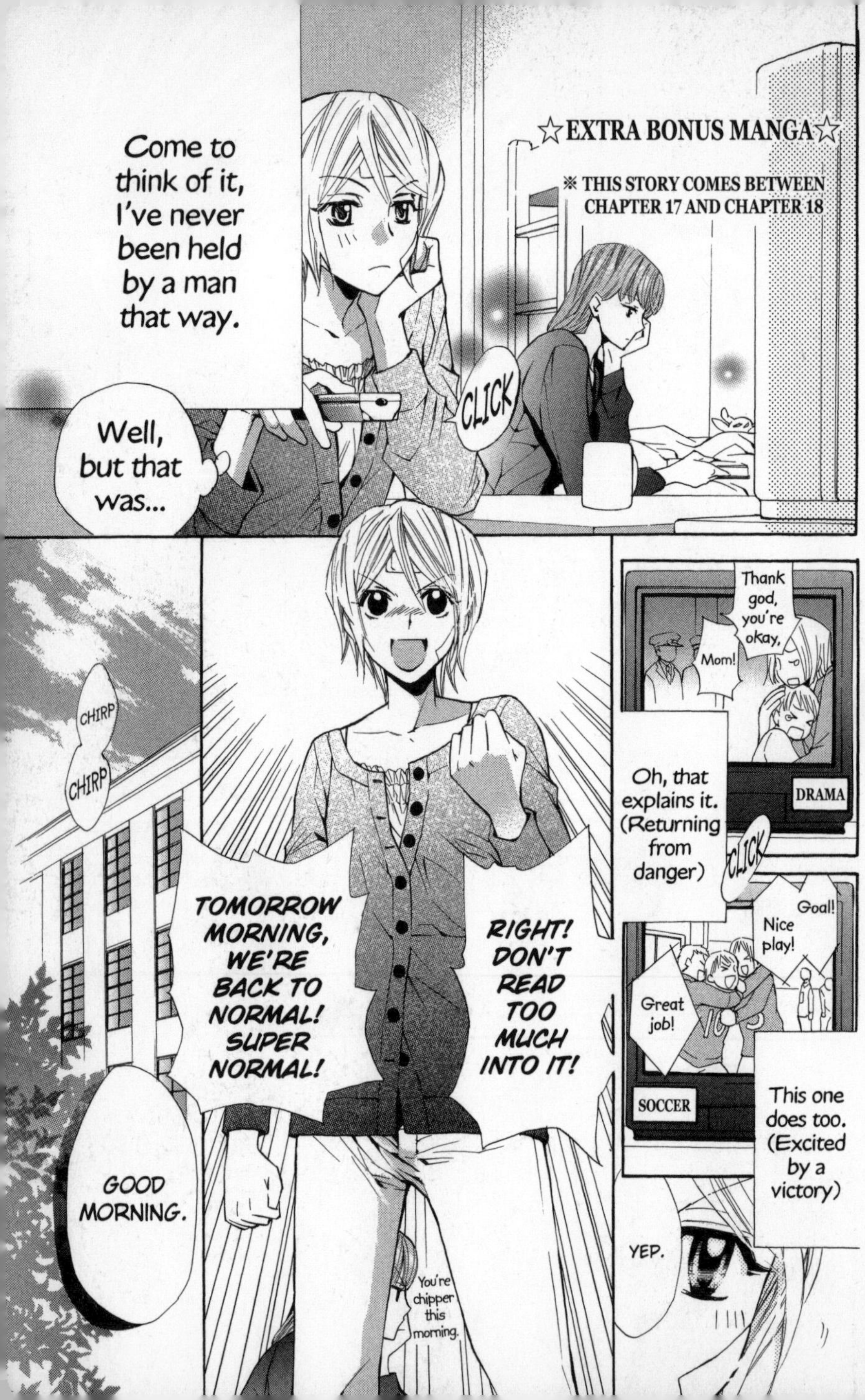
☆EXTRA BONUS MANGA☆
※ THIS STORY COMES BETWEEN CHAPTER 17 AND CHAPTER 18
Come to think of it, I've never been held by a man that way.
CLICK
Well, but that was...
Thank god, you're okay,
Mom!
DRAMA
Oh, that explains it. (Returning from danger)
CLICK
Goal!
Nice play!
Great job!
SOCCER
This one does too. (Excited by a victory)
RIGHT! DON'T READ TOO MUCH INTO IT!
TOMORROW MORNING, WE'RE BACK TO NORMAL! SUPER NORMAL!
CHIRP
CHIRP
GOOD MORNING.
You're chipper this morning.
YEP.

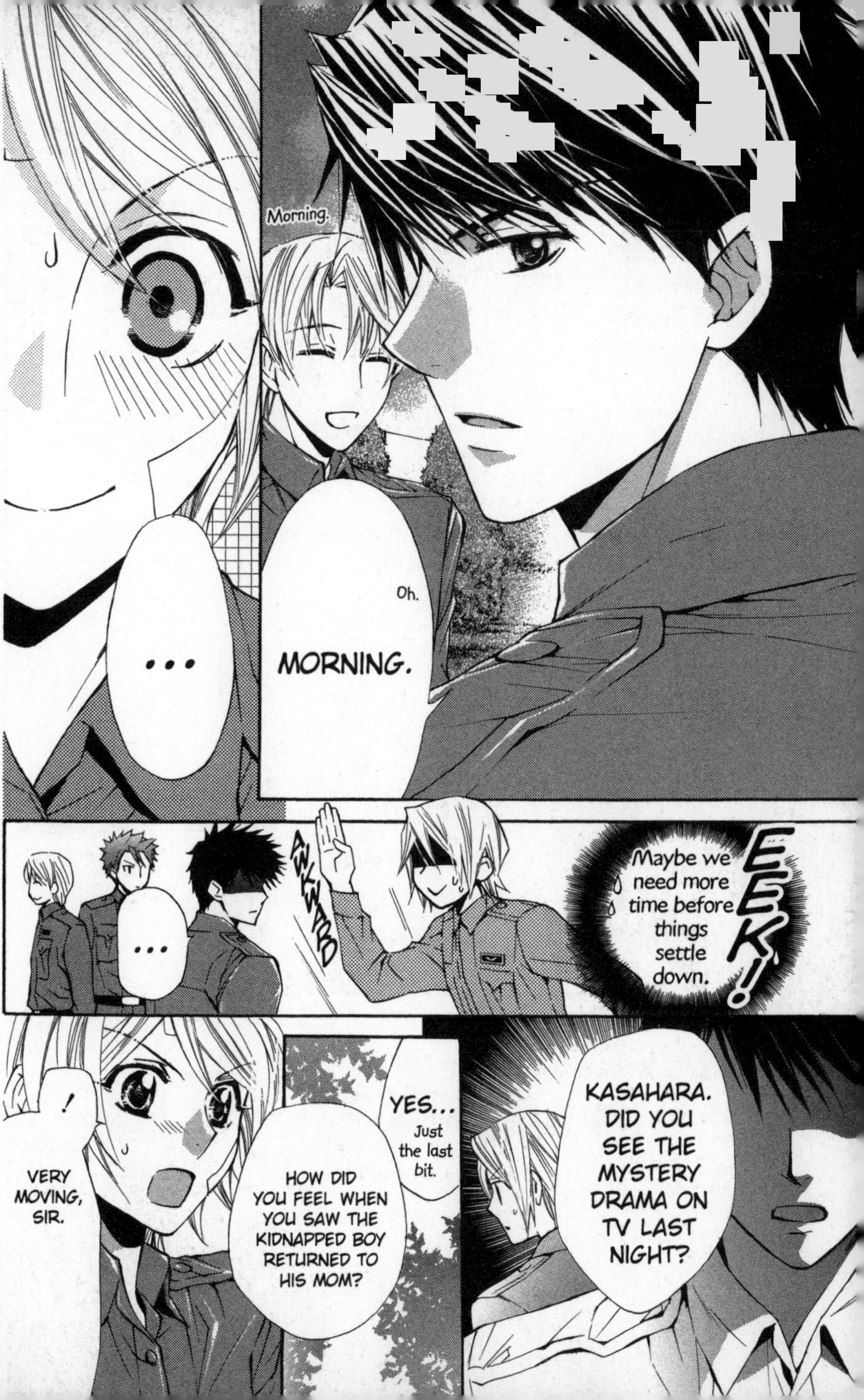
Morning.
Oh.
MORNING.
...
EEK!
Maybe we need more time before things settle down.
AWKWARD
...
KASAHARA. DID YOU SEE THE MYSTERY DRAMA ON TV LAST NIGHT?
YES...
Just the last bit.
HOW DID YOU FEEL WHEN YOU SAW THE KIDNAPPED BOY RETURNED TO HIS MOM?
!
VERY MOVING, SIR.

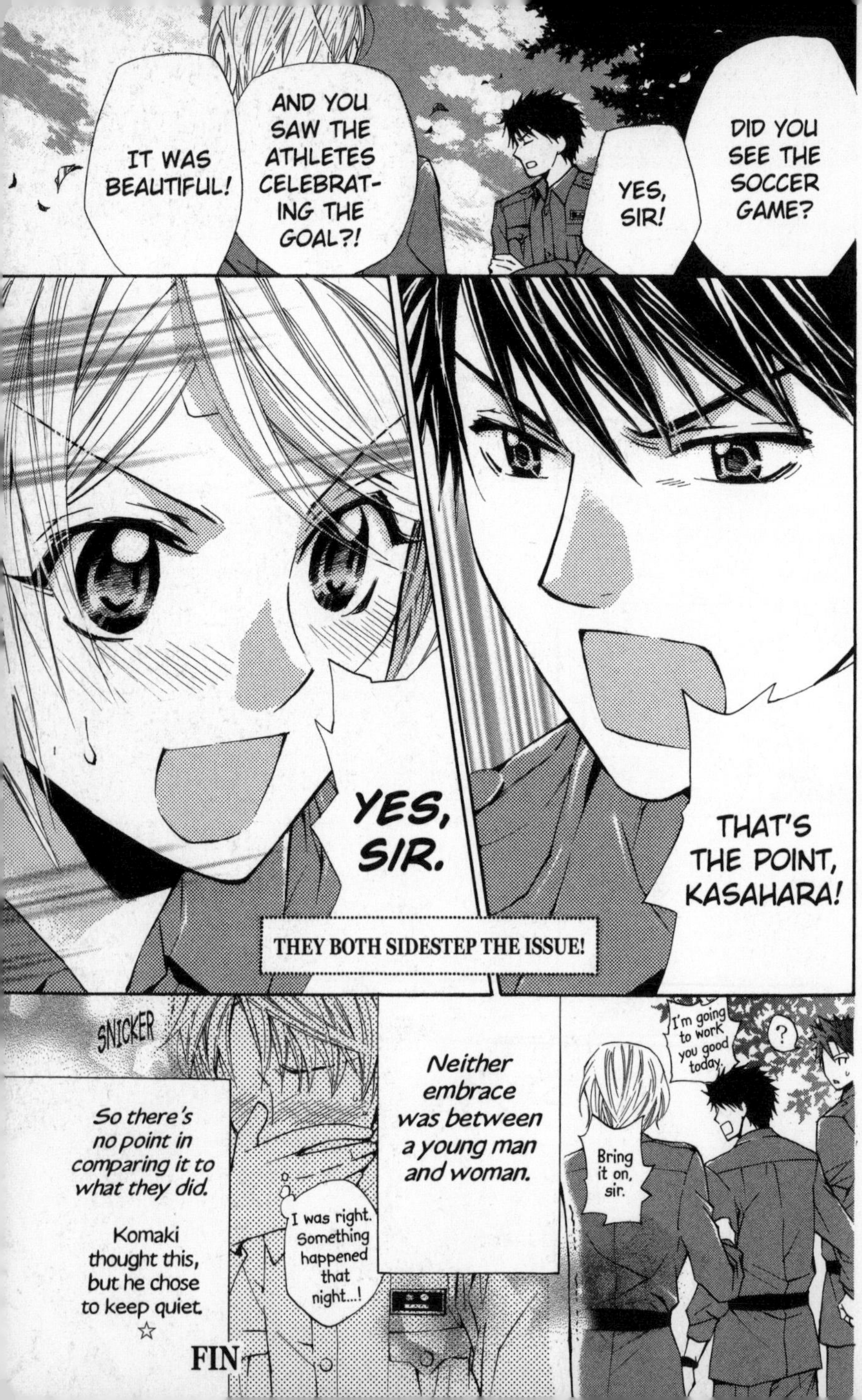
DID YOU SEE THE SOCCER GAME?
YES, SIR!
AND YOU SAW THE ATHLETES CELEBRAT-ING THE GOAL?!
IT WAS BEAUTIFUL!
THAT'S THE POINT, KASAHARA!
YES, SIR.
THEY BOTH SIDESTEP THE ISSUE!
I'm going to work you good today.
?
Bring it on, sir.
Neither embrace was between a young man and woman.
So there's no point in comparing it to what they did.
Komaki thought this, but he chose to keep quiet ☆
SNICKER
I was right. Something happened that night...!
FIN

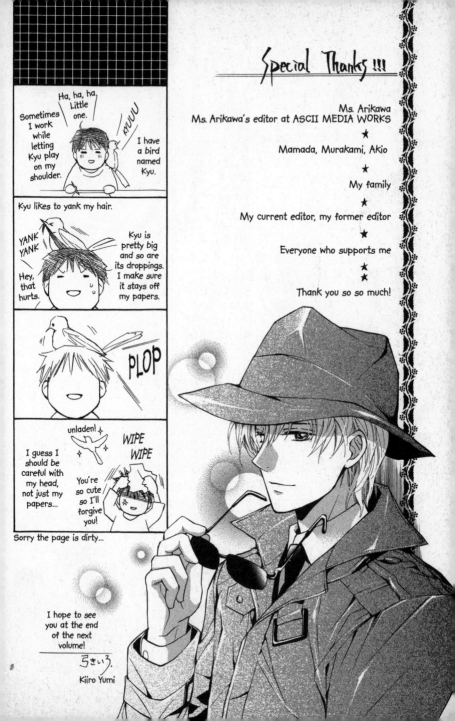

Special Thanks!!!

Ms. Arikawa
Ms. Arikawa's editor at ASCII MEDIA WORKS

★

Mamada, Murakami, Akio

★

My family

★

My current editor, my former editor

★

Everyone who supports me

★
★

Thank you so so much!

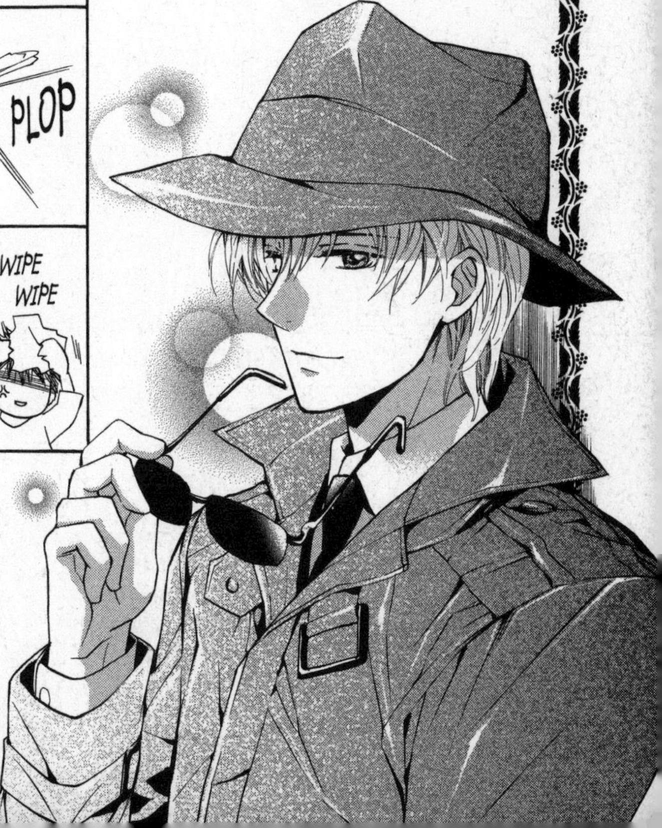

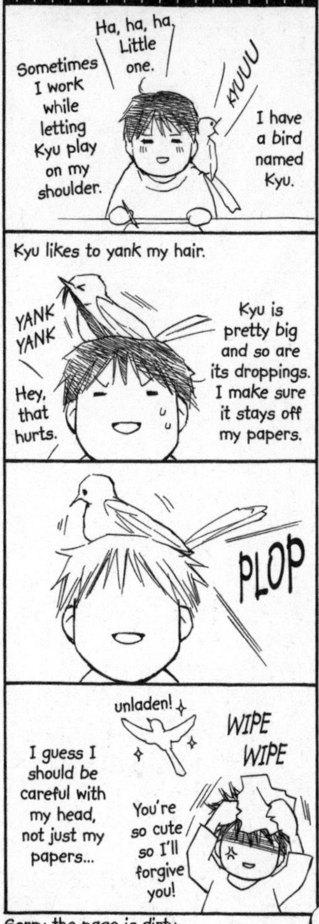

I have a bird named Kyu.
KYUUU
Ha, ha, ha, Little one.
Sometimes I work while letting Kyu play on my shoulder.
Kyu likes to yank my hair.
Kyu is pretty big and so are its droppings. I make sure it stays off my papers.
YANK YANK
Hey, that hurts.
PLOP
WIPE WIPE
unladen!
You're so cute so I'll forgive you!
I guess I should be careful with my head, not just my papers...

Sorry the page is dirty...

I hope to see you at the end of the next volume!

弓きいろ
Kiiro Yumi

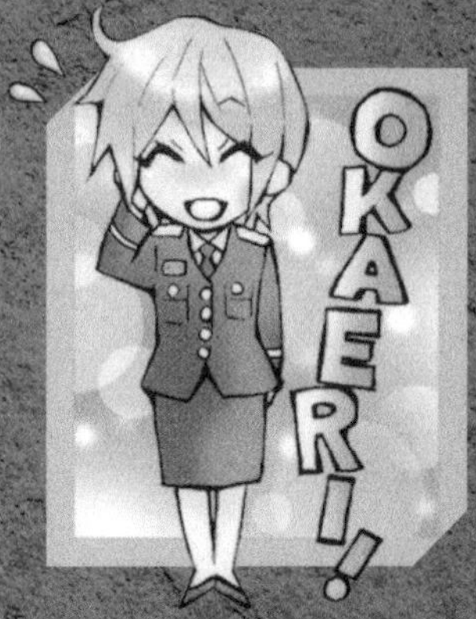
OKAERI!

Kiiro Yumi won the 42nd *LaLa* Manga Grand Prix Fresh Debut award for her manga *Billy Bocchan no Yuutsu* (Little Billy's Depression). Her latest series is *Toshokan Senso Love&War (Library Wars: Love & War)*, which runs in *LaLa* magazine in Japan and is published in English by VIZ Media.

Hiro Arikawa won the 10th Dengeki Novel Prize for her work *Shio no Machi: Wish on My Precious* in 2003 and debuted with the same novel in 2004. Of her many works, Arikawa is best known for the *Library Wars* series and her *Jieitai Sanbusaku* trilogy, which consists of *Sora no Naka* (In the Sky), *Umi no Soko* (The Bottom of the Sea) and *Shio no Machi* (City of Salt).

library wars

Volume 4
Shojo Beat Edition

Story & Art by **Kiiro Yumi**
Original Concept by **Hiro Arikawa**

ENGLISH TRANSLATION Kinami Watabe
ADAPTATION & LETTERING Sean McCoy
DESIGN Amy Martin
EDITOR Pancha Diaz

Toshokan Sensou LOVE&WAR by Kiiro Yumi and Hiro Arikawa

First published in Japan in 2009 by HAKUSENSHA, Inc., Tokyo.
English language translation rights arranged with HAKUSENSHA, Inc., Tokyo.

Printed in the U.S.A.

Published by VIZ Media, LLC
P.O. Box 77010
San Francisco, CA 94107

10 9 8 7 6 5 4 3 2 1
First printing, March 2011

www.shojobeat.com www.viz.com

PARENTAL ADVISORY
LIBRARY WARS: LOVE & WAR is rated T+ for Older Teen and is recommended for ages 16 and up. This volume contains violence.

RATED T+ FOR OLDER TEEN

ratings.viz.com